PUBLICATIONS
OF THE
ARMY RECORDS SOCIETY
VOL. 4

AN EIGHTEENTH-CENTURY
SECRETARY AT WAR
THE PAPERS OF WILLIAM,
VISCOUNT BARRINGTON

The Army Records Society was founded in 1984 in order to publish original records describing the development, organisation, administration and activities of the British Army from early times.

Any person wishing to become a Member of the Society is requested to apply to the Hon. Secretary, c/o The National Army Museum, Royal Hospital Road, London, SW3 4HT. The annual subscription entitles the Member to receive a copy of each volume issued by the Society in that year, and to purchase back volumes at reduced prices. Current subscription details, whether for individuals living within the British Isles, for individuals living overseas, or for institutions, will be furnished on request.

The Council of the Army Records Society wish it to be clearly understood that they are not answerable for opinions or observations that may appear in the Society's publications. For these the responsibility rests entirely with the Editors of the several works.

Viscount Barrington in 1791, aged 74, portrait by
Sir Thomas Lawrence. By kind permission of Lord
Barrington and the Hon. Mrs Jean Strutt.

AN EIGHTEENTH-CENTURY SECRETARY AT WAR THE PAPERS OF WILLIAM, VISCOUNT BARRINGTON

Edited by
TONY HAYTER

Published by
THE BODLEY HEAD
for the
ARMY RECORDS SOCIETY
1988

A C.I.P. catalogue record for this book
is available from the British Library.

ISBN 0-370-31227-9

© The Army Records Society 1988
Printed in Great Britain for
The Bodley Head Ltd
32 Bedford Square, London WC1B 3EL
by Mackays of Chatham Ltd, Chatham, Kent
Set in Linotron Ehrhardt
by Rowland Phototypesetting Ltd
Bury St Edmunds, Suffolk
First published 1988

FOR

Contents

Editor's Note and Acknowledgements

In the preparation of this edition of the Barrington Papers, documents have generally been reproduced exactly as written. Clerks in the eighteenth century copied carelessly, often spelling the same word or name differently in the same passage. Capitals were used without system. Sometimes grammar and syntax were quite wrong. This state of things has been left alone in the present edition, and the use of [sic], which can become irritating, has been reduced to a minimum. Only in a few cases, such as the inadvertent writing of the same word twice, or the habit of repeating quote marks at the beginning of every line, or the various modes of expressing money sums, has any tidying-up been done. And sometimes the layout of certain pages—for example where tables are used—has been altered for convenience where no sense was thereby lost. Some marginal notes or underlining added much later in the letter books have also been omitted. So also have been the customary beginnings and graceful valedictory endings of letters. Substantial omissions however have been indicated by asterisks. The headings of documents, unless within quote marks, and the dates are expressed in simple modern terms. Round brackets within documents indicate the work of eighteenth-century hands, square brackets, of the twentieth century. Generally letters wholly in the hand of the sender are expressed as 'holograph'. 'Copy in clerk's hand' is used in some cases, but documents from W.O. 4, W.O. 5, W.O. 26 and W.O. 71, where everything was clerk-copied are described only as 'copy'. In some cases Barrington made his own copy: this is expressed as 'copy in Barrington's hand'. In the case of the long letter book Ipswich 107, everything therein is in Barrington's hand and is described as 'copy'.

As to the general treatment, there has been some concession to chronology, but the immense variety of business handled by the War Office made a thematic treatment more appropriate.

* * *

I acknowledge with gratitude permission given by the Trustees of the British Library Board to reproduce material from the Francis and Newcastle papers, by the Suffolk County Council in respect of the Barrington collection at the Record Office in Ipswich, and Her Majesty's Stationery Office in respect of material from the files of the War Office and State Papers in the Public Record Office. I also record my thanks for the kind permission of Lord Barrington to photograph the two fine portraits of his ancestor at Berwick Place.

Other persons whose help, advice, hospitality and/or kindness in general I gladly mention include the staff of the East Suffolk Record Office, particularly Pat Woodgate; the staff of the British Library, including the Map Section; the Staff of the Public Record Office at Chancery Lane and at Kew, particularly Hilary Jones and Philip Clayton-Gore; Mark Fiennes for impressive photographic help; Dr Alan Guy of the National Army Museum; Patricia Methven of the Liddell Hart Centre for Military Archives at King's College London; Jennifer Ramkallawon of the National Portrait Gallery; Jennifer Tanfield of the House of Commons Library; the Hon. Mrs Charles Strutt; the Hon. Mr Guy Strutt; Captain Robin Alderson; Patricia Bickers; and Mary Fraser. The manuscript was patiently and effectively typed by Angela Brown, Linda Marchant and Elizabeth Stewart. Lastly I acknowledge the patience and forbearance, even though she had on hand a similar demanding project, of my wife Philippa.

The Barrington Papers

The bulk of the Barrington papers are to be found in the War Office series in the Public Record Office at Kew, in particular the out-letter books (W.O. 4). The process of supervising the Army can be followed outwards from this nucleus to such sources as the papers of the Secretaries of State, the Treasury, the Paymaster-General, the Ordnance and the Admiralty. Unfortunately there do not appear to exist any papers of Law Officers of the Crown for this period, and almost nothing of the Commander-in-Chief. Even the War Office in-letters are scanty, although happily for the purposes of the present work, they became a little less so in 1756.

The Barrington archive in the East Suffolk Record Office is a valuable supplement to the more formal public material to be found at Kew. Here can be found much more raw data—drafts (some of which are reproduced in this book), papers written by a man for collecting his thoughts on an issue, and more sensitive papers that he did not wish to be seen. Even at the War Office there were private letter books (eg W.O. 4/988). But at Ipswich can be seen the loose private letters (Ipswich 3a-d) for his first period at the War Office, and the private letter book (Ipswich 107) dating from 1766, now crumbling and much affected by damp, which Barrington kept at home in Cavendish Square. This valuable source contains a correspondence with officers on difficult points of promotion, as well as a number of letters of great interest for the study of the last few years of British rule in the Thirteen Colonies. It ends in 1775; there may well have been another volume extending to 1778, now lost. The Ipswich archive also contains a surprising number of letters on patronage, in spite of Barrington's hearty dislike of it.

Taken together with other examples found in the Chatham and Newcastle papers, Barrington materials are voluminous. A conscientious administrator who occupies an office for two decades will produce a good deal of paper. Also Barrington, though often regarded by historians as a private and evasive man who left few clues about himself, was in fact quite lavish with statements about the principles which guided his official conduct. Those statements, delivered sometimes with an air of moral reproof which irritated correspondents, are now a useful element for the student of his papers.

Only a small sample of his output can be reproduced here. Correspondence with Thomas Gage[1] and with Governor Bernard[2] are therefore not included here. Neither are the letters printed in the biography of Barrington produced in 1814, with the exception of the famous letter to Charles Gould on officer-preferment (Document 210).

In contrast to the manuscript sources, published biographical materials on Barrington are scarce. A short and uninformative notice of him appeared at the time of his death in the *Gentleman's Magazine*.[3] A biography was produced two decades later by his brother Shute Barrington, the Bishop of Durham, with the help of a kinsman, Sir Thomas Bernard.[4] It is a finely printed edition by William Bulmer, but it relies mainly on long quotations from his papers. It had some merit, as the papers now in Ipswich remained in the hands of the family until 1934. But Bishop Barrington's main purpose was to assemble materials for a fraternal eulogy of a man to whom he owed a good deal: Barrington had solicited for his brother the Canonry of Christchurch from the Duke of Newcastle in 1759, and this was a significant step towards future preferment for him. Consequently the book avoids mention of Barrington's shortcomings and numerous enemies.

In more modern times Barrington has only been noticed in the wider context of administration, politics and warfare, usually, it must be said, presenting him in a fair and just light, although the occasional popular history will still be found to rely on the less kind opinions of Horace Walpole and other contemporaries. The most full treatment hitherto in modern times has been that of Lewis Namier in the *History of Parliament*.[5]

1
Barrington's Life and Career

William Wildman, Viscount Barrington of the peerage of Ireland was born in 1717. His father was the first Viscount, and the family had only fairly recently emerged from comparative obscurity, partly through fortunate legacies.[1] His mother was of a Bristol family.[2] Three other sons were born of this marriage: John, who became a Major-General, Samuel, later a Vice-Admiral of the White, Daines, a judge, natural philosopher and intimate of Gilbert White, and Shute, Bishop of Durham. Colourful tales circulated in later years of Barrington's nepotism towards his siblings,[3] but with the exception of Shute's preferment through Barrington's influence with Newcastle, these accounts were exaggerated. There were also three sisters, Sarah (the mother of Uvedale Price, the artist), Anne and Mary.

The family were probably not able to feel proud of their father, who had become notorious for his equivocal part in a lottery scandal in 1723. Horace Walpole, who called him 'a very dirty fellow', embarrassed Barrington years later by requesting of him a list of his father's writings for inclusion in a revised edition of *Royal and Noble Authors*. 'The answer I received was that his Lordship would be obliged to me if I would continue to omit all mention of his father—and to oblige his Lordship I did.' This, continued Walpole, was 'a strong presumption that he was ashamed of him'.[4] It is difficult to estimate how much the father's reputation affected the son: certainly he grew up to be a proud but sensitive and slightly awkward man, and this had an important effect on the level at which his apparently-promising career stopped, and on the manner in which he conducted his official life.

Barrington succeeded to the peerage in 1734, made the grand tour, and was brought into Parliament as a member for Berwick in 1740. At this time the government of Robert Walpole was in decline and opposition was the fashion. Filial piety may have helped to impel Barrington to join in the attacks on a minister who years before had

3

persuaded members to expel his father from the House of Commons for his part in the lottery scandal.

For some time Barrington's name was associated with that of the Cobham set, but in 1745 his career took on a more calm and measured tone with his appointment as a Lord of the Admiralty. He was appointed Master of the Great Wardrobe in 1753. It cannot be said with certainty when he abandoned a political and took up a more administrative route in his career, but it is possible that he discovered in himself at a fairly early age a talent for business and insensibly began to take that direction, reducing the emphasis upon a more parliamentary career which had not been notably successful.

In 1740 he married Mary, the daughter of Henry Lovell and widow of the Hon. Samuel Grimston. It seems to have become a somewhat bleak and loveless marriage. His brother and biographer, who lost no chance of praising Barrington's virtues, avoids all mention of his marriage. There were no children, and some years later in 1759 Barrington was observed to have formed an attachment to Lady Harrington.[5] For some time his wife's money was useful to him, his annual income falling short of his expenditure by a good sum. Year after year in the accounts the deficit to be made good is referred to in his wife's handwriting, for example, 'Pd. this year from my Separate Estate, & wch. Ld. Barrington has no right to, two Hundred and eight pounds eight shillings and eight pence. M. Barrington'.[6] In 1752 the sum was over £538. In 1754 Barrington gave up his stable establishment. His appointment as Secretary at War with a substantial salary (see Section 3) was timely for him, and by 1758 Lady Barrington's contribution had fallen to £4. In the 1760s Barrington began to enjoy more of the pleasures of life, gave parties in his London home in Cavendish Square,[7] and subscribed to an opera club, attending rehearsals as well as performances.[8] Lady Barrington died in 1764.

It is fair to record that as his position improved Barrington began to be generous towards his brothers, and to his mother, who survived until 1763.

The circumstances of his appointment to the War Office are something of a mystery. In 1754 he asked for a seat on the Treasury Board as part of the scheme of rearrangement on the death of Henry Pelham (Document 1). The Duke of Newcastle put him off, preferring Lord Dupplin. Barrington got his chance in the following year when Henry

Fox, after eight years in the War Office, was able to achieve the Secretaryship of State. In November 1755 Barrington kissed hands as Secretary at War after anxious consultations with the Duke about a Deputy in the office (2). Newcastle thought that the best part of the transaction lay in the fact that the Duke of Cumberland and Fox had had no hand in the appointment.

This was the beginning of a long association with the army, which continued until March 1761, and from July 1765 to December 1778. What was regarded by Newcastle as a factor in making a strong political combination soon became for Barrington a personal opportunity for useful and congenial departmental work. But this beginning was not a happy one. The disaster of Minorca occurred in the spring of the following year, and he played an unfortunate though not crucial part in it. A series of three letters, if their purport was construed jointly, from him to Governor Fowke of Gibraltar, left it unclear whether or not the Governor could or should make a detachment from his command for the relief of Minorca. The possible ambiguities in these letters were bound to come under public scrutiny when Fowke's trial followed that of Admiral Byng.[9] It was remembered against Barrington that he had taken a hard line against Byng, but he was able to justify himself. Fowke's decision not to support Minorca had not in fact had any connection with the letters, and he had only been prevailed upon by others to advance them in his defence, regretting it afterwards. But Barrington was to suffer taunts on this score for years afterwards, from Junius, from Barré and other enemies.

* * *

During 1756 he settled into the office, and mastered its intricate patterns of work. No such thing as an Army Board existed as with the Treasury and Admiralty, although certain technical points of detail could be referred to the Board of General Officers. There were thus good opportunities for independence and innovation, but also no chance of sharing the responsibility for mistakes and disasters. The office part of the business, as will be shown later, suited Barrington very well. He performed less happily in Parliament, before whom he laid his first Estimate, on 27 November 1755.[10] His parliamentary speeches were admired by Horace Walpole, and were well prepared and delivered. There are some striking passages in some of them. Unfortunately for Barrington, delivering set-pieces was only part of the role. The traditional unpopularity of the army ensured that raising military matters in the Commons nearly always led on to question and argument. Such record of proceedings as we have shows that under attack Barrington became rattled, overreaching himself and sometimes having to apologize for rude expressions.[11] As politics became more bitter and venomous in the next two decades Barrington-baiting became a form of sport in the Commons and in the newspapers, and may have contributed to his growing weariness with the political scene after 1775.

* * *

An aspect of Barrington unfavourably commented upon at the time was his apparent adroitness in surviving changes of ministry. Particularly in the 1760s did he stand out as a rock in a torrent that swept others away. Later historians have picked up and commented on this Vicar of Bray image. The formation of the Pitt ministry in October 1756 nearly ensured that Barrington's career at the War Office was one of the shortest of the century, but he was saved. John Calcraft wrote, 'Lord Barrington I rather think will continue Secretary at War, for the present, D. of N. has beg'd the King to keep him, or he was condemn'd.'[12] Barrington had a deep sense of personal obligation to the Duke after this, and Newcastle was glad to be able to rely on his dog-like devotion. In spite of all the attention he had paid over the years to the task of building up his connection, Newcastle needed friends after 1756. After having had first Fox then Pitt thrust upon him he never felt quite secure again. But when the crash came for the Duke in 1762 even Barrington stayed with the administration. For this he was much criticized: he was Newcastle's protégé, he ought also to have withdrawn. One should 'go out with friends', not to do so was vulgar careerism. So ran the argument. It is worth examining the opposite view, which, although it commanded little respect at the time, would perhaps be more sympathetically regarded in a later age. Barrington's notion of his role was a 'civil service' departmental one. There was a job of work to be done, and the public good, as represented by the King, to be served. 'Zeal' was one of Barrington's favourite words. His enemies talked of his unprincipled servility, he spoke of their faction. In this he resembled several other new professionals or 'court and administration men', such as Bradshaw, Charles Jenkinson and John Robinson, all of whom voiced similar sentiments,[13] and equally were derided by Burke and the Rockinghams. There could never have been any common meeting-ground between

Burke and Barrington—the one usually out of office, for whom the political process was essentially public and rhetorical, consisting in statements on great issues, or searching enquiries into the dark and noisome places of secret government: the other, part of the ruling group, a man happiest operating as a bureaucratic official behind closed doors. But Burke and his friends were determined to knock upon these polished panels. Within lurked the 'interior managers', that sinister group of whom Barrington was one, his offence compounded by the fact that he represented the army, the most obnoxious part of the executive in a free constitution. Men who were developing a doctrine of party could hardly be expected to have much respect for a minister who stayed with the Court through thick and thin, and had constant access to the King.

Other enemies, equally aggressive, had less ideological justification. Horace Walpole, who called him flimsy and contemptible—'fawning Lord Barrington'[14]—remembered that Barrington had joined the pack who brought down Sir Robert Walpole, his father. Also he considered that Barrington had prejudiced the reputation of his friend Henry Seymour Conway by slighting the competence of general officers in 1770.[15] Calcraft was involved with the army through the agency business, and was simply concerned to make as much money as rapidly as possible. Restraints and regulations placed in his way by Barrington merely maddened him. And large numbers of discontented officers whose pretensions to promotions could not be satisfied murmured in coffee houses and sent forth to the newspapers an increasing stream of complaints.

* * *

In 1756 the worst effects of this tendency were in the future. Barrington's idea of politics as work was useful in his new and laborious task where an attention to fine detail was essential. The clerks, many of them of long standing, were quite capable of dealing with routine business. If they ran into snags they consulted the Deputy Secretary. If the matter was one of important principle the consultation extended to the Secretary at War, with the Deputy Secretary at hand to supply precedents. Many of the out-letters of the period arose in this way. Most of the others were common-form letters requiring his signature for the sake of form. In this way work could go on from day to day without the constant attendance of the Secretary at War. But in one way or another work was always being held up, and Barrington began to devise ways of improving the performance of his office. In some cases a new and more subtle form was needed for dealing with a case. This was true of much of the financial business of the office. In other, more embarrassing instances, where personal considerations were involved, a line of conduct had to be fixed upon and adhered to. This applied particularly to dealings with officers clamorous for preferment. His first period at the War Office gave him ideas for developing his own policies, but necessary subservience to the Duke of Cumberland until the autumn of 1757 and to the old King hampered him. After the accession of George III in 1760 there were signs that Barrington was beginning to plan changes in the work of the office. Many of these came to fruition in his second period after 1765.

* * *

Barrington left the War Office on 18 March 1761. Lord Holdernesse also stepped down to make way for Bute, the first of the sacrifices to be made of the old group that had held power for so long. But Barrington's career was not at an end. Somewhat to his surprise he was made Chancellor of the Exchequer. He expressed his surprise at this in a letter to Andrew Mitchell: 'but no man knows what is good for him. My invariable rule therefore is, to ask nothing, to refuse nothing, to let others place me, and to do my best wherever I am placed.'[16]

The next reshuffle was more alarming. The Duke of Newcastle resigned and Bute became First Lord. Barrington moved from the Exchequer but was made Treasurer of the Navy. As has been mentioned, the Duke was disappointed at the reluctance of old colleagues to follow him and show the world how indispensable he was. But with Barrington the public and private contexts were separate. By this time, at the age of 45, he had arranged the major part of his public attitude to his liking. He had also begun to compose his own script in a series of documents recording important conversations and events in his career. They are to be found in the *Life* by his brother[17] and are therefore not included here. In sum, he tried to convey his attitude of a disinterested public servant to Newcastle and Bute, who both seem to have found it difficult to believe. A coolness grew up between Barrington and Newcastle after this, although he undertook to support the Duke if he was attacked in Parliament on the organization of supplies for the army in Germany during the war. But he made it clear he would not join in a general scheme of opposition. 'The Duke then told me he wished me well; but would never more talk with me on business ... He said he should always be glad to see me: but that our conversation would not be interesting.'[18] For Newcastle it was fidelity or treachery.

Another proscription of politicians took place at the time of the fall of Bute in 1763, but Barrington was saved by the intervention of the young King, who had begun to appreciate him. By this time, apart from being regarded as an agreeable and useful member of the team, he had succeeded in getting others to accept the view he had of himself as a hardworking official, and attached to the general good as represented by the Crown. When the Grenville government fell in the summer of 1765 and the Court was crowded with men wishing to be noticed, Barrington characteristically was careful not even to be seen in London. On his return on the morning of the 17 July he found that the major appointments had been made and that the King wished him to return to the War Office.

The Rockinghams were strange bedfellows for Barrington. Several, such as Burke and Dowdeswell, were to become bitter enemies. But their power only lasted for a year. The departure of the Marquis of Rockingham was not followed by a great massacre, and Barrington kept his place at the War Office. A year later he had a narrow escape when there was a move to return him to the Exchequer in the place of Charles Townshend. Barrington did not relish the plan, nor did he have good memories of his earlier time in that office. After a day or so of uncertainty Lord North was prevailed upon to take the office. Barrington remained with obvious relief at the War Office.[19] No-one ever offered to displace him again – he was too useful. Years later when his departure came about it was at his own instance.

* * *

By the mid-1760s Barrington's lack of advancement was beginning to distress him in a particular, though not in a general sense. He was not anxious for power for its own sake, indeed he seems to have been one of those rare individuals who were sufficiently aware of their own limitations to know where to stop in career-advancement. The rest of the world was unaware of this and expected Barrington to continue to climb, using the War Office as others had before him, as a spring-board. By 1768, such was the King's confidence in him that Lord Chesterfield thought that he would be Secretary of State if Shelburne were removed.[20] In September William Knox wrote, 'Lord Shelburne is again on the hinge, and Lord Barrington is talked of for his successor.'[21] But Barrington knew better. He was not statesman-material. His preferred method was rather to influence those who had real power. But his behind-the-scenes mode, which had served him well enough before with the Duke of Newcastle, became in course of time less effective, particularly on the subject of America. And America was a matter upon which Barrington considered he had special knowledge. His long correspondence with his kinsman Governor Bernard of Massachusetts, and with General Thomas Gage, the Commander-in-Chief in America after the Seven Years' War, gave him a good deal of detailed knowledge of the American situation. He could also bring to bear upon these details his undoubted grasp of army matters, and his experience of public-order problems, particularly those made worse by incompetent direction from magistrates. Officers in America placed in difficult positions when acting in support of the civil power ought to be supported by a Secretary at War who called himself the friend of the Army, just as in London in 1768 (3). It is perhaps easy after the event to blame Barrington for not seeing that these problems existed in a radically different form on the other side of the Atlantic, or for not simply taking a larger, less detail-bound attitude. The Gage and Bernard papers, for the most part published elsewhere and not included here, show Barrington battling manfully but a little myopically with what he saw as a gigantic public-order problem. He had always taken a hard line on America, startling the Rockinghams by voting against them on the question of repeal of the Stamp Act in February 1766. But he tried to be realistic as well. His paper on America, of May 1766, sent to Shelburne and Pitt, and submitted to Gage in America for his comments, was the first of Barrington's attempts to influence public policy in a wider sense beyond his department.[22] He wrote not as Secretary at War, although knowledge acquired in his office showed clearly in the paper, but as an acquaintance of a number of influential men on both sides of the Atlantic. Technically he was on the outside of the power group. A Secretary at War of his office is not supposed to make policy. But he was older now, a little more confident, seeing the King sometimes as often as once a week. Oblique and informal influence with colleagues might work.

The paper recommended withdrawing the army from many of its existing posts in America, where they were too scattered and isolated. If they were concentrated in Canada, Nova Scotia and Florida they could better improve their discipline and training, and could move into a particular area if domestic trouble threatened. At present they were isolated in scattered and vulnerable units, unsupported by the civil power, exposed to insult at the least, and at worst liable to be over-whelmed. The even smaller groups on the Appalachian frontier, now that the French and Spanish threat had ceased, should also be brought out, leaving the West as a 'desert'.[23] General Gage however did not give unqualified support to the plan, and Barrington did not feel strong enough in 1766 to press it upon the government. He continued however to try to influence ministers, particularly Hillsborough, on American subjects.

* * *

He was on surer ground in his own department. He returned to the War Office in 1765 determined to avoid some of the difficulties which had plagued his first term. The hand-to-mouth haste of wartime was over, the size of the army had decreased greatly, and it was a good time for frugality and careful management, and for developing those 'rules of the service' to which he frequently referred in correspondence. Those rules often originated in Barrington's own head, or arose in conversation with the Adjutant-General. They were then canvassed in the Closet, and subsequently became promulgated as official. These were the years in which a bold attempt was made to tighten up on the purchase and sale of commissions, and on other procedures involved in recommending for preferment. The myriad financial problems which arose from the work of the Treasury and from regiments and which were sent to the War Office for solution were passed in review, and rulings for the future worked out. Inevitably the application of new procedures made enemies. Aspiring officers were disappointed, greedy agents were brought to book, regimental paymasters and contractors were urged to be more businesslike.

There were enemies within the office as well. Philip Francis, First Clerk from 1763 to 1772, is now regarded as the most likely candidate for the mysterious Junius who contributed by his clever and rancorous writing in the *Public Advertiser* to the savage political atmosphere of the early 1770s.[24] The authorship may never be entirely proved, but certainly information seemed to be leaking into the newspapers from the War Office at an alarming rate. It may have been Francis who passed to the papers Barrington's well-known letter praising the conduct of the Guards in dealing with the Wilkes riots in 1768. This represented a serious blow for Barrington. He had been accustomed to being unpopular with disappointed individuals. Now he increasingly became public property in the press. The Rockinghams closed in for an attack over the same riots, the first occasion in which Burke led in the House of Commons on a major matter. The whole question of the use of military power in suppressing riots, and of the army as a legitimate part of the constitution of a civilized state was ably discussed. The House divided decisively in Barrington's favour. Burke wrote later: 'I never made more than two motions. As to that on St. Georges fields, I did in effect repeat it, and I never slept so happily as after I had discharged myself of that accusation ... To its Object it proved very innoxious. It has not diminished a Shilling of Lord Barringtons salary.'[25]

But although the attack failed it had been an unpleasant experience for Barrington, and probably made him more secretive and more impatient of Parliament's role of scrutiny. In 1770, stung by attacks over his proposals for the augmentation of the army as a result of the Falkland Islands dispute, he let slip the following revealing remarks: 'But what this gentleman or that may say here, should not, I think, be a consideration with the servants of the Crown, but what they consider most conducive to the safety of their King and country . . . I have always been of opinion, that ministers should do the right thing, let it please or displease.'[26]

But the sense of being observed by the public increased when Junius entered the contest. Having poured his scorn on the front rank of a corrupt administration – Grafton, Weymouth, Sandwich and others – he now turned upon the 'base wretches' such as Barrington and Bradshaw ('the cream-coloured parasite') who lurked in support. In November 1770 Barrington rather unwisely remarked in a debate that he did not know of a single general fit to command the army, a gaffe gleefully taken up by the *Public Advertiser*.[27] In January 1772 a private letter from Junius to Woodfall the printer announcing the next salvo was more ominous: 'Having nothing better to do, I propose to entertain myself & the public, with torturing that bloody wretch Barrington. He has just appointed a french Broker his deputy, for no reason but his relation to Bradshaw. I hear from all quarters, that it is looked upon as a most impudent insult to the army.'[28]

Barrington had parted company in December 1771 with his Deputy Secretary Christopher D'Oyly. D'Oyly had served him capably and the circumstances of the rupture are not known, except that they parted on cool terms. Francis and D'Oyly had been on friendly terms in the office, so the episode strengthens the case for identifying the former as Junius. Instead of appointing Francis in D'Oyly's place Barrington had brought in an outsider, Anthony Chamier the financier and brother-in-law to Thomas Bradshaw, who was Barrington's man-of-business. Contemporaries were mystified by this appointment: it certainly infuriated Francis, who left the War Office in March.[29] Meanwhile more Junius letters were published. Sixteen were promised but only five appeared. They dwelt upon all the alleged shortcomings of the Secretary at War: his obsequiousness at Court and autocratic sternness at the War Office, his abandoning of friends in order to hold on to office, his relations with Lady Harrington (wife of the Commander of the Horse Grenadier Guards), the St George's Fields Massacre, his slighting of the generals, his nepotism towards Chamier and Bradshaw, his destruction of General Fowke.[30] The disappearance of Junius from the literary scene in 1772 must have been a relief to Barrington.[31]

* * *

Throughout the 1760s and early 1770s Barrington was encouraged and sustained by his relationship with George III. The King worked hard at his army and had already mastered most of the detail by the time Barrington returned to the War Office in 1765. Ministers might put the army to use in wartime, but nearly all the points of day-to-day administration in peace or in war were settled by the monarch and the Secretary at War. This became clear some years later during the King's illness in 1788, at which time Army business came almost to a halt. The King had a liking as well as a respect for Barrington, and employed him in several delicate matters of negotiation, for example in sounding Lord North on his willingness to take office in 1770,[32] a further change of government which had no effect on the incumbent at the War Office. For his part Barrington was careful not to ask for anything himself, although he was prepared to use his interest for his family (4). But this relationship, once so useful and congenial to each party to it, began to be a nuisance to the Secretary at War just as it was to Lord North with the outbreak of the war with America.

The decade of the 1770s was an increasingly unfortunate time for

Barrington. Attacked in the Press, with friends falling away from him or in some cases dying, he awaited the American conflict with dread. For his brother the Admiral it was the best part of his career. For Barrington it was political death. Others resigned their appointments or merely declined to have any part in the affair, such as Rockingham and Keppel. The Earl of Effingham also objected to the war and the King at once deprived him of his regiment. Barrington, conveying this information to the Earl, may have felt a twinge of envy. In view of his position and perhaps too-constantly advertised fidelity to the Crown, such a line of conduct was not available to him. His suggestion to ministers that direct military action would be unwise and that a naval blockade was preferable was not liked. But his sense of duty compelled him to try to bring pressure in areas where he saw danger. Public-order points were as always in the mind of this man, experienced by now in dealing with years of rioting in Britain. Denuding the mother-country of troops might be fatal if a general insurrection broke out, and the first years of the decade had already been notable for widespread disorders over food prices.[33] And having spent many years reminding officers that in cases of riot they must only fire on mobs with the concurrence of magistrates, he urged Lord Dartmouth to reverse his ambiguous instructions to officers in America. Otherwise officers uncertain of their powers might be over-whelmed (5). A few days before, he had called for responses to his questions about the legal position of officers on riot-duty, questions which had lain unanswered for two weeks with the Law Officers of the Crown (6). The essential weakness of Barrington's position over American strategy, already exposed in 1766–67, became even clearer to him in 1774–75: he was only half-responsible, as the man who under the British constitution most resembled a minister for the army, but who had no power of policy, except by persuasion. He recorded a conversation with the King in 1776, when he made his distaste for his position quite clear: 'I have, said I, my own opinions, in respect to the disputes with America: I give them, such as they are, to Ministers in conversation or in writing; I am summoned to meetings, where I sometimes think it my duty to declare them openly, before perhaps twenty or thirty persons; and the next day, I am forced either to vote contrary to them, or to vote with an Opposition which I abhor. I know the use and necessity of practicability; but it may be carried too far. Your Majesty has condescended to be my patron; I will have no other: be pleased to determine for me, how as a man of honour, conscience, and feeling, I am to act.'[34]

After December 1774 Barrington continued to make representations to Dartmouth, but only about the state of the Army, not about the use to which it might be put, of which indeed he was often kept in ignorance.[35] He seemed to prefer sometimes not to know what was going forward in America, allowing his role to shrink once more to a departmental one.

The parliamentary records show that Barrington would not lead for the government as he had done in Newcastle's day. He presented departmental business, but if it was attacked on grounds of policy he would fall silent and North and his friends had to come forward to justify and explain. They made the policies, after all. Barrington had lost his chance of being in the front rank, which probably suited him. He had now also no chance of achieving much by influence, which did not suit him. He was quite logical in avoiding the trouble attendant upon a position wherein he did not possess power either formally or informally.

As early as October in 1776 after the spring session of Parliament he spoke to the King in the same terms.[36] His words showed that the attacks and jealousies of political life were at last beginning to unnerve him. Although he had tried to distance himself from the direction of the war, he could not feel free of responsibility. In December 1777 he wrote: 'I cannot write or talk about the dreadful catastrophe of Burgoyne's army, and I wish I could think of any other thing.'[37] The King's suggestion that Barrington should stay in the War Office but quit the House of Commons, where he had become so exposed to attack, was rejected by North. So thought the Commons: they wished to have the Secretary at War more, not less responsible than he already was. Barrington, having signified his desire for retirement, left the date of it to be determined by the King. But George III was too intent upon the war, and too suspicious of any sign of faint-hearted behaviour, to be of any help to him. Miserable and depressed, his main energies concentrated on contriving his own withdrawal, Barrington dragged out the last few months of his official life, while the business of the War Office was mainly carried on by the clerks and by Chamier's successor Matthew Lewis. There are many laconic but weary entries in his diary about this time—'Long day in the House'—and once, for a period of two weeks from 28 January to 8 February 1778, 'Forgot & not entered from great business.'[38] He was badly savaged in February in a debate to vote additional supplies. By May the King had agreed in principle to his withdrawal, and at length let him go, not with a very good grace, on 16 December 1778 (7).[39]

Barrington cleared his desk at the War Office, helped himself to two silver inkstands and two silver taper-pots, the accepted spoils of office, and quitted the place he had held for a total of eighteen years. Apart from a brief spell as joint Postmaster-General in 1782, as part of a last desperate attempt to shore up North's administration, he never again held public office. He was therefore not involved with the triumph of the Rockinghams and the administrative inquisition which accompanied it, or with the peace with America.

* * *

Barrington kept on his town house in Cavendish Square, but withdrew more and more to his country seat at Beckett, near Faringdon in Berkshire, a small and somewhat inconvenient damp house, half of which had been burnt down in the Civil War. The family dismantled the rest of it in the nineteenth century. His engagement diaries show that he kept up a wide circle of friends, continued to subscribe to the opera club, and was the centre of a local dining club in Berkshire. But his declining days must have been saddened by memories of the latter part of his official life. Domestic problems also forced themselves upon him. Not having the solace of children of his own, he increasingly had to bear the burden of his brother's children, to whom he was guardian. General John Barrington had never recovered from the rigours of the West Indian climate in 1759 and died in 1764. The younger boys, William, who succeeded as the third Viscount after Barrington's death, and Richard were his chief headache. Several bundles of correspondence[40] tell a dreary tale of protested bills (which were sent to Barrington: after a while he refused them all), of bailiffs and drunken brawls, and of reports from discreet and embarrassed agents engaged on shadowing the nephews. For William he made a considerable effort, having him educated at Louis Lochée's military academy in Chelsea before getting him into the army. In spite of his strictures and protests on the subject Barrington was not unwilling to indulge in nepotism on occasion.[41] William's military career was brief and not meritorious. His brother Richard was eventually paid by Barrington to stay abroad. Louise gave him a great deal of uneasiness although at length she made a safe though not brilliant marriage, and Barrington and his brothers Shute and Daines made a reasonable settlement on her.

Other worries intruded upon his retirement. His accounts as Treasurer of the Navy had never been made up. Settlement of public accounts often took years, and like the parallel office of Paymaster-General, the personal fortune of the Treasurer was liable for any shortfall. Only six months before his death Barrington had to pay £2,915 into the Receipt of the Exchequer to balance his account with the public, after years of wrangling with auditors and threats of distraint by bailiffs, which must have wounded him deeply.[42]

* * *

Barrington died at his house in London on 3 February 1793. Even Horace Walpole admitted that he missed a man who had been an enemy so long that he had become an old friend.[43] He lived in the traditional world of authority and due subordination, and died at the beginning of a new era of change. We do not know what was his response to the French Revolution, but it may fairly be guessed that a man born in the Augustan Age and who had spent much of his official life in combating civil disorder would have regarded it as the consummation of a tendency about which he had been uttering dire warnings for years. Of its deeper significance he would have been utterly uncomprehending. The forces of change alarmed and disgusted him. He may have been forward-looking in his official methods, but in his basic ideas he was with the old order. His papers[44] contain ideas and proposals for dealing with poachers and for preventing stage-coaches from carrying game which might have been poached, and for destruction of suspicious dogs belonging to the poor. He was interested in schemes for building houses of correction, to which should be sent any trespasser 'not giving such an account of his Ramble as does satisfye such Justice before whom he shall be brought'—whipping and hard labour should follow. In many other ways he might appear unpleasingly severe. He thought Byng should be shot. He played a part in the ruin of Lord George Sackville in 1759–60, which perhaps accounts for a lack of receptiveness to Barrington's ideas in Sackville some years later when as Lord George Germain he was the minister for America. He personally conducted the parliamentary attack on Wilkes which resulted in his expulsion. He was against the presence of strangers in the House. His 'adherence to strict rules' seemed to some merely stubborn obstructiveness. His enemies, Burke, Isaac Barré,

Wilkes, Junius, Sir Robert Rich, Sir John Dalrymple, and others have left memorials of their dislike of him. And Whig historians noticed him, when they did so at all, as one of the villains in their drama.

But he was capable of inspiring friendship, even devotion, and left behind a memory of acts of charitable kindness in his part of Berkshire. His friends,[45] however, were not simply the sort of people little relished by contemporaries (or by Whig historians); they also left no very obvious or public records of their liking for him. The opinions that were remembered dwelt upon his small-mindedness, his myopic concern for office detail, his coldness. Horace Walpole thought that even his agreeable manners were a pose. But the record of his papers shows a kindness and humanity towards the army, as well as an impressive administrative achievement. Peacetime was best for this and Barrington's best years were perhaps between 1765 and 1768. Problems could be addressed and solutions proffered after consultation with friends and officials as well as after private rumination. It was easier at such a time to be kindly and urbane towards the troubled and the unfortunate, as well as the clamorous. This friendly feeling not only extended to officers, some at least of whom took a fair and understanding view of his position, but also to the common soldier. The outcasts of society could at times have their lot improved by a minister who in some subtle way may have felt himself to be an outcast. It is true that he did not rise to the height where he could forget detail and take grand decisions. Perhaps it was his merit that he recognized that he was not capable of it. But those who do wield power know quite well the value of men like Barrington, and that the running of a good office requires an immense and laborious attention to detail. Office work may be composed of trivia, but the sum of the trivia, properly assembled, is the enabling factor in great strategy.

I

Barrington to the Duke of Newcastle

[Holograph] 13 March 1754

As it is now Understood in the world that the great Arrangements are taken, I am perswaded I shall not be among the first who troubles your Grace with their pretensions to the vacancies which they shall occasion. I take the Liberty of offering my Claim in this manner as it is so late in the day, but I hope your Grace will permit me to wait on you in person tomorrow morning.

I had the honour to inform your Grace some time since of the promise of the next seat in the Treasury, made by Mr Pelham when Lord Barnard came there. It was very explicit, never repeald, but on several occasions confirm'd. I have not the least doubt but it would have been fully perform'd if any ardent wishes could have kept him here; & I hope that his kind intentions in my favour will have the same weight with your Grace that I know they have on other Subjects. I am the more confident of this, as there is no man in England who from his situation in office, length of Service there, (on this occasion I will add useful service) or constant attachment to his Majesty's Measures & Government, has so good a Claim to this small step, which I have long & patiently expected; Nor should I now perhaps give your Grace this trouble, if my Interest only was concern'd; but I feel that my honour is affected in the most essential Manner.

I will not trouble you with assurances of my Attachment to your Grace, for I am sure you do me justice in that particular: If it were less, Gratitude would produce the same Effect, if I reced from your Grace what I am desirous to receive as a favour: To which I beg leave to add, that in return for eight Years laborious & useful Service both in Office & in Parliament I have never reced one favour from the Administration.

Add. Mss. 32734, ff. 229–230

2

Barrington to the Duke of Newcastle

[Holograph]   Beckett
9 October 1755

I should have deserved the utmost blame if I had engaged the Employment of under Secretary at War without consulting your Grace; & more especially after I had beg'd & you had so kindly promised your Advice and Assistance, without which I should dispair of getting well through the difficulties of the nice situation I am soon to be in. Mr Fox never recommended anybody to me for that Station; he only advised me not to engage myself hastily to Mr Lloyd, who he say'd was altogether unfit for the office he was in. My answer was that I would not engage myself for anything till I was Secretary at War; but that in respect to Mr Lloyd I would not determine at all till I had fully talk'd with him. He never gave the least hint of Mr Calcraft's succeeding as undersecretary, & I never had the least intention of that kind. Mr Myddleton wrote to me & inclosed a letter from Your Grace. I am sure he is perfectly satisfy'd with my Answer, & Mr Lloyd ought to be satisfy'd with one I have written to him tho' I have in both these Letters very clearly express'd my resolution to keep myself absolutely unengaged till I am in the office to which I am destin'd. I will endeavour to form such a Plan as I think will best answer the King's Service, be approved by the world in general, & satisfy the Persons most nearly concern'd; but I will determine nothing till after I have lay'd the whole before your Grace for your advice & approbation. I am not much obliged to the person who inform'd your Grace of a supposed Engagement to Mr Calcraft; but I am glad he misrepresented *me*, for I know your Grace will believe what I say, & consequently that you will be cautious of believing informations of others which you may receive from the same quarter.

I could not receive greater pleasure than by finding that things go on so well, & I am infinitely honour'd & flatter'd by your wishing that I was in Town, & thinking that I might be of some use to you. Indeed my Lord, your Goodness to me is above all expression, & so is my grateful sense of it. I have done some

Business which render'd my return hither necessary, & I would go back to London on what your Grace is pleas'd to say, if I did not know that you will be at Claremount before I come there, & if my house was not full of Company. I believe they will leave me next week, & then I will present myself to receive your Commands, but if you have any which will not admit of this short delay a Line by Saturday's Post shall make me immediately leave all to follow you.

* * *

I fear I must beg a line from your Grace at all Events by Saturdays Post, for I could not be easy here if I were not clear that you did not want me elsewhere. I can be in Town by Wednesday morning at yr Coffee time.

Add. MSS. 32859, ff. 444

3

Barrington to Lieutenant-Colonel
Dalrymple of the 14th Foot
[at Boston]

[Copy]   War Office
                                                    28 April 1770

[Margin note: Triplicate sent by Mr Pownal at Lord Hillsborough's Office on 15th May]

I have the honour to acknowledge the receipt of your Letter of the 13th of March together with the Papers enclosed. I cannot express the concern I feel on Account of the unfortunate disputes between the Troops and the People of Boston, which have had such fatal Consequences.

In Candour and Justice, no Man should think ill of others without proof, and nothing less than proof shall make me conceive any ill Impressions concerning the 29th: Regt. The good Character which Captain Preston universally bears, entitles him in particular to the most favourable Construction of his Actions.

As I am persuaded the Earl of Hillsborough Secretary of State for America will signify the King's pleasure relative to this

unfortunate Affair, I need add no more than that the Troops
under your Command, as part of His Majesty's Forces entrusted
to my Care, may depend on every proper Assistance and support
which I can give them.

W.O. 4/87, p. 8

4

Barrington to the King

[Holograph copy]   Beckett
                                                    23 September 1765

Above a year ago, Mr Grenville acquainted Doctor Barrington
(who by your Majesty's goodness is a Cannon of Christ Church)
that you intended he should be Dean of Windsor when Doctor
Booth should dye. I have this moment heard that he is dead. I
had not the least hand in this application, being determin'd never
to trouble your Majesty about myself or family who have been
much favour'd already by the Crown. Mr Grenville has long
known & loved my brother, which alone occasion'd his being
mention'd to your Majesty for the Deanery of Windsor.

In the present state of things, it may probably be inconvenient
to your Majesty that this your gracious Intention should take
place. I therefore must humbly implore in my brother's name as
well as my own, that you will not consider any former arrangement, so as to occasion the least difficulty in the present Course of
your Majesty's business.

I humbly hope, Sir, you will pardon my well meant presumption in writing this Letter; and permit me to add that I am with the
utmost duty & respect [etc]

Ipswich 112, no. 22

5

Barrington to Lord Dartmouth

[Copy]   Cavendish Square
                                                28 March 1775

If my former representations & entreaties have not already had
effect; may I conjure your Lordship not to let the Major Generals
proceed to America, without carrying Orders for the Troops to
act against Persons unlawfully in Arms in New England, without
any direction from the Civil Magistrate. I am certain that no
Officer will take the command of a Detachment against Insur-
gents in that Country without asking whether he may or may not
proceed in that manner; And I am as certain that General Gage
will not give any clear explicit Instructions on that head unless he
has received the most clear & explicit Intructions from home.

I am ashamed to trouble your Lõp so often on this matter, but it
seems to me so important that General Gage should have no
doubts how he should Act in the present Juncture, that I must
omit nothing which can tend to his information. I am at the same
time perfectly persuaded that he will do with zeal & fidelity
whatever he thinks himself authorised to do for the public
Service.

Ipswich 107

6

Barrington to Lord Dartmouth

[Copy]   Cavendish Square
                                                1 April 1775

I have been considering what you were pleased to mention to me
yesterday; but I cannot make the questions which I think should
be put to the Attorney & Sollicitor General more clear or explicit
than those which I had the honor to send to You about a fortnight
ago. I enclose a copy* of them least they should have been lost or
mislaid.

Pray, my Dear Lord, do not think me impertinent if I now repeat my idea of the necessity there is for a Suspension of the Habeas Corpus Act in New England, & a power to bring over to this Country for trial persons taken up there for High Treason.

* * *

*In the present Situation of the Massachussets Bay, May Troops act against persons in Arms without any direction from a Civil Magistrate?
May they in Connecticut?
May they in Rhode Island?
May they in New Hampshire?

Ipswich 107

7

The King to Barrington

[Holograph]   Queen's House
                                                  16 December 1778

Lord Barrington cannot be surprised after my having experienced His attachment, and faithful discharge of the Employment he hath held for eighteen Years of my Reign, that I feel hurt at having this day consented to his retreat; but as I intend to shew him a mark of my approbation of his conduct, arising from that consideration alone, and unsolicited by Him, I chuse to take this method of acquainting him, that I have directed Lord North to have a Warrant prepared granting a Pension of two thousand pounds per Annum untill he shall be appointed to some other Employment. Lord Barrington may rest assured that He will always be esteemed by Me.

Berwick Place MSS (unclassified)

2

The Paradoxes of the Secretaryship

The office to which Barrington came in 1755 has always seemed anomalous and baffling to historians. Contemporaries often did not understand it either, and the War Office received many letters from otherwise knowledgeable officials which were patiently readdressed to the other government departments to which they properly should have been sent. This ill-defined situation had probably been allowed to grow up deliberately. In the generation after the Revolution Settlement, Parliament became more inquisitive about the Army. At the same time the chain of agencies involved with the military establishment multiplied. Checks and balances in the constitution were admired in the eighteenth century, but in this case a loss of accountability in Parliament inevitably resulted. In other respects the ambiguity led to much inefficiency in business. But for various reasons connected with England's troubled history in the seventeenth century, efficiency within the executive, especially the military part of it, would not have been admired. Standing armies were associated with despotism and were disliked for generations after the disappearance of the Stuarts. Consequently no Ministry existed with the task of developing the army as a force, and the Minister who supervised it was intended to have little or nothing to do with its actual use in wartime. To call him a Secretary at War seems odd: he had nothing to do with war policy in a wider sense. Secretary to the Army would have been a more accurate title.

So nothing reliable can be said about the effective role in practice of the Secretary at War without referring to the curious position he occupied in government, to his relations with the other great offices of state, and to the constitutional pressures and inhibitions which had brought this about.[1]

If the office ever had a chance of becoming a Secretaryship of State, it lost that chance at the end of the seventeenth century, due to the correct and unambitious behaviour of William Blathwayt, who was Secretary at War from 1683 to 1704. The Nine Years' War gave Blathwayt opportunities for the exercise of power far beyond the usual scope of the War Office either before or since, but he did not attempt to make his position permanent, and after William III's death the Secretaries of State speedily re-established their lost power. The Secretary at War never had another such opportunity.[2] It became clear that his work fell into two areas, one military, the other civil. Originally a clerk to the Commander-in-Chief, or to the King (as Commander-in-Chief), he continued to be paid as a staff officer, and to be appointed by a military commission, which commission wisely made no attempt to enumerate his multitudinous responsibilities (8). He was however almost invariably a civilian, a fact which helped in part to allay the fears of military encroachment. Although the role changed and became more bureaucratic in the eighteenth century, it never lost the earlier character of military secretary to the monarch. This aspect of the office attracted unfavourable notice later in the eighteenth century. Many believed with Blackstone that although the prerogative was less a matter for concern, royal influence had been increased by the existence of a standing army.[3] And the indefinable and camouflaged nature of the office led to overheated speculation about the improper extent of the Secretary's influence. Also, as with other areas of the constitution, the position was not constant. The custom and practice of the office responded to the greater flow of military business as the years passed, and attacks by Parliament had a modifying effect. There were demarcations, but they were shadowy, like the marches of a medieval country. An ambitious Secretary at War could gain more power: an unassuming one could permit the area of his operation to shrink. At different times and for different reasons Barrington did both.

One of his chief strengths was that he provided the nearest thing to a co-ordinating ministry. But this was only true in a limited administrative sense. In the absence of a Ministry of War, little or no policy-direction of the army took place in peace-time. The King, the Secretaries of State, the Commanders in Chief, the Master-General of the Ordnance, the Treasury and the Paymaster-General all had parts to play in maintaining the army, and many of these lines of supervision crossed in the War Office. In time of war the position changed and became more dynamic, but to the prejudice of the power of the Secretary at War. The great objectives of the nation's army were decided in meetings of Cabinet, to which he might often not be invited. At these meetings expeditions to distant theatres were ordered, and the Secretaries of State hurried away to their offices to set on foot the first stages of them. At this point the Secretary at War would come forward, as befitted a departmental official of the second rank, to issue the detailed instructions to activate their plans. If he was intimate with the Secretaries of State he might learn a good deal about these plans, and they would be wise to let him know anyway. But he was not of his office entitled to know about them, and in cases was kept in ignorance for some time of the destination of expeditions.

However, although it is broadly true that the Secretary at War did not set the army onto its military tasks, he had a good deal of influence upon what sort of an army it was. And if he did not make policy, he had influence over it. More powerful men might plan the strokes of strategy, but they turned to the Secretary at War to make sure that they were building on firm foundations. The military part of his function required him to have the detailed knowledge for supplying military demands. The civil and political part, juxtaposed with and overlapping the former, required him to know how to account for every item of expenditure to the Treasury, and to appear before Parliament with good estimates. The two roles combined to give him a surprising amount of power, which could enable him to modify events, because he alone had the statistical and technical knowledge to advise on the potential of several possible lines of policy. Before a Secretary of State decided what he would do, he was forced to discover from the War Office what he could do. But although some Secretaries at War, notably Barrington, were prepared to use their unique position to try and achieve organisational reforms, they were not ambitious to alter the basis of power of the office. They were quick to point out in Parliament that, in Charles Jenkinson's words, they were not ministers 'and therefore could not be expected to have a competent knowledge of the destination of the army, and how the war was carried on.'[4] Barrington said much the same a few years earlier: 'A Secretary at War must obey the King's orders signified by a secretary of state or resign. The secretary at war is not a Cabinet councillor. He is only a ministerial officer. He is not a proper judge of the propriety of a measure.'[5] He was not therefore the minister for the army in the sense that Parliament would have liked. Direct responsibility for failure in wartime was difficult to fix upon him, although he could not escape being partially and obliquely implicated.

When Barrington was first at the War Office he was careful to be entirely directed by the Duke of Cumberland. The Duke was an object of dislike and suspicion in many quarters, but he was a powerful figure and Barrington was new to his job and wished to be directed. For nearly two years many of Barrington's letters are the result of direct instructions from Cumberland (9). When the Duke was disgraced the position altered. By the autumn of 1757 Barrington was more confident in his office. He worked closely with the old King, now in his mid-seventies, and had a great respect for him. But he regarded the new Commander-in-Chief, Lord Ligonier, in an entirely different light. For Barrington, Ligonier was a military officer responsible for command and discipline. He himself had a much wider brief, to supervise the army and to answer for it in Parliament and to the public, lest the military should become either too extravagant or too arrogant. Ligonier tried to behave as if the wording of the Secretary at War's commission from the King—'to observe and follow such Orders and Directions as you shall, from time to time, receive from Us, or the General of Our said Forces for the time being'—ought to be construed literally, so that Barrington could be treated as his clerk. Over the question of promotions there was little dispute. Ligonier decided, and Barrington carried the recommendations to the King (10, 11). Over the issue of army medical arrangements, which Barrington considered fell within his department, they clashed badly (12).[6] But the lines dividing the activities of the Commander-in-Chief and the Secretary at War were never very clear, and the latter had acquired by long usage a number of functions that might appear purely military, such as the pursuit of deserters (13, 14), communicating with the King over courts-martial and signifying respites and mitigations of sentence (15), even the making of odd clandestine bargains to save the lives of condemned soldiers (16). He also scolded officers for bad behaviour in public, composed their quarrels and granted them extended periods of leave, besides ordering colonels to discharge recruits who had been improperly enlisted. Ligonier never offered to disturb these arrangements. But the contest between them over the relative positions of War Office and Commander-in-Chief was a small-scale skirmish compared to the battle launched by Palmerston years later.[7]

With his political chiefs he was careful to be correct in his behaviour, even showing a touch of irritation if they tried to cast improper responsibilities upon him (17). He had no way of compelling the compliance of the other departments of state and was forced to call upon the Secretary of State to issue necessary instructions to the Lord Lieutenant of Ireland, the Admiralty and the Ordnance (18, 19, 20). Even the Auditors of the Imprest sometimes needed more than an office letter from the Secretary at War (22). On the other hand a note to a friendly official might set events in motion in advance of authority from the Secretary of State, thus saving delays (21). Generally he acted towards the Secretaries of State as a departmental official, asking advice when unsure of his powers and working closely but with deference with them (23, 24, 25, 26, 27, 28, 29, 30). In 1773 he and Lord Rochford agreed an arrangement for cooperation between their two offices, but only in the particular and vexed area of troop-transport to overseas stations (31).[8] Relations between the War Office and Secretary of State's Office in all other respects continued to be conducted in accordance with the way in which the customary course of business had developed.

With George III things were more clear cut. It was his army and he usually knew his own mind about it. Barrington gave a good deal of advice on matters of detail, to which the King listened. But on the question of the American rebellion Barrington had little influence, indeed did not appear to wish to have influence (32, 33, 34).

The high point of Barrington's influence beyond a narrow departmental role had been during the Seven Years' War and arose from his close association with the Duke of Newcastle. Numerous papers on recruitment and for saving money came from the pen of the Secretary at War at this time, showing a firm grasp of essential facts (35, 36, 37, 38, 39). Barrington was always more at ease with Newcastle. Apart from gratitude to the Duke for his patronage, Barrington shared his love of detail. Significantly they both began to panic about the cost of the war about the same time; in fact Barrington's letters on this subject are more alarmist than the Duke's.

After Newcastle's resignation in 1762 Barrington never again successfully influenced the men of power. He tried on occasions to get onto the same terms with Lord North (40) but received much less encouragement.

At the Treasury Barrington was regarded as a trusted representative for the army, and was allowed a good deal of administrative discretion, a theme taken up in Section 4.

8

Barrington's Commission for his second term as Secretary at War

[Original engrossment, signed by the King and the Duke of Grafton]

GEORGE R   Court of St. James
                                              19 July 1765

LS GEORGE THE THIRD, by the Grace of God, King of Great Britain, France and Ireland, Defender of the Faith &c. To Our Right Trusty and Welbeloved Cousin and Councillor William Viscount Barrington, Greeting: We being well satisfied with Your Loyalty, Integrity and Ability, do hereby constitute and appoint You Secretary at War to all Our Forces raised, or to be raised, in Our Kingdom of Great Britain and Dominion of Wales. You are, therefore, by Virtue of this Our Commission, to receive the said Place into Your Charge, & You are diligently to intend the Execution thereof, and faithfully and duly to execute and perform all Things incident and belonging thereto; And You are to observe and follow such Orders and Directions as you shall, from time to time, receive from Us, or the General of Our said Forces for the Time being, according to the Discipline of War, in pursuance of the Trust reposed in you, and your Duty to Us. Given at Our Court at St. James's the Nineteenth Day of July 1765, In the Fifth Year of Our Reign.

By His Majesty's Command
Entered in the Office of   Grafton
Thomas Gore Esqr.
Cõmry Gẽnl of Musters.
John Fr. Hesse

Ipswich 100

9

Barrington to Lieutenant-General Hawley
[at Canterbury]

[Copy]   War Office
                                                        6 January 1756

The Duke being made acquainted that the small Pox is broke out,
attended with very bad Symptoms, at Canterbury, HRHss has
Ordered me to desire you would provide an Hospital to receive all
the Soldiers, that may fall ill of that Distemper, to prevent as
much as possible, the Distemper from Spreading, by keeping all
those that may be Infected, Separate & by themselves. If by this
Direction any small Expence shall be incurr'd I am ordered to
take care that it be satisfied, and that no necessary expense be
spared.

W.O. 4/51, p. 121

10

Field Marshal Ligonier to Barrington

[Holograph]   N.p.
                                                        28 April 1759

Lord Ligonier present's his compliments to Lord Barrington and
beg's the favour of His Lordship that He would take the King's
pleasure on Serjeant Major Harpar of the First Regiment of Foot
Guards to succeed Mr. Thos. Hayward as Provost Marshal to
the Three Regiments of Foot-Guards, whose Commission Ld.
Ligonier has inclos'd to His Lordship. And also that Drum-
Major Laurence Higgins Eldest Drum-Major to the Guards,
may succeed Drum Major General Jno. Conquest, deceas'd.

Ipswich 3b, no. 47

11

Field Marshal Ligonier to Barrington

[Holograph]   London
                                                            9 July 1759

Lord Ligonier presents his compliments to Lord Barrington and
beg's the favour of His Lordsp. to take the King's commands on
the following Promotions in Major General Whitmore's Regiment; by which Lord Barrington will see the Attention paid to his
Lordship's List, which postpone's the Promotion of such as are
recommended to Lord Ligonier.

Lieutenant John Hunt.	Lambton's	)
Lieut. Hampden Evans	Boscawen's	)
Ens Downe . . .	Bentinck's . . .	) 5th Octr. 1757
Ensign Geo. Hastings	Lambton's . . .	) 23rd July 1758
Nichs. Delacherois		)
Gabl. Hamilton		) To be
Eusce. Chute	Whitmore's	) Lieutenants
Thos. Lewis		)
Joseph Fish	. . . .	) 12th Jany. 1758
Thos. Whitmore	Nephew to ye General	
Gilbert Burd	D. of Newcastle	
– Lumley –	Ld. Hallifax	Ensigns
– Corbet –	Ld. Powis	
John Pleydell		

Ensign William Melville to be Lieutenant vice Hunt
    Mr. Josiah Winslow to be Ensign vice Melville.
Ensign Willm Campbel to be Lieutenant vice Evans
    Mr. James Nailor to be Ensign vice Campbel In Bentincks
    Mr. Heneage Campbell to be Ensign vice Hastings.

Lord Ligonier beg's the favour also of Lord Barrington to
take the King's commands that Lieut. James Johnston of Col.
Colville's Regiment may be appointed Lieut. in Lt. General
Campbel's Light Troop: But for the rest of the Promotions of
Lieutents. to the Light Troops, Lord Ligonier recommends the

Eldest Cornets in their respective Regimts. tho' they happen to be in Germany, and the Second Cornets to be made eldest Cornets. This makes a Vacancy in every Regiment except the Greys.

Ipswich 3b, no. 13

12

Barrington to Ligonier

[Copy in clerk's hand] N.p.
15 July 1758

As I had not the honour to see your Lordship at Court, & as I am going to morrow into the Country, unless you have some unexpected commands which will keep me in town, I must trouble you with a Letter.

Capt. Gore of Home's notified as Major of Brigade, Mr. Fuller recommended by Lord Buckingham to your Lordship, & lately disappointed thro' a mistake of mine, is an Ensign in Brudenell's, Mr. Charteris is an Ensign in Stuart's, & Mr. Burleton is a Surgeon in the Hospital for Germany as your Lordship desir'd.

I have sent Mr. Adair to Dr. Pringle, to know whether he will serve in Germany, or the Isle of Wight. If the Doctor does not chuse either service, as I imagine from a Letter of his I received yesterday, I have then directed that Dr. Clephane shall be sent immediately to the Isle of Wight, & I have order'd Adair in that case to wait on Dr. Shaw with my request that he will recommend a Physician on whom we may depend, to serve with Dr. W. in Germany. As I find your Lordship chuses to be acquainted with whatever concerns the Army Hospital, I will take care you shall know every thing for the future, before it is done. You would have known all the past, if I had imagined you had leisure or inclination for such details.

* * *

P.S.   I have just received a paper from your Lordship by General Napier. On great part of it I have spoken & written so fully to your Lordship, that I need add nothing now but that I continue in the same opinion. Till I change my opinion, I never change my Conduct.

I cannot enlarge the Establishmt. for the German Hospital, because it is already as large as your Lordship's was in 1746: If the Duke of Marlborough finds a necessity to enlarge it, the necessity may justify his Grace. No such necessity appears to me. If it be thought expedient, Mr. Adair shall go over himself to inspect the Hospitals.

Ipswich 3b, no. 197

13

Barrington to the Mayor of Chester

[Copy] War Office
30 November 1765

Having been informed by Lieut Colo Blackett who Commands the Invalids at Chester, and to whose care the several deserters passing to & from Ireland are committed, that the Keeper of the County Goal has refused taking any more deserters under his care, except such as are committed by the Magistrates of the County, I beg leave to acquaint You therewith, and to represent to you that, as the Blackhole is by no means a place fit for the Confinement of deserters, the refusal to admit them into the County Goal will occasion great prejudice to His Majesty's Service. I must beg therefore that you will be pleased to give your assistance towards removing this inconvenience and on my part you may be assured that, if any difficulty should arise with respect to the regular payment of the Subsistence of such deserters, while in the Goal (which I hope has never yet been the Case) I shall take Care to have it immediately set right.

W.O. 4/78, p. 131

14

Christopher D'Oyly to Arthur Roon J. P.
[at Haverfordwest]

[Copy]   War Office
                                                    23 April 1771

I am directed by the Secretary at War to acknowledge the favr. of
your Letter of the 16th Instant relative to the committment of
John Downs and John Grace Deserters from the 69th Regimt of
Foot, to the Goal at Haverfordwest. Lord Barrington returns you
his thanks for your Attention to His Majesty's Service, but as
Troops are seldom Quartered in your Neighbourhood and as
these Men may remain a long time in Confinement before the
necessary Order can sent for their removal, I beg leave to trouble
you with the enclosed Route for their joining a Party of the said
Regiment now at Gloucester, and I should take it as a particular
favour if you will be pleased to acquaint them that in case they join
the Party at that Place there is great reason to believe that their
Desertion may be pardoned. I must likewise beg that you will be
pleased to advance each of these men 7s to carry them to
Gloucester, which, together with the Expences incurr'd during
their Confinement will be immediately paid on your drawing on
Mr. Meyrick of Channel Row Westminster Agent to the Regiment for the Amount who has received Orders for that purpose.

W.O. 4/600 [no page number: this letter book
unnumbered after p. 157]

15

Barrington to the Judge Advocate General

[Copy]   War Office
                                                    30 December 1755

Having had the Honour to lay before His Majesty the proceedings of a Genl. Court Martial held in Privy Garden on the 9th &
15 Days of this inst. when Henry Robinson, James Carmichael,

James Crumpton of the 3d Regt. of Foot Guards, William Davis & John Mack Glew (Als William Hayes) of the first Regt. of Foot Guards were tryed & found Guilty of Desertion; I am to Acquaint you His Maty has been pleased to Mitigate the Sentences of the Court Martial upon the said Henry Robinson, James Carmichael, Wm Davies [sic] & James Crumpton, by ordering them to receive one half of the Punishment they are Severally adjudged to receive Vizt. Henry Robinson 100 Lashes on his bare back from the Regt. to which he belongs instead of 200, James Carmichael 400 Lashes with a Cat of nine Tails on his bare back from the three Regts. of Foot Guards instead of 800, Wm. Davies 300 Lashes with a Cat of Nine Tails on his bare back from the three Regts of Foot Guards instead of 600 & James Crumpton 300 Lashes with a Cat of Nine Tails on his bare back from the Three Regts. of Foot Guards instead of 600 at the several times and in the manner prescribed by the Sentences, & to confirm the Sentence of the said Court Martial on John Mack Glew (Als Wm Hayes) whereby he is adjudged to Suffer Death.

W.O. 4/51, p. 105

16

Lord Sandys to Barrington

[Holograph]   Ombersley Court [Near Worcester]
25 October 1773

One of my neighbours has had the misfortune to have a very undutiful son, who from a love of rambling has inlisted two or three times from the army and is now in Worcester Gaol confin'd for Debt, where he has been discover'd by the Army to have deserted from Gen. Maitland's Regt, since when he has inlisted into the Guard's, and I believe has deserted from them; his father who is an honest Man, and has a tolerable fortune, will be very happy to pay what losses the different Regiments have sustain'd, could he be assured that the Capital Punishment he has incurr'd might be chang'd into the milder punishment which has been indulg'd of late years, that of Banishment into the W.Indies, I shall be much oblig'd to your Lordship if you can contrive to obtain this favour upon my application the person's name is Cornelius Hasledine formerly of the 49th Regt since of the Guards.

Ipswich 6a2, no. 235

17

Barrington to Lord North

[Copy]   Beckett
                                                        27 August 1775

***

My Letter of Monday 21st to your Lōp, contained everything I could suggest on the Subject of augmenting & recruiting: I stated all the Objections to every kind which occurr'd to me. This was *my* duty; it is *yours* to determine: You have decided in favour of New Corps & particularly those offered by Mr. Ackland, General Fraser, & Lieut Colonel Campbell: I have not a word more to say against any of these Proposals; And the Proposers shall find every proper facility in me: I do not know the terms required by any of these, but I shall object to none which your Lōp approves. In short your measures shall find at the War Office, while I am there, the same zealous assistance which I gave in the last War to the Duke of Newcastle's & Lord Chatham's.

Ipswich 107

18

Barrington to Lord Weymouth

[Clerk's hand, signed by Barrington]   War Office
                                                        11 March 1778

Partys of Captain Commandant Dalrymple's Corps of Infantry being under Orders to embark for Ireland to recruit in that Kingdom, I have the honor to acquaint your Lordship therewith, and am to desire you will be pleased to receive and transmit His Majesty's Commands to His excellency the Lord Lieutenant of Ireland, that the said Party may be furnished with the necessary Beating Orders on their Arrival in Dublin.

S.P. 41/27 [pages not numbered]

19

Barrington to Lord George Germain

[Copy]   War Office
                                                              15 January 1777

It being intended that one hundred Remount Horses shall be sent to No. America for the two Regiments of Light Dragoons on Service there, I have the honor to acquaint your Lordship therewith, and am to desire you will be pleased to receive his Majesty's Commands thereupon, and signify the same to the Rt. Honble the Lords Commissioners of the Admiralty, that Transports may be forthwith ordered for this service, and that directions may be given for six vacant Stalls in each Transport, that provisions may be provided for One hundred Men who are to embark with and take care of the Horses, during the Passage to America, and that accommodations may be made for two Officers who are likewise to embark on board each of such transports.

W.O. 4/99, p. 2

20

Barrington to Lord Weymouth

[Copy]   War Office
                                                              28 January 1777

The Arms &c undermentioned being wanted for the 29th Regt. of Foot to replace a like Number which have been sent to America, I have the honor to acquaint your Lordship therewith, and am to desire you will be pleased to receive HM Command thereupon and signify the same to the Master General of the Ordnance that the said Arms etc. may be delivered out of HM Stores for the use of the said Regt., and the Expence charged to the Estimate of Ordnance for Parliament.

* * *

63 Firelocks with Bayonetts,
Scabbards, & Cartouch Boxes

W.O. 4/99, p. 72

21

Barrington to Charles Frederick

[Copy]   War Office
                                              27 February 1761

Lord Barrington presents his Compliments to Mr. Frederick and sends him herewith Copies of two Letters which he has this day wrote to Lord Holdernesse for Arms and Ammunition for five Hundred and Forty two Men, being Draughts from the Regimts. of Foot Guards to recruit the Battalions serving in Germany. Lord Barrington desires Mr. Frederick will be pleased to give the Necessary Directions for issuing the said Arms and Ammunition immediately, to the Officer Commanding the said Draughts, without waiting for the Forms of Office.

W.O. 4/981 [pages not numbered]

22

Warrant to allow the Auditors of
the Imprest to allow in the Paymaster's
accounts money for a Commissary

[Copy]   June 1757

GEORGE R

Warrant for allowing in the accompts of Wm. Pitt Esq. late Paymaster General of the Forces £946.10s. issued by him to Capt. Ruvigny De Cosne in pursuance of the King's Pleasure signified in a Letter from Henry Fox Esq. late Secretary at War.

WHEREAS by Our Warrant bearing date the 11th of April 1747 We were pleased to direct that the sum of £3 a day should be paid unto Capt. Ruvigny De Cosne from the 20th of February 1746/7 (the date of his Commission as Commissary for conducting Prisoners of War from hence to Calais &c) to the 20th of August following inclusive, And by a Letter from Henry Fox Esq. Our late Secretary at War dated the 10th of June 1748 We were pleased to signify Our Pleasure to Wm. Pitt Esq. Our late Paymaster General of Our Forces to Issue to the said Capt. Ruvigny De Cosne the sum of £1.10.0 a day from the 21st of August 1747 to the 13th of May following, both days inclusive, amounting to £946.10.0, for the abovesaid service, which sum was accordingly issued by him to the said Ruvigny De Cosne, And it having been represented unto Us that Our late Secretary at War's Letter abovementioned will not be deemed a sufficient Voucher for your passing and allowing the said sum of £946.10.0 in the accompt of Our said late Paymaster General, Our Will and Pleasure therefore is, and We do hereby authorize and require you or either of you to give plenary allowance in any future accompt or accompts of Our said late Paymaster General Wm. Pitt Esqr. for the said sum of

£946.10.0 by him issued, in obedience to our Commands as above set forth, to the said Ruvigny De Cosne; And for so doing, This shall be as well to you as to all others whom it doth or may concern a sufficient Warrant, Authority, and Direction. Given at Our Court at Kensington this   day of June 1757 in the Thirtieth year of Our Reign.

By His Majesty's Command
Barrington

W.O .26/23, pp. 203–204

23

Barrington to Robert Wood

[Copy]   War Office
                                                    10 March 1761

Lord Barrington presents his Compliments to Mr. Wood & desires he will be pleased to take Mr. Pitt's opinion, for how many months Subsistence should be sent out for the Forces under Major Genl. Hodgson & what Sum for the Contingencies of the Expedition under his Command, as it will depend upon the time the Expedition will Continue & the Possibility of the Paymaster getting money where the Forces are going, for his bills upon the Paymaster General here.

Lord Barrington desires Mr. Wood will obtain him this Information as soon as possible, that no time may be lost in writing the proper Letters to the Treasury & Pay Office.

W.O. 4/981 [pages not numbered]

24

Barrington to William Pitt

[Holograph]   War Office
14 February 1757

It has been represented to me from Major Grant of the 1st
Highland Battalion that the Scotch Dutch Officers, at present
recruiting in Scotland, are a great hindrance to him; as they can
afford to give as much money as he can, and enlist only for a term
of years. I have given directions some time ago that no new
Beating Orders should be issued to these Officers, but these, of
which the Major complains, having been granted for a term
not yet expired, I know not how to recall them; and therefore I
have the honour to transmitt this account to you, for your
consideration.

S.P. 41/23 [pages not numbered]

25

William Pitt to Barrington

[Draft in clerk's hand]   Whitehall
15 February 1757

I have received your Lordship's Letter, with Regard to the
Hindrance Major Grant, of the 1st Battalion, finds from the
Officers of the Scotch Dutch, now recruiting in Scotland, under
beating Orders, given to them, some time ago, and not yet
expired, which your Lordship does not know how to recall:- I do
not apprehend the Ground of your Lordship's Difficulty upon
this Occasion, as I do not conceive, there is any Defect of Power
in the War Office to recall the Beating Orders, granted to the
Scotch Dutch in the like manner as is practised, with Regard to
any other beating Orders given in that Kingdom; But if your
Lordship imagines there may be any difficulty as to the Republic

of Holland, Your Lordship will be pleased to apply to Ld. Holdernesse thereupon, Holland being in the Northern Department.

S.P. 41/23 [pages not numbered]

26

Barrington to William Pitt

[Holograph]

N.p.
16 March 1757

My first Clerk has just sent me an Acct. of your Verbal Message that you agree to the Plan proposed, and desire to Know what Orders from you are necessary to the Admiralty or to me. To the Admiralty none are needful at present, because the passage from Scotland to Ireland being a kind of ferry, will be provided by me: But you will signify to the War Office his Majesty's pleasure that the Highland Battalions should march as soon as they are in readiness, from their present quarters to Port Patrick, and be there embark'd for Donachdee. You will acquaint the Lord Lieutenant that they should be disembarked at Donachdee and march thro' Ireland to Cork, to be there embark'd on board such transports as will be there to receive them. I imagine the Orders for the Passage to America should come from the Admiralty but of this I am not certain. This night the Agents of both Batts. will be directed to send the second Clothing to Leith with the utmost Expedition, & I will tomorrow write an Office Letter to the Admiralty for the Convoy they have promised.

P.R.O. 30/8/18, pp. 172–173

Barrington to William Pitt

[Holograph]   War Office
11 April 1759

Upon the repeated applications of the Agents to the Regiments in
North America, setting forth the great hardships the Officers on
that Service suffer from the want of their Arrears, I obtain'd His
Majesty's Warrant for making out Debentures Compleat for
these Regiments up to the 24th December 1757; But as I have
reason to believe that very large Sums remain in the hands of the
Paymaster General, on account of several of the said Regiments, I
think it proper to acquaint you, that it is my intention that the
Officers shall receive only the Amount of their Arrears; and that I
shall not move His Majesty to grant his Warrant for Clearing any
of the said Regiments, until I have seen their Non Effective &
Recruiting Accounts, which I have order'd to be lay'd before me.

As the Examination of these Accounts may possibly take up a
great deal of time, and the Officers are in immediate Want of their
Arrears, I should be glad to know whether you have any Objection
to issuing the Arrears of the Officers to each Regiment, upon a
Letter from me, signifying the Kings Pleasure to that effect, as has
been sometimes done upon other Occasions.

S.P. 41/23 [pages not numbered]

28

William Pitt to Barrington

[Holograph]   Hayes Place, Kent
3 September 1759

Understanding since I troubled your Lordship yesterday, that the
Wiltshire Battalion stands in need of some repairs of divers
things, as well as of a little refreshment in easier quarters, after a
long and fatiguing, close duty at Winchester, I woud strongly
recommend their being sent into quarters at Salisbury and

Devizes, where they will be ready for instant service, on occasion: nor do I think the *occasion* far off. Warwickshire and Berkeshire may take their turn of duty: the first at Hilsey, the latter at Winchester. I hope the Norfolk Battalions will be willing, and in a condition, with a little refreshment, to stay out the winter, and be quartered as near as conveniently may be, towards the Hampshire Coast. Dorsetshire, having requested to serve during the winter, if any militia stay out, can not be so well as where they are. Glocestershire may also remain on Duty, at least for some considerable time longer till They want refreshment. I beg you my dear Lord to be of the Number of Those, who believe France in earnest to push a desperate stroke, with a chance at least to embarras us; and in this belief I extremely wish to keep on foot, during the winter, all possible force, and to avail ourselves of every kind of Zeal for raising immediately still more, in order to have every man of the Army at liberty to move against the enemy, the Instant any Landing happens. in my opinion Lord Lauderdale's offer shoud still be accepted, as well as Lord Aberdour's and I shoud be obliged to you if you woud talk to the Duke of Newcastle upon it.

* * *

P.S.
Any expence which gives
security & confidence will
be largely compensated in the
price of our Loan.

Ipswich 112, no. 48

29

Barrington to William Pitt

[Holograph]   Cavendish Square
                                               4 August 1757

The last letter from the Duke brought over a plan of Augmentation of which I have the honour to send you a copy herewith; to which I have added a Calculation of the Expence and a

Comparison between this Plan & that of last Year. I need not recommend a speedy consideration of it to you or the rest of the King's servants. I have not been able to shew it to any of them till today, & then only to the Duke of Newcastle. This plan is for a larger number than was proposed to the King, or than I by his Majestys Command mention'd to His R.H. However I conclude it may be lessened in case the present situation of affairs shd not require so large an Encrease. I will attend you at a moments warning on this or any Affairs.

* * *

P.S. I shall not mention the Duke's Plan
to the King till I know the opinion of
his Servants thereon, I wish on that Acct.
as well as others to know it soon.

P.R.O. 30/8/18, pp. 180–181

30

Barrington to Lord Rochford

[Holograph]   War Office
                                                31 August 1773

The 29th Regiment of Foot being hourly expected from North America, and the Impressing of Carriages at this Season of the Year being very detrimental to the Harvest, I have the Honour to submit to your Lordship whether it will not be proper immediately to signify His Majesty's Pleasure to the Lords Commissioners of the Admiralty that, in Case the Transports which bring home the said Regiment should put in to Plymouth or Portsmouth, Orders may be sent to those Ports for their sailing round to Dover, where they may disembark the Regiment, if it should be judged adviseable for the transports to come round to the River.

S.P. 41/26 [pages not numbered]

31

Paper on division of responsibilities between public offices for transport of troops

[Copy in clerk's hand]   Secretary of State's Office
                                          February 1773

Arrangement proposed for ascertaining with the greater precision the Line of Duty in the Several Offices of the ancient Secretaries of State, the Secretary of State for the Colonies, the Lords of the Admiralty, and the Secretary at War, respecting the Execution of His Majesty's Commands concerning Troops to be transported to the Colonies in Africa and America, from Great Britain or Ireland; and to Troops returning to Great Britain or Ireland from the said Colonies.

Case of Troops sent to the Colonies from Great Britain or Ireland when Relief is not the Object

1st   That in all Cases where Troops are to be sent from Great Britain, or Ireland to the Colonies in Africa or America, *and in which Cases relief is not the Object* the Secretary at War do notify to one or other of the ancient Secretaries of State, and also to the Secretary of State for the Colonies, the Regiments or Corps, that are to be so sent, and that the Letter from the Secretary at War to the Office of the Ancient Secretary of State, do desire that such Secretary of State do take the King's Pleasure for all the necessary Orders to the proper Offices here, for providing Vessels for their transportation, and for their embarkation; And that the Letter from the Secretary at War to the office of the Secretary of State for the Colonies, do desire that such Secretary of State would take The King's Pleasure for all the necessary Orders to the Commander in Chief in America, or to the Governor of the Colony to which the said Regiments or Corps are to be sent, for their reception &

47

accommodation and touching the Service on which they are due to be employed.

Case of Troops sent to the Colonies when Relief is the Object

2d.   That in all Cases of Troops sent from Great Britain or Ireland to the Colonies in Africa or America, *When Relief is the Object*, the Secretary at War do in like manner, notify to one or other of the Ancient Secretaries of State, and also the Secretary of State for the Colonies, as well the Regiments or Corps which are to be sent, as those which are to return, desiring in his Letter to the Ancient Secretary of State, that he would take the King's Pleasure for the necessary Orders to the several Officers here respecting the transportation, and also for the embarkation of the Troops to be sent from hence: And desiring in his Letter to the Secretary of State for the Colonies, that he would take the King's Pleasure for such Orders as may be necessary to be given to the Commander in Chief in America, or to the Governors of the Colonies respecting the Disposition of the said Troops sent from Europe upon their arrival, together with such Orders as may be necessary, as well to the Offices here, as to the Commander in Chief in America, or the Governors of the Colonies, respecting the embarkation and transportation from thence, of the Regiments which are to return.

Case of Troops returning to Great Britain, or Ireland from the Colonies.

3d.   That in all Cases of Troops ordered to return to Great Britain or Ireland from the Colonies *where no Relief is sent out* the Secretary at War do in like manner notify to both Offices the Regiments or Corps which are to return, desiring in his letter to the Secretary of State for the Colonies, that he would take the King's Pleasure for such Orders, as well to the proper Offices here as to the Commander in

Chief in America, or the Governor of the Colony, as may be necessary for the embarkation and transportation of the Troops from the said Colonies to Great Britain or Ireland, & desiring in his letter to the Ancient Secretary of State, that he would take The King's Pleasure for the necessary Orders touching the reception and disposition of the said Troops upon their arrival in Great Britain or Ireland.

NB   No proposition is made with respect to the Case of removal of Troops from one Colony or place in Africa or America, to another, as no question has arisen upon that Case; and it is presumed that all Orders respecting that Service will continue as hitherto to be issued from the Office of the Secretary of State for the Colonies only.

If this arrangement is approved it is proposed that all the Letters which have been dispatched to and from the different Offices, respecting the Orders for the relief that is to go out in April, be revoked, and fresh Dispatches wrote agreeable to the above arrangement.

S.P. 41/26 [pages not numbered]

32

The King to Barrington

[Holograph]   Queen's House
                                          30 January 1775

Lord Barrington: I have received Your plan of the utmost force that can be collected in New England for the Service of this Year, I wish You would deferr laying a Copy of it before Lord North and

Lord Dartmouth untill I have seen You on Wednesday, as I shall then wish to have some explanation of this paper. Lord Dartmouth has acquainted Sir Jeffry Amherst with the occasion of my wishing to see him tomorrow and it appears as if he will do his utmost to avoid going to America; but I hope to put so strongly before his eyes that the having freed that part of the Globe of so dangerous neighbours as the French is not more honorable than the bringing these Colonies to a sense of their duty and thus by his weight preventing an effusion of blood which if unavoidable cannot be but be[sic] disagreable.

Ipswich 111, no. 52

33

The King to Barrington

[Holograph]
Kew
8.10, 29 July 1775

Lord Barrington, Having received last night a letter from Lord Rochford which shews Sir J. Blacquiere means to evade raising the Recruits in the County of Kerry untill October I think it right to apprize You of it that if possible the Scheme I gave You yesterday may be effected for sending above 2,000 Men to Boston this Autumn, the more I reflect upon it the more I am confirmed in my idea that two compleat Regiments and Recruits to put the Army now there is a much better plan than five fresh Regiments and the troops now there in the present broken situation; but if upon canvassing the matter what I have proposed cannot be brought to bear in time for Sailing this Autumn, then desire Lt. G. Harvey to devise the best method of getting 2,000 from Ireland for N. America; but then I insist upon Roche's plan for recruiting being solely turned to compleating during the Winter the Regiments in N. America in either case Lt. G. Gage must have notice to keep the private men of the 18th 59th and any other Regiments unfit for Service and send the Officers & non Comms. &c Home.

Ipswich 111, no. 56

34

The King to Barrington

[Holograph]   Queen's House
                                          2 February 1776

Lord Barrington, The Considerable Draft that has been made
from some of the Eight Regiments now under Orders for foreign
Service has occasioned my changing the Destination of the 21st
and 31st Regiments from going to Ireland to be part of the eight
Regiments to Serve in Canada; I have in consequence of this
Resolution this Morning directed the Lord Lieut. of Ireland to
have the 3d. 9th. 11th. 20th. 24th. 34th. 53d. and 62d. to be
inspected by M. G. Cunninghame, and that if on his Report they
are equally fit for Service the 3d. and 11th. as last on the Four for
Service to be kept in Ireland in lieu of the 21st. and 31st.
Regiments, but should of the eight any two Regiments be in worse
order than the rest, those two are to be ordered to remain in
Ireland.

Ipswich 111, no. 70

35

Barrington to the Duke of Newcastle:
Paper on recruitment

[Copy in clerk's hand]   N.p., n.d. [November 1759]

Tho' at present there are wanting to compleat the British forces in
Germany no more than 337 men, double that number will not
compleat them in the Spring, even on a supposition that they do
not suffer from the Enemy. As the Army still keeps the field, no
Officers are come over to recruit, & if they came little success
would be expected.

There is no way of keeping this Corps effective, with such men
as will preserve the reputation it has acquired, but by sending
Voluntiers draughted from the Regts. in Great Britain. The

manner in which the last draught was made, tho' somewhat troublesome, is the most equal & least felt by each Corps.

The East India Battns. under Draper & Coote, especially the former, will want recruits – I think it would be right to give an additional Company to each, which might be sent over to India as soon as compleated; & on their arrival, if the War continues, a like number of Commission Officers might be sent from India to Europe to raise their Companies here. This was practised when Adlercron's Regt. was in India.

I have good accounts of Morris's Battn. & think there is a prospect of it's being raised within the time stipulated by him; but I have great doubts whether any part of it can be at the place of embarkation in the month of January. I have sent an intelligent Officer, a Welshman, into Wales, to see what can be done immediately in that part of the Country by giving Commissions to Gentlemen there. I flatter myself we shall have some success; but the month of January is coming on fast; & this important Service, I see plainly, must not be left to uncertain contingencies.

The King will not send the old Regts. or any part of them. The young Regts. are most of them too weak to bear draughts, or detachments; & if any of them were sent as a Corps, & the Colonel could be left behind as being a General Officer, their Lieut. Colonels would be older than Coote, if not older than Draper. We do not want Field Officers in India.

If five Companies of Craufurd's, consisting of 100 men each, were sent by the first ships, with Officers of no higher rank than Captains, that Regt. would remain in England with three Field Officers & nine Companies, & be on the same Establishment with all the other Regts. in Great Britain. The Companies sent to India might still belong to that Regt. so that Col. Craufurd's profits will not be diminish'd; & means might be found for keeping some young Officers of Quallity, as Lord Warkworth & others, at home, without disgracing them. This number of 500 is in all probabillity as many as the first India ships can carry; & we shall probably get Highlanders or Welshmen time enough for those Ships which go later in the Spring.

I dare say the first Returns from Guadaloupe will shew us that 600 or 700 men are wanted to compleat the three Regts. station'd there. I know not how they can be supply'd, unless our successes in No. America should enable us to send some men from thence.

The Garrison of Senegal, tho' more healthy than it was, will want 300 or 400 men. There are no Officers here recruiting for that Garrison; & even those who are recruiting for Gibraltar have little or no success, because most men chuse to stay at home, & therefore inlist in Regts. here on the terms allow'd by the Proclamation.

I almost despair of getting any more Voluntiers for the Regts. at Jamaica & Antigua, where 750 men are wanted to compleat three Regiments.

Recruits in general come in slow. Last week produced 271; the week before 242; & yet November is the best recruiting month in the year, & has sometimes produced near 1000 men a week. The men inlisted by the City are included in this number. As to the Westminster Subscription, it has had little effect, which makes me doubt whether the freedom offer'd by the City has not been a stronger inducement than the money. When recruiting flags very much in the City, I should advise closing both Subscriptions because the large sums offer'd by them do certainly more or less affect recruiting by Regimental Funds, which can not afford any thing like that Levy Money.

There are now on the Establishment near 150,000 British Subjects in red coats, including the Irish Army, the Marines, & the Militia. The Militia consisting chiefly of substitutes keeps men from inlisting in the Army, at present, tho' hereafter it may be a Nursery for the Army. I fear we have not the means of keeping up so large a body of men by Voluntiers; & I never think of compulsive methods, being of opinion that they would do much more harm than good in this Country.

The number of Effectives wanting to compleat the Army at home are near 8000 men. 'Till they are got I submit whether any more new Corps of Infantry should be raised. The only way of getting men at all for new Corps is by giving great preferment to inexperienced Officers, who have fortunes & interests in their Country. I take the Militia to be as good as any Corps so composed, either is or will be during the probable continuance of this War. The Militia brings no charge of Half pay, & does not discontent old Officers like these Regts. If any more Cavalry is wanting, I must strongly recommend Col. Johnston's scheme of adding a Cornet to each Troop of Dragoons, & 10 men & horses raised by him at his own expence. This is the best method, & cheapest both now & hereafter.

If any men should be raised for the local defence of Great Britain, without intention of sending them from thence, it is of consequence that they should not be allow'd any advantages but those granted to the fencible men of Argyllshire & Sutherland, even tho' they might agree that there should be no stipulation against their serving abroad: At least it should be stipulated that the Officers shall have no Half Pay, unless the Corps does *actually* serve abroad.

I can not advise a recruiting Bill this session. Those Bills always produce trouble & tyranny in the Country. Those pass'd in 1757 & 1758 produced little more than 200 men each year & would in all probabillity produce fewer this. I can think of but one means to quicken recruiting, which is, by allowing the marching Regts. to give a guinea for every good recruit to the man who brings him. This has been try'd in the Guards, & I am told with good effect.

I would also advise that the Publick shall give as far as a guinea each to every soldier inlisted for home Service, who will enter into a new engagemt. to serve abroad if requir'd.

Ipswich 3c, no. 236

36

Barrington to the Duke of Newcastle: Paper on recruits for Germany

[Holograph]   N.p.
                                            25 August 1760

The number of Effectives in South Britain, Officers included is

Cavalry	3,869
Infantry	18,351
	22,220

Horse &
Grenadier
Guards   635
Foot
Guards   3753
Invalids   2372

From which deducting the 4 Battns. of foot Guards, the Horse & Grenadier Guards, & the Invalids, there remain 15,460 men. Of these 3224 are Cavalry, 12,226 Infantry.

At present 2,635 of the above 12,226 foot are in Garrison at Land Guard fort, Dover Castle, Tynmouth & Plymouth. Remain in Camp or in Quarters 9,751.

If it shall be thought proper to send abroad the 1400 foot desir'd by Prince Ferdinand; I think it will be least objectionable to send Craufurd's Regiment, which amounts to about that number, to act as a Corps. The Battalions already in Germany, contain one with another near 800 *rank & file*, without being recruited from hence. My reasons for preferring this way of reinforcing Prince Ferdinand are these.

1st Our present numbers will not admit of Draughts from Our Battalions here without tearing them to pieces.

2d I cannot think it adviseable to send any of the Old Corps remaining in South Britain, from thence: They are only Eight in number, and are none of them compleat.

3d The young Regiments here are all so weak (Craufurd's excepted) that it will require two of the strongest among them, to furnish the number demanded. If Craufurd's Regiment goes abroad, there will then remain in South Britain 10,779 foot Effectives (Officers included) After deducting the Foot Guards & Invalids.

Deducting from thence the 2,635 now in

Garrison, at the places before mention'd, the number then remaining would be 8,144.

Dover Castle
457
Tynmouth
[sic] 281
Land Guard
Fort 450
Plymouth

1447
2,635

The Effectives of the Militia (officers included) are 21,524. If Dover, Tynmouth, Land Guard Fort, or Plymouth might be entrusted solely to them, in that case, the number of Regulars now station'd in any or all of these places would be added to the above 8,144.

As to the Cavalry, If it be thought expedient to give the 400 men & horses desir'd for them, (exclusive of what shall be wanting to remount Eliotts) there is no way of furnishing them, but by Draughts from Albemarle's and Rich's, the only Regiments of heavy Dragoons in Sth. Britain. Their Effectives, rank & file, are about 900; and it would be extremely difficult to recruit any Draught made from them.

Eliott's Regiment may be best recruited from Burgoyne's, a Corps rais'd on the same Plan; And I think those Draughts would be replac'd here, with tolerable ease; there being still a great disposition in the people to enlist in the Light Cavalry.

There can be little difficulty in sending horses to Germany; the difficulty lyes in supplying the men. I am surpriz'd to find by a Letter of Lord Granby's to Lord Ligonier that his Lordship, & the Colonels of Cavalry with him, desire to get their horses them selves, tho' they propose to draught their Riders from Our Corps. Surely season'd horses, already train'd to Service, taken from the Regiments here, would be more immediately useful, both for the heavy & light Cavalry in Germany. New Horses bought by the Regiments at home to replace those sent abroad, would soon be train'd & season' here; but most of them would be spoilt by immediate Service in Germany, before they could be useful in that Country.

[*Endorsed*]: Lord Barrington's Paper relative to the Recruits ask'd by Prince Ferdinand.

Add. MSS. 32910, ff. 274–275

37

Barrington to the Duke of Newcastle: Paper on policy

[In Newcastle's hand]   N.p.

12 September 1760

Land Forces –   At Home
                                   In Germany
                                   In America
                                   In the East Indies
                                   Lord Barrington to be con-
                                   sulted; & to suggest what Sav-
                                   ings, if any, can be made.

[In Barrington's hand]

At Home   It is more probable that the Troops at Home will be augmented than diminish'd, because all the foreign Services are supply'd from thence. We have not at present more troops in Great Britain than are wanted for its defence.

In Germany.   while the french remain superior in that part of the World it is more to be wish'd that Reinforcements could be sent thither than that any troops should be brought from thence

In America. America must be divided into the Islands & the Continent. As to the Islands (among which Guadeloupe is included) there can be no diminution of Forces or Expence. On the contrary, fresh demands will come from thence, particularly from Jamaica where the Negroes are very troublesome.

If Canada be reduced this Summer, a less force than what is now on the Continent of America will probably be sufficient there; because our Colonies will want no defence, and less than 20,000 Men (the amount of our Effectives there including the 2000 lately sailed thither) will probably be sufficient to keep the conquer'd Country (disarm'd & tir'd with the War) in order. But I doubt whether any savings can be expected, because if some Regiments could be spared from that part of the world, they will be wanted in others; especially if any new Enterprizes should be undertaken. However there will be a great saving of Expence in Provincial troops, victualing of them, extraordinaries, (which include Carriage of all sorts) &c &c &c, in case the War in Canada should be over this Summer.

I will here venture to submit to consideration, whether all the troops possible should not be sent from N. America, if the War ends there before it ends in *other* parts of the world, & whether as many Soldiers as possible should not be disbanded there, if a general Peace be concluded before they are removed from *that* part of the world.

The Reason is this. In time of Peace, reduced Soldiers are a burthen to the mother Country, because for one that takes to industry at home, ten take to evil courses.

East Indies. I am less able to judge of the objects of War there than elsewhere; but I should think we are more likely to send forces thither than to bring any from thence before a General Peace.

[*Endorsed*]: Extract for Septr. 9th. 1760 Lord Barrington Return'd to the Duke of Newcastle with observations Septr. 12. 1760

Add. MSS. 32911, ff. 263–264

38

Barrington to the Duke of Newcastle:
Paper on Policy

[Holograph]   N.p.
2 October 1760

When I last had the honour to communicate my thoughts to your Grace, on what Savings might be made in the Army, I consider'd whether any and what reductions of Corps were practicable in the different parts which are the Seat of War. I have since turn'd my thoughts to what reductions of expence were practicable in Regiments still kept on foot, and I think some may be made without lessening our present force.

At the beginning of the War, the Establishments of many Regiments sent to America were greatly encreas'd in hopes of raising men to compleat them either there, or at home. This expectation has never answer'd at all. Nobody here will enlist for America, when they have such great encouragement to enter into Service without going abroad, or at least nearer home; and in America it is so much more advantageous to enlist in the Provincial than in the Regular Regiments, that no recruiting for the Army has gone on there, for the last two years. The Troops have during that time been supplied by draughts from hence, and lately by a Battalion and some Companies sent thither, which cannot well be incorporated into the old Corps, at least on the Continent: There is no prospect of sending any more draughts from hence to that part of the World.

If therefore the original intention of enlarging the Regiments in America, neither has been, or can be answer'd, why should they remain on that high Establishment? The pay of the Non-Effective men, tho' stop'd in the hands of the Paymaster, is an unnecessary Grant of Parliament, and the money given for their Cloathing is an unnecessary profit to the Colonel at the Expence of the Public.

If it be thought expedient to reduce these Regiments, the manner of doing it, in my opinion is as follows.

All the Regiments Serving in North America consist of Companies containing either 100 or 70 private men in each.

To a Company of 100 private men, are allotted 1 Captain, 2 Lieutenants, 1 Ensign or 2d Lieutenant, 4 Serjeants, 4 Corporals, and two Drummers. to a Company of 70 private Men 1 Captain, 1 Lieutenant, 1 Ensign, 3 Serjeants, 3 Corporals, and 2 Drummers.

It is propos'd in the Companies which consist of 100 private men, to reduce 1 Ensign or 2d Lieutenant, 1 Serjeant, 1 Corporal, & 30 private men. The reduction of the Serjeant, Corporal, and private men, may very well take place from Christmas next. With regard to the Ensigns it is submitted whether they should not be continued on the Establishment another Year, the Commander in Chief being directed not to fill up any vacancies which may happen in that rank, and to remove the Supernumeraries, as opportunity may offer, into other Regiments which are allowed Ensigns.

In the Companies which consist of 70 private men, a reduction of 10 private [men *omitted*] may be made very safely. If they should be so much farther weakened this Campaign, as to admit of a reduction of 20 private men, 1 Serjeant and 1 Corporal may be reduced at the same time.

By the foremention'd reduction of 1 Serjeant, 1 Corporal, & 30 private men from the Companies of 100 men; & of 10 private men from the Companies of 70 men, the following Savings will be made upon the Estimate for Parliament, of the Forces in North America for the ensuing Year.

			Per Diem		
			£	s	d
From 14 Battalions of 1000 in each	{ 140 Serjeants 140 Corporals 4200 private men }		157	10	
From 1 Battalion of 900 men	{ 9 Serjeants 9 Corporals 270 Private men }		10	2	6
From 2 Battalions of 1400 men in each	{ 28 Serjeants 28 Corporals 840 Private men }		31	10	
From 7 Battalions of	700 private men		13	6	8
	6364 men per diem		212	9	2
	For 365 days		£77,547	5	10

But the real Saving to the Public by this reduction for the year 1761, will be no more than £67,625.4.2, as the Colonels have assigned for their present Cloathing, a part of the Offreckonings of their respective Regiments for the ensuing year, amounting to £10,522.1.8, which in case the propos'd reduction should take place, must be made good by Warrant out the Extraordinaries of the Army. The above mention'd number of 6,364 are less by 300 Men than were wanting to compleat the Regiments in North America, when they took the field this Summer.

The Regiments serving in the Islands of Jamaica and Antigua, are likewise very low in point of numbers; and there is not the least prospect of compleating them. It is therefore propos'd to reduce the Companies of the 38th Regiment at Antigua 10 private men each; the Companies of the 49th Regiment at Jamaica, which at present consist of 4 Serjeants, 4 Corporals, 2 Drummers and 100 private men each, to 3 Serjeants, 3 Corporals, 2 Drummers and 70 private men each; and the Companies of the 74th Regiment at Jamaica and Senegal, which at present consist of 4 Serjeants, 4 Corporals, 2 Drummers & 100 private men, to 2 Serjeants, 2 Corporals, 2 Drummers & 50 private men each, by which reduction the following Savings will be made upon the Estimate for Parliament of the forces in the Plantations for the Year 1761.

		Per Diem		
		£	s	d
From the 38th Regt at Antigua	100 men	3	6	8
From the 49th Regt at Jamaica	10 Serjeants 10 Corporals 300 private men	11	5	
From the 74th Regt at Jamaica & Senegal	20 Serjeants 20 Corporals 500 private men	19	3	4
	960	£ 33	15	
For 365 days		£12,318	15	

But as the Colonels have assigned for their present Cloathing, a part of the next years' Offreckonings amounting to £969.18.0 which must be made good by Warrant if this reduction takes place, the real Saving to the Public for the ensuing year will be

	11,348	16	4
Savings upon the Forces in North America	£67,025	4	2
Savings upon the Regiments in the Islands	11,348	16	4
Total Savings	£78,374	0	6

All the reductions propos'd in this paper may be safely made without diminishing in the least, the number of Effective men in the respective Corps. If any unexpected means should be found to compleat them to their present numbers, in the whole or in part, their Establishment may be again rais'd at any time with the greatest ease.

I have considered all the other Regiments both at home and abroad, but I cannot advise reductions on any of them at this time. [*Endorsed*]: Paper Concerning Reductions which may be made in the Expence of the Army. Given to the Duke of Newcastle by Lord Barrington. Octr. 2 1760

Add. MSS. 32912, ff. 287–289

39

Barrington to the Duke of Newcastle

[Copy in Barrington's hand]   N.p.
                                                     February 1761

By the latest Returns from Germany dated the 1st of December, the British Troops there, wanted 2,391 men, to compleat them to the allowance. Of these 380 were Cavalry, & 2,011 were Infantry.

The sick at that time amounted to 5,596; 571 of whom were Cavalry, & 5,025 Infantry.

The usual computation is, that two thirds of the sick will recover, so as to serve again next Campaign. The third part of 571 is 190; the third part of 5,025 is 1675: so that according to this method of Calculation 570 men will be wanting to compleat the Cavalry, & 4,154 to compleat the Infantry, over and above such, who tho' not ill on the 1st of December, may die before the opening of next Campaign.

Method propos'd for compleating the Cavalry.

The Blues to be compleated (over and above the Recruits they may raise) by draughts from the two Regimts of Rich & Albemarle, now in Great Britain.

The Regiments of Irish Horse, to be compleated by draughts from the Horse in Ireland. The Inniskilling Regiment of Dragoons is always compleated from thence. It is apprehended the Irish Horse will find it easy to replace in Ireland, the draughts they send to Germany.

The Regiments of Bland, Waldegrave, Howard, Conway, Campbell, Mostyn, Mordaunt and Ancram, to be compleated from their own Light Troops; & Eliott's by Draughts from Burgoyne's & Lord Robert Sutton's. There is great reason to hope that these Regiments and Troops of Light Dragoons would be soon full again, as the taste for serving in those Corps still continues, and as no new ones are raising.

What is propos'd for the Infantry is as follows:

The Guards to be compleated out of the Battalions at home, which can always recruit themselves.

The two Highland Battalions to be recruited by draughting the best men of the Nine Highland Independent Companies rais'd, & raising in the Highlands, who are under Orders to come Southward, as soon as they are compleat.

There remains 12 Battalions of foot; their Non Effectives amount to 1,444, and the third part of their sick to 1,172, which added, make 2,616 men. As to these Corps, I propose as follows.

There are 12 Independent Companies raising for the Regimts in Germany; they will produce 1200 private men.

Tho' these Companies are compos'd of better stuff than those rais'd for the other parts of the world; yet, being very raw and totally ignorant of every military duty, I would propose to turn them into Regts at home, in lieu of an equal number draughted from thence, in such manner and proportion as shall be thought proper. The aforesaid Draughts should be made by impartial persons, & sent over with careful officers to Germany.

Craufurd's Regt consisting of five Companies more than any other Corps, the men of those Companies may be sent to Germany, the Officers remaining here, & endeavouring to raise the same number afresh.

These men might do well enough, for Hatmen; but, in order to supply the Grenadiers, a sufficient number might be draughted from the *Irish* Soldiers of the Battalions in Ireland: And if this were done with discretion, perhaps the Irish Army might not be the worse for it. If Ireland could furnish 900 men for the Infantry in Germany, the account would stand thus.

Wanted for the 12 Marching Regts in Germany		2,616
Independt. Comps	1,200	
Crawfurds	500	
Irish Draughts	900	2,600
Wanting to compleat the 12 Battns in Germany		16

Tho' the foregoing Proposal is founded on the best Data we have, I am sensible how uncertain all such calculations are, and therefore I will now add some additional methods of furnishing men for Germany.

There will remain in South Britain after the departure of the Expedition, six new Regts of foot, vizt. Gray's, La Faussille's, Lambton's, Trapaud's, Richmond's, & Craufurds. Of these, the two last are the strongest, & therefore I will not propose taking a man from them. The other four are very weak, and I see no prospect of compleating them. The private men of these Regts amount to 2,188 who might be dispos'd of partly to the Regts in Germany, & partly to the Regts at home, none of which last are compleat. The Officers might be reduc'd to half pay for the present, which must be their fate whenever the War ends; And, if the Field Officers were assur'd of being provided for in other Corps as Vacancies happen'd, they would be gainers by the reduction. As to the Captains & Subalterns, they are not in general, men of much service, & those among them who have pretensions, might be provided for in other Corps. This measure would also produce a large saving to the Publick.

But if this total reduction of these four Regmts were thought too great a hardship; Or, if from other motives it be deem'd inexpedient, one hundred men would be sufficient to enable each Corps to recruit afresh; & then the remaining 1778 might be applied to the purposes abovemention'd.

In case it shall be thought unnecessary, or inexpedient to compleat all the British Corps in Germany, from hence, the following method might help to compleat some of them.

Send home the officers of three Marching Regts, leaving the men to be incorporated into the remaining nine, except just so many as with the Non Commission Officers, shall be sufficient to enable them to go a recruiting after they return. I think this cannot produce less than 1000 men.

Another Idea is to keep all the 12 Marching Regiments abroad, reducing the number of private Soldiers in each, below the present Establishment. But, I submit whether the same number of men be not more useful in Nine strong, then in 12 weak Battalions; especially as the Grenadiers form Corps apart. The strongest British Battalion that was engag'd near Wesel did not fight more than 500 private men, tho' it took the field in the Spring compleated up to 900.

If the bringing over three Regiments hither, be approv'd, Lord Granby should be directed to make choice of them.

[*Endorsed*]: Proposals for Recruiting the Army in Germany. Feb. 1761

Ipswich 3b, no.1

40

Barrington to Lord North

[Copy]   Beckett
                                                 23 December 1774

As I presume the Army in No America is one of the matters now under the consideration of the King's Servants, I think it may be of some use to remind your Lōp, that four Battalions which belong to the Forces here, make part of that Army.

After deducting from the 17,000 men at home, the Horse & Foot Guards which are fixed to the Capital, a Regt of Light Dragoons which escorts the King, the forces in Scotland, Guernsey & Jersey; what remains in South Britain is but barely sufficient to answer the common requisitions of the Civil Magistrates in the different parts of the Kingdom. I cannot therefore without uneasiness reflect that near 2000 taken from the small number are so far distant, when the high price of Bread, & a Stop to all orders from No America give room to apprehend more than ordinary Commotion among various Setts of Manufacturers.

If it be judged necessary to Support the authority of Parliament by Land forces acting vigorously on the other side of the Atlantic, nothing can be spared from the Troops now there; but in that case it should be consider'd whether an addition ought not to be made to the Army in So. Britain equal to the four Regmts which are lent to another Service.

If the Plan should be to reduce the North Americans to a proper sense of their duty by the operations of the Marine, it should then be consider'd whether the four Battalions might not return home.

Ipswich 107

3

The War Office and Its Work

For most of Barrington's official career the War Office was situated in the Horse Guards. It had migrated there by way of several addresses from the time of Charles II. An earlier Secretary at War, William Blathwayt, had even established the War Office in his own house. When Barrington was appointed in 1755 the office was in Number 7 Whitehall, where it had been since 1721. Within a year it moved to the newly completed Horse Guards where shortly afterwards Barrington arranged with Gold Stick in Waiting for parking rights for his coach (41). Here in a suite of rooms comparable in size to that of a modern set of barristers' chambers the Secretary at War and a handful of clerks conducted the greater part of the day-to-day running of the Georgian army.

Many other departments and officials were conveniently close at hand in Whitehall and Pall Mall. The Adjutant-General, whose office had at various times been in the old Horse Guards and Cleveland Court, was in another part of the new Horse Guards, and the Paymaster-General's handsome office building was next door in Whitehall. The Judge Advocate General, after a series of wanderings in Privy Gardens and the Strand, had come to rest in premises nearby in Whitehall: the Board of General Officers also met in his office. The offices of the Secretaries of State were at the Cockpit and Cleveland Row. The whereabouts of the Commander-in-Chief is less certain. Presumably he was at the Horse Guards as in later years, although there is no evidence of letters proceeding from there in Ligonier's time. The Board of Ordnance moved to Palace Yard, Westminster some time in the 1750s. Many of the agents with whom the Secretary at War was in constant touch —Calcraft, Adair, James Merrick, Cox and Drummond—could be reached by only a few minutes walk for a War Office messenger. And Barrington's town house was only a short drive away. He sometimes refers in correspondence to his 'office day',[1] but in fact he came into the office one, two or three days a week, sometimes more, if there was such an emergency as the great recruiting drive of 1757.

The staff of clerks awaiting him in the office included several veterans. He declined to take on Henry Fox's Deputy Secretary Edward Lloyd (2), and appointed Thomas Sherwin, who had been a clerk since 1731 when Henry Pelham had been at the War Office. Sherwin did not live much longer, however,[2] and Thomas Tyrwhitt, the writer of classical commentaries, succeeded him,[3] surviving until the end of Barrington's first term, when Charles Townshend brought in his own appointment. Tyrwhitt had an important role in advising Barrington, settling work programmes for big projects such as augmentations or foreign expeditions (42), producing precedents and conducting research projects.[4] His successor Welbore Ellis appointed Christopher D'Oyly as the Deputy Secretary in 1763,[5] and Barrington kept him on when he resumed office in 1765. Relations with D'Oyly deteriorated: the appearance of Philip Francis as First Clerk, a friend of D'Oyly, may have had some connection with this, for both seem to have united in their dislike of Barrington. The appointment of Anthony Chamier the banker[6] in the room of D'Oyly puzzled contemporaries (Section 1), for Chamier clearly had no need to work. But he seems to have regarded it as an interesting hobby for a gentleman[7] and served efficiently for three years. Matthew Lewis, the father of 'Monk' Lewis, the gothic novelist, was Barrington's last appointment.[8]

The First Clerk was the next most important man in the office, and could reasonably expect to succeed the Deputy in due course: Sherwin, D'Oyly and Lewis had all been First Clerks. Thomas Bradshaw, Barrington's protégé might also have succeeded to the post had he not been appointed a Chief Clerk to the Treasury in 1761 after two years at the War Office. Philip Francis, appointed by Ellis, quickly mastered the complexities of the work of the office. The detailed statement he drew up when he had only been with the War Office for a year ranges impressively over every aspect of the work of the office. It was probably written at the instance of Ellis, to serve as a guide.[9] Barrington was soon aware of his First Clerk's excellent grasp of business. By 1766 he was writing to the Secretary to the Treasury declining to enter into a complicated discussion of army finance until Francis returned from holiday (43): later in the year he relied heavily on him during the emergency of the food riots (44). However the nineteenth-century biographers of Francis[10] gave a rather too partial account of the part he played in the War Office. They depicted him as a brilliant master of the official letter, handling most of the intricate correspondence, while Barrington and Christopher D'Oyly spent their time receiving suitors. The best letters going out over Barrington's signature were, they allege, composed by Francis. They go so far as to claim that Barrington's literary style was impoverished and even grammatically incorrect. The quality of numerous drafts in the Barrington archive in his own hand give the lie to this notion, where there is no evidence of lack of grasp of issues or of grammar. The stature of Francis does not need to be exaggerated, by denigration of his master. He was certainly clever and pushing, and too big for the walls of the War Office. If he was Junius then he would also have been ill conditioned and vengeful. It is surprising that he lasted so long at the War Office.

* * *

Few clues survive as to the accommodation and office arrangements in Barrington's time (45, 46). And it is odd that although he was so meticulous in some matters he seems never to have called for a general statement of the office routine together with job descriptions of his staff. In 1779 Charles Jenkinson, Barrington's successor, caused the first of these statements to be drawn up, although it only extended to personnel, salaries and fees (47). The document, probably prepared by Matthew Lewis, alleged that no similar document had been found in the records except for a list from 1720: this was not quite true, but the list made in 1759 was of the same type, a bare statement of clerks and salaries (48).

Barrington's own salary passed in the Estimates for £365 a year—no more than that of the Adjutant-General[11] but this was only a small part of the annual sum he received. Since the seventeenth century the Secretary at War had been paid 'allowances' which together with the official salary made an amount not far inferior to that paid to a Secretary of State. If the public did not know before what Barrington's true emolument was, Junius was on hand to tell them.[12]

A much more detailed watch bill for the War Office, drawn up four years after Barrington's retirement, gives an insight into the extraordinary system of perquisites and fees which had grown up over many years in the office, fees which sometimes amounted to much greater sums than the salaries (49, 50). These papers dwell more upon the fees than upon the work done by the recipients. To arrive at an exact idea of a clerk's entitlement was important: Matthew Lewis had to break in upon Barrington's retirement to ask for his view on Leonard Morse's fees on entry of officers' commissions (51).

The eighteenth-century view of a post as a piece of property meant that many clerks remained immovably fixed in their jobs for many years, collecting sums which were substantial in peace-time and in wartime were enormous. In 1796 Parliament became curious about this state of affairs and learned some interesting facts. Several of Barrington's clerks—Harman Leece, who had been in the office for fifty years, Charles Marsh (thirty-five years), Andrew Clinton (forty years), and Charles Plenderleath (thirty years) had only just retired. In that year the Deputy Secretary at War received £2,837 in fees, the Examiner of Army Accounts £4,757 and the First Clerk the astounding amount of £14,482.[13] The reluctance of clerks to retire is unsurprising. And yet their work was arduous and repetitive. It also carried with it some element of risk. The fate which overtook William Johnston, who lost his post after irregularities had been detected in the passing of contingent bills, must have been remembered in the office for years (52, 53, 54). Johnston's letter of defence gives a vivid impression of a chaotic and overstrained system of work, of which he had become an inadvertent victim. It is more than half-convincing. Perhaps an increase in the establishment of staff would have been fair. Edmund Burke, for all his dislike of the institution, was unable some years later to detect any obesities in the War Office that needed reduction.

41

Lord Cadogan's Orders

[Copy] N.p.
16 November 1757

That the Commanding Officers of the Horse Guards at Whitehall is [sic] to Order the Centries always to permit the Secretary at War's Coach to come into the Court Yard at Whitehall, there to remain during the Time His Coach is in Waiting. Also, to let all Gentlemen's Coaches (but no Hackney Coaches) into Whitehall Yard, that have Business at the War Office, and when the Coach is Empty, they [sic] are to go out of the Court Yard and stand in the Street way. Neither the Secretary at War's Coach, nor any other Gentleman's Coach, having Business at the War Office be permitted to go thro' the gate into St James's Park.

The Centries are to open the Gates at any time in the Night for the Clerks, whose Business is at the War Office to go in or out.

W.O. 26/23, p. 333

42

Internal War Office memorandum about the Rochefort expedition

N.p.
16 July 1757

[Written columnwise: text on left in
one hand (Bowles?): a few comments and ticks on
right in another (Tyrwhitt?)]
Lord Barrington
To leave Blank March Routes for
Bentincks, Amhersts The Second √
Battn. of Effinghams & for
Loudons Regimt. to march from the

Camp at Barham Downs to ----------
--- and for Homes, Hodgsons &
Brudenells to march from ye Camp √
at Chatham to ---------
--- For the First Battn. of Chas.
Hays, the Second Battn. of Do.; √
for the First Battn. of
Cornwallis's, the Second Battn.
of ditto; for the First Batt of
Stuarts and for the Second Battn.
of Do & march from the Camp near
Amersham to --------- and Blank
Routes for the First Battn. of
the Buffs, the First Battn. of √
the Kings own Regiment and the
First Battn. of Kingsleys to
march from the Camp at
Dorchester.
To order the Apothecary Gnl to √
provide [double *added in the
second hand*] Medicine Chests for
the 12 Battalions under orders.
To make out the List of the
Staff; and the Instructions for √
the Cōmander in chief for the
time being
To let the Admiralty know that
Tonnage be provided for 3 Women p √
Company of the Ten Battalions,
more than the Establishment of
Officers & Men, and that Tonnage
will be wanted for 6 Officers &
112 Dragons with [140 *added in
the second hand*] 186 Horses. That
Tonnage be laid in for these
horses & Bread for the whole
Troops for ------- [3 Months
added in first hand] days.

*The instructions come from
the Secretary of State*

Hospital Ship for 300 Men. A √
Warrt. to Lt. Gl. Mordaunt or
Cõmanding Offr for the time being
to hold Gnl. Cts. Martial & put
the Sentences in execution, and
three Blank Deputations from the
Judge Advocate General.

A Paymaster, Money for Sub-   *This Sir J. must settle with*
sisting the Troops and for   *the Treasury & Pay Office*
Contingencies to be provided, to
be settled with the Pay Office.

The Hospital to be regulated   *This will be done with the*
for 500 men, with Mr. Cathcart   *assistance of Dr. Pringle*
Mr. Comissary Hume about Bread &
Forrage for the Troops when
encamped or on the March.

[*Endorsed* Mems for Ld. B. July 16]

Ipswich 3b, no. 209

43

Barrington to Grey Cooper

[Copy]   War Office
                                                11 July 1766

I am to acknowledge the Receipt of Your Letter of the 27th. of last
month, relative to the Liquidation of the Demands of Ireland in
Great Britain, and to desire you will inform the Rt. Honorable the
Lords Commissioners of HM's Treasury that as soon as Mr.
Francis returns from the Country, which will be in a fortnight, I
shall direct him to wait on Sir Robert Wilmot and enter on that
Business.

W.O. 4/80, p. 77

44

Barrington to Philip Francis

[Holograph]
Cavendish Square
24 September 1766

Lord Barrington desires that Mr. Francis will prepare an order in consequence of the letter herewith enclosed, consulting with General Harvey and the quartermaster general how it can best be done. He will come to the Office at noon to sign it. There must also be ready an answer to Lord Shelburne acquainting him how the King's Orders have been obey'd. Lord Barrington thinks the Duke of Gloucester's regiment is the nearest, Trowbridge being in Wiltshire. He also desires Mr. Francis will prepare against he comes at noon a short state of what Troops have been order'd to march in consequence of corn riots since they began, & to what places.

W.O. 1/873, no. 471

45

Barrington to George Shevlocke Esq

[Copy]
War Office
17 January 1756

The business requiring it, I have appointed Mr Wm. Bowles, of my Office (who writes this) to be one of my Franking Clerks. I acquaint you therewith that the Letters frank'd by him, in my Name, may not be Charged.

W.O. 4/51, p. 137

46

War Office Memorandum

[Copy in hand of William Bowles:
Barrington's signature] 15 October 1757

I have this day agreed to permit my first Clerk Mr Bowles to
inhabit the Rooms in the attick Story in the new War Office
during the pleasure of the Secretary at War for the Time being,
and on Condition that it bring no additional Charge on the Public
for Coals and Candles, or any other Account.

Barrington

I thankfully accept the use of those Rooms on these Conditions; and I promise to deliver them, or any part of them
up immediately whenever I shall be required so to do by the
Secretary at War for the time being.

Wm. Bowles

W.O. 26/23, p. 309

47

War Office Memorandum on Staff and Salaries

[Copy] War Office
5 January 1779

An Acct. of the number and Names of the Persons in the
Department of the Secretary at War, on the 5th Jañry 1779, with
their respective Salaries, distinguishing the time when any increase in the Number of such persons, or in their Salaries was first
made, as far as the same can be prepared from any Documents in
the War Office.

	Present Salaries		
Right Honble Mr Jenkinson	£2476		
Mr Lewis as Deputy Secretary	321	2	
Do as first Clerk	98	5	4

	Present Salaries	
Mr Smith Examiner of Army Accounts	520	
[*In margin*: Clerks on the Establishment]		
Mr Leece	90	
Mr Marsh	110	
Mr Davis augmented at Lady day 1776 from 71 to	92	
Mr Morse augmented at Michms. 1772 from £50 to £250, at Christmas 1777 to	280	
Mr Channing	111	
Mr Clinton augmented at Xmas 1778 from £120 to	220	
Mr Bowles augmd. at Lady day 1774 from £54.12. to £73.10; at Xmas 1775 to	150	
Mr Taylor augmented at Lady day 1773 from £50 to £120, at Midsummer 1777 to	200	
Mr Clements augmd. at Lady day 1776 from £104.12. to	154	12
Mr Weir augmd. at Michms. 1775 from £54.12. to	73	10
Mr Plendleath [ie, Plenderleath] augmd. at Midsumr. 1775 fr. £54.12. to £73.10; at Lady day 1776 to	100	
[*In margin*: Supernumeraries]		
Mr Shuckborough augmd. at Midsumr. 1775 fr. £54.12 to £73.10. at Midsumr. 1778 to	100	
Mr Dods do do	100	
Mr Green augmd. at do. from £54.12 to	73	10
Mr Collins do do	73	10
Mr Watkins	54	12
Mr Winder	54	12

NB   There never has been kept in the War Office any Register of the Clerks employed therein or of their Salaries: Nor is there any Document of any kind in the Office of more than six or Seven Years back, in any manner relative thereto, excepting a List of Clerks in the Year 1720, hereunto annexed.

* * *

W.O. 26/30, pp. 92–93

48

Barrington to Thomas Bowlby [at Mr Holland's in Carlisle Street, Soho Square]

[Copy]   War Office
                                            27 September 1759

I send you enclosed, according to yr. request, an Account of the Persons employed in this Office with the places they hold, and the Salaries, Fees, Wages, Pensions & Gratuities respectively paid to them by the Crown for those places.

The above Salaries &c being paid by His Majesty's Paymaster General, the proper deductions have been, and will be made by him from such Places in this Office as exceed one hundred Pounds per Annum.

* * *

	£	s	d
The Lord Viscount Barrington, Secretary at War	2002	11	6
Thomas Tyrwhitt, Deputy Secretary	225		
Thomas Bradshaw 1st Clerk	121		
Gilbert Elliott	100		
James Reynolds	90		
Harman Leece	80		
Vacant	60		
John Davies	50		
Robt. Pierce	50		
Leonard Morse	50		
Thomas Johnson	50		
Sebastian Channing	50		
William Berkeley	50		
Thomas Bowles	50		

W.O. 4/59, p. 82

'Account of the Persons employ'd in the War Office, their Business, Salaries and Perquisites'

[Copy]   20 July 1782

The Secretary at War. His Salary is £2476 p Ann clear He receives no Fees whatever, except on the Renewal of Commissions at the Demise of the Crown.

He has the whole Direction under the King of the Department of War, and appoints the Under Secretary and all the other Principal & Supernumerary Clerks, Messengers & other Persons employ'd in the Office.

The Several Persons at present employ'd in the Office are as follows Viz.

Deputy Secretary at War M. Lewis Esq. His Salary is £320 p Ann but he is entitled to Fees arising from the Entry of Comissions—This makes his Place to be worth £500 p Ann in Time of Peace and £900 p Ann in Time of War. And he has also a Contingent Warrant for £200 p Ann. more during the Time of the Militia being called out.

First Clerk M Lewis Esq. His Salary is £100 p Ann but he is entitled to Fees which make this Place worth £800 p Ann in time of Peace and £2000 p Ann in Time of War.

He has the Care of the Detail of the General Business of the Office and superintends the Conduct of all the Clerks.

Principal Clerk and Examiner of Army Accts. R Taylor Esq. His Salary is £520 p Ann with a certain Share of Fees which makes his Place worth £630 p Ann in time of Peace and about £750 in Time of War. He also receives a Moiety of the Emoluments of the Deputy Secretary.

The whole Department of Accounts is under his Controul nor is he considered as subject to the Directions of the Deputy Secretary, as the other Clerks are but only of the Secretary at War himself.

Principal clerk Assistt. to the Examiner of Army Accts. Mr

Collings. His Salary is £200 p Ann besides which he is entitled to Fees on attested Copies of the Beating Orders – which Fees amount to about £120 p Ann in time of Peace and £250 in Time of War.

Private Secretary & Clerk established, Mr Merry. His Salary is £200 p Ann by means of the following Arrangement. The late Clerk examinant has retired with the King's leave retaining £300 p Ann of his Salary from Midsummer 1782 The remainder of his Salary is given to Mr Taylor who succeeds him retaining his former Salary as Assistant but giving up his Fees on Beating Orders as follows Viz

Mr Collings succeeding to the Office as Assistant to Mr Taylor engages to pay to the Private Secretary £125 p An out of the Fees for Beating Orders, and £25 p An to Mr Plenderleath now Assistant to Mr Marsh. The remainder he takes as his Salary – on Condition that if the Surplus fall short of £50 it shall be made good to him out of the Contingent Office Bills – So that the Salary of the Private Secretary will be as follows £73.10. as Clerk in the Room of Mr Collings £21 as Attendant on the Secretary at War and £125 to be paid by Mr Collings out of the Fees for Beating Orders. In all £200 p Ann untill some better Provision can be made for the Private Secretary.

Principal Clerk Mr Marsh. Salary £110 p An with Fees which make the Place worth £600 p Ann in Time of Peace and as far as £1500 p Ann in Time of War and he has at Present the apartments of the Deputy Secretary at War with Coals and Candles.

He is responsible for the Estimates & Establishments – Collects the Returns of the Garrisons & of the Staff at Home & abroad & prepares Warrants for their Payment. Furnishes the Secretary at War with Lists of Quarters and assists the first Clerk in directing the Current business of the Office. He has been in the Office ever since 1759.

Principal Clerk. Mr Leece. He is the Oldest Clerk in the Office. His Salary is £90 p Ann His fees are the same as Mr Marsh's. Consequently his Place is of the same Value.

His Business is to superintend the Letter writers Desk to take an Account of & receive the Fees upon the Several Warrants & to administer the Oaths to Widows & Officers which he does *Gratis* *[an ironical pencilled comment added in an early nineteenth-century hand*: how liberal]

Principal Clerk. Mr Morse. His Salary is £80 p Ann with Fees on the Entry of Commissions & on Warrants for Courts Martial which makes his place worth about £300 p Ann besides which he has an allowance of £100 p An for compiling the List of the Army & he has all the Profits of Printing it. He has also £100 for his trouble in keeping a Book for the King containing a Register of the Services of the Several Officers of the Army another £100 for extra Clerks employed by him in Entering the several Changes & Additions to the King's Book.

His Business is to take and Enter Commissions and to receive the Deputy Secretary at War's Fees upon them, & a small Fee for himself. The Deputy Secretary's Fees on Commissions are one Day's Pay according to the Rank of the Commission.

He has been in the Office ever since the year 1753.

Established Clerk. Mr Channing. Has been in the Office ever since 1756. His Salary is £110 and Fees to the Amount of about £50 p Ann more for Keeping the Account of Expences on Deserters sent from their several Establishments.

Anor. Clerk Established. Mr Davies. His Salary is £110 p Ann with £20 allow'd him by the First Clerk for paying the allowances on the Compassionate List. He likewise pays the Widows of the Army under the appointment of the Paymaster of the Widows Pensions (Mr. H Fox)

Anor. Clerk Established. Mr Clinton. His Salary is £120 p Ann. He was private Secretary to Lord Barrington & has obtained an Additional Salary of £100 till better provided for.

His Business is to make out the Contingent Bills of the Office and to receive the Salary for the Secretary at War. He also keeps an Index of the Business of the Office arranged according to the several Regiments which is called the journal Book.

Anor. Clerk Establish'd. Mr Clements. His Salary is £154.12. He writes the Notifications & takes Charge of all the Papers relating to them. Registers the Leaves of Absence & Publishes Promotions in the Gazette.

Anor. Clerk Establish'd. Mr Bowles. His salary is £150. He

writes in the Deputy Secretary's Room endorses & Keeps all his Papers.

Anor. Clerk Establish'd. Mr Weir. His Salary is £73.10. He keeps an Account of Compassionate Cases which with copying Papers & Letters gives him full employment.

Anor. Clerk Establish'd. Mr Plenderleath. His Salary is £100 p An he is Assistant to Mr Marsh in the Estimates Business & in the Accounts of the Establishments.

There are also six Supernumerary Clerks, whose Salaries are as follows viz.

Mr Dodd Mr Green	at £100 p. An. Each.
Mr Watkins [space blank]	at £73.10. Each
Mr Winder Mr W Mackay	at £52.10. Each

Their Business is to transcribe, Copy and enter all Letters & Orders into the Books of the Office which is done very regularly. The Senior of these (Mr. Dodd) also keeps the Account & has the Care of all the Correspondence relating to Deserters. Mr. H. Mackay. Has also £52.10 p An. for preparing all the Books of Returns & is frequently employed on *extra* Business for which he has *extra* Pay allowed him when employ'd.

Office Keepers	Mr Green at £100 Profits included Mrs Green at £30 p An Do.
Establish'd Messenger	Mr Stacey. Salary £60 p An.
Acting Messenger	Mr George Doyle worth about £150 p An.
Assistant Messenger	Mr Jas. Harrington. Salary £10 p An. & Wages of 12s. p Week.
Two Porters	at 12s. p Week Wages.

W.O. 2/42, pp. 3–9

50

War Office Fees 1782

[Copy]   [20 July 1782]

The Fees said to be Received & divided between the Deputy Secretary at War, First Clerk and the Principal Clerk, arise & are shared as follows Viz.

There is a Fee on Money Warrants of one Guinea for every £100.

One Guinea p Company or Troop on Augmentation Warrants & the same on Debentures. And on Warrants for Clearances & Repayments of Poundages & other Stoppages, there is a Fee of one Guinea p Regiment.

These Fees are shared & divided as follows viz

On Money & other Warrants (except Clearances & Augmentations) The First Clerk has two fifths and the remaining three fifths are divided equally between Mr. Marsh & Mr. Leece.

On the Warrants for clearances and Augmentations the first Clerk has two fifths and the remaining three fifths are equally divided between the Principal Clerk examiner, and Mr. Marsh and Mr. Leece.

W.O. 2/42, p. 11

51

Matthew Lewis, Deputy Secretary at War
to Barrington

[Holograph]   War Office
                                                  7 October 1779

I am under the necessity of troubling your Lordship with a business which plagued you not a little while you were at the head of this Office.

Mr. Morse's *Book* Warrant is to be settled. Mr. Jenkinson is an entire Stranger to the nature of his Claims, & has called upon me as well to supply him with the information within my power, as to endeavour to obtain Your Lordship's ideas upon it.

I have therefore prepared two Papers—N.1 is prepared from *Records*, and I can therefore vouch for it's accuracy—N.2 is drawn up from Memory; and it is upon that Paper, I wish your Lordship to authorize me to say from yourself that it is the real state of the case; or to point out where it is mistaken—Mr. Jenkinson would be very happy if Your Lordship would be obliging enough to add whether if you had continued here, you would have made any further allowance to Morse than the £200.

The Plea of the new Book may entitle him to something beyond it—What should, in reason, be called an adequate & liberal allowance for it, 150£ which He asks though not expressly upon that ground, or £50—or £100?

Your Lordship can conceive how aukwardly I feel in being the person to give that intelligence which is to prelude the hopes of Lord Amherst's Secretary; and you know at the same time, that no consideration can induce me to sink or gloss over a single circumstance respecting what has passed within my own knowledge and to the best of my recollection—Perhaps Your Lordship will not thank me for drawing you in for a share in this business; but I really think as it was conducted so entirely under your Lordship's direction, it would neither be consistent with propriety on the part of the present Secretary at War, nor with justice to Mr. Morse, to have the point determined, without reference to Your Lordship.

Our affairs stand still everywhere; I might almost say, go backward—A Fever is got among the Fleet; insomuch that I hear four Ships are too sickly to put to Sea—

* * *

Ipswich 7, no. 104

52

Barrington to William Johnston

[Copy]   War Office
                                              6 September 1765

I am informed from undoubted authority that the Public has been defrauded to the amount of several hundred pounds in the Contingent Bills of the following Regts. of Militia, Vizt.

Westmoreland from	25th June 1761 to	24th June 1762
Do	25th June 1762	24 Decr. 1762
Durham	25th Augt. 1761	Do
Do	Contingent Disbursements	
Listers	1. Sep. 1761	24 June 1762
Do	25 June 1762	24 Decr. 1762
Cumberland	25 Decr. 1761	Do
Sir Digby Legard	25 June 1761	14 Novr. 1762
Do	15 Nov. 1762	24 Decr. 1762
Leicestershire	25 Decr. 1761	Do

The Warrants for these Bills were not obtained by Mr. Ellis till after they had been examin'd & approv'd by you. There can be no doubt of the fact, because the Agent to these Regiments gave notice of the fraud with great honour the moment he discovered it. I am also inform'd that the Clerk who Sollicited the passing of these Bills gave you five Guineas before they were passed.

You will let me know in writing on what grounds these Contingent Bills were approv'd by you, and whether you received the aforesaid money

W.O. 4/988, p. 19

53

William Johnston to Barrington

[Copy]   16 September 1765

By your Lordship's Letter, I am commanded to deliver in writing upon what grounds the ten contingent Bills of five Militia Regiments recited by your Lordship, were approved by me; Your Lordship having undoubted Authority to induce you to believe, that by them the Public has been defrauded several Hundred Pounds; and to answer to the Charge of my having received, previously to my passing those Accounts, the Sum of Five Guineas.

Before I enter upon my particular Exculpation, as to the Fact specified, your Lordship will, I hope, forgive me in observing, that altho' your Lordship seems to be of Opinion, that Warrants could not be obtained for these Bills, until examined and approved by me; yet nothing is more certain, than that such Warrants have been granted, without any previous Examination of mine, and the Multiplicity of Business I was engaged in, might often have prevented me from giving that Attention to the separate Accounts, which they deserved, had they been presented to me, and might therefore not have been totally exempt from Faults. I do not by this Observation, my Lord, mean to insinuate, that the Bills in question were not passed by me; at this Distance of Time, my Memory is insufficient to furnish me with Proofs either for, or against the Question, but your Lordship will give me leave to presume, that if they were examined and approved by me, the official Method of transacting that Business was strictly adhered to, and I therefore hope, my Lord, I shall stand acquitted of Errors, necessarily arising from my acting conformably to a Precedent, of which I had complained, and yet was obliged to comply with.

The Exorbitancy of Contingent Bills in general, and the very vague and indeterminate Manner of examining them, unassisted by the necessary Check of Vouchers, in support of the Articles charged, were with me an early Subject of Complaint to the whole

Office. Mr. Bradshaw, Mr. Tyrwhitt, Mr. D'Oyly, and Mr. Francis, will, I am persuaded, if applied to, testify that I have often troubled them on this Account, endeavouring to obtain a new Regulation and Arrangement of this great and growing Expence; that so an effectual Stop might be put to the possible Impositions of the Officers upon the Agents, or of them upon Government: and if your Lordship will be pleased to have recourse to sundry Remarks, communicated by me to Mr. Bradshaw, and now in the Possession of Mr. D'Oyly, you will, I flatter myself, be convinced, that as far as remonstrating to my superiors, against the Propriety of passing these Species of Bills without Vouchers, may be judged an Evidence of my not countenancing them, or of wishing to be benefited by any Deception of Government thro' them, I shall stand exculpated.

But the absolute Necessity I lay under of passing these Bills, pursuant to the Mode established in the Office will appear to your Lordship from a Recital of the following Transaction. At my first coming into the War Office in the Year 1761, I observed that the Contingent Bill for the Invalids had been encreased from about £150 to upwards of £840 without an Alteration of Service or a Difference in the Proportion of Numbers, that might justify this Encrease, and I applied to Mr. Bradshaw, signifying my Apprehensions, and requesting to be instructed as to the Mode of examining that Account. I received for answer to look Back to Precedents, and to conform to the custom of the Office. I complied with my Directions, and found that the Term, Manner, and Charge of these Bills, corresponded with the Accounts of the preceeding Year, and that there was no Precedent of a Voucher for any of the Articles, being ever demanded, except the Signature of the Agent at the Bottom of the Bill. I had therefore only to examine if the Sums were carried out right, if the Articles corresponded with those of the preceeding Year, and the Total was cast up with Exactness: The corrections they received from me made them right in these Respects, as the Bills in the Office will fully prove. Nothing more was in my Power from the Precedents and Customs of Office, which were given in command for me to follow, and to attempt an Innovation, might, in my Situation, have been imprudent. I was obliged therefore, tho' dissatisfied, to pass these Accounts.

Thus your Lordship will readily see that if these Bills of Mr. Drummond have been passed by me pursuant to the established official Form which I will presume to be the case, I must hope to be acquitted of any Neglect in the Discharge of my Duty, that the Open for Fraud has been too long authorized by Precedent, and has been by Direction complied with, in Opposition to my repeated Remonstrances; and lastly, that, if Mr. Drummond, well versed in the Business of Agency, and furnished with the Accounts and Vouchers, upon which these Contingent Bills are founded, could sign them without discovering the Fraud, as it now appears he did, I . . . . [erasure] may hope to stand excused as to any known or intentional Fraud, or of having it in my Power to detect it, especially as I had neither the Accounts nor Vouchers to recur to, nor by the Precedents of the Office, any right to demand them, or any other Authority for the Bills being just and true, but Mr. Drummond's Signature.

As to the Sum of Five Guineas, said to be received by me of Mr Drummond's Clerk, before the Passing of the Contingent Bills in question, I must beg your Lordship's Indulgence in reciting every Circumstance relative to this Charge with as much exactness as faithfulness.

Mr Drummond's Clerk a considerable Time ago, (but whether before, during the Time, or after passing those Contingent Bills, is more than I can at this Distance of Time, being two Years, exactly say) called on me one Morning, when busied at my Desk, and having acknowledged the Trouble, he had at different Times given me, he requested my Acceptance of a Paper containing I presume, the Sum mentioned by your Lordship: Upon my rejecting his Offer, as a Matter I had no right or pretension to, he, unobserved by me, seized an Opportunity, during Our sub-sequent Conversation, of slipping the rejected Paper into my Desk; in a day or two after, I found five Guineas wrapped up in Paper within my Desk, and recollecting the Offer of the Clerk, I, as soon as he came again to the Office, charged him with the leaving of them there, assured him that I was not conscious of having done any Thing that ought to entitle me to such an

Acknowledgement, and insisted on his re-accepting of them. He refused me, urging, that he had been desired to give me that Sum, by one I had greatly obliged, without naming the Person, or specifying the Manner in which it was supposed I had conferred the Favour, and on my pressing him to take the Money from me, he rushed out of the Door and left me thus abruptly. How far Money thus given may be construed, I must leave to your Lordship's Justice and Candour to interpret.

The Detail my Lord, of this Transaction, is so true, that the said Clerk will, I am persuaded, on Enquiry verify it in every Particular, and if your Lordship requires it to be authenticated by me in the most solemn Manner, I am very ready to give your Lordship that Satisfaction.

And thus my Lord, I hope you will be induced to beleive, that if I passed the Bills in Question, I acted agreeably to official Method and Precedent; that altho' the Public has suffered in this Case, and may have been defrauded in similar Ones, it was never thro' my Connivance or Encouragement; having always, as far as it lay in my Power remonstrated against the open I saw for the commission of Frauds, Besides the Applications I made to the Gentlemen already named, when Mr Ellis came into the office, I took the Liberty, as he ordered me to attend him with Contingent Bills &c of opening to him the Nature and Manner of those Bills, and of passing them, by which it was manifest how exposed the Government was to Frauds and Impositions: and I also told him that I heard, that in Ireland, they were never allowed, without the Oath of the Commanding Officer of the Corps, that the Articles charged were just and true, which I judged to be a proper and effectual Cheque.

I must farther beg leave to observe to your Lordship, that supposing my Integrity, until now, I thank God, unimpeached, stood in no Degree of Estimation, your Lordship will I presume, think, that I have not so much folly in my Composition, as to run the Risque of an Employment which is my sole support, for the Sum of Five Guineas, or to connive at any Mans defrauding of the Public of £1,700, for so inadequate a Bribe.

If in the foregoing Vindication of my Conduct, there be any Part of it insufficiently explicit, your Lordship will, I am persuaded, from your wonted Humanity, honour me with your Commands for farther Explanation, that I may have a new Opportunity of endeavouring to remove every Doubt that may remain in your Lordship's Breast, injurious to the Integrity of him who has the Honour to be with the greatest Respect [etc]

W.O. 4/988, pp. 38–42

54

Barrington to William Johnston

[Copy] War Office
19 September 1765

I have received your Letter of the 16th Instant, in which you do not deny the two Facts mentioned in mine. The one is, that the Accounts were passed by you: Of this, if there were any Doubt, Mr D'Oyly could convince you. The other Fact is, your receiving five Guineas from the Agent's Clerk who sollicited the passing these Accounts.

I am certain there never was any Rule or Direction in the War Office, which prevented your checking Contingent Bills by Vouchers always in your Power. I mean the Marching Books, and Ogilvie's Survey. If these had been consulted, Frauds of such Magnitude as those in Question must have been discovered. However I might have passed over your Neglect with Reprehension and Exhortation, if you had never received a Present from a Person whose Accounts you were to controul, That Circumstance destroys all future Confidence, and if it were pardoned in any one Person at the War Office, would destroy all Order and Discipline there.

I must therefore dismiss you from the Employment you hold under me, which I do with great Concern. Besides the Feelings of Compassion, I am very sorry to lose a Person of your Abilities, whom I wished myself to have brought into the War Office, and whose Entrance there I facilitated, after I had left it.

W.O. 4/988, p. 43

4

The Financial Role of the War Office

The most numerous War Office records are those bearing on army finance, in spite of the destruction of great quantities of statistical material at some unknown date in the past. In fact the major part of the Secretary at War's work was financial. Yet the establishment of clerks, as has been shown, was hardly generous. Nor was Barrington likely to be given more staff, or to be allowed to set up a more effective system of financial control. The problem of how to be a modern state which would be militarily formidable to the rest of the world without being constitutionally objectionable to itself impinged upon this as upon other areas of army administration. It seems to have suited government and people to have a system which was slow, confused and liable to corruption, rather than one which was smooth and efficient, but a threat to a free constitution. Consequently the army of the eighteenth century was separated from public money by a chain of official agencies. Clode regarded these intervening authorities as 'safeguards or outworks to the Treasury', and remarked with his characteristic portentousness of the advantages of 'protecting the Public Treasure from too close a proximity to the Standing Army'.[1]

The system inherited from the seventeenth century had undergone some overhauling in the time of George I and George II. Barrington in due course added his own contribution of reform and it is tempting to speculate upon what he might have achieved in a more radical climate of general administrative reform. A basic description of the system is possible: it was the complexity of operating it which baffled the despairing commissioners of Public Accounts in the 1780s. The principle was that money for pay passed from the Exchequer by way of the office of the Paymaster-General and the regimental agents to the regimental paymasters. At length it was disbursed by the captains of companies within the regiments. Supplies of money for warlike stores and for barrack maintenance also originated from the Treasury, but were handled by the Ordnance Office. Further, the Treasury arranged by way of contractors a large class of provisions for major foreign expeditions.[2]

The importance of the War Office lay in the fact that although it did not generate funds or make decisions about expenditure, it alone had the special knowledge required to complete the procedure of disbursing money for military purposes economically and accurately. The department, possessing no funds of its own, made out a detailed case to the department holding funds but without information. This involved providing good statistics, and a great deal of War Office time was spent in this way.[3]

The first major exercise for the War Office was to prepare accurate Estimates.[4] Presented to Parliament by the Secretary at War, usually at an early stage in the autumn session, they were intended to cover foreseeable expenditures for the ensuing year from 24 December. Notice was given in advance by the War Office to the Lords Commissioners of the Treasury (55), and copies of the Estimates lodged with them. Once Parliament had voted the supply for the Estimates the Treasury authorized the Paymaster-General to issue the first instalment of it, according to the Establishments (see below) prepared by the War Office. The money then began its slow journey from the Exchequer to the regiments.

Estimates had a deceptively simple appearance. There was almost no reference to the manifold items which might be supposed to be consumed by the army in the course of a year, only a list of regiments and other units with a sum of money for each based on the expected complement of men. In January 1767 for example the army in Great Britain appears on the face of it to cost about £594,000. The pay of a typical regiment of foot of 529 men is described as amounting to £11,321.[5]

But within these sums lay concealed a situation of considerable complexity. 'Pay and Subsistence' covered a variety of categories, for each of which deductions had to be made.[6] Deductions included 1s in the £ (the 'poundage') to the Paymaster-General, 1 day's pay a year from all officers and men for the maintenance of Chelsea Hospital, a number of allowances for officers' servants, for cost of clothing lost when men deserted, for recruiting money, for extra money for the regimental agent (56), and for the support of officers' widows. These did not constitute the sum total of deductions from pay: the balance, or off-reckonings, were still liable to considerable inroads by the colonels, who used it to service their arrangements with contractors for clothing the men. In the circumstances it is not surprising that little or no pay was left in the hands of the common soldier.[7] There was not much that an eighteenth-century Secretary at War could do about this. His regulation by several warrants, which are discussed below, of regimental finance was at best a crude overall direction. Pay and subsistence were bound to vary a good deal, according to whether troops were in quarters, under canvas or on the march, what the season of the year was, what provisions were locally available, and what the attitude of innkeepers was. And many colonels were apt to have extravagant ideas about fripperies (for which the men often had to pay) which they considered conduced to smartness on parade. All these factors impinged adversely on the already pitifully tiny personal economy of the man in the ranks.

This extraordinary system, whereby an inclusive sum was nominally made out to each regiment, which was then expected from it to generate its own income and indeed its own reserves, had the merit of presenting a camouflaged target in Parliament, which it was hoped would make for a smoother and more trouble-free presentation of Estimates.

* * *

Outside Parliament the Secretary at War, operating as a bureaucrat, was in constant touch with a Treasury anxious for his advice. Sometimes he proffered his own without waiting to be asked. Finance in fact seems to have been what Barrington was best at and what he liked dealing with. He took his role as guardian of public money and seeker after economies seriously. And it had the advantage of strengthening and emphasizing the civilian aspect of his status, and so enabled him at least in part to disentangle himself from an overbearing Commander-in-Chief such as Ligonier.

Saving money became important after 1763. In spite of the considerable and rather brutal reduction of the army after the Peace of 1763 the cost of it in the view of many politicians was not declining fast enough. In fact army expenditure was never again to achieve the level of 1754, the last 'normal' year of peace. In 1766 Lord Shelburne, newly appointed Secretary of State, was determined to try and achieve some economies. The cost of Britain's new imperial commitments was clearly an important element in her military expenditure. Barrington, who had for some time been urging action on this without success, circulated his own paper recommending the abandoning of the western 'desert'[8] (see p. 11). He became increasingly involved in the task of trying to identify the detail of expenditure, and in the summer of 1766 the Treasury asked him to obtain the best estimates he could from General Gage in New York and Governor Melville in the West Indies. The Lords Commissioners discovered that Barrington had already taken the initiative by writing to the governors for that purpose[9] (57, 58). Gage was unable to assemble all the information he needed from outlying stations (59) but Barrington nevertheless proceeded in January 1767 to lay before a slightly-startled House of Commons, not only the usual seven army estimates covering the expected outgoings for the year, but also Gage's estimates, which amounted to twenty-three different categories and were still not complete.[10] Barrington made no attempt to move the House on these papers: no doubt he considered that he had achieved his purpose of embarrassing ministers from whom he could get no clear directive on American policy(60). This was his boldest attempt to use his role as a financial manager to influence imperial policy. Generally he confined himself to a departmental role in discharging the annual business of passing accounts, and of making the best guess he could of probable expenditure for the ensuing year. He was well aware that the presentation of Estimates was a prime opportunity for a parliamentary attack upon the military establishment, on ideological as well as financial grounds. The surviving notes for his speeches on these occasions, which were for him the most difficult part of each parliamentary year, show the care he took to be properly prepared (61, 62, 63).

* * *

The next stage was that of Establishments. Having presented his Estimates in what he hoped was an inconspicuous and unexceptionable manner the Secretary at War would return to his office to supervise the task of preparing the Establishments. These were grounded on the Estimates, but were drawn out in far greater detail. An Estimate was an evasive statement for public consumption: an Establishment was a comprehensive authorization for use by anyone disbursing public money for the army.

Once they had been worked out by the clerks in the War Office and inspected by the Secretary at War they were carried to the King for signature. They then became operative to authorize the Treasury and the Pay Office[11] (64).

The Clerks made up the Establishments from information derived from the monthly returns from regiments. Periodic mustering of regiments by deputy commissaries responsible to the Commissary General of the Musters was supposed to be a check on this, but this was frustrated by the inefficiency, and often the venality, of those officials.[12] Another and more valuable check was the review.[13] By the middle of the eighteenth century it had become a way of checking the administrative efficiency of a regiment as well as its battle-worthiness, and the instructions to the reviewing generals were complicated (65).

The annual presentation of Estimates – and of Extraordinaries, a handy device whereby Parliament retrospectively voted money for charges not foreseen in the Estimates – by no means exhausted the tale of the financial cares of the Secretary at War. Standing midway between the Treasury and the Army, he often memorialized the former on behalf of the latter, and more frequently urged the latter to be economical and careful of their accounting. A large part of his correspondence was with agents, requiring from them good vouchers to strengthen his negotiating position with the Treasury. Agents were important in providing for the day-to-day housekeeping requirements of the Army[14]—camp necessaries, bedding and utensils, or wood for firing (66, 67, 68, 69, 70, 71, 72) or sometimes more unusual items, such as a boat for the convenience of Landguard Fort (73). Hardships could quickly fall upon troops if advances of pay and subsistence were not arranged (74, 75). Remote foreign stations complained of waiting in vain for money-supplies, and he carried their complaints to the Treasury (76, 77, 78, 79, 80), which nearly always accepted his advice. In some cases delay in supplying colonial troops had been caused by distance and weather, or by political factors (81, 82), but dilatory agents were often to blame. Barrrington was ambivalent in his feeling towards agents, and tried hard to preserve his control over them (83). They were a vital link in the chain of financial control. But some of them at least aroused his disapproval. Several had been trained as clerks in the public service, set up their own private enterprises and acquired great fortunes. His dislike of John Calcraft, the wealthiest of them, seems to have been at least partly due to jealousy. But there were other sounder reasons for being wary of agents. The very circumstances of their appointment, which was by private treaty with the colonels of regiments, was likely to irritate both King and Secretary at War, who were bent on extending the State's control over private arrangements. Barrington's efforts to do this in 1760 (84, 85, 86) however met with little success, for the amount of security to be given by the agents was left to be decided between the colonels as before.[15]

As indicated above, relations between Barrington and the Treasury officials were cordial and trusting, and his opinions were nearly always accepted by them (87). They gratefully recognized his grasp of essential points in the detailed and impartial papers he prepared for them. Worrying away at complex problems and producing solutions was Barrington's strong suit and there are many examples in the papers, two of which may be given here: the financial arrangements for hiring German mercenaries in the Seven Years War, and the settling of accounts between units on the British and Irish military establishments.

Barrington became involved in the first of these two cases almost as soon as he came to the War Office, even before the official commencement of the Seven Years War, when the possibility still existed of obtaining Russian as well as German levies (88). The War Office had the task of arranging the details of the reception of the Germans for the defence of Britain, and of reducing the friction between foreign guests and a chauvinistic local population.[16] But the worst difficulties were financial, and arose after the departure of the mercenaries to take their part in the campaign of the Combined Army in Germany. The adjustment and settling of accounts with several German chanceries was one of Barrington's most intractably difficult tasks (89, 90), not made easier by receiving incomplete information from Lord Holdernesse, the Secretary of State for the Northern Department and from the Treasury (90, 91). The matter dragged on and became merged in the general chaos of enquiry into supplies for the German campaign,[17] in which Barrington gave loyal help to Newcastle when he was attacked for mismanagement[18] (93, 94).

The second case arose from the custom of keeping a number of regiments on the Irish establishment. This had the effect of creating a hidden reserve and helped to render the army a little less visible to the public eye. But it became a problem when regiments in Ireland were expanded and then raided for drafting to foreign stations. The hand of Philip Francis, who was well-versed in the practice of the Irish establishment, can be discovered in the preparing of Barrington's solution (95).

Generally Barrington in his role of watchdog of public money made proposals to save money (96). But on his return to office in 1765 he was not afraid to make an important proposal to the Treasury arguing the case of the unfortunate officers who had suffered in their careers as a result of the reduction of regiments on the British establishment from ten companies to nine (97). As usual the Lords Commissioners assented to his proposal,[19] but ruled that the sum be estimated for Parliament, which Barrington had made clear he considered an inconvenient mode (98, 99, 100).

* * *

The War Office was expected to provide rapid and detailed information of the financial implications of augmenting or diminishing the army's manpower. At the beginning of Barrington's first term one of the biggest augmentations of the century was taking place (101, 102, 103), and comparison of the advantages of many different schemes took place in the War Office[20] (104). A decade later he was involved in the reverse process. He was not at the War Office when the great reduction of 1763 took place, but the pressure, though on a smaller scale, was still urgent in 1766 and 1767 to effect economies (105, 106). Fresh recruiting took place in 1770 because of the Falkland Islands scare (107) and in 1775[21] (108).

* * *

Economy therefore meant careful book-keeping. It also meant vigilance. Colonels as well as agents overstepped the mark and had to be checked. In 1760 a collusion of colonels came to light in the extraordinary case of the forage scandal, which needed some tact in handling. A number of officers, some of them of considerable seniority, joined in a scheme to charge for a much greater number of forage rations than had really been consumed during a summer encampment. Two officers declined to be a part of this fraud, and through them the War Office came to know of it.[22] The Board of General Officers could not withstand the weight of evidence with which they were deluged by the War Office, but suggested that the affair was due to inadvertence.[23] The enormity of the fraud was such that it seemed better to pretend that this was the case, and Barrington allowed the matter to rest after reprimands had been administered for the sake of form (109, 110, 111, 112), and the offending colonels had been ordered to repay the excess money.[24]

There were however dividends and perquisites which officers more justifiably believed themselves to deserve, generated by the system of regimental finance. The system whereby the colonel organized the clothing of the men was an opportunity for him to make profits for himself. The off-reckonings of the regimental pay and subsistence serviced the fund for this (113, 114). It has been shown,[25] however, that the colonels with ample private means of their own benefited most: they could settle immediately with the contractors and collect the off-reckonings as they built up. For the colonel lacking his own resources the chronology was reversed: the assignment of off-reckonings was a security only, and by the day of final settlement with the clothing contractor interest had accrued. The position was ably reviewed in 1771 by Philip Francis (115). The authorship of a similar but more extensive paper on the subject produced in April 1772 is not certain—Francis left the War Office on 20 March 1772—but it may have been written for the guidance of Anthony Chamier, the new Deputy Secretary at War (116).

Dividends for captains declined during the century, and it became increasingly difficult for them to live on their basic pay. The small amount of money arising from the management of a company was therefore particularly important for the professional officer without means. The work of regulating the extent to which captains could claim balances from the non-effective funds after all other legitimate calls had been made upon them extended back to 1749, so Barrington had precedents to work upon. The Royal Warrant of March 1761 (117) permitted dividends to be distributed equally up to £30 per captain, and was based on earlier warrants.[26] The background to this was a long conflict over winter stoppages in Germany. The prolonged campaigns of the German war had created disadvantageous conditions for allowing any profits of company command to arise. Lord George Sackville had not been able to solve these problems, and they were inherited by his successor Lord Granby. The chief complaint of the captains was that they ought to have been credited with the sixpences stopped from the men's pay to cover the greater cost of keeping cavalry in winter quarters[27] (118). Barrington was uncertain about precedents (119, 120), but as a Secretary at War fond of calling himself the 'Army's friend', he must have been embarrassed by Granby's reminder of the deserving nature of the captains' case (121). The war ended with no resolution of the matter, and a number of captains must have returned from hard campaigning in the German theatre feeling cheated. Barrington quitted office soon after drafting the warrant of 1761, and was dismayed to find on returning to office in 1765 that the problem still existed. In the next two years he applied himself to it at intervals (122, 123, 124, 125, 126, 127). The most far-reaching warrants in this reforming period were the two for regulating the Non-effective Fund of the infantry and the Stock-purse of the cavalry (128, 129), which permitted fixed equal dividends in peace-time after payment of all the outgoings which experience had by that date identified as common and legitimate in the regimental economy. Strict adherence was enjoined upon agents.[28] These warrants remained the guide for regulating regimental dividends for many years. Their effectiveness may be judged by their inclusion in printed editions of regulations up to the time of the French wars in the 1790s.

The documents therefore firstly show Barrington dealing with day-to-day problems as they were presented to him by others or as he perceived them himself. Guided by experienced clerks, his predecessors had done similar things. But the record also shows him as a reformer. The accurate drafting of a good warrant, which might clear up problems in the future, was a congenial task to him. His role need not be exaggerated, however. His reliance on the expert knowledge of Philip Francis has already been referred to. Edward Harvey, the Adjutant-General, was also an important agent in the process of reform. Shortly after the commencement of Barrington's second term Harvey placed before him a memorandum suggesting some of the reforms in finance mentioned above, as well as in officer-preferment and other matters (130). It was in fact a complete statement about the post-war log-jam in the army, and Barrington took it as his guide. He was never too proud to learn. A large part of his success lay in being responsive to the innovatory impulses of others, and in transmuting them into good administrative forms.

55

Barrington to Grey Cooper

[Copy]   War Office
                                                      10 November 1772

I send you herewith Copies of such Estimates of the Charge of the Forces for the ensuing Year 1773, as can with Propriety be made up before Christmas, Viz.

Guards and Garrisons
Forces in the Plantations &c
Forces serving out of Ireland on the British Establishment.
The General and General Staff Officers in Great Britain.

You will be pleased to lay the same before the Right Hõnble the Lords Commissrs. of His Majesty's Treasury, and acquaint their Lordships that upon the whole there is a Decrease of these Estimates, amounting to between three & four Thousand Pounds, principally occasioned by the Deduction of one Day's Pay charged last Year for Leap Year, and by some Change judged proper to be made in the Charge for Provisions for the Forces in North America, Gibraltar, and the Ceded Islands, on account of the late Change of the Establishment of the Regt. of Foot, and by withdrawing two Battalions from N. America. I am also to add that one Battalion of Foot, viz. the 50th. hath been sent from Ireland to the West Indies.

It is intended that Ireland shall continue to pay the said Regiment, Great Britain making good to the Regt. whilst on Service, the Difference between British and Irish Pay. One Company of the 42d. has in the meantime been ordered from the Isle of Man to Ireland, which Company is to be discontinued on the British Establishment fom the 25th. of next Month. By this Arrangement Ireland will still have the twelve Thousand Men established for the Service of that Kingdom, notwithstanding the Absence of the 50th. Regiment which is to be replaced from hence as soon as the relieved Regiments return from the West Indies.

W.O. 4/90, p. 232

56

Warrant for payment of allowances to agent, Directed to the Earl of Darlington and Viscount Dupplin, Joint Paymasters-General

[Copy]   2 August 1756

GEORGE R

WHEREAS We are pleased to allow unto Peregrine Furye Esqr. Agent and Sollicitor to Our Regiment and Independent Companies of Invalids, One Man p. Company in Our regiment and Twenty five Old Independt. Companys of Invalids, over and above the Man p. Company upon the Establishment in consideration of his great Pains and trouble in the Performance of his Duty as Agent and Sollicitor AND WHEREAS We are humbly besought to make him the same allowance of One Man p. Company in Our fourteen New Indep Company of Invalids over and above the Man p. Company upon the Establishment, which We thinking reasonable are graciously pleased to Grant OUR WILL & PLEASURE THEREFORE IS, and We do hereby Authorize and Direct, that in the Debentures to be made out by you from time to time, for the Pay of Our said Fourteen New Indep. Compys of Invalids, you take Care to allow the Full Pay of One Man for Each Company of Our said Fourteen New Indept. Companys of Invalids over & above the Allowance to the Agent and Sollicitor borne on The Establishment and notwithstanding the same may be Respited, or not borne upon the Muster Rolls, Yet the Amount of the Full Pay of the said Men of Our Fourteen New Independt. Companies of Invalids is to be Computed and included in the Debenture or Debentures to be made out by you for The Pay of the said Indept. Companies from time To time, and as often as the same shall be paid & Cleared, It being Our Intention that the Agent & Sollicitor of Our Companies of Invalids now and for the time being shall have and Receive the aforesaid Allowance. And for so doing, this Shall be Your Warrant.

  Given at Our Court at Kensington This 2d Day of August 1756, in the Thirtieth Year of our Reign

By His Majesty's Command
Barrington

Earl of Darlington &
Ld. Viscot. Dupplin PayMaster
General, and Pay Master
General for the time being.

W.O. 26/23, pp. 99–100

57

Barrington to Grey Cooper

[Copy]   War Office
                                            16 July 1766

In Answer to the favor of your letter of the 15th. instant, wherein you signify to me the desire of the Rt. Hon.ble the Lords Commrs. of H.M. Treasury, that I should direct Genl. Gage & Govr. Melvil to prepare Estimates of such Military Services as can be foreseen within their several Commands, with as much exactness & precision as the Nature of the cases will admit of, & to transmit the same to me in order to their being laid before the next Session of Parliament; I am to acquaint you for the information of their Lordships, that in my dispatches of the 26th. March last to the Commander in Chief in No. America, (of which I send you an Extract) I informed His Excellency Major Genl. Gage, that a very particular Estimate of the many Expences incurred by the various and extensive Establishments in No. America, would be expected by Parliamt. next year, & desired him to send me as soon as he conveniently could, after he had finally settled every thing, an exact Account of all certain contingent Expences, & an Estimate, as far as a probable Guess would go, of those which are in their Nature uncertain, and I shall not fail to repeat my Directions to him on this head by the next Pacquet, as a thing required by their Lordships.

Provision having been made these two last years for the Garrisons in the ceded Islands, & for victualling the Troops stationed there, I did not think it necessary to call upon Govr. Melvil for any such Estimate, but that the whole Expence may be ascertained to Parliament with as much exactness & precision as the Nature of the business will admit of, I shall in Obedience to their Lordships Commands, take the earliest opportunity of communicating to Governer Melvil, their Lordships Directions on this Subject.

W.O. 4/80, pp. 97–98

58

Barrington to Major-General Gage

[Copy: enclosed with 57 above] War Office
26 March 1766

When the Estimates of this year were considered in the house of Commons, it was objected that no particular mention was made in the Plantation Estimate of the many Expences incurred by the various & extensive Establishments in No. America & it was said that you had been directed to send Materials for that purpose. To this it was answered that you had sent a great Variety of Estimates which had been again referred back to you with Directions that you should cutt off from them whatever appeared to you superfluous, & that time had not yet permitted a Return from you. With this the house was satisfied for the present, but a very particular Estimate is expected next year. I desire your Excellency will please to bear this in Mind, & that you will send me as soon as you conveniently can after you have finally settled every thing, an exact Amount of all certain contingent Expences, & an Estimate as far as probable Guess will go, of those which are in their nature uncertain. Provisions & Firing, for the Troops are very material Articles, & must be particularly stated.

W.O. 4/80, pp. 99–100

59

Barrington to Grey Cooper

[Copy]   War Office
                                                    25 September 1766

I send you herewith Copies of the several Military Estimates
indended to be laid before Parliament for the Year 1767, so far as
the same can b. at present ascertained. As I cannot yet be
furnished with Materials for forming the Estimates of the Allowances to the Widows, for the Half Pay &c, and for the Charge of
Chelsea Hospital, with any degree of exactness, and as I must
suppose that the Sums of each will be rather diminished than
encreased for the next Year, I shall beg leave to deferr laying them
before Parliament till after Christmas, if the Rt. Hōnble the Lords
Commissioners of the Treasury have no Objection.

W.O. 4/80, p. 324

60

Barrington's notes for speech in the Commons

[Holograph: a small folio page folded lengthwise into four and
written in four columns]

                                                    [January 1767]

Mr. Ellis in Decr. 1764 directed an account to be sent of the
amount of contingent expenses in N. America.

Estimates from the different departments arrived in Letters
dated Ap. 1 & May 5th. 1765 went to the Treasury 26 June were
refer'd back to the W.O. 27 July, a report was made Sep. 7.

The Treasury approved this report. Many things were struck
out & the Genl. was order'd to cut off as much more as he cd.

Reason why these Estimates were not layd before the House last year—New Estimates sent for first in March 1766 by W.O. & afterwards in July by T. order. Melville also order'd to send Estimates.

Genl. Gage sent his dated 11th & 28 Oct. & 9 Novr. and they were recd. 22 Decr.—He says that he has been long examining & curtailing Expences and he thinks these Estimates as exact as they can be made.

They consist of 23 different Papers and yet several Estimates are not yet come to his hands.—None are come from the W. Indies or any ansr. from G. Melville.

To make these Papers more intelligible to the Comns. I have classed them according to their several Services, postponing Comy. Leake's Estimate of Provisions.

Mr. March's Paper

In regard to the Estimate of Provisions Mr. Leake recons the Expence (after deducting the Stoppages from the Troops) at 42 800£. W Florida excepted.

The Sum voted for all the Troops in N.A. is 22242£. consequently a deficiency of 20638£ which is to be accounted for thus.

Condemnation, wastage, losses in transportation to the outposts &c equal to a 4th part.

Provisions given to persons not on the Estimate voted in Parliament & from whom no stopages can be made as Indians, Seamen, Artificers, batteau men, Waggoners &c.

N.B. In the Plantation Estimate no more is provided for than the usual sum for Provisions & Contingencies. If therefore these Estimates shd. be approved the Sum voted for them must be 22658£ short.

I have laid these Estimates before Parliament as the best lights into what is doing in N. America, tho' many relate to Services not within my department or proper to be moved by me, as Indian Correspondence, reparation of Forts Barracks &c.

The whole amount of the Estimates is 98,646£. without those of the Ilinois, West Florida & Southern Indian Correspondence: Also ceded Islands.

This is a great Sum, but the Contingent expences of N.A. not come within it. Ilinois.

No Man can estimate his private or publick Expences. If you will save money you must lessen the Articles.

But there are services not thought of as passage of Recruits to no less than 40 different Posts.

I will not move any thing on these Papers because They are none of them Estimates for the year 1767.
I cannot vouch for any of them.

I am not a judge of many Articles & there are some which if I understand them I do not intirely approve. No. 11. 13. 16.

I think voting money on these estimates is authorizing & approving them.

Ipswich 6a2, no. 363

61

Barrington's notes for speech in the Commons

[Holograph: folded columnwise as Document 60; columns alternately written and left blank: figures crossed through and amended included]

[1776]

These Estimates must be open'd more fully & less minutely than usual.

The Guards Garrisons &c in Great Britain ~~22,783~~ 20,752 more less by ~~853~~ 1178 than last year: But there are at present only 7 marching Regiments in the Island. In due time are expected 3B. from Gibraltar 3 from Minorca 2 from North America & 2 from the West Indies; but the four last will come *Skeletons*. These 20 Bats. will be augmented to 677 each, & Elliots 90 additionals to do the whole light Cavalry duty.

The Plantation Estimate added to the Irish Regimts. lent to England amount to ~~32,105~~ 34,636 being 18727 more than last year.

Guernsey the same as last year, in Jersey 120 more being in all 348. Affrica is the same.———In the West Indies four augmented Bats. of Royal Americans making 324 more than the force of last year.——— These Batts. have always behaved incomparably well; the officers both English & Foreigners serving well together: Prevost—Haldimand's Services & merits. establishment for him.

At Gibraltar 8 men less at Minorca 79 less; but 5 Bat of Hanoverians (of equal numbers with English except two). serve there. Three Bats. of these troops at Gibraltar releive three; two at Minorca & Invalids releive three other English Regiments.

These Corps not taken by Treaty or Contract but by Treasury minute. Nothing paid for them but levy money for the men— no half pay hereafter. Compare them with the last of our Augmentations.

Consider the point of legality. & of taking the measure without consent of Parliament; if not illegal or dangerous why delay? Indemnity not necessary: Martial Law.

No insecure force at these Stations.

In North America great Changes: In 1773 there was 13 Bat. 4 more sent for the Relief and kept—(a Regt. of Dragoons) * in March last 3 Bat. went from Ireland. In July 4 more: In Oct 5—in all 29——— Five more to go from Ireland in December, 1 from the West Indies 1 from Scotland being 1150 Men. Total 36. But two viz 18th & 59th: very weak one's will return which deducted leaves 34—The number of these 34 ~~make 23492 which~~ added to 574 Dragoons makes ~~24065~~ 25126 according to the Establishment. (Deducting the addl Comps 4654) * Add to these 11000 Marines. [*added in margin]

That these Corps may be always kept as compleat as possible two additional Companies have been appointed to each which are to stay in Europe to recruit.

How these Companies were officer'd.
Having thus stated all I must own that the numbers are as yet very incompleat tho' all endeavours have been used to raise Men

Encrease of bounty Money
Lowering of Standard
Irish Recruits
Foreign Recruits

This difficulty does not arise now for the first time: Has been long felt and particularly in 1771 when we were to have recruited by Irish & Foreigners. Works, Manufactures, encrease of Wages account in part but the great cause is our high Establishment in time of Peace.
——— State the Paper.

The whole number of Men for 1776 is 55,388, the expence including all the Estimates is 1,436,669 the encrease of men this year is 17549 men. of Money is 331,201£.

But why vote these forces the war being
Unjust
Unnecessary for you may treat
Impracticable. How will you carry it on
Minorca. Preston Pans.

Ipswich 6a2, no. 697

62

Barrington's notes for speech in the Commons

[Holograph: paper folded as before into four columns: no blanks left]

[8 November 1776]

The whole Estimates for 1777

	Men	Money
British ----- -----	63,335	1,656,382
Foreign ----- -----	20,694	571,566
Forn. Artillery -----	730	31,205
	86,759	2,259,153

being more than last year by 333 men—34,864£

Guards Garrisons &c in G. B. 20734 Men 648,009£. Less by 18 men, 11,190£ than last year when the troops were voted. but 10 Bat. were then absent now only three. There are also adl. Companies to Regiments abroad 5914 when compleat. The decrease of expence this year on Gar: & Gars. chiefly arises from Burgoyne's transfer'd to the Plantation Estimate.

Plantation and Irish Estimates together 44,601. Men 996,890£. more by 351 Men & 46,086£ than last year. This chiefly arises from Burgoyne's transfer'd Prestons augmented 4 adl. Companies to the 71st. Adl. Staff and Hospital, & provisions for 8 Bats. & the Guards sent last year after the Estimates for this year were voted.

The foreign Estimates 20,694 Men 571,566£. more 289 Men but decrease of expence 14,124£—In these Estimates appear two Articles (worded according to 1760 precedent) which want explanation. The words are *to make good deficiencies in the grants of last year for troops of Hesse and Hannau.*—Last year there was no provision for 273 Hessian & 16 Hannau Valets de bass for carrying tents &c, for thro haste they were omitted in the *Etats,* but were actually raised, musterd and sent. The Expence of these for pay & levy money 4489£—The Second Division of Hessians marched sooner by 13 days than was expected; this makes 2484£ for pay—The Hannau Regt. march'd five days sooner than calculated, 164£ & the Subsidy was calculated from 6th March instead of 5 feb. to date of treaty. This amounts 369£. and the 3 Articles as above to 7631.£

Foreign Artillery 730 Men 31,205£ contains arrears for last year as well as provision for the next—The Treaties stipulated Artillery if wanted: They were first refused then demanded; Money voted 7th May 13,973 for Hesse, 9th May 3383 for Hannau: this was for pay; but 5875 was due for Subsidy tho' thro haste not then demanded.

I must mention one Article of expence that cannot be estimated but will appear in Services incurred but not provided, viz allowance to Officers who lose an Eye or Limb and to Widows & Orphans of Men slain in fight.

Having thus stated the different Estimates, it may be expected that I should state the force employ'd in different parts; particularly N. America the seat of War.

Guernsey, Jersey, Gibraltar, Minorca and Affrica as last year: West Indies more by 578 Men Dalrymples Corps.

Under Sir Guy Carleton's orders 13172 including 1 Bat. of Maclean's Corps—Under Sir Wm. Howe's 41,199 including 1 Bat of McLeans and 1 of Goreham's—These together amount to 54272 Men [sic] including 2000 Marines ashore. Some more provincial Corps are raised or raising.

But this is the force on Paper: I will therefore state what was the real force in September last effectives officers included under the immediate Command of these Generals—Under Carleton 12,760 besides the 8th. Regt. in the forts: but all these are not with Carleton: The effective force with Howe the day before the action on the 15th of Sepr. was 26,200 Men besides 5540 Hessians Cavalry &c daily expected.

All these troops were healthy full of spirit and zeal few deserting, wanting for nothing but action and confiding in their officers, especially their Generals.

Ipswich 6a2, no. 698

63

Barrington's notes for speech in the Commons

[Holograph: paper folded as before: no blanks left]

[3 December 1777]

The whole Estimate for 1778

Men		Money
British	65135	1659481
Foreign	23220	652852
Do. Artil.	774	27379
	89129	2,338,712

(being less than last year 132 Men 15,475£)

Guards Garrison &c in G. Britain 20,057 Men 634,240£. being less by 677 Men—13,769£. than last year, the 48th. Regiment being left in the W. Indies at 477 Men. There are also 77adl. Companies to the Regts. in N. America being 5177 if compleat.

Plantation and Irish Estimates together 45,078 Men, 1,082707£. are more by 477 (the 48th) & 16,868£ than last year 5745 of which arises from correcting the old error of Ireland paying english money for Corps lent to us.

The foreign Estimates are 23994 Artillery included, expence 680,231£. being more by 68 Hessian and 1 Hannau Chasseurs (expence 5075£) but the whole expence of foreign troops is decreased—18574 arising chiefly from omiting levy money and expences made good last year. (By the returns in July the last recd they wanted but 1210 Men reconing all recruits sent out as received). Besides, I believe there are abt. 900 Marines on Shore 1654 Provincials, being 2 Bat of McLeans and 1 of Gorehams. of the other Provincials I have no Account.

(The real force in July when the last returns were sent to the War Office were effectives officers included—under Sr. G. Carleton 14200—being abt. 730 (adl. Companies) more than last year.

Under Sir W. Howe 35,000 besides Marines & Provincials being abt. 3000 more than last year viz 2500 foreigners & the debris of the 7th. & 26th. Regiments—exchanged from Captivity.)

Ipswich 6a2, no. 699

64

Barrington to Samuel Martin

[Copy]   War Office
                                                                    21 May 1760

His Majesty having been pleased to sign three Establishments for the pay of Lieut. Colo. Fraser's & Lieut. Colo. Montgomery's Highland Battalions of Foot, from 25th Oct 1756 to 24th of Decemr. following one being for the use of the Treasury, one for the Paymaster Genl. the other for this Office, I transmit the same to you, & desire you will be pleased to take the first Opportunity to lay them before the Rt. Honble. the Lords Commrs of His Majesty's Treasury that they may be countersigned by their Lordships, as soon as it shall be convenient, as they are at present much wanted.

W.O. 4/61, p. 124

65

Order for a Review, to the Earl of Ancram

[Copy]   Kensington Palace
                                          6 October 1756

Orders and   OUR WILL AND PLEASURE IS that upon Re-
Instructions for ceipt of these Our Instructions, You do as
Reviewing the   soon as Conveniently may be Repair to the
Several Corps   Quarters of Our Regt. of Dragoon Guards
within   and Regiments of Dragoons mentioned in
mentioned   the Margin hereof.
                         That upon your Arrival at the Quarters of
Sir Charles   any Division or Troop, or Company of Our
Howards   said Corps you do give the Necessary orders
                   for Drawing them together in some Con-
Lt. Genl   venient place under Arms and Acquaint them
Hawley's   what Number of Cartridges you would have
M. G. Earl   them bring into the Field.
Albemarle's   That you cause them to Pass in Review
                   before you, and take an Exact Account of their
                   Numbers, with the goodness, Size, Age, and
                   Make of their Men and Horses, the Condition
                   of the Cloathing, Accoutrements, and Horse
                   Furniture, the Time they were last Cloathed,
                   and whether all the Particulars have been
                   delivered according to Our Regulation, and
                   whether the same be well fitted, and if the
                   Accoutrements are compleat and Uniform,
                   such as Pouches, Belts, Slings and Cartouch
                   Boxes; the time they were last furnished, and if
                   the Serjts have Sashes.
                         That you cause the Colonel or Officer
                   Commanding Our said Corps respectively to
                   lay before you list of all the Non Commission
                   Officers and Private Men, that have been
                   inlisted,   discharged   Recommended   to

Chelsea, or have died or deserted since last Review.

That you take an Exact Account whether their Arms are in good order, the Time they were last Supplyed, and whether all the Men have swords according to Our Intention.

That you cause the Division or Troop to be Exercised before you and carefully Observe whether the Officers as well as Serjeants, and Private Men are perfect in the Manual and Evolutions, According to our Book of Exercise, and in the Several Firings, Marching, etc. as ordered by Our Captain General, taking Notice of any defect or negligence in the discharge of this part of their Duty and Strictly Command & Enjoin the Officers to Use their utmost Diligence & Endeavours to teach and perfect their Men and themselves in the knowledge and Use of their Arms, that they may be ready and Expert in all the parts of Discipline which Our Service requires.

That you cause the Agent or Paymaster of Our said Corps to lay before you the last Years Accts of the disposal of the Money arising by their Noneffectives and the Allowance borne on the Establishment to the Captains for keeping their Troops Compleat, signed by himself and the Commanding Officer.

Your are carefully to Examine whether Our Intention be complyed with, of the Men Allowed upon the Establishment to the Captains for keeping their Troops Compleat, as well as the Non effective Subsistence of Men and Horses, being reserved in the Agents hands both as a Fund for Recruiting and to Answer the Respits which the Commissaries of their Musters are ordered to make.

That you do report to Us, what & how many

of the Respits made on the Muster Rolls of Our said Corps from Midsummer 1755 to Midsumr 1756 ought in your Opinion to be taken off. You are likewise to Examine whether the Directions of Our Regulations for the Stoppages &c. for Our Regt. of Dragoon Guards and Regiment of Dragoons dated the 19 June 1749 be duly Observed and Complyed with.

The Commanding Officer of each Division or Troop of the Corps mentioned in the Margin hereof, is to deliver you returns upon Honour of the Commission officers Non Commission Officers and Private Men who shall happen to be Absent, mentioning the Time of Absence by whose leave, and Whether they have Exceeded such leave.

That if any Complaint is made that the Regimt or any of the Men are not duly, & justly Accounted with, or any illegal Stoppages are made from them, you are to Enquire into the truth of the Fact and upon due Examination thereof, if the said Complaint is found reasonable you are to order Justice to be done, and upon Refusal of any Officer, Report the same for Our further Direction.

You are to take particular care to Examine into the Officers Compliance with the directions of the Act of Parliament for the due and Punctual Payment of their Quarters and report the least neglect of their Duty, herein Strictly Charging and commanding them to the most Exact performance thereof.

That in case of any difference between the Troops and the Inhabitants where they are Quartered You are to use your utmost endeavours to reconcile them and earnestly recommend to the Officers to Observe and keep up such good order and Discipline amongst their Men as may prevent all just Occasions of Complaint in their Quarters and render Our Service easy and Acceptable to all Our Subjects.

And this Service being performed you are to make a just and Impartial Report in writing to us of all and every Particular hereby recommended to your Charge, with such further Observations as you shall judge may be any ways Conducing to the Benefit of Our Service, and for the good order Governmt and Discipline of Our Service And for so doing This shall be to all whom it may concern a sufficient Warrant Given at Our Court at Kensington this 6 day of October 1756 in the Thirtieth Year of Our Reign.

By His Majesty's Command
Barrington

W.O. 26/23, pp. 116–119

66

Barrington to Mr Ross (and five other agents)

[Copy]   War Office
                                               24 May 1756

By the Duke's Direction I enclose a List and the Prices of the Camp Necessaries for a Light Troop of Dragoons, which His Royal Highness Orders to be immediately provided for the Light Troop to Lieut Genl. Hawley's and to the Earl of Ancram's Regiment of Dragoons to which you are Agent, together with sixteen Pickett Ropes of Hemp and Hair, for each of these two Regiments which were omitted when the said Regiments provided themselves with Camp Necessaries, the Expence of which for each Regiment amounting to One Hundred and Four Pounds ten Shillings will be defray'd as soon as proper Certificates of their being provided and delivered are brought to this office.

W.O. 4/51, p. 515

67

Barrington to John Trotter

[Copy]   War Office
                                              20 January 1777

I desire you will immediately provide for the Service in North America, the Several Setts of Bedding, and Articles of Wooden & Tin Ware mention'd in the enclos'd Paper, and upon your transmitting to me an Account of their having been provided and sent to North America, with an Account of the Expence, I will lay the proper Warrant before the King for your reimbursement.

*   *   *   *   *   *

By Order of Robt. Adair Esq
To John Trotter
To provide for the Service in No. America

900 Setts of Bedding each consisting of One pallias & Bolster Case, three Sheets, 2 Blankets & 1 Coverlet. 100 Setts of Bedding each One Mattras & Bolster, three Sheets, two Blankets and One Coverlet

Wooden Ware	*Tin Ware*
400 Quart Bowls	40 One gallon Kettles in covers
1000 Pint Do	60 Four Do Do
1000 Trenchers	60 Three Do Do
4000 Spoons	250 Quart Pots
300 White Platters	600 Pint do
48 Mops	200 1/2 Pint Do
	30 Sauce Pans
	50 One Spout Lamps
	50 Flat Candlesticks
	50 Lanthorns

W.O. 4/99, p. 38

68

Barrington to John Varley

[Copy]   War Office
                                                11 May 1756

Colonel Noel of the Coldstream Regt of Foot Guards Adjutant
acquaints me that only one pair of Sheets for each Bed was
specified in the Return of Utensils, Beds &c sent to me &
afterwards transmitted to you in my Letter of the 10th of last
Month as likewise that there was omitted a Scavenger to take away
the Dirt; I am Commanded to signify to you it is HMP that you
Provide the further number of 333 Pairs of Sheets for the Use of
the Battalion to be Cantoned in the New Horse Guards as
likewise to provide a Scavenger to take away the dirt, the Expence
of which is to be incerted in the Account directed in my Letter of
the 10th of April last.

W.O. 4/51, p. 464

69

Barrington to Mr Rice

[Copy]   War Office
                                                2 December 1765

I send You enclosed an Account of Furniture to be provided &
Repairs necessary to be made in the Officers Rooms in the Horse
Guards & desire that you will make an Estimate of the Expence
attending the same & transmit it to me for my Information.

* * *

Horse Guards Whitehall
November 16th 1765   Necessary Repairs wanting

In the Officers Rooms
The Rooms to be painted & Whitewashed
The Cornet's Chimney altered to prevent it's smokeing

Back Room & passage below Stairs to be painted & Whitewashed
The Privy to be painted.

In the Horse Guards Room
Benches and Tables repaired.
6 Chairs—New
2 Warming Pots for shaving new
Snuffers & Candlesticks new
Lines to Sky Lights
Quilts & Covers—repaired
Brushes for Cloaths—new
Two Blankets—new
Hooks & Numbers for Arms—new
Two Lamps in the Passage repaired
A Table for Quarter Master's Room & the Chimney altered to
prevent smokeing.

Grenadier's Rooms
The Sink in the Powdering Room repaired & Pipe put to do. to
take off the waste Water.
4 Blankets wanted new
Windows to be repaired & Frame & Wire to Stair Case Window
to be new.
Looking Glass for Serjeant's Room.
Bedsteads & Steps—repaired.
A Shaving Pot—new
A Bin in the Passage for Coals—new.

W.O. 4/78, pp. 136–137

70

Barrington to James West

[Copy]   War Office
                                                 3 May 1756

I enclose a letter from Mr Abraham Hume, Commissary General
for Stores &c to me with one to him from Mr Godfrey appointed
to be Commissary for Firing and Straw, and I am to desire you will

be pleased to lay them before the Rt. Honble. the Lords Commissioners of the Treasury that their Lordships may give such directions as they shall think proper.

W.O. 4/51, p. 412

71

Abraham Hume to Barrington

[Copy]   Hill Street
                                                    29 April 1756

Mr Godfrey having wrote to me the Inclosed Letters, relative to the Supplying the Troops with Fuel, Straw and Lights that they may want in their Cantonments and in their Encampments, it being a Necessary Service, and which your Lordship as well as myself has often heard His Royal Highness the Duke of Cumberland say, it was time Someone should be appointed to provide, and that he thought Mr Godfrey very capable of doing it; I therefore lay it before your Lordship, that the same may be taken into Consideration, and Directions given, as I believe those Articles may be soon wanted.

W.O. 4/51, p. 413

72

W. Godfrey to Abraham Hume

[Copy]   N.p.
                                                    29 April 1756

His Majesty's British Troops and those in His Majesty's Pay will want during their Cantonment and in the Field, Fireing, Straw, Lights and other Necessaries for the providing of which no Person is yet appointed, having formerly being employed for those purposes; I take the Liberty of acquainting you that unless some measures are soon taken for Securing of those Articles the Troops may Suffer, therefore beg leave to put you in mind by this that you may lay the same before whom you think proper, as I hope my former Services in those Articles were agreeable, I take the Liberty to offer them again on this occasion. It is impossible for me to say what number of People may be necessary, nor what wages to give them, But suppose at each place where Magazines are to be made that it will be proper to have One head Clerk to take on account of what is received into the Magazine and what is delivered out and to have one or more persons under him to assist as the Service may require, so that the whole may be conducted with regularity and without confusion. I suppose a head Clerk may be had at about 7s.6d. p day, and those under him at 5s p day; and what Labourers may be necessary at the current price of the Country, as to myself, altho I have had Commissions frequently for providing of Forage, Wood & Straw with an allowance of £3 a day, yet I am willing to take for this Service what may be judged adequate to the trouble.

W.O. 4/51, p. 414

73

Governor Singleton to Barrington

[Copy]   Landguard Fort
                                                30 June 1767

Since I have been honoured with your Lordship's Letter of the 25th, I have made repeated enquiries among the oldest of the Soldiers in this Garrison who all remember a Boat belonging to it & likewise the seizure of the Boat for being concerned in helping to land unaccustomed Goods. Whether the money allowed to defray the expence of this Boat came thro' your Lordship's Office or from the Boards of Ordnance I do not know, but imagine from the latter, and think it may have been charged under some other denomination, as she was commonly worked by men who were paid as *labourers* by the Board of Ordnance. In either case I thought it was my duty to make my application to your Lordship, which I shall urge no farther than by saying that I believe no other man would take the Sutlers place off his hands upon the Terms he has it, if any would, we should be sorry to make the exchange; as the present man has always given general satisfaction to every body in the place, and rather than part with him we would willingly make up his losses out of our own pockets in order to keep him with us. If a Boat shou'd be allowed us it would answer the double end of supplying us with Bread and for bringing Our Letters from Harwich, for which latter purpose twenty Pounds A Year is allowed to the Postmaster there, who employs a fellow for ten or twelve, who does it in a very negligent, careless unsafe manner, and sometimes neglects us entirely for two or three posts together. If this twenty Pounds p year was allowed to Us, the additional expence attending the Boat would be trifling. And we should in every respect be much better served this and the other reasons for urging the above request is humbly submitted to your Lordship.

W.O. 4/82, pp. 179–181

74

Barrington to Lord Darlington and Lord Dupplin
(Joint Paymasters-General)

[Copy]   War Office
                                              20 April 1756

His Majesty having thought fit to Appoint the several Gentlemen mentioned in the annexed List, to be Additional Officers to the Hospital for the Service of the Land Forces in North America, and they being Order'd immediately to repair to their Posts, I am Commanded to Signify to your Lordships, It is H My P that you do Issue to the said Gentlemen Six Months Pay from the 25th of December last, to the 24th of June next, at the daily allowance against Each of their Names set down, to Enable them to purchase Necessaries

*　*　*　*　*

Surgeon Richard Huck at 10sh. p Diem
Surgeon William Russell at 10 do
Ditto's Mate, Jonathan Mallett at 5sh per Diem
Ditto's Mate, Arthur Nicholson at 5 per do
Ditto's Mate, William Austin at 5 do
Apothecary's Mate ---- Lock at 5s Do
Ditto's Mate ---- Walker at 5s Do
Ditto's Mate ---- Trail at 5s Do

W.O. 4/51, p. 391

75

Barrington to Richard Rigby (Paymaster-General)

[Copy]   War Office
                                                    5 May 1777

Several Parties of Recruits raised for the Additional Companies
of the 71st Regiment of Foot being ordered to embark to North
America under the Command of two Lieutenants, two Serjeants,
and two Corporals; I have the honor to signify to you HMP, that
you do issue £200 on Account to the Agent of the said Corps,
and place the same to the Account of the Subsistence of the
Regiment.

W.O. 4/100, p. 8

76

Barrington to Charles Townshend (Paymaster-General)

[Copy]   War Office
                                                    16 June 1766

Mr Richardson Agent to the 32nd Regt. of Foot having represented to me that no remittances having been received for 19
Weeks past at St Vincents for the Subsistence of the Regt the

Commanding Officer was obliged to draw Bills upon him to the Amount of £1509-15- on that Account, which Bills Mr Richardson has by direction accepted, I am to signify to you the K:P. that you do stop that sum out of the next Issue made to the persons who have contracted to remit the Subsistence of the above Regt. & pay it into Mr Richardson's hands, for the purpose of answering the bills drawn upon him.

W.O. 4/80, p. 4

77

Barrington to Grey Cooper

[Copy]   War Office
                                             19 July 1766

I am to acknowledge the rect. of your letter of the 17th instant, enclosing a Copy of the Minute which the Rt. Honble the Lords Commissioners of the Treasury have resolved upon, relative to the Inconveniencies which their Lordships are apprehensive may arise from the power given to the Military Commanders, & Lieut. Govrs. in America & the ceded Islands, to draw Bills on the Treasury; and I am to desire you will be pleased to acquaint their Lordships that the Orders therein contained shall be sent, by the 1st Packet, to the said Commanders, & Lieut. Govrs. & that I will take care the same be transmitted, from time to time upon every change of such Commanders, & Lieut. Govrs., agreable to their Lordships desire.

W.O. 4/80, p. 123

78

Treasury Minute referred to in Document 77

[Copy]
Treasury Chambers
Whitehall
15 July 1766

Present
Mr. Chancellor of the Exchequer
Mr. Townshend
Mr. Onslow

Write to General Gage and Governor Melville and inform them that my Lords apprehend great Inconveniencies from the Power given to the Military Commanders and Lieutenant Governors in America and the Ceded Islands under their several Commands to draw Bills on the Treasury; and that my Lords for the future direct that such Commanders and Lt. Governors when they have occasion to incurr any Extraordinary Military Expences, shall respectively inform Genl. Gage or Govr. Melville of such occasion, of the Sums wanted, and of the Services intended to be supplied by them; and that Genl. Gage and Governor Melville being in their respective Commands convinced of the necessity of such Services, shall, in such Cases as will admit of delay, transmit on account thereof, to this Board, that His Majesty's pleasure may be taken thereupon, and that proper Estimates may be laid before Parliament, to the end that such Sums may be granted as Parliament shall think necessary for that purpose, and in such as will not admit of delay, the Genl. and Governor shall give to such Commanders & Lt. Governors, Bills on the Treasury for the necessary Sums & transmit an Account thereof to this Board, as well as to the proper Office to whose Department the Service so undertaken particularly belongs, with the reason why consistently with the good of the Service, it was not possible to delay the incurring such Expence until such time as the Regulations abovementioned could be complied with, and such Commanders & Lt. Governors are to be directed to indorse on the said Bills the rate of Exchange at which they shall negotiate the same.

Let these orders be sent also to the said Commanders and Lt.

Governors. For that purpose, write to Lord Barrington, and desire his Lordship to transmit the same, and to take Care that the same be from time to time transmitted upon every Change of such Commanders and Lt. Governors.

Like Letter of the same date and like inclosure to His Excellency Governor Melville.

W.O. 4/80, pp. 136–137

79

**Barrington to the Lords Commissioners
of the Treasury**

[Copy]   War Office
27 April 1757

May it Please Your Lordships

The Several Agents to the Regiments in Garrison at Gibraltar having presented to me the annexed papers & Memorial, & praying my Interposition to prevent dishonour falling on the said Regiments, by Bills being protested, which were drawn on them for one month's subsistence for those Regiments, by the Regimental Paymasters, by order of Lord Tyrawley; I consulted the Paymaster General of His Majesty's Forces thereon, & am informed by him, that he has pursuant to your Lordships direction of the 25th of March last, issued to John Bristow Esqr; to be by him remitted for the use of the Garrison of Gibraltar, Four Months subsistence to the 24th of August next, & that he has no money in his hands to answer these draughts.

I therefore humbly pray Your Lordships will be pleased to take the same into your consideration, & to give such direction as you shall think proper, that the said Bills may not be returned protested.

W.O. 26/23, p. 185

80

Memorial of Agents referred to in Document 79

[Copy]   N.d.

To the Right Honble. Lord Viscount Barrington
His Majesty's Secretary at War
Memorial of the Agents to the Regiments
in Garrison at Gibraltar

Sheweth

That the Commanding Officers of these several Regiments having made a Representation to Lord Tyrawley, a Copy of which is hereunto annexed, and in Consequence thereof His Lordship having issued his orders also annexed, that the Paymasters of the severall Regiments should draw upon your Memorialists Bills for one Months subsistence which they have accordingly done, and Application has been made to the Paymaster General for a month's Subsistence to discharge the said Bills, But the said Subsistence being issued to the Contractors—he could not comply with our Request

> Your Memorialists therefore humbly pray your Lordship to take this Matter into Consn. So as to prevent any Dishonour falling upon the said Corps from their Bills being protested.
> Wm Adair
> Thos. Wilson
> John Calcraft
> John Winter

The annexed Papers to the above Memorial were:
The Representation of the Colonels and Commanding Officers then in Garrison at Gibraltar Dated 2d March 1757.
A Copy of a Letter from Lord Tyrawley in Answer to the said Representation Dated Gibraltar 3d. March 1757.
A Copy of a Letter from John Campbell Colo. of 56th Regt. Charles Jefferys Colo. of 14th Regt. John Crawfurd and Thomas Wilkinson to John Calcraft Esqr. Dat. Gibraltar 5th March 1757.

81

Barrington to Grey Cooper

[Copy]   War Office
                                                  10 February 1766

I apprehend that the Contractors for Victualling Troops in the
West Indies and other parts of America depend in a great
Measure on the Supplies they get from the Northern Colonies. If
so, the Difficulties arising from the present Situation may occasion great Distress to the Troops, unless Timely Measures be
taken to secure a certain Supply of Provisions for them from other
Parts.

I therefore think it my Duty to apprize the Lords of the
Treasury of my Apprehensions, and to submit it to their
Lordships whether it will not be expedient that the several
aforesaid Contractors should be questioned from whence they
have ordered Provisions: After which, my Lords may give such
Directions as the Circumstances of the Case shall require.

W.O. 4/78, p. 381

82

Treasury Minutes

[Copy]   Treasury Chambers
                                                        Whitehall
                                                 February 11 1766

          Present: Mr. Dowdeswell
                    Lord John Cavendish
                    Mr. Townshend
                    Mr. Onslow
                      *   *   *

READ a letter from Lord Barrington Secretary at War 10th Febry.
1766 apprising My Lords of his Apprehensions that the Contractors for Victualling the Troops in the West Indies & other parts of

America will be under great Difficulties to secure a sufficient & certain Supply of Provisions for Men in the present State of the Northern Colonies.

WRITE to Mr. Henniker Impowering him to send from England or Ireland such Quantities of Beef & Flour as He shall judge necessary for the Supply of the Troops in West Florida.

LET the Contractors for supplying His Majesty's troops in the West Indies & in East & West Florida with Provisions be written to & desired to attend My Lords to Morrow at Twelve o'Clock.

* * *

February 12, 1766

THE CONTRACTORS for supplying His Majesty's Troops & Fleets in the West Indies & in America, attended the Board; and being severally examined, as to the present State of Their Magazines of Supply respectively, they declared, that They believed that notwithstanding the distressed State of the Northern Provinces in America & the Embargo laid upon the Ports from which they principally ship their Provisions, there was at present a sufficient Supply in all Their Magazines. They were directed by Mr Lords to make Application to the Board as soon as They had any Apprehensions of Their not being able to perform their Contracts.

* * *

T. 29/37, pp. 335–336

83

Barrington to Messrs Ross and Gray, Agents

[Copy]   War Office
                                                 10 November 1772

A Claim having been made by you for the Sum of Two Hundred Eighty Five Pounds Eighteen Shillings & Nine Pence, stopt by the Pay Office from the 66th Regiment on account of Victualling in the Year 1765, which had been before stopt in America, I am to acquaint you, that I should have had no Difficulty in laying a

Warrant before the King for your Reimbursement, had the Fund been remaining in the Hands of the Paymaster General, as in the Case of the 22d. Regiment. But the Claim not having been made by you till after those Sums had been applyed to the Public Service, your Application under these Circumstances should properly be made to the Treasury.

The farther Claim of One Hundred Thirty One Pounds Twelve Shillings and Four Pence, stated to have been issued on account of the Recruiting to Captain Robert Campbell in the Year 1764, I cannot take into Consideration, till an Account has been produced of the Expenditure, agreeable to the Purpose for which the Money was issued.

W.O. 4/90, p. 233

84

Barrington to Judge Advocate General

[Copy]   War Office
                                                      24 May 1760

It having been represented to the King that great inconveniences do frequently arise upon the death of Agents, as the money which they are possessed of on a Regiml. Acct. passes with their other Effects to their Executors or Administrators, from whom it cannot be recovered but after many unavoidable delays, occasioned either by the forms of Law, or by the difficulty of stating an Exact Acct. of the same, distinct from the personal Estate of the deceased, by which means, not only the recruiting and other Regiml. Funds, but also the pay & Subsce. of the Troops are often for a long time locked up in the hands of Strangers, to the manifest injury and obstruction of H.M. Service, I am commanded to signify to you, It is H.M.P that you do forthwith summon the Board of Genl. Officers, who are to take this matter into consideration, and to report their opinion, in what manner the inconveniences abovementioned, and others which may arise upon the death of Agents to Regts. may best be guarded against,

& particularly whether it would not be for the good of the Service in this respect, if Agencies to Regts. were managed in partnership, so that in case of the death of one partner the business might always be carried on without interruption by the Survivor.

W.O. 4/61, p. 154

85

Barrington to Judge Advocate General

[Copy]   War Office
                                                      20 June 1760

Having had the honour to lay before the King the Report of the Board of General Officers of the 12th instant, I am commanded by H.M. to acquaint you It is H.M.P. that the said General Officers do consider and report for H.M. information what Sums of money an Agent should deposit, or vest in the publick Funds, for a Troop of Horse Guards, for a Troop of Horse Grenadier Guards, for a Regiment of Horse, for the first Regt. of Dragoon Guards, for a Regt. of Dragoons for the first Regt. of Foot Guards, for the Coldstream & third Regts. of Foot Guards, for a Regt. of Foot of two Battalions, & for a marching Regt. of Foot, as a Security and for obviating the inconveniencies suggested in my Letter to you of the 14th [sic] of last Month.

W.O. 4/61, p.302

86

Barrington to Lt.-General Lord Delawarr
and 97 other Colonels of Regiments

[Copy]   War Office
                                                      10th July 1760

The King being desirous to prevent the inconveniencies which may arise upon the death of Agents to Regiments was pleased to direct the Board of General Officers to take this matter into consideration & to report their opinion in what manner the said inconveniencies may best be guarded against. And the Board accordingly have reported to His Majesty that they have not been able to discover any better method of obviating the inconveniencies, the foresight of which occasioned this reference, than by the Colonel taking a sufficient security by a deposit of Money or by the Agent vesting a sum in the publick Funds, in the names of Trustees applicable upon demand of the Colonel to make good any deficiency arising from the failure or death of the Agent.

The Board being further directed to Consider what sums of money an Agent should deposit or vest in the publick Funds, as a security for the several Corps in His Majesty's service, report that they have not been able to fix any certain sum which may be adapted to the several circumstances that may occurr. And have submitted it to His Majesty as their opinion, that the Sum to be deposited by the Agent cannot be so properly determined by any person as by the Colonel of each Corps whose interest as well as regard for the Service must induce him to require a sufficient security.

When I had the honour to lay this report of the Board of General Officers before the King His Majesty was pleased to order that the same should be communicated to the Colonels of the several Corps in His Service, that if any of them have omitted to require sufficient security from their Agents, they may be apprised of the necessity of their speedily taking that precaution, as, in case of any accident His Majesty agreable to the opinion of the Board must look upon the Colonel as the only person accountable not only for the pay of his Regiment, the Regimental Funds, & other money with which the Agent is usually entrusted but also for every obstruction & inconvenience which may arise to His Majesty's service from the Death, or failure of the said Agent.

W.O. 4/61, pp. 367–368.

87

Barrington to Charles Lowndes

[Copy]   War Office
                                                      15 July 1767

I send you enclosed a list of Warrants signed by the King since my
letter of the 27th May last for the Marches &c of different
Regiments to the periods therein mentioned which I beg you will
lay before the Right Honble. the Lords Commissioners of His
Majesty's Treasury that their Lordships may be pleased to give
directions for their being immediately satisfied, as the Bills upon
which these Warrants are granted appear upon a strict examination to be drawn up in conformity to the Regulation which I had
the honor to transmit to their Lordships in my Letter of the 1st
February 1766.

W.O. 4/82, p. 183

88

Barrington's notes for speech in Parliament

[Holograph]   [1755]

[Endorsed]: Minutes of my opening on the Hessian and Russian
Subsidies in the House of Commons 1755.

The Treaty with Hesse stipulates 8000 Men for 4 years & 4000
more if required

It is like other subsidiary German Treaties except in the Subsidy
which is the same for 8000 Men & a power of requiring 12000 as
in 1740 for 6000 Men.

The Particular use of Hessians is for quotas &c.

Invasions particularly at the time when signed, June 18th.

This Treaty must deter especi
ally as it gives liberty to Austria.
— No Provocation.

But do not defend Hanover
ans.ⁿ Then you must buy it
back with your advantages.

It will be mine — Palatinate
Bavaria.

Has Hanover deserved this?
We get the Royal family:
They get 3 Kingdoms. Hano-
ver gets nothing.

They lose their Prince's presence
his Court, his Subsidies, their
own Security. & G. B. will
not give 100,000 a year to
save them.

But the K. might pay it. ans.ⁿ
He augments his Troops &
Fortifications.

Your honour will not let him
pay, & it would be dangerous.

Recapitulation

Measures of Politicks at least
Problematical — You must
have Confidence — The mi-
nisters deserve it in foreign
affairs — Better than it
was expected, cannot be by
chance.

Excerpt from Barrington's handwritten notes for a speech in Parliament, 1755 (see Document 88). *Courtesy of the Suffolk Record Office*

These Motives solely British: The third Motive is British and Hanovern.

Right to mention Hanover.

The Russian Treaty is founded on that of 1742 which is purely defensive. Art. 3d—Russia furnishes 12000 Men without Subsidy.

This Treaty never complain'd of. rather liked, but not sufficient at present—Men too few, & perhaps American dispute not included.

The Treaty of 1755 having the same views gives 55,000 *additional* Men and Galleys, wch. Fixes the amount of the additional Succour.

Unusual Stipulation of continuing the operations tho' attackd at home—& that the Commander shall receive orders from H.M.

For this you are to pay after they leave their own Territories the Empress being poor, but you only pay three months after the return.

Comparison of Expence between these & German troops—this shews the Ally not mercenary.

To this nobody would object, nor would you come to Parliament —It is the Subsidy of 100,000£—Compare it.

As it could not be avoided. See if the objects are addequate, that is the question.

Objects are new: *Ballance* of Power in Europe, Grand *Alliance*.

The Object is to keep things quiet where you are weak to be active where you are strong.

Being known to have the Force may prevent calling for it. Exemp. gra.

Powers of the Baltick—when you had not Sweeden you had Danemark.

Neutral Bottoms granted to the Dutch in [blank] Inconveniences —One or both may assist France if not deter'd.

You cannot deter with your Fleet—Invasion—Trade— Plantations—Superior wherever France can go or be.

Subsidies cannot, they are engaged. Russia luckily not engaged.

The words *Diversion & Galleys* shew this to be a principal object of the Treaty.

Why not hire Russian Ships? Ansr. Troops ansr. more effectually.

If this be a true british Object it justifys the Treaty, but another remains—Hanover.

All agree Hanover shd. be defended in some Cases; A Majority think so in this.

2 It shd. where the Cause is intirely British & it can be done.

1 Hanover an Inconvenience. England has notwithstanding grown happy and strong. Advantage must be bought.

France will not go into Germany without Assistance there.

Only one Power can assist them. This treaty must deter especially as it gives liberty to Austria.—No Provocation.

But do not defend Hanover. Ansr. Then you must buy it back with your Advantages.

It will be ruind—Palatinate Bavaria.

Has Hanover deserved this? We get the Royal Family. They get 3 Kingdoms. Hanover gets nothing.

They lost their Princes' presence, his Court, his Subsidies, their own Security, & G.B. will not give 100,000 a year to save them.

But the K. might pay it. Ansr. He augments his Troops & Fortifications.

Your honour will not let him pay, & it would be dangerous. Recapitulation.

Measures of Politicks at least Problematical—You must have Confidence—the Ministers deserve it in foreign affairs—Better than was expected, cannot be by chance.

Ipswich 3b, no. 214

89

Barrington to Lord Holdernesse

[Copy]   War Office
                                                 10 December 1759

In Obedience to your Lordships Commands, I have examined the Establishmt. of the Brunswick Troops which are intended to be taken into the Pay of Great Britain, & they appear to me to be at least as advantageous as those of the Hessian Corps in our Service; indeed, as the Brunswick Regt. consist of fewer Companies, & Troops, than those of the Landgrave of Hesse Cassel of nearly the same Number of Men, upon Comparing the Officers allotted to each Company, & Troop, there will be a saving in favr. of the Brunswick Forces; Your Lordship will be pleased to Observe, that this is upon a Supposition, that the Pay of the

Brunswick Troops will be the same, as that of the Hessians; for their denomination and Numbers are only mentioned, in the papers I had the honour to receive from your Lordship.

The Sum demanded for Levy Money for these Troops, is perfectly right, upon the footing of the Hessian Treaty, Vizt. 80 Crowns each Man, & horse, & 30 Crowns for each Foot Soldier.

As to the Subsidy they demand, their Calculation is just, if the principle be admitted, upon which it is made; the Hessian Treaty no where mentions, that a Horseman, is to be reckon'd as three Foot Soldiers; or that the Subsidy which we pay to the Landgrave, is calculated at so much a head for his Troops, valueing each of his Cavalry, at the price of three of his Infantry.

My first Clerk has seen Mr Murhead, Monsieur Alts Secretary, who says, that the amount of the Subsidy paid to the Landgrave of Hesse Cassel is not ascertained by a Calculation of so much a head for the Number of Troops he furnishes, but a Certain Sum agreed upon by the two powers, without any Calculation: as a proof of which, the Landgrave received during the last War, the same Subsidy for 6000 Men which is now paid him for the body of 8000 Men, under the Treaty of 1755.

W.O. 4/59, pp. 483-484

90

Barrington to Lord Holdernesse

[Copy]   War Office
                                    17 January 1760

I am to acquaint you that the Materials which I have received from yr Office for forming an Establishment of the Charge of the Brunswick Troops are very deficient. The Tabelle specifies the Establishmt. of the several Corps, but does not fix the Pay which the Officers and private Men of the different species of Troops are to receive; which all the other Tabelles of Foreign Troops that have passed through my Office have done.

In the 7th Article of the Treaty with the Duke of Brunswick it is said these Troops are engaged on the foot of the Hessian Troops.

Upon comparing the Tabelles of the three Bodies of Hessian Forces now in the pay of Great Britain with that of these Troops, it appears not only that the several Brunswick Corps are on a different Establishment from those which bear the same name among the Hessians, but that there are some Corps not to be found among the Hessian Troops in Our Pay.

It is therefore impossible for me to form an Estimate with any precision, even admitting the Hessian Tabelles to be the Standard with regard to pay; & I must beg your Lordship will procure me as soon as possible a Tabelle specifying the Pay of the Brunswick Troops, that I may be enabled to prepare the Estimate for Parliament.

I must also desire yr Ldship will be pleased to acquaint me on what day the Requisition was made to the Duke of Brunswick, for the Infantry, & on what day the Cavalry.

W.O. 4/59, pp. 540–541.

91

Barrington to Samuel Martin

[Copy]   War Office
                                              26 July 1760

I have received your letter of Yesterdays date, together with some papers delivered by Monsieur de Ferone, to the Duke of Newcastle, containing the demands of the Duke of Brunswick, for the Service of his Troops, and desiring that their amount in German currency might be computed in Sterling money for the information of the Duke of Newcastle.

I return you herewith the said papers, together with the amount of the several demands in Sterling money.

I must desire you will acquaint the Duke of Newcastle that the Tabelle which was sent me by Lord Holdernesse, in order to my preparing an Estimate of the Brunswick Troops, did not express the pay which those Troops were to receive, it specified only their numbers and ranks. As the Brunswic Troops were engaged upon the foot of the Hannoverians I got the best information I could obtain from the Hanoverian Office, of what pay Troops of their respective denominations would receive according to the Hanoverian Establishment; and upon that authority I formed the best Estimate I could to be laid before Parliament, until a more compleat Tabelle should be received from Germany.

Upon looking over the Tabelle you sent me yesterday in which the pay is expressed I find so great a difference between the allowances demanded for the Brunswic Corps, and what Hanoverian Troops of the same denomination receive, that I think it will be proper to make a more strict enquiry into this matter, than the time between this and Monday will admit of. You will therefore be pleased when you have laid this matter before the Duke of Newcastle, to return me again the Tabelle which I herewith send you, as it will be necessary at a Conference I propose to have with Mr Ferone on that Subject.

The Levy money is perfectly right both with regard to the Treaty, and the Estimate laid before Parliament.

The additional Subsidy from the day of requisition until the Brunswick Troops enter into the pay of Great Britain, is calculated by Monsieur Ferrone for the Cavalry and Infantry *separately* altho the Treaty fixes it in general for the whole Corps. I am not therefore able to make a report on the paper you sent me; as it neither mentions the day of requisition, for the Troops, nor the rules by which the Subsidy is calculated for the Cavalry and Infantry separately.

The Duke of Brunswick is entitled to £34,375,11.3 for Subsidy to the 24th Decr. and if the advances to him up to that period, do not exceed that Sum, the publick can be no loser.

Upon the whole, the Sum now demanded by Monsieur Ferrone may very safely be paid to him, as a much larger Sum will be soon due to the Duke of Brunswick, but then I think it should be paid upon account only, and not on the footing of his demands, until they shall be further discussed and finally settled.

* * *

	£	s	d
Agent de Levee 1,200 Cs at 4s.9¾	288	15	-
Subsidies jusqu'au 9eme Aout 1760	20,985	2	4
Solde jusques'au 23d October 1760	28,067	17	4
	49,341	14	8

W.O. 4/61, pp. 497–499

92

Statement on Supplies for German campaign

[Holograph: Barrington's hand]   n.d. [1762]

The 21st of February 1757, the House of Commons voted £200,000 to assist the late King in forming & maintaining an Army of Observation in Germany.

Some time after, it being determin'd to . . . . . . strengthen that Army, the Hessians then in England were sent to Germany; their pay was changed from British to German, and they were augmented to 12,000 men. The vote for this was in May.

These Troops when employ'd in the Empire, were by Treaty entitled to demand from us, the same treatment with the King's Electoral Troops, who, like all other Troops, have bread, forage, firewood &c, when in the field.

The *then* Treasury therefore, gave orders to General Amherst then Commissary of Musters to the Hessian Troops, that he should make contracts for supplying them with Bread, forage & other Extraordinaries.

General Amherst thought the best way in which he could supply them was by desiring the Hanoverian Chancery of War, to furnish these necessaries to the Hessians, whenever they should encamp with, or be joined to the Hanoverians, *in the same manner & at the same price*, to which the Hanoverian Chancery consented.

In the following year, Colo Boyd who succeeded General Amherst, with the same Instructions, having made a like application to the German Chancery, they continued to furnish Extraordinaries to the Hessians, in the same manner as the year before.

In order to repay the German Chancery this expence, various sums were at different times paid by Our Commissaries Amherst & Boyd, as appears by the *services incurred*, and *Accounts of the disposition of the Million* for 1757 and 1758, laid before Parliament in 1758 & 1759. Those sums, together with a demand on our part, on the German Chancery, mentioned in the Paper now under consideration of the House, amount to £322,397; but there still remains a ballance of £336,479 due to the Electoral Chancery, and this is what we are now to pay.

The utmost care has been taken in examining these Accounts, both by Our Commissaries abroad, & the Treasury here: Nothing can be more fair than the manner in which those Accounts have been kept by the German Chancery.

Part of the Bread was bought, & part was baked. We are charged only for that part of either, which was delivered to those Troops whom we were to supply.

The Accounts state the first Cost of the Grain & Meal; the price of the Wood used in baking; the loss on Bread taken by the Enemy; losses on Resale which was sometimes necessary, or by waste in the Magazines, expences of the Magazines, Servants, Utensils, &ca. Of these incident expences, no more is charged to our Account, than according to our proportion of the Bread received by us.

Wood is charged according to the same rule; & forage, according to the quantities actually delivered to Our Troops.

Our Commissaries abroad having carefully examined all the Books & Accounts of the German Chancery, certify that in all articles of expence, no more is charged to us than our share, or at any other price than what the late King paid as Elector, for his own Troops. The said Accounts have agreed with the books of the several Officers who accounted with the Hanoverian Chancery.

Besides the Hessians, a small Corps of Prussian Troops, paid by the King of Prussian, & making part of the Army of Observation in the years 1757 & 1758 were supplied with these Extraordinaries by us, in consequence of an agreement between the Courts of London & Berlin. This expence was authorized by the Votes of 1757, & 1758, granting money on account, to 'enable His late Majesty to defray any extraordinary expences of the War, incurred, or to be incurred for the service of those years, & to take all such measures as may be necessary to disappoint or defeat any Enterprizes or designs of his enemies, or as the exigency of Affairs may require'. All like Votes ever since that time, have passed in the same terms.

These Prussian Troops were furnished by the Hanoverian Chancery, with bread, forage, wood &ca, exactly in the same manner & proportion, as the Hessians; And our bearing this part of their expence, was not unknown to Parliament, because money was voted in 1759 for some of that expence incurred in 1758, & not provided for, by the German Chancery.

If it be said that these Hessian & Prussian Extraordinaries were to be paid out of the £200,000 voted in 1757, for the extraordinary expences of the Army of Observation, let it be remembered;

First, That the £200,000 was voted while the Hessian Troops were here, & before it was determin'd by Parliament that they should return to Germany.

Secondly, That this sum was very insufficient to defray the Extraordinaries even of 38,000 men to which number the Troops of that Army were to amount exclusive of the Hessians, & Prussians.

But what makes it clear to a demonstration that the Hessian & Prussian Extraordinaries were not included, is an Estimate of the Extraordinary Charge for 30,000 men of the Troops of Hanover, Wolfenbuttle Saxe Gotha, & Count of Buckeburg, for the year 1758, which extraordinary charge, is explained to include Forage, bread-Waggons, Wood & Straw for those Troops. The sum voted for these Extraordinaries was £386,915, being near double what was given for the same services the year before. The Estimate is very particular; & calculated to include every expence which was intended to be defray'd by it: Tho' all the other forces which compos'd the Army of Observation are enumerated in it, no mention is made of the Hessian and Prussian Troops, or their Extraordinaries, altho' they made a part of the Army of Observation from its first formation.

It has been said the demand of this ballance of £336,000 due to the Electoral Chancery, should have been made sooner; an objection more natural to come from the other side of the water, than to be raised on this. The truth is, it require'd a great length of time to state such voluminous Accounts, & to give the proofs requir'd in each particular. The late King was obliged to borrow £200,000 in England, at 4 p cent Interest, because he had laid out a still greater sum for these Extraordinaries, at our request, & for our convenience; and His present Majesty must have demanded £111,000 more than has been laid this year before Parliament, & to the payment of which, the Parliament could have no Objection, if it had not been understood that this payment would enable His Majesty to defray those expences out of His Electoral Treasury.

Ipswich 3c, no. 56

93

Barrington to the Duke of Newcastle

[Rough draft, including corrections, in Barrington's hand]

N.p.
11 October 1763

The meeting of Parliament approaching I have thought it right to read over peruse and consider examine the Report from the Committee appointed last session to consider the Several Estimates & Accounts presented to the House of Commons and relating to the application or expenditure of Publick Money since the commencement of the late War.

I find that mention is made therein of the Contract enter'd into by the Treasury in Decr. 1760 with Sr. Lawrence Dundass for furnishing Horses to the Hanoverian Artillery. That This contract appears to be cheaper by 17½ per Cent than that made by the Board of Ordnance about the same time with Messrs Oswald and Mill for the Horses of the British Artillery: However as Sir Lawrence tells every body it is by this Contract he has acquired his immense fortune being a loser as he says on the Proviant Train inland, ~~I have thought it right to~~ shall endeavour to make myself thoroughly a Master of ~~whatever can be found relative thereto~~ all the Papers relative thereto, ~~which Papers I expect to have soon. In a day or two I expect to have some the Papers relative~~. I will also converse with Colonel Pierson if necessary, & leaving nothing unexamin'd which can tend to my Instruction in this Matter. The transaction past before I came into the Treasury, but I shall always consider it my duty to support every part of Your Grace's Administration with the same equal Industry & Zeal. ~~I have accordingly desired & obtain'd permission to examine the German corr Treasury Books relative to previous to Lord Butes presiding there so far as they concern the German War, & in a day or two I they will such parts they will be ready for my Inspection. I have not mention'd the practical point in my contemplation, for tho' I do not suspect any the least design of giving your Grace any trouble, it is most prudent not to lead the ministers to such consideration of that return.~~ Whatever I find worthy of your Grace's knowledge shall be communicated to you, and if ~~there be anything in which~~ I can be useful to ~~your Grace~~ your Grace in anything I beg ~~leave to assure~~ you ~~with that sincerity you have always found in me~~ will believe there never can be a time when I shall not be equally happy to receive and obey your Commands.

~~I send herewith a printed Copy of the Report which possibly your Grace may desire to see & whi~~ As your Grace may possibly wish to see the Report & not have it by you I send a printed Copy of it herewith.

I am intirely ignorant of any design to revive the Committee next Session, or to substitute any other mode of enquiry; but as somewhat of that sort does not seem improbable I presume your Grace will not be unprepared against the meeting of Parliament. Whatever Part your friends take on that occasion shall be ~~punctually~~ the exact ruler of my Conduct.

I beg leave to add my humble respects to the Dutchess of N. who as well as your G. I hope to be in perfect health.

Ipswich 112, no. 41

94

Barrington to the Duke of Newcastle

[Rough draft in Barrington's hand including corrections]

N.p.
15 October 1763

Since I had the honour to write to your Grace I have got all the ~~Treasury Papers~~ materials relative to the Contracts with Sir Lawrence Dundass both for the Artillery and proviant Trains. I find ~~them made the~~ your Treasury to have acted therein as I expected, with all possible regard to the publick ~~oeconomy~~ and every prudent precaution with relation to them selves. I will carry the Papers ~~into Berk~~ [Berkshire] with me to Beckett ~~and ponder~~ where I am going and will make a short abstract of them there; such as will bring the whole transaction within half a Sheet of Paper, for the ease of your Grace ~~Mr Legge~~ or any other Person whom you would have consulted thereupon. ~~At my return~~ I shall return to London in the beginning of November & when I hear your Grace is at Newcastle House, will pay my Duty to you there, and hope for your Commands if I can be useful to you.

I happened to meet Pownal in the Park the day I came to London abt. a fortnight ago, when he told me he was appointed by the Treasury with others to examine & state the foreign Demands, since which I heard nothing of that Commission till I was honoured by your Grace's Letter of the 12th Instant; ~~I have~~ which has occasion'd my enquiring fully into ~~that~~ it. I find that the Comrs are authorized among other things 'to state distinguish and ascertain the nature of the said (German) Accounts Claims & Demands and of the Warrants Orders ~~and~~ Authorities & Voutchers on which the same are founded, together with the opinion what is proper to be done thereon'. It seems to me that those Powers would be necessary ~~for the examination of~~ to enable the Comrs to examine into Warrants orders authorities & Voutchers issuing from Persons in Germany, who are the proper objects of their enquiries, but ~~they might also~~ the Powers extend to subject any such Acts of the Treasury touching German expenditure to their enquiry and report as shall be lay'd before them. I cannot find that any ~~such~~ thing ~~of that nature~~ was in Contemplation: if it was, nothing can be more mean or dirty and it will recoil on the wretched designers. Pownal ~~will~~ wd. make no ill use of these Powers ~~if~~ in complaisance to any body, & I believe the same of Cuthbert. I have enquired who the third Comr. is & I find him to be the relation or friend of ~~one of the Secretaries to~~ a person ~~much trusted by the Treasury~~ belonging to the Treasury which (the pay being two pounds a day) may account ~~pretty well~~ for his appointment.

Ipswich 112, no. 67

95

Barrington to Charles Lowndes

[Copy]   War Office
                                                    19 April 1766

I am to acknowledge the Receipt of your Letter of the 19th of last Month, inclosing a Copy of a Letter from His Excellency the Lord Lieutenant of Ireland to the Right Honourable the Lords Commissioners of His Majesty's Treasury, with two Papers containing a State of the Demands made by Ireland upon Great Britain, on the Head of Levy Money and Cloathing for Draughts made at different Times from Irish Regiments, of Subsistence advanced by Ireland to Regiments ordered from thence upon Foreign Service, and of Levy Money to replace the Augmentations made to those Regiments, before they embarked, by Draughts from other Irish Regiments.

I have fully considered the different Matters contained in the Papers; and, in the first Place, shall beg leave to submit to their Lordships my Opinion with respect to the Rule or Principle which I think should be adhered to in settling each of the above Demands, conformably to the Practice of the Army. I shall afterwards propose to their Lordships that Method of liquidating and adjusting the whole Account which I apprehend will be most likely to prevent Difficulty and Delay.

In the Course of the late War it was frequently found necessary to recruit the Regiments serving abroad, by Draughts from Ireland, and it was then settled that the Irish Regiments so draughted, should be allowed five Pounds in lieu of Levy Money for each Man, to be paid out of the Non Effective Fund of the Regiments that received the Draughts. This Demand therefore, as far as it can be authenticated, appears to be well founded, and ought to be made good either out of the Non Effective Fund of the British Regiments, or, if that Fund shall be insufficient, by the Publick.

With respect to the Claim for a compleat Cloathing for each Man draughted, I did formerly, by my Letter of 16. March 1761, inform Mr Rigby 'that no Allowance is made on that Account to Regiments in England, except seven Shillings a Man for a Waistcoat,' consequently that no greater Allowance could be made to Irish Regiments, and I still adhere to that Opinion. The Charge at the rate of seven Shillings p man for a Waistcoat, when liquidated, must be made good in the same Manner with the Charge for Levy Money.

The Demands contained in the second Paper transmitted by His Excellency the Lord Lieutenant of Ireland, relate entirely to Regiments ordered from thence since the Conclusion of the Peace, to relieve others stationed abroad, & sent to Ireland in their Room. That their Lordships may see in one View, how these Demands arise, I beg leave to state to them the original Plan, upon which it was determined that the whole Relief should be conducted, wherein their Lordships will perceive that it was determined to carry on that Service with as little additional Expence as possible, to the Publick.

By the first Plan of the Relief it was settled that the Regiments sent from Ireland to relieve others on the British Establishment in North America and the West Indies should, in the first Place, be augmented by Draughts in Ireland to the Establishment of the Regiments serving in North America; that the relieving Regiments with their Augmentations, should continue on the Irish Establishment untill the Day of their landing at the Place of their Destination inclusive, on which Day the relieved Regiment quitted the British, and came upon the Irish Establishment; by which Means the Account *as to Pay*, was exactly even; and if Ireland, in Exchange for their compleat Regiment, had received another compleat Regiment of 500 Men, Ireland would then have had no Demand at all upon England. But the relieved Regiments being very incompleat, it was agreed that Ireland should be allowed five Pounds for every Man wanting in the relieved Regiments, to compleat to the American Establishment, in order to enable that Kingdom to replace the Draughts they had made from their other Regiments to augment those sent on Foreign Service. Whatever this Allowance amounts to, is undoubtedly due to Ireland, and must be made good out of the English Non Effective Fund of the relieved Regiments. It was also understood as a Concession made by Great Britain, that the Number of Men wanting to compleat should be taken from the Return of each Regiment as it landed in Ireland, and not as it embarked, which would have been more strictly regular; and by this Means Great Britain risqued the Loss of any Men who might have died during the Passage.

But I must here observe that, altho' it be admitted that five Pounds should be allowed for every Man wanting to compleat to the American Establishment in each Regiment, landed in Ireland, to be taken on the day of their landing, this Indulgence ought by no Means to be extended any farther. And Whereas his Excellency the Lord Lieutenant of Ireland alledges that the 44th and 45th Regiments were, after their Arrival in Ireland, obliged to discharge a farther very considerable Number of Men as unfit for Service, for which Men, Ireland makes a Demand of Levy Money, I am clearly of Opinion that this Claim, not being justified by the original Plan of the Relief, ought not to be admitted; and that no Levy Money ought to be allowed by England, except for such Men as have actually received their Discharges from their Commanding Officers, before their respective Regiments landed in Ireland.

The 62d Regiment not being in the Case of the relieving Regiment, the Claim of five Pounds a Man for 171 Men, with which that Regiment was augmented, before its Embarkation from Ireland, is well founded, and must be made good by Government.

The only Demand which now remains for me to take Notice of, is, for the Balance of Subsistence advanced by Ireland to the Regiments, ordered from thence, and arises thus. As they were to continue on the Irish Establishment until the day of their Disembarkation abroad, it was thought convenient that Ireland should advance them a certain Sum upon Account of Subsistence, but it appears that the Sum so advanced exceeded the Pay due from Ireland to those Regiments. That Exceeding therefore is in fact, a Loan made by Ireland, for which that Government must of Course be reimbursed, and for this Purpose I apprehend nothing more will be necessary than for their Lordships to give Directions to His Majesty's Paymaster General to liquidate and adjust the same.

Having thus stated to their Lordships the Principles upon which I think the Demands made by Ireland ought to be satisfied, I beg leave farther to propose, as the easiest Way of compleating this whole Business, that His Excellency the Lord Lieutenant of Ireland should be desired to appoint some Person here, who might be furnished with all the Materials and Documents necessary to verify and settle each specific Demand. Sir Robert Wilmot is versed in this Sort of Business, and if it should be thought adviseable to appoint him or any other Person for this Purpose, I shall direct Mr Francis of my Office to assist him in examining the Accompts, and in reporting to the Lords of the Treasury what final Steps may be necessary for satisfying all the Demands of Ireland, at once.

I beg their Lordships Pardon for not sending an earlier Answer to your Letter of the 19th: of March last, but the Matter required a good deal of Consideration and Enquiry, and I thought it was better to delay my Report a Month, than to send it less correct, intelligible, or satisfactory, than the Nature of the Case would admit.

W.O. 4/988, pp. 91–94

96

Barrington to Charles Lowndes

[Copy]   War Office
                                              11 October 1765

I beg leave thro' you to acquaint the Right Honorable the Lords
Commissioners of H.M.'s Treasury that upon conversing with
Genl. Harvey, who is lately returned from the Isle of Man, & is
fully informed of the situation of H.M. Forces lately stationed
there, & of the nature of the duty to be done by them;—it appears
to me that one Company of Foot stationed at each of the following
places; vizt. Castle Town, Douglas, Ramsay, & Peel, will sufficiently answer the ends & design of sending the Troops to that
Island, which, I understand to have been that of preventing the
illegal practices of smugling. I think it my Duty therefore to
submit to their Lordship's consideration, whether if their
Lordships should be of the same opinion with me on this head, it
may not be proper to move the King for the removal of the
Remainder of the Forces, Vizt. the Two Troops of Light Dragoons, & five Companies of the Queen's Regt. of Foot from
thence back to Ireland, as soon as possible, whereby a considerable Saving may be made to the Public in the several Articles
which the ensuing Season will call for to be furnished to the
Troops in a great measure at the Public Expence, Vizt. Bread,
Forage, lodging, Coals & Candles, as likewise the difference
between the British & Irish Pay, for the said Forces, so long as
they shall be on Service out of the Kingdom of Ireland.

I take this opportunity of sending you herewith a Regulation
settled by the Adjutant General, relative to the proportions of the
several Articles above mentioned, which are to be delivered by the
Contractor to such part of H.M. Forces as it may be judged
necessary should remain in the Isle of Man, & am to desire their
Lordships will be pleased to give their Directions to the Contractor, to conform himself thereunto upon every occasion.

W.O. 4/78, pp. 2–3

97

Barrington to William Mellish

[Copy]   War Office
                                              18 September 1765

The last time I wrote to the Treasury, I advised a Reduction of various Expences for the benefit of the Public: I am now going to propose some Encrease of Expence, for the equitable advantage of certain Officers. A Secretary at War should be the Advocate of the Public, or of the Army occasionally, as justice requires; and both have an undoubted Right to his assistance even unasked.

In the Year 1757, the Establishment of all marching Regiments at home, was changed from Ten Companies to Nine; the tenth or youngest Captain was continued a Supernumerary in the Corps till a Vacancy happened, and received his full pay by Warrant. There were at that time, means of providing for the Subalterns of the Reduced Companies, by means of Augmentations then making in the Army.

During the War, Regiments consisting of ten Companies frequently came home. On their arrival here, they were constantly reduced to Nine; the Officers of the 10th were provided for as before mentioned, and none of them were ever placed on Half Pay. After the Peace, all the Regiments of foot in the King's Service were made to consist of Nine Companies only; but the Reduced Officers of the Tenth have had no provision made for them other than the half Pay. This was done with views of the most commendable public oeconomy, but in my Opinion is a grievous and unjustifiable hardship laid on many Officers who served in old Regiments subsisting before the late War; in which Regiments some of them bought Commissions at great Expence, concluding they would stand at the Peace: These Gentlemen find themselves out of Employment, and on Half Pay, while Officers in many new Corps formed during the late War, enjoy all the Advantages of the Service.

The practice of the Army founded in equity, has always been to reduce the Youngest Corps first, but in this instance the Reduction has been made by disbanding the Youngest Officers of the oldest Corps, (amongst others, of the Royal or 1st Regt. of foot,) every one of which Officers, according to my conception, has a better right to remain in the Service, than the oldest Officer of the same Rank in the 2nd, or any other Corps of the Army. The Alteration in the Establishment, by which these Officers have suffered, was intended for public conveniency: but such Alterations should be always made without doing injustice to Individuals.

If it were in my power to remedy the evil without adding to the Expences of the State, I would not trouble the Lords of the Treasury on a Subject foreign to their Department; but where the smallest additional Burden is laid on the Public, I ought to bring the matter under their Lordship's Consideration, and take no farther Step without their Authority.

The only way of doing Justice to the reduced Officers before mentioned, is to make them Supernumeraries in their respective Corps, with allowance of full Pay till Vacancies shall happen in like manner as was practised, during the War; the annual Expence of this would be £3,650 ..., over and above the Half-pay they now receive. That Sum is not great, when it is considered as a Redemption from penury and almost despair of Sixty three Officers who have all served during the War; of whom many might claim reward, as well as justice from the public, if the national Burthens would permit. A consideration of these Burthens ought to check Acts of Bounty but will not excuse a denial of Right.

In case the Treasury approve this Plan, you will please Sir, to remind them, that there are two ways of carrying it into Execution: The one is by Voting the necessary Sum on Estimate laid before Parliament; the other by making a Warrant for the purpose, the Amount of which afterwards becomes an Article among the Services incurred but not provided. I should recommend the first of these methods, if it were not for one consideration: the Expence on this head would be continually diminishing as Vacancies happen in Regimts. or by death. Now, if the whole Sum be voted in Estimate, the Savings will remain in the Pay Office, but if what is needful only, be paid by Warrant, no more than that precise Sum will go out of the Exchequer.

Ipswich 6e, no. 32

98

Charles Lowndes to Barrington

[Copy in Barrington's hand]   Treasury Chambers
                                               10 December 1765

The Lords Commrs. of His Majesty's Treasury having read your Lordships Letter of the 18th Septemr. last, setting forth the hardships attending the Situation of several Captains in the Army who serv'd during the late War in the Regts. consisting of 10 Companies; Which Regts. being reduced to 9 Companies when they came from abroad, these Officers were at the end of the War left on half Pay; And proposing to My Lords to make them Supernumeraries in their respective Regts, with allowance of full Pay till vacancies shall happen, in like manner as was practis'd with them, from the reduction of their respective Regiments to the end of the War: I am directed to inform your Lordship, that the Lords of the Treasury approve of putting the said Officers on full Pay, and are of opinion, that the proper method of carrying this Proposal into execution will be by laying before Parliament, an Estimate of the expence thereof.

Ipswich 6e, no. 33

99

Draft Estimate called for in Document 98

[Copy]

'Estimate of the Charge of Full Pay for 365 days for the Year 1766 to Officers reduced with the 10th Company of several Battalions reduced from ten to nine Companies, and who remained on Half Pay at the 21st December 1765.'

	Per diem			Per 365 days		
	£	s	d	£	s	d
20 Captains at 10s p. diem each	10			3,650		
18 Lieutenants at 4s 8d p. diem each	4	4		1,533		
8 Ensigns at . . . 3s 8d p. diem each	1	9	4	535	6	8

N.B.
As the Half-Pay of the above
46 Officers amounts to £2,859.3.4
p. Annum, the real Encrease of
Expence to the Public will be
no more than £2,859.3.4 or one
half of the above Total.

Ipswich 6e, no. 30

100

Barrington to Major-General Rufane
(Colonel of the 6th Regiment of Foot)

[Copy]   War Office
                                                         18 June 1766

It having been thought expedient for the Good of the Service, to
alter the Establishment of all the marching Regts. of Foot, so that
from the 25th of April 1763 inclusive, each Battn. might consist of
nine Compys only, whereby several Captains, Lieuts & Ensigns of
Merit & long Service, were reduced to half pay, And Whereas,
upon representation made of the hardship incurred by the several
Officers so reduced & that upon like reductions in 1757, &
afterwards, the Officers of the 10th Companies were paid as
Supernumeraries, out of the Contingencies of the Army, & did
duty with their respective Corps until they were provided therein
on the 1st Vacancies, Provision of full Pay hath been made by
Parliament from the 25th Decr. 1765, for the aforesaid Officers

reduced soon after the late Peace, & still unprovided for; I have the honor to acquaint you therewith, & to signify to you, It is H.M.P. that such of the Officers who were reduced, with the 10th Company of the Regt. of Foot under your Command, who remained on half Pay, at the 24th Decr. last, & who are entitled to the benefit of full Pay provided for them as above mentioned, shall attend, & do duty with any Company of your Regt., to which you, or the Officer commanding your said Regt., shall think proper to appoint them, until such time as Vacancies shall happen therein, when they are to be appointed respectively according to their Rank, to the first vacant Company, Lieutenantcy, or Ensigncy. And I am to acquaint you It is H.M.P. that these Supernumerary Officers do take rank in the Regt. from the said 25th day of Decr. 1765, as the junior Captain, Lieut. & Ensign, in like manner as if they came from half Pay, & that they shall proceed, as to their future rank therein, regimentally.

I am also to inform you, that the Paymaster General will have Orders to issue to you or your Assigns, the Pay of the said Supernumerary Officers, along with the Subsistence of your Regt., in Order to it's being paid over to them, or such of them as shall be entitled thereto, until they shall be provided for by Vacancies in the Regt. But in Order that all the Officers of your Regt. may be in the same State, in regard to their Pay, as they would have been, in case the 10th Company had never been reduced, I am to acquaint you, It is H.M.P., that the money voted for the aforesaid Supernumerary Officers should be considered as part of the General Fund of the Regt., & paid to the Officers serving therein, in such manner as it would have been paid, in case the 10th Company had never been reduced.

* * *

Like Letters of same date to the Colonels of the following Regts. of Foot.
7th. 13th. 17th. 27th. 28th. 35th. 42d. 46th. 53d. 54th. 57th. 60th. or Royal American, 2 Battns.

W.O. 4/80, pp. 44–46.

101

Barrington to James West

[Copy]   War Office
                                                5 January 1756

His Majesty having thought fit to Order Ten Regts. of Foot to be
forthwith raised under the Command of Colonels Abercrombie,
Napier, Lambton, Whitmore, Campbell, Perry, Lord Charles
Manners, Arabin, Anstruther and Montague, towards forming of
which Regts. H.M. hath directed the Thirty Eight Addl. Companies to the present Regts. of Foot in Great Britain to be
incorporated into the new Regts. and three Pounds Levy Money
for each Private Man wanting to Compleat the new Regiments, I
inclose an Estimate of the Charge of the Ten Regiments with
Levy Money, and am to desire you will be pleased to acquaint the
Rt. Honble. the Lords Commissioners of His Maty's Treasury
therewith.

W.O. 4/51, p. 113.

102

Barrington to Robert Ince

[Copy]   War Office
                                                5 January 1756

His Majesty having been pleased to order Ten Regts. of Foot to
be immediately Raised under the Command of Colonels Abercrombie, Napier, Lambton, Whitmore, Campbell, Perry, Lord
Charles Manners, Arabin, Anstruther, and Montague, each
Regiment to consist of Ten Companies of Three Serjeants, three
Corporals, Two Drummers and Seventy Private Men in each,
And as the Cloathing and Accoutrements &c for those Regiments
must be immediately Provided, I am Commanded to signify to
you, It is His Maty's Pleasure that you forthwith Summon a Board
of General Officers to Inspect the Patterns which shall be
exhibited and do everything else which shall be necessary that

the said cloathing and Accoutrements &c may be immediately provided.

W.O. 4/51, p. 114.

103

Barrington to Henry Fox

[Copy]   War Office
                                                                10 January 1756

His Majesty having thought fit to order Ten Regiments of Foot mentioned in the Annexed list, to be forthwith raised and Consist of Ten Companies of three Sergts, three Corporals, two Drummers & 70 Effective Private Men besides Commissioned Officers and to be partly formed by the 38 Comps lately added to the Nineteen Regts. of Foot in Great Britain: I have the Honour to Acquaint you therewith, that you may be pleased to receive His Majesty's Commands thereupon, & signify the same to the Master General of the Ordnance, that the arms &c mentioned in the Annexed List for the said Ten Regiments may be delivered out of His Majesty's Stores & the Expence thereof Charged to the Estimate of Ordnance for Parliamt.

* * *

Regt.	Iron Ramrods	Firelocks & Bayonetts	Cartouch Boxes & Straps	Halberts	Drums
Col Abercrombie	314	314	314	14	12
Col. Napier	418	418	418	18	14
Col Lambton	314	314	314	14	12
Col Whitmore	314	314	314	14	12
Col Campbell	314	314	314	14	12
Col Perrys	314	314	314	14	12
Lord Charles Manners	314	314	314	14	12
Col Arabin	314	314	314	14	12
Col Anstruthers	418	418	418	18	14
Col Montagues	314	314	314	14	12
	3348	3348	3348	148	124

W.O. 4/51, pp. 128–129

104

War Office comparison of augmentation plans

[Copy]   n.d. [probably August 1757]

	Per diem			For 365 Days		
	£.	s.	d.	£.	s.	d.
The Charge of raising Ten 2d Battalions formed like those of last Winter*, to consist of 8140 Men Officers included.	402	6	8	146,851	13	4
The Charge of Augmenting 37 Batts. with 8,113 Men according to HRH's Plan	316	11	–	115,540	15	0
Saved by Augmenting the Batts.	£85	15	8	31,310	18	4

A 2d. Battn, consists of the following Commn. & Non Commn. Officers

Major	Capt	Lieuts	Ensigns	Surgeons Mates	Serjts.	Corpls	Drūms
1	9	11	9	2	30	30	20

A Battn. of Nine Companies according to HRHss's Plan, will consist of

Colo	Lt Colo	Major	Capt	Lieuts	Ensns	Surgeon
1	1	1	6	19	8	1

Mates	Serjts	Corpls	Fifs	Drūms
2	36	36	2	18

To raise Ten 2nd Batts. it will be necessary to appoint. vizt.

Majors	Capt	Lieuts	Ensns	Surgeons Mates	Serjeants	Corpls	Drūms
10	90	110	90	20	300	300	200

To Augment 37 Batts. The additional Officers will be. vizt.

Lieuts	Surgeons	Mates	Serjeants	Corpls
296	15	22	222	222

Ipswich 3b, no. 178.

105

Barrington to Grey Cooper

[Copy]   War Office
                                                          15 July 1767

His Majesty having been pleased to direct that the 53rd & 54th Regiments of Foot shall be reduced to the same Numbers as the other Regiments of Foot serving on the Irish Establishment consist of, viz. 2 Serjeants, 2 Corporals, 1 Drummer and 28 Private Men in each Company besides the usual Commissioned Officers, I am to acquaint you therewith for the Information of the Rt. Hōnble the Lord Commissrs. of His Majesty's Treasury.

Enclosed I send you an Estimate of the Pay of each of the said Corps from the 25th August next inclusive, from which Period It is His Majesty's Pleasure the reduced Establishment of the said Regiments shall commence.

W.O. 4/82, p. 185

106

Estimate referred to in Document 105

Estimate of the Charge of the Pay of the 53rd Regiment of Foot, commanded by Major General Toovey, from 25th August 1767, inclusive.

	Pay per Diem		
	£.	s.	d.
1 Colonel and Captain	1	4	–
1 Lieut Colonel & Captain	–	17	–
1 Major & Captain	–	15	–

6 Captains	each 10s	3	–	–
10 Lieutenants	each 4.8	2	6	8
8 Ensigns	each 3.8	1	9	4
1 Chaplain			6	8
1 Adjutant		–	4	–
1 Quartermaster		–	4	8
1 Surgeon		–	4	–
1 Mate		–	3	6
18 Serjeants	each 1s. 6d.	1	7	–
18 Corporals	each 1s		18	–
9 Drummers	each 1s		9	–
252 Private Men	each 8d	8	8	–
329		21	16	10
Allowance to the Widows		–	12	–
Allowance to the Colonels		–	10	6
Allowance to the Captains		–	9	–
Allowance to the Agent		–	4	6
		23	12	10

One Regiment of Foot more commanded by Major General Parslow, of the like Rate & Numbers as the Regiment above mentioned	23	12	10

Barrington

W.O. 4/82, p. 186

107

Augmentation statistics, 1771

[Copy]
War Office
November 1770

Estimate of the Charge of an Augmentation proposed to be made to His Majesty's Land Forces for the Service of the Year 1771.

	Numbers	£	s.	d
An Augmentation to the Royal Regiment of Horse Guards from 25th December 1770 to 24th December 1771 both inclusive being 365 days	81	3,777	15	
To Lieutenant General Mostyn's Regiment of Dragoons Guards	81	2,669	1	3
To Earl Waldegrave's Regiment of Dragoon Guards	54	1,779	7	6
To Nine Regiments of Dragoon Guards and Dragoons more of the like Numbers	486	16,014	7	6
To Two Regiments of Light Dragoons	264	8,760	–	–
	966	33,000	11	3
To the Three Regiments of Foot Guards	640	9,733	6	8
An Additional Company to each of the 44 Battalions of Foot	2,332	48,046	3	4
An Augmentation to the 44 Battalions of Foot	8,800	107,066	13	4
An Augmentation to the Regiment and 20 Independent Companies of Invalids	580	6,174	11	
	12,352	171,020	15	
Total	13,318	204,021	6	3

Ipswich 6e, no. 155

108

Augmentation statistics 1775

[Copy]   N.p., n.d. [1775]

Estimate of the Charge of an Augmentation to His Majesty's
Forces for the Year 1775

		Numbers	*Pay for 365 Days*		
	Augmentation to Sir Jeffery Amherst's Regiment of Foot	200	£2,646	5	–
	Do. to Lt Genl A'Court Ashe's Regt	200	2,646	5	–
	Do. to Majr. Genl. Mackay's Regt	200	2,646	5	–
	Do. to Majr. Genl. Evelyn's Regt	200	2,646	5	–
	Do. to Lt. Genl. Parslow's Regt	200	2,646	5	–
	Do. to Sir Adolphus Oughton's Regt.	200	2,646	5	–
Foot	Do. to Colonel Robinson's Regt	200	2,646	5	–
	Do. to Lt. Genl. Pierson's Regt	200	2,646	5	–
	Do. to Lord Adam Gordon's Regt	200	2,646	5	–
	Do. to Colonel Maxwell's Regt	200	2,646	5	–
	Do. to Lt. Genl. Lambton's Regt	200	2,646	5	–
	Do. to Lt. Genl. Trapaud's Regt	200	2,646	5	–
		2,400	£31,755	0	0

Levy Money for 2,400 Men at £5. per Man		£12,000	0	0

One Independent Company of Invalids	100	£1,438	14	2
Nineteen more Independent Companies of Invalids	1,900	27,335	9	2
	2,000	28,774	3	4
Total	4,400	£72,529	3	4

Ipswich 6e, no. 247

109

Barrington to Judge Advocate General

[Copy]   War Office
                                                        29 May 1760

It having been represented to the King that a Composition was entered into by the Contractor for Forage the last Summer, with some of the Troops, by which the publick was to have been made to pay for a much greater number of Rations, than were really issued, or than the Troops were entitled to for their Effective horses, I am commanded to Signifie to you It is H.M.P. that you do forthwith summon the board of Genl. Offrs. who are to enquire into this matter, and to report the state there of with their opinion what is fit to be done thereupon.

I send you herewith a Copy of a paper, containing a summary View of this transaction transmitted by me, to the Lds. Commissrs. of H.M. Treasury, which, if you think proper you may lay before the board.

Since that paper was drawn up, I have discovered that the orders of the Field Marshal Ld. Visct. Ligonier therein recited, are only an abstract of the Genl. orders given out on the 7th. of Novr. last, I have therefore annexed an exact Copy of the orders of that day as far as they relate to the affairs of Forage, by which it appears that none of the Regts. except the 9th. and 66th. were authorized by those orders to receive the value of the Forage due to them in Money.

I also send you for the information of the Board in this enquiry a letter from the Duke of Richmond Colo. of the 72d. Regt. of Foot, to me with the Inclosures marked 1.2.3.4. and also the returns of Effective horses made to the Genl. Officers Commanding at the several Encampmts. the last Summer, as they were delivered to me, by the sd. Genl. Officers, together with an Acct. of the highest number of Rations of Forage the several Regts. drew for p.diem, during their Encampment, according to the returns made to Mr Hume Comissary Genl. by his deputies, as also an Abstract of the final Acct. settled by the Contractor with the Regts. therein named as delivered into my office by the sd. Contractor.

W.O. 4/61, pp. 166–167

110

First paper enclosed with Document 109

[Copy]   [1760]

In the Spring of the last year, the Lords Commissioners of H.M.s Treasury entered into a Contract with John Wellan, for supplying such Troops as should be Encamped during the Summer, with Forrage at the rate of 10¼d per Ration of Hay and Oats, and accordingly Magazines were formed in the Neighbourhood of the several Encampments.

With regard to the issuing of the Forrage the same regulations which had been constantly practised in former Encampments at home, were put in force, the Regts. which Encamped, were directed to make weekly returns to the Generals Commanding at each Camp, of their Effective Horses, and to draw Forrage for them only, while they did not exceed the number allowed to a Regt. of Foot. Mr Hume the Commissary Genl. had a deputy at each Camp, who was to be a check upon the Contractor, both as to the goodness of the Forrage, and the Sufficiency of the

Weight and measure, and also to take care that the Regt. drew for their Effective Horses only according to their Returns to the Genl. and that their number did not exceed the Regulation. Each deputy Commissary made weekly returns to Mr. Hume in London of the issues from the Magazines to the respective Regts. as it was his duty to be present at every issue, that Mr. Hume might be enabled from his returns to know exactly the number of Rations each Corps received during their Encampment, in order to Check the Contractor's Accts. when they should be referred to him by the Lords of the Treasury previous to their being finally settled.

The Regts. accordingly made weekly returns to the Genls. commanding at each Camp, of their effective Horses, and drew for Forrage from the Magazines according to their returns.

The 11. of Novr. last the following order was given out by the Adjut. Genl. by Command of Ld. Ligonier.

The Marshal hath this day ordered, that the Genl. Officers, Staff & Regts. which were Encamped, or were ordered to have their Batt. or Baggage Horses, should receive Forrage for their Effective Horses only, (upon honour) and those not to exceed the regulation, from 16th. June to 19th. Novr. following inclusive. If they receive for more than their Effective Horses, and that within the regulation, they will pay the exceedings to the Contractors. If they have received less than for their Effective Horses, they may demand and receive the same, or the value of it, according to the allowance made by the Governmt. to the Contractors.

This order could only be construed to authorize such Regts. as had encamped very late in the Summer and such other Regts. as had not encamped at all, but had kept their Horses in readiness, to receive Forrages, or an allowance in the lieu of it, for their effective horses only during that part of the time mentioned in the order, for which they had not received Forrages in kind. However the order has been much misunderstood, or a very improper use has been made of it by many of those Corps which were encamped the last Summer. The order expressly forbids their receiving more Forrage at the Expence of the Governmt. than for their Effective horses even within the regulation notwithstanding which the Corps mentioned in the list annexed have demanded and received from the contractor in consequence of returns Signed by the Commanding Officer, Forrage in kind, and in money, not only for more than their Effective horses, but even for more horses than they are allowed by the regulation (which is 82 per Regt.) and some more than double the number of horses which they returned, as Effective in their Weekly returns, and for which they drew Forrage from the Magazines during the time they were encamped. This will more fully appear from a Comparison of the returns of effective horses to the several Generals, and of the final returns to the contractors in the paper hereunto annexed.

It must be observed that the highest number of horses which the Regts. ever returned as effective, or drew Forrage for, is there set down and that for the greatest part of the time they were in Camp, many of the Regts. did not return as effective above half that number.

This matter came to the knowledge of the Secretary at War (who was totally unacquainted with any part of it, or even with the above mentioned order of the Commander in chief) through the Duke of Richmond who acquainted him, that the 72d Regt. under his Graces Command having 39 effective horses during the last Summer, was entitled to 6,123 Rations of Forrage, of which having encamped very late, they had received only 1738 in kind, and therefore agreable to the the Field Marshals order, had a demand upon the Contractor for the Value of the remaining 4,385 Rations. Upon Application to the contractor's Agents they refused to pay the Regt. more than at the rate of 3s. for every 7 Rations, altho the Contractor was to receive from the Governmt. 10¼d for each Ration; but soon after, one of them (Wm. Wase) wrote to Captn. Poole, the paymaster of his Graces Regt. telling him, that all the Corps that were in Camp, drew for the full Number of horses allowed by the regulation, and proposing that the 72d. Regt. should alter their return from 39, which was their real number of Effective horses, to any number they pleased; and that he would pay the ballance to the Regt. according to the Acct. so altered.

By this Scheme if the commanding Officer could have persuaded himself to sign a false return (which was left to his honour) the Contractor, and the Regt. might have terminated their dispute about the rate at which Forrage was to be paid for to their mutual Profit, at the expence only of the Governmt. If the Commanding Officer would have altered his return from 39 to 82, the Regt. instead of £93. 18. which they received, or instead of £187. 5. 6¼d which they claimed as the full value of the Forrages at 10¼d a Ration might have received £238. 13. The Contractor instead of £93. 7. 6¼d which was his profit upon the smaller number of Rations, would have put £236. 14. 10 into his pockett and the Governmt. instead of £187. 5. 6¼d would have paid £475. 7. 10.

The Duke of Richmond forbid the Signing any such false Certificates, and refused to accept more than the Regt. was allowed to take for their Effective horses, which was paid by the contractor at the rate of 3s. for every 7 Rations.

Lord George Lennox Lt Colo. of the 33d. Regt. was also offered by the contractor 6d. a Ration for the full allowance of horses to that Regt. altho it does not appear that they had more than 41 effective horses during their whole Encampment. This Offer his Lordship refused, and acquainted the Secretary at War with it, which is a proof that altho his Lordship did (probably inadvertently) sign a Return of 91 Horses, he never intended to receive one Ration more than he was avowedly allowed to take.

Upon this discovery of a Fraud which was evidently carrying on between the Contractor for Forrage, and some of the Troops to the prejudice of the Governmt. the Secretary at War thought it necessary to search the affair to the bottom, and accordingly he immediately wrote to the Generals, who had Commanded the several Camps, for the weekly returns made by the Regts. under their respective Commands of their effective horses, and also called upon the contractor for the returns made to him by the Regts. when they finally settled their accts. and gave him (the said contractor) a Genl. receipt for the Forrage said to be issued to them, which receipts are to be his Vouchers to the Auditors. These Returns are now in the Secretary at Wars possession and from an abstract of them, the annexed comparison has been formed, which shews at one view the extent of this very pernicious fraud. The Officers who have signed the varying returns have undoubtedly been guilty of Fraud, or great inadvertency; the contractor most certainly of Fraud.

As the Accts. of the latter are not yet passed the publick may be prevented, in the present instance, from suffering by this fraud. the Books of the Commissary Genl. being formed upon the weekly returns of his deputies, will ascertain what quantity of Forrage has really been issued, and it is apprehended that the contractor cannot claim, under his contract, to be allowed for more. Whatever demand he may have upon the Regts. for the money which he has paid in consequence of his Composition with them, it cannot be conceived that a fictitious acct. founded upon falsified returns ought to be any ways binding upon the Publick, especially when it is to entitle the Accomptant to an immoderate and fraudulent profit.

For the future it will be very easy to guard against any abuse of this kind, by strictly forbidding all compositions of money in lieu of Forrage between the Contractor and the Troops. Whenever the circumstances of the Service may require that the Troops should receive an allowance of money instead of Forrage, it will certainly be adviseable that such an allowance as is intended to be given them, should be paid to them immediately by the Government. If the Contractors proposal to the Duke of Richmond as above stated had taken place (and it is to be feared that a like proposal did take place in some Regts.) it is very evident that the Governmt. would have paid 150 per Cent more than the real value of the Forrage to which the Regts. was entitled, of which Sum above four fifths would have fallen to the share of the Contractor.

Barrington

(a) Regiments
(b) Highest number of Effective Horses, for which the Regt. that encamped drew Forrage during the Encampment.
(c) No. of Horses which they have since returned as Effective to the Contractor and for which they have demanded or received the Ballce. in money for the whole time mentioned in the order.

(a)	(b)	(c)
5th	89	
33d	41	91
34th	45	89
19th	58	86
24th	64	86
11th	72	87
36th	83	89
50th	63	89

The 9th & 66th Regts. not having encamped made no returns of their Horses, so that it does not appear what number they really had effective during the last Summer. They have both returned to the Contractor more than are allowed by the regulation; the 9th 89, & the 66th 87, & have received their respective Ballances due to them in money; it is presumed at the same rate of 3s. for every seven Rations, as was offered by the Contractor to the Duke of Richmond.

W.O. 4/60, pp. 586–594

III

Second Paper [enclosed with Document 109]

[Copy]

7th November 1759. H.M. having been pleased to order the Troops in South Britain into Winter Quarters it is His Excellency's Field Marshal Ld. Visct. Ligonier's orders, that they keep their horses, repair and Compleat their Camp Equipage as soon as possible (the charge of which the Commanding Officers will Sign and return to the War Office and to the adjutant Genl.) and hold themselves in readiness to march upon a moments warning.

The Commanding Officers of the Regts. which were encamped, will make up their Accts. with the respective

Commissaries for the Bread, Wood & Straw received til the time of their breaking up Camp, and give genl. rects. accordingly.

The Genl. Offrs. Staff & Regt. will also make up their accts. of Forage from 16th June (when the first of the Corps encamped) till the 19th Novr. when the last Regt. at Ripley Camp breaks up, in which accts. the Genl. Offrs. &c. will take Forage for their Effective horses, only upon Honour as formerly ordered, and those not to exceed the Numbers allowed by the Regulation, if any of them have received for more than their Effectives they will repay such exceeding, and if others have not recd. for their Effectives within the Numbers allowed they may receive such deficiency (in kind only) from the Magazines giving receipts accordingly.

If Whitmores Regt. (which is under the command of Lt. General Onslow and M.Gl. Duroure) or La Fausille's Regt. which is under M.Gl. Whitmore (which Regts. were ordered to have their Bat. & Baggage horses) have not recd. Forage from the Contractors for the time before mentioned they may receive it, or the Value according to the allowance which the Governmt. gives the Contractors under the above regulations,

General Orders of 11th Novr. 1759.

No 1 The Marshal hath this day ordered that the General Officers Staff and Regts. which were encamped or were ordered to have their Bat or Baggage horses should receive Forage for their Effective horses (only upon honour) and those not to exceed the regulation from 16 June to the 19th Novr. following inclusive. If they receive for more than their Effective horses, and that within the regulation, they will pay the exceedings to the Contractors. If they have recd. less than for their Effective horses, they may demand and receive the same or the Value of it according to the allowance made by the Governmt. to the Contractors.

Robert Napier
Adjt. Genl.

No 2 Number of horses returned by the 72nd Regt. of Foot at Southsea Camp July 25th 1759

Horses 51

Number of horses allowed by the Government for a Regt. of Foot 82

Number of horses returned by the 72nd Regt. at Bedhampton Camp, for which Forage was recd. from the 16th of June to 19th Novr. 1759, being One hundred and fifty seven days

Number of horses for Officers 35

For the Grand Sutler . . . . <u>4</u>

Total <u>39</u>

Number of Rations for the above 39 Horses for 157 days 6123

Of the above Rations were recd.
In Hay and Oats 1738

The remaining 4385 Rations were received in money at the rate of 3s for every 7 Rations amounting to £93.18

A. Wall Qr.Mr. to 72nd Regt.

[Copy]
Capt. Poole   Portsmouth 12 Jan, 1760
No 3 Sir

Last Night I saw Major Prescott, and I was telling him that all the Regts. that were in Camp drew for their full Number of horses, none drew for less than 70 horses, and some 84 so as your accts. are not delivered in if you think proper the same may be altered. I have sent Mr. Wall a form of the same so please to mention the No. of horses more, and I will send you a bill for the ballance if you approve of it.

I am &c,
Signed
(pray excuse haste)   W Wase

Copy of a rect. given by Qr.Mr.Wall to the Contractor Bedhampton Camp Novr. 17th 1759. Recd. from Mr. John Wellin Contractor for hay and oates Six thousand one hundred and twenty three Rations of Hay & Oates being the allowance for thirty nine Horses of His Grace the Duke of Richmond's Regt. for one hundred & Fifty seven days from the 16 June to 19 Nov. 1759. Both days inclusive.

Rations of Hay 6123

Rations of Oates 6123

Note the Commissary's Names that refused giving any more than 3s for every 7 Rations are

W Wasse. Andrew Ross.

My Lord   Feb. 2nd 1760

By order of Field Marshal Ld. Visct. Ligonier dated the 11th Novr. 1759 (of which a Copy is inclosed) the Regts. that were encamped last Summer were to receive Forage for their Effective horses only, and such as had not received the full allowance for sd. Effective horses were to be paid by the Contractors for Forage according to the allowance made by the Governmt: the 72nd Regt. had a demand for £4385 [sic] Rations of Forage, being the Quantity the Regt. was intitled to for their Effective horses, over and above the Rations they had recd. from the Magazines, and upon the Regts. making a demand for that allowance W. Wase and Andrew Ross two of the Commissaries refused to pay it and did not pay any more than at the rate of 3s for every 7 Rations, which is considerably less than the Governmts. allowance.

By a letter of W. Wase to Captain Pool, the paymaster of the Regt. (a Copy is inclosed) your Lordship will see that some Regts. have been paid for 84 horses the full Number, and none less than 70, and that there is a proposal for altering the accts. of the 72nd. Regt. (which could not be done without the Commanding Officers Signing a false return which was left to his honour) and paying them according to the acct. so altered by which there would be a Considerable gain.

I am to desire your Lordship will order the Contractors to pay the Regt. for the No. of Rations they have an actual Claim to, agreable to the Field Marshals order. And as other Regiments appear to have been paid for a greater Number of horses than their Effectives, I hope the 72nd Regt. will not suffer, from their regularity in strictly conforming to the Marshal's order.

> I have the honour to be with the utmost respect
> My Lord
> Your Lordships
> most obedient and
> Sincere Servant
> Richmond &c.

An Acct. of What Forage of Hay and Oats have been issued to the Sundry Regts. Specifying what part of the said Forage was issued in kind and what part also was Settled to the respective Officers and Regiments in Cash

Regiments Names	No. of horses	days	Rations in kind	Rations in cash
1st Regt. of F. Guards	250	24	6,000	
ditto	278	133	36,974	
2nd. or Coldstream	179	24	4,296	
ditto	197	133	26,201	
3rd Regt. of F.Gds	184	24	4,416	
do	202	133	26,866	
5th Regt. late Benticks	89	157	13,973	
8th late Wolfes	–	–	11,099	
9th Colo. Whitmores	89	157	–	13,973
11th Colo. Bocland's	87	157	9,217	4,442
24th Gl. Cornwallis	86	157	6,520	6,982
19th Ld. Beauclerck's	86	–	6,939	6,563
30th Ld. Loudoun's	–	–	10,955	arrear unsettled
34th Ld. Effingham's	89	–	4,516	9,457
33rd Ld. Ch. Hays	91	–	4,262	arrear unsettled
36th Ld. Rob. Manners	89	157	9,508	4,465
50th Late Hodgsons	89	–	8,677	arrear unsettled

66 Late La Fausills	87	157	– 13,695
67 Wolfe's	32	157	5,024
Do. Capt. Baldwin	8	76	608
72 D of Richmond's	39	157	6,123
Ld. Bruces Militia	78	76	5,928
Colo. Berkerley's do.	68	39	2,652
Col. Colvills Detacht	–	–	3

The Highest Number of Rations of Forage
the following Regts. took per day 1759

The 5th Regt. late Bentick's Sandheath 89
The 8th Regt. late Wolfes at do 68
The 33rd do or Hays . . . . . at do 41
The 34th do. or Effingham at do 45
The 19th do or Beauclercks at Warley 58
The 34th Regt. . . . . at do 64
The 11th do . . . . at Chatham 72
The 30th do . . . . at Dartford & Chatham 77
The 36th do . . . . at do 83
The 50th . . . . uncertain by rects. 63
The 72nd Regt. . . . . at S.S.Common 39
The 67th do . . . . at do 40
The 1st Regt. of F. Guards in London 284
The 2nd do . . . . do 197
The 3rd do . . . . do 202
The Wiltshire Militia 78
The Gloucester S. Battn. of Militia 68
The Staff according to the Regulation

W.O. 4/61, pp. 168–175

112

Barrington to Samuel Martin

[Copy]   War Office
                                                              27 June 1760

I desire you will acquaint the Lords Commissioners of His
Majesty's Treasury, that the Board of Genl. Officers, to whom
His M. was pleased to refer the Consideration of the transactions
between the Contractor for Forage the last summer and some of
the Troops, as stated in my Letter to you of the 30th April last,
have lately made their report to His Majesty, by which it apears to
be their Opinion that the Number of Rations received from the
Contractor, have exceeded the Number of Effective horses and in
some Instances the Number allow'd by the regulation, but that
this has been done inadvertently, the Officers being misled by the
general practice of the Army heretofore, and not with any Intention of Fraud: the Board have also given it as their Opinion, that
so much of the Forage received either in kind or in Money as
exceeds the Allowance for the real Effectives, should be repaid by
the several Corps to the Contractor, and not allowed in the
Accounts with the Publick.

The King is willing to hope that the Opinion of the Board is
well founded in attributing the part which the Officers have acted
in this Affair to inadvertence, but as such inadvertence in matters
of duty is itself highly culpable, His M. hath ordered that all the
Officers who have been anyway concerned in this transaction,
should receive a severe reprimand from their respective Colonels.

His M. hath also ordered that so much of the Forage, received
by the several Regts., either in kind or in Money, as exceeds the
Allowance for their effective horses, should be forthwith repaid to
the Contractor, agreable to the Opinion of the Board of Genl.
Officers.

W.O. 4/61, pp. 338–339

113

Warrant for Assignment of Off-reckonings for Light troops of Dragoon Guards and Dragoons

[Copy]   27 April 1756

GEORGE R

Dragoon Guards
Lt.Gl. Blands
M.Gl. Herberts
Sr.Cs. Howards
Dragoons
Lt. Genl Hawleys
Lt. Gl Campbells
E Albemarle's
Sr. R Richs
Lt G Cholmondeleys
Sr John Copes
Sr John Mordaunts
E Ancrams

WHEREAS we have been pleased to Order a Light Troop of Dragoons to be Raised and Added to Each of Our regiments of Dragoon Guards, and Regiments of Dragoons mentioned in the Margin hereof, each Troop to consist of Two Sergeants, Three Corporals, Two Drummers and sixty Private Men, besides Commission Officers And it being represented that in Order to furnish the Non Commission Officers and Private Men of the said Light Troop, with Cloathing, Accoutrements and other appointments conformable to Our Regulations bearing date the 14th Instant, and to defray the Charge thereof, it will require Assignments of the Offreckonings for the said Non Commission Officers and Private Men, for Two Years from the 25th December 1755, the day the Establishment of the said Light Troops did Commence to the 24th of December 1757, which We thinking reasonable are graciously pleased to grant. OUR WILL & PLEASURE therefore is, That the General Officers of the Cloathing Board do Pass and allow the Assignments of the Offreckonings for the Non Commission Officers and Private Men of Each Troop of Light Dragoons as before mentioned, From the 25th of December 1755 to the 24th of Decr. 1757, both inclusive. For Passing and allowing of which this shall be as well to the said General Officers of the Cloathing Board, the Pay Master General of Our Land Forces, the Auditors of Our Imprests, and all others whom it may concern a Sufficient Warrant Authority

and Direction Given at Our Court at Kensington this 27th Day of
April 1756 in the Twenty ninth Year of Our Reign
By His Majesty's Command
Barrington

W.O. 26/23, pp. 72–73

114

Warrant for Agent to Assign Off-reckonings of independent companies at New York

[Copy]   21 January 1758

GEORGE R

WHEREAS it hath been most humbly represented unto us, that the
Patterns of Cloathing for the four Independent companies at New
York, hath been exhibited by John Calcraft Esqr. Agent to the said
Companies and view'd and approved of, by the General Officers
appointed by us to have the Inspection of the Cloathing of our
Forces, And Whereas, it hath been usual to contract for the
Cloathing immediately after the said Patterns are approved, But
no person being fully authorized to act herein, the Government of
New York being Vacant, We are most humbly besought to grant
Our Warrant, to empower and enable the said John Calcraft to
contract for the Cloathing of the said Companies which We
thinking reasonable, are graciously pleased to consent to. O. W. &
P. therefore is, that you do pass and allow of such Assignment as
the said John Calcraft hath, or shall make for the Offreckonings
or Cloathing Money of the said four Independent Companies at
New York from 6th July 1758 to 5th July 1759 both days inclusive,
in order to prevent any Inconveniency which might otherwise
attend the Service of Our said Independent Companies, for want
of a sufficient power from a Governor of New York for the above
mentioned purpose; And of this Our pleasure the General
Officers appointed by us to have the Inspection of the Cloathing
of Our Army, the paymaster General of our Forces, the Auditors
of our Imprests, and all others whom it may or shall concern, are

to take Notice and shall be to them a sufficient Warrant, Authority and Direction, Given at our Court at St. James's this 21st day of January 1758 in the thirty first year of our Reign.

By His Majesty's Command

Barrington

W.O. 26/23, p. 36

115

Note apparently in the hand of Philip Francis

[Holograph]   n.d. [?1771]

[Endorsed]: 'A Suggestion of the Meaning of the Clause in the 36th Paragraph of the Mutiny Act relative to the due and well Cloathing of the Army.'

It is I apprehend very plain, that the Clause in the 36th Paragraph of the Mutiny Act, which is said to be made for the Encouragement of the due and well Cloathing of the Army, was not intended to create a new Law relative to the Cloathing, as it speaks of Offreckonings as Things customary and well known before, without explaining them, and of an Assignment without naming an Assignor, but was most probably designed to remedy some Inconveniency, Neglect or Fraud which had crept in upon the Method and before that Time.

By ancient Custom so far back as the Year 1676, which is presumed to be previous to any Mutiny Act, the Paymaster General was authorized by the Crown to pay the Offreckonings, as the Colonel of the Regiment should from Time to Time signify his Approbation. The Consequence of this Method might be, that the Offreckonings were obtained before any Security was given for the Delivery of the proper Cloathing in due Time; which made it necessary for the following Clause to be inserted in the Mutiny Act, especially as since the Time above stated, the Custom of Assignment has prevailed. The Clause runs thus —'The respective Paymasters are hereby directed to make Deductions of all Offreckonings, and to pay the same to such Person or Persons only, as have a regular Assignment for Cloaths by him or them delivered to the said Regiment, Troop, or Company; and the Receipt of such Person or Persons having or being lawfully entitled to such Assignment, to be from Time to Time taken for the same. And when no such Assignment appears, the Offreckonings to remain in the Hands of the said Paymaster respectively, for the Use of the Regiment, Troop, or Company, until a new Contract for Cloathing and Assignment is made'.

The Custom being formerly to pay the Offreckonings, as the Colonel of the Regiment should signify his Approbation, without any Assignment previously made for the due Cloathing &ca of the Regiment, this Clause seems to be made to remedy this Inconveniency, by directing the Paymaster as before to make Deductions for Offreckonings, but not to pay them, until an actual Delivery of Cloathing &ca. is made, under a regular Assignment for that Purpose. Nor will the Paymaster pay the Offreckonings till he has received a Certificate from the Cloathing Board that the due Regulations relative to the Cloathing are complied with by the Colonel; and I apprehend it is this Direction to the Paymaster to pay the Offreckonings that makes the Assignment of Force; for before this is done, the Assignment is to be considered merely as a Security to the Clothier, Contractor, or Agent that, upon the proper Cloathing being delivered, and all Regulations for that Purpose observed, he will have a valid Interest in the Offreckonings, under the Colonel's Assignment.

This Construction of the above Clause seems to me to comprehend the full Intention of it, by remedying the Evil; and is rather confirmed by the latter Part of the Clause, which directs the Offreckonings to remain in the Paymaster's Hands for the Use of the Regiment, when no such Assignment appears. And the Words *for Cloaths by him or them delivered to the Regiment* must in common Construction refer to the *Payment* and not to the *Assignment* vizt. *to pay the same to such Person or Persons for Cloaths by him or them delivered, as have a regular* Assignment for that Purpose.

The Nett Offreckonings were, most probably, originally considered as not much more than sufficient to bear all the Expence of proper Cloathing and Accoutrements, and all other Charges incidentally or accidentally relative thereunto, and if by Chance or good Management (all Regulations being complied with) it amounted to a little more than sufficient, the Remainder became the Colonel's Property, in Consequence of his Risque in undertaking to furnish the proper Cloathing, Accoutrements &ca. for such Deductions.

If the Intention of the Clause was to prevent such Remainders, if any, from falling into the Colonel's Hands, or continuing to be his Property, it would most undoubtedly have prohibited it in express Terms, and appropriated such Remainder to other Purposes, the not doing of which appears to me a very strong Proof that no such Thing was intended, but that the true Meaning of the Clause was, as I have observed, to prevent the Offreckonings from falling into the Colonels Hands before an actual Delivery of the proper Cloathing &ca. had been made, and all Regulations relative thereunto complied with, and the Caution taken by the present Regulations seems effectually to carry the Design of this Clause into Execution.

Ipswich 3b, no. 382

116

War Office memorandum on Off-reckonings

[Copy]   25 April 1772

The Custom and Practice of the Army concerning Offreckonings.

Parliament votes the Numbers and the Expence of the Army for a year.

The Distribution of the Men and appropriation of the Money thro' all its Branches is left to the Crown.

The Vote of Parliament is a gross Sum for the whole Army upon Estimate, stating the Pay of each Corps without particulars.

The Crown authorizes what is deemed the Establishment by a Sign Manual, appropriating to each Rank their particular Pay.

Subdivision is afterwards made, by the same authority, of the Pay of each person, vizt.

That of the Pay of Commissioned Officers into what is called

Subsistence, and Arrears.

That of the Noncommissioned officers and Private Men into Subsistence and Offreckonings, with other Appropriations or Stoppages for Poundage and Chelsea Hospital, which are also made upon Arrears.

The Offreckonings after the same Deductions constitute a Fund to reimburse the Expence of Clothes & Accountrements, their loss and repairs, package, freight, insurance &c, for the Noncommissioned Officers and private Men.

The whole Pay of the Regiment some time after it has become due, is by the King's Warrant, called a clearing Warrant, made payable to the Colonel or his Assign.

The Ballance, part of which arises on the Offreckonings, after every Regulation made by the Crown hath been complied with, of course falls to the Colonel.

By ancient Custom so far back as the year 1676, which is presumed to be previous to any Mutiny Act, the Pay Master General was authorized by the Crown to pay the Offreckonings, as the Colonel of the regiment shoud from time to time signify his approbation.

Since this, the Custom of Assignment has prevailed, and stands at present, as follows.

When a Regiment is newly raised and formed, the Amount of 18 or 20 Months Offreckonings (or 12 Months more for Dragoons) is judged necessary to furnish what is wanted to fit out the Man for Service. The Foot are clothed every year, the Dragoons every two years.

The Colonel upon forming his Corps receives in Money, not from the Men but from the Public, the Value of 6 or 8 Months Offreckonings, and at the same time is authorized by the Crown to assign to some other Person, usually his Clothier, or his Agent, the 12 or 24 Months Offreckonings next accruing.

The same Assignment is executed every year, or every two years ensuing, by Virtue of the same direction, which continues in force altho' the Colonel is frequently changed.

The Colonel of every Regt. respectively is allowed to make an Assignment as above as soon as Patterns of Clothes have been inspected and sealed by the Clothing Board, and a Certificate of the delivery of the last year's Clothing, (if any) has been produced.

To enable the Colonel to contract and produce to his Clothier a Security for his Money, this Assignment passes in the November preceding the June when the Cloths are to be put on.

The Money for the Cloths &c does not accrue completely till the June following the putting on the Clothes (or the next June for the Dragoon Clothing) and is seldom issued to the Colonel or his Assign within a twelve Month after it has become due.

During all this time, which is very often 2½ years for the Foot, or 3½ years for the Dragoons, the Assignment passes as Paper Currency from one hand to another to the great convenience of all Parties concerned.

But as the Money is not yet to be come at, and the Assignment is a mere Security, Interest is paid for the Value of the Clothes from the time of the delivery to the time when the Clothier is paid or the Assignment is discharged, and paid off by the Public.

The Method of proceeding hath some times been, that when the Colonel assigned over to his Clothier or other Person all the Offreckonings for a certain yearly Period, the Assignor used to require from the Assigns a Defeazance.

From its being universally understood that the Clothier hath no farther interest in the Assignment than to the Amount of the Clothes delivered, the Custom of requiring a Defeazance is in general disused. But on payment being made for the Clothing, a Reassignment is made to the Colonel upon a specific consideration.

Thus the Colonel, when the intent of the Security has been answered, realises the power of receiving the Offreckonings which he had before delegated, and comes into possession of the whole Money that had accrued on Account of Clothing, by which means he is reimbursed what he had laid out, and is enabled to make good the old, or provide new Accountrements and to comply with the several Regulations of the Crown untill all Claim shall have been discharged by the Royal Authority given to the Paymaster General as his Voucher to the Auditor.

No Colonel ever claimed to be the Assignor till authorized and directed by the Crown, and the power of receiving the Offreckonings previous to the clearing of the Regiment, hath been sometimes withdrawn, or suspended till Justice be done to the Men, according to the intentions of the Crown.

If therefore any Complaint should arise from the Regiment against the Colonel for Neglect, or otherwise, Or if by any intervening Change of Colonel, the Money accruing shou'd fall under the disposal of One Party, and the Care of the Regiment with the duty of providing Clothes, Accountrements, or for repairs &c under another.

The King, to whom the whole care of the appropriating the Public Money belongs, has directed the issue of such Offreckonings as have not yet been paid, to be stopped, and refers the Matter to his Military Council, the Board of General Officers, and the Colonels, or their Assigns have usually acquiesced in the Decision of these customary Judges.

Since the drawing up of the above, a Passage hath been met with in a Tract written by Mr. Hutcheson (Member for Hastings) in the year 1718, by which it appears that, after every Regulation of the Crown relative to Clothing had been complied with, the Remainder of the Offreckonings was by long usage become esteemed a very legal Perquisite, and to which the Colonels were thought to have as good a Right as to any part of their personal Pay. The Tract is entitled, Abstracts of the Number and yearly Pay of the Land Forces of Horse, Foot and Dragoons in Great Britain for the year 1718, with some Remarks relating to the same, Reprinted in 1720.

W.O. 30/105, pages unnumbered.

117

Regulation for applying the non-effective balances of Infantry Regiments

[Copy]   Court of St. James
                                           17 March 1761

WHEREAS Our late Royal Grandfather by a Regulation in 1743, was pleased to order that the Non effective Accounts of Our several Regts. of Infantry should be annually stated on the 24th day of June; and that whatever ballance remained (after deducting five pounds for every man wanting to compleat to be carried to the Credit of the suceeding Account) should be divided among the Captains, partly in Aid of their extraordinary expences & partly as a reward and their care & diligence in compleating their Companies, AND WHEREAS the difficulty of recruiting on Account of the scarcity of men, hath of late made it impracticable to compleat the said Regiments, by which means the ballances of their Non effective Funds have encreased to a very considerable Amount so that Our said late Royal Grandfather thought proper from time to time to suspend the distribution thereof among the Captains, until his farther Pleasure should be known; AND WHEREAS it hath been represented unto Us that the said Ballances since the 24th. day of June 1757, are still undistributed We therefore thinking it reasonable that a proper Allowance should be made to the Captains out of their said Ballances, according to the intent of Our late Royal Grandfather's regulation & that the remainder, if any, should be applied to the Publick Service, do hereby direct, that in Our Regts. of Infantry serving abroad, the ballance of their Non effective Accounts stated annually, according to Our late Royal Grandfather's Regulation shall be distributed equally among the Captains provided the said ballance does not exceed the Sum of £30 to each Captain, whose Company consists of one hundred private Men, & in proportion where the Companies are of a lower Establishment, And that in Our Regts. at home the said ballance shall in like manr. be distributed among the Captains, provided it does not exceed the Sum of twenty pounds, to each Captain of a Company of 100 private men, & also provided that the said Company did consist of ninety effective private men, or upwards, on the 24th day of June to which the Account is made up; And that in all cases where the Non effective ballances of any Regt. shall exceed the Sums which we are hereby pleased to allow to the Captain, the surplus shall be brought to Account, at a Saving to the Publick to be disposed of as We shall hereafter direct. Whereof the Colonels, & Agents of Our several Regiments of Infantry, & all others Our Officers whom it doth, or may concern, are to take notice and govern themselves accordingly;

Given at Our Ct. at St. James's this 17th day of March 1761 in the
first year of our Reign.

B.H.M.C.

Barrington

W.O. 26/24, pp. 387–388

118

Marquis of Granby to the Duke of Newcastle

[Holograph] Rotheim
25 September 1759

Upon repeated application made to me from the Commanding
Officers of Cavalry for the Sixpences Stopped in their Winter
Quarters I must beg leave to represent to your Grace that tho
Government usually applyd that Stoppage to reimburse itself in
part for the expence of Magazines yet as there were none formd
last Year and that the Campaign was both long and Expensive I
hope your Grace will think it just and for the Good of the Service
that the amount of these Sixpences should be applyd to the paying
the Contingent bills of the Cavalry and the remainder thrown into
the Stock purses of the Several Regiments in order to help
remount em.

Add. Mss. 32911, f. 82r

119

Barrington to Lord Granby

[Copy] War Office
12 September 1760

Having been applied to by the Agents to the Regts. of Cavalry
which went first to Germany to procure H. M.'s Warrant for
assessing a certain part of the Winter Stoppages in 1758 & 1759

to defray the contingent Expences of the sd. Regt. agreable, as it is said, to yr. Ldship's orders in consequence of the directions of the Lds. Commrs. of the Treasury, I thought it my duty in the first place to inform myself as well as I could, of whatever might be proper to guide me in a matter of which my Office afforded no precedent.

The result of my enquiries is contained in the enclosed paper which I take the liberty of transmitting to yr. Lordship. One of the Impediments to my preparing at present such a Warrant as is desired, yr. Ldship will see arises from the Agents here not having a distinct Accot. of the Summer & Winter Stoppages. your Lordship will therefore be pleased to direct the sevl. Regts. to send over a proper Account to their Agents.

The great difficulty however arises from the contingent Bills which the Regts. have delivered in. Upon this head I must beg leave to remind yr. Ldship that every saving from the Pay granted by Parliament for the Troops is publick Money, and therefore my very great regard for yr. Ldship, as well as my concern for my Self, makes me desirous that we should not be liable to the least blame for any misapplication of the Winter Stoppages. It is true that the Treasury have directed that a part of this money should be applied to satisfy the Contingent Bills of the several Regts. but as their Ldships have not specified what part is to be applied to this purpose, I do not think so general a direction will Justify me in preparing a Warrant for the payment of any Contingent Bills that are not reasonable & agreable to the Custom of the Army.

It appears by the inclosed paper that the present Allowance of £35 a year to the Captains of Dragoons for Contingencies is agreeable to His Majesty's regulation in consequence of the report of the Genl. Officers, Colonels of Dragoons in 1749, but rather in favour of the Captains. Yr. Ldship will judge from thence whether H.M. will be easily induced to set aside a regulation which he has so lately established upon so good grounds. for my own part, I must declare that I cannot venture to propose such a Step to H.M. until I am furnished with better Arguments than I am yet Master of, to evince the expediency of it.

The other Articles specified in the Contingent Bills, which I have seen, are the Pay of Bat Men & Waggon Drivers with Troop

Stores Shoeing & furniture of the Bas Horses & a new Bas Horse to each Troop the 2nd year, How far all or any of these Articles are fit to be Allowed your Lordship is the best Judge. I must only beg leave to observe to yr. Lordship that I do not conceive it was the intention of the Treasury that any Articles of Expence should be allowed in those Bills which are not either Warranted by former custom, or peculiar to the present Service. Your Lordship's prudence perhaps may add another Restriction by not permitting any charges to be made which are not peculiar to the Dragoon Service, for if the Captains of Dragoons obtain an Allowance from the Publick, for any Expences which the Captains of Infantry are equally subject to, the latter will probably expect the same Indulgence, tho' it will not be so easy to find a fund for paying them.

W.O. 4/62, 90–92

120

Paper enclosed with Document 119

[Copy]

It was customary abroad in the last War to apply the money arising from the Stoppages of 6d.p.diem from the Non Commd. Officers & private Men of the Dragoons for Forage, during the Summer in the following manner Vizt. two thirds to the remounting fund & one third towards providing Camp Necessaries. It does not appear whether this Application was authorized by any Warrant, or only by former custom. there seems to have been no Stoppage in Winter probably, because the Troops being canton'd in the Austrian & Dutch Territories were obliged to find their own Forage.

During the present War in Germany the Stoppage of 6d.p.diem hath been made from the Dragoons both in Summer & Winter they having received Forage in Summer from Our own Magazines & in Winter from the Country where they were Quartered in the way of Contribution &c.

Though it was understood that the Summer Stoppage was to be applied according to the Precedent of the last War, it was thought necessary to consult the Lords of the Treasury with regard to the Application of the Winter Stoppage, of which there was no Precedent. Their Lordships upon being consulted on this head were of opinion that the sixpences stopped from the Regts. of Dragoons during the Winter shou'd be applied in the first place to satisfy the contingt. Regimental Bills of those Corps, & that the remainder shou'd be carried to the Stockpurses of the Regts. as an additional fund for recruiting & remounting them, in consideration whereof, the Publick should not be charged with making good any Losses of Horses belonging to the said Regts. & their Lordships have desired the Secretary at War to prepare the necessary Warrant to be signed by H.M. for the disposal & application of the said Monies in the manner above mentioned.

The Regts. have since given in their contingent Bills for two years in which after Specifying some Articles of expence, an Allowance of £65 per Annum is proposed to be given to the Captains, in addition to the £35 which they at present receive out of the Stockpurse, as this Sum in the opinion of the said Captains may be a sufficient Fund to answer the Expence of certain other Articles not charged in these Bills.

It may be observed upon these contingt. Bills in general that none of the Regts. abroad in the last War were allowed to bring in Bills of this kind, & that it seems difficult to assign a reason why the Cavalry should now have this Indulgence more than the Infantry, expecially as the Articles of Expence charged in these Bills must be common to both Services.

With regard to the additional Allowance of £65 per Annum which is proposed to be given to the Captains for Contingencies, it shou'd be remembered that by the report of the Colonels of Dragoons in the year 1749, the Allowance to the Captain for all the Contingencies which they could conceive him liable to, was fixed at £25 p Annum, a Troop then consisted of 41 Rank & File [added above the line: a Troop now consists of 57 Rank & File] & the Captain's Allowance is rather more than proportionably encreased to £35 p Annum. If this Allowance is to be still further encreased to £100 p Annum, it ought surely first to be proved, that the Expences for defraying which, it was given, are four times greater than they were in the year 1749, or that the Captains are now subject to some new Charges, which the Colonels of that time could not foresee.

As the Stoppages in Summer & Winter are not distinguished in the Accounts delivered in by the Agents, it cannot be said precisely how much of the Winter Stoppage will remain to be carried to the Stock purse after the Contingt. Bills & the Contingent Allowance to the Captains shall have been paid. This however seems necessary to be known, that it may appear how far this Fund will be able to answer the intentions of the Treasury, by Securing the Publick from any Demand on account of Horses lost upon Service. It should also be known whether the Treasury mean that this Fund should only be applied to make good future Losses of Horses, or whether it is to be charged with all the losses which have happen'd since the Regts. went to Germany in which Case the Sums which the Regts. have received on this Account, by Warrant, must be paid back to the Publick.

Another reason why the Summer and Winter Stoppages should be distinguished, is, that the Allowance for Camp Necessaries, according to the Custom of the last War, should be one third of the Summer Stoppages only, whereas in the Accounts delivered by the Agents the Summer & Winter Stoppages being confounded together they claim one third of the whole for Camp necessaries, which, if allowed will greatly diminish the Fund which is proposed to be made out of the Winter Stoppages.

W.O. 4/62, pp. 93–96

121

The Marquis of Granby to Barrington

[Holograph]   Warburg
                                               25 October 1760

Private

My information that your Lordship objected to the 200 days forage money came from his Grace of Newcastle, who in his letter of the 12th of September, which I have now before me, acquainted Me that Mr West would receive orders to transmit a sum for the payment of the forage Money; but in a Postscript his Grace writes, (on talking with Ld Barrington I find he doubts whether the foot are entitled to the 200 days forage Money the beginning of the campaign & his Lordship thinks that Lord George Sackvilles precedent will not do for that was the first year of their being abroad). on this I acquainted his Grace that I flattered myself if Ld George had a power to grant the troops 200 days forage money, the same was & would be invested in me & therefore beg'd that his Grace would give orders that a sum might be transmitted for the payment of that money by my warrant on the Deputy Pay Master as that I was informed was the method, I was not acquainted that it was to come through your Lordship to the treasury but understood Ld Georges application was immediately to the Treasury who in consequence transmitted the money; I likewise mentioned to his Grace by the same letter that your Lordship had put a Stop to the Agents paying the Contingent Bills &c &c to the captains of Cavalry out of the winter sixpences which the Lords of the Treasury had consented to my disposing of in that manner, acquainting his Grace likewise that though I thought that no stop should have been put to my disposal of those sixpences, after I had the power of disposing of them granted to me by the treasury, & though I was thoroughly convinced of the rectitude of the Measure & the necessity of it for the good of the service, yet I would acquiesce till I had transmitted to your Lordship & his Grace a clear state of this affair signd by the Commanding officers of Cavalry, for which purpose I desired them All to meet, which they intended doing, but were immediately after so dispersed, that it has been impossible to bring it about. As they are not likely soon to meet together & as we are likely to have a winters Campaign, convinced as I am of the necessity there is to pay the contingent Bills &c &c to the Captains of Cavalry I must beg (that as I was authorized by the Lords of the Treasury to dispose of these sixpences) that the Agents may be allowed to pay according to my orders part of those sixpences to the Captains of Cavalry the rest as agreed upon to the Stockpurse; in regard to the 200 days forage Money, I will by the next messenger write to your Lordship an office letter on the occasion; I will only add in regard to the contingent Bills &c &c the Captains of Cavalry have well deserved every mark of Favor & regard.

Ipswich 112, no. 80

122

Barrington to Charles Lowndes

[Copy]   War Office
                                              20 January 1766

Having very carefully examined and considered the several Accounts, relative to the Stoppages made from the Cavalry serving in Germany in the last War, together with the Claims of those Regiments for Remounting, for Camp Necessaries, and for satisfying the Captains Contingent Demands, I beg Leave to lay the following State of this whole Matter before you for the Information and Direction of the Lords Commissioners of His Majesty's Treasury.

I find upon Enquiry, that, in the Course of former Wars, 9d. p. Day has been stopt during the Summer Months for each Horse, of which 3d. p. Day has been given to each Private Dragoon in Addition to his 8d. personal Subsistence, 4d. p. Day has been set apart for a Fund for Remounting, and the remaining 2d. the Colonel has received to defray the Expence of Camp Necessaries; but it does not appear, that any Stoppage was then made in the Winter Months.

In the last War the like Stoppage was made and continued in Winter, as well as in Summer; the Troops having constantly been furnished with Forage by Contribution, or from our own Magazines at public Expence: the Partition and Application of which was not at first distinguished by the Agents in their Accounts; for they carry'd ⅔ds of the whole, Winter & Summer, Sixpenny Stoppage to the Remounting Fund, and the remaining ⅓d to the furnishing of Camp Necessaries. This I have not allowed; for such an Application even of the Summer Stoppages is no otherwise authorized than by the Practice of former Wars: As the Winter Stoppage was only made during the last War, there cannot be any Precedent for the Disposition of it. In Consequence of this, I directed the Agents to consider only the Stoppage for 8 Months, commencing 24th February, and ending 24th October both inclusive, as Summer Stoppages applicable as formerly; and to keep entire the Winter Stoppage for the remaining 4 Months of the Year, without any Charge set against it.

The Agents having pursued the above Direction, it appears, that the Winter Stoppage made upon the Cavalry serving in Germany during the last War amounts to about £55,529.9.3 which is however much augmented by stating the Winter Stoppage for four Months, though the Troops sometimes continued in the Field during the last War above nine Months; and also by confining the particular Months which were to be considered as Summer Months, between February and October; for by this Means, as the Troops went abroad about July, and returned in February and March, the Summer Stoppage for one of the Years during their Continuance in Germany can only exist for about 3 Months. This renders the ⅔ds of the whole Summer Stoppage, carry'd to the Remounting Fund, unequal to the Charges made upon it (if the Agents Accounts, not yet liquidated, shall appear exact) to the Amount of about £10,553 And also the remaining ⅓d apply'd to Camp Necessaries, unequal to the actual Charge of them about £1,732—Exceedings, which make a Ballance due to the Regiments on both those Accounts, of between twelve and thirteen Pounds.

At the Conclusion of the former War, when the like Stoppages were made during the Summer, the whole Savings on the Stockpurse Account of the Cavalry, as also the Overplus which arose from the Sale of the reduced Horses after giving £3 to each of the reduced Men, and preserving £63 p. Troop to begin a new Stockpurse, were by Order of the Crown divided among the Captains, as a proper Reward for their good Behaviour, and Compensation for their Losses in Service. But, under the present Circumstances of the Stockpurse Accounts, there appears to be a Deficiency to answer the Charges made upon the, occasioned by the Number of Horses lost in Action, the increased Expence of them when bought, the longer Continuance of the Summer Campaigns, and the Method of confining the Summer Months between February and October. By these Circumstances the usual Dividends to the Captains of the Cavalry are cut off, and yet their extraordinary good Behaviour and Hardships during the last War (which the very Circumstances, that occasion the Deficiency, most strongly confirm) certainly demand some Acknowledgement from the Public, as a Mark of Approbation. I therefore think it my Duty to recommend those Officers to the Notice of the Lords Commissrs. of His Majesty's Treasury, and assure them, that, in my Opinion, if £100 p. Troop be given to each Captain, it will not be an Indulgence beyond their Merits; & will fall short of what their Predecessors have had in former Times.

The Treasury, during the last War, approved of an Allowance, after the Rate of £50 p. Troop p. annum, in Addition for their Contingencies; and the Marquis of Granby, then Commander in Chief, was pleased, by Warrants dated 18th August 1762, to order Payment to each of the Captains to that Time; and £37.10. out of the Stockpurse for the Subsistence of a Bat Man, and supplying the Bat Horses. The first of these Allowances was made on account of heavy and constant contingent Expences in a War where the Campains lasted much the greatest Part of the Year: The second was a Fund to maintain two Bat Horses, and a Bat Man, instead of taking a Dragoon for that Purpose. I give no Opinion on these Articles, and possibly it may not be thought proper in another War to allow them; but having been authorized by the Treasury, the Captains very naturally conceived they would continue to the End of the War, & have squared their Expences accordingly. I am therefore of Opinion, that all Arrears of these Allowances, to the Day, when the Cavalry arrived here, should be pay'd; and also, that a Sum of £63 p. Troop should be given, as a Fund to begin a new Stockpurse. The Colonels of these Regiments think they should be allowed £100 for that Purpose, and perhaps I may be obliged hereafter to ask that Sum from the Treasury; but I do not choose to recommend an unusual Addition upon this Account at present.

If the Lords of the Treasury consent to these Proposals, I think, they will not do more than is reasonable; and yet they will give great Satisfaction to the Officers concerned, as complying in a great Measure with the Prayer of a Memorial to His Majesty, presented by the Colonels of Cavalry serving in Germany. But if any such Demands should be hereafter made, and the Indulgence I now recommend be cited as a Precedent, I hope, the whole of the Case will be thoroughly considered, and that no future Treasury, or Secretary at War will give any Countenance to a similar Claim, except under similar Circumstances.

The Consequence of granting these Indulgences will amount to about £17,500 which added to the Sum of about £12,800 before stated as due to the Regts. will make together above £30,000. That Sum taken from the Saving, made upon the Winter Stoppages of £55,529.9.3 will leave a Ballance to the Public of about £25,000.

Having thus stated through You the whole of these Matters to the Lords of the Treasury for their Consideration, I must beg to know, whether their Lordships approve, that the Allowances I have now recommended be made to the Captains of Cavalry serving in Germany during the late War, should be pay'd out of the abovementioned Fund.

W.O. 4/78, pp. 313-317

123

Barrington to Charles Lowndes

[Copy] War Office
17 February 1766

By your answer to my Letter of the 20th Janry last concerning the application of the Winter Stoppages you informed me that the Lords Commissioners of His Majesty's Treasury had been pleased to approve of the allowances of £100 to the Captain of each Troop serving during the last War in Germany and of £63 per Troop to begin a new Stock Purse, but their Lordships have taken no notice of the other parts of my proposal, viz, of paying to the Captains the Arrears of the £50 and £37.10 per Annum due from August 1762 the time to which they were paid by Lord Granby's Warrant, till their arrival in England, & also the making good to those Regiments, which have been over pay'd, the Ballances which appear to be due by their Agent's Accounts, as yet unliquidated, I must therefore desire you to acquaint me, If I have their Lordship's approbation of these other parts of the proposal, and to move their Lordships for their direction for the payment of the whole out of the Winter Stoppages.

W.O. 4/78, p. 409

124

Warrant for the application of the winter stoppage

[Copy]   Court of St James
                                              20 June 1766

WHEREAS it hath been represented unto Us, that a stoppage was made in the last War, as well in the Winter, as in the Summer, from the Pay of the Non Commissioned officers and private Men of our Regiments of Cavalry serving in Germany, for the application of which Winter Stoppage there is no Precedent, nor hath any Warrant been issued, either by Us, or our late Royal Grandfather for that purpose; in consequence of which the Ballances in the hands of the Agents have encreased to a considerable amount. And whereas it hath been further represented unto Us, that by the extraordinary length of the Campaigns, and the severity of the Service, the expences have been considerably augmented, so that the usual allowances to the Stock purse vizt. of two thirds of the summer Stoppage carried to it (according to the present limitation of that Stoppage to eight particular Months vizt. from 24th Febry to 25th October in each Year both inclusive) is found unequal to the charges made upon that account, for remounting and for Payment of the Arrears of thirty seven pounds ten shillings per Annum to each Captain for the subsistence of Bat

Men and replacing Bat Horses from the respective times of their last payment to their Embarkation for England; and that there are also remaining due arrears to the same Period, of the annual allowance of fifty pounds to each Captain for the encreased expence of Contingencies; And it having been further represented unto Us, that the Extraordinary good behaviour of the Officers strongly recommended them to the consideration of our Royal Bounty; And we having been humbly besought that some allowance should be made to them as a Mark of our approbation of their Services, which We thinking reasonable are pleased to consent to; O.W. & P therefore is that out of such monies as have come in to your hands arising from the said Winter Stoppage, after leaving sixty three pounds pr Troop to begin a new Stock purse you do retain so much as shall be necessary to ballance the respective Stock Purse Accounts to the 24 June 1763 (giving Credit for the same till those accounts shall receive a final liquidation) And also that you do deduct and pay over out of the said Fund the arrears due to the Captains for the subsistence of Bat Men and replacing Bat Horses, and for additional contingencies from the respective times of their last Payment to their Embarkation for England after the Rates per Annum, that each Captain has been respectively paid before on those accounts, and also the sum of one hundred pounds for each Troop as of our Royal Bounty to be proportioned and paid to the Captains agreable to their times of Service in each particular Troop, or to their legal representatives, And whereas it hath been further represented unto Us that by the Precedent of former Wars, one third of the Summer Stoppage hath been usually allowed to the Colonels for the furnishing of Camp Necessaries, and as by the limitation of the summer Stoppage to eight particular Months the one third of the Summer Stoppage hath in most Regiments been insufficient for the purpose of supplying Camp Necessaries; And We having been humbly besought on that account to make good such deficiency and also to permit such Colonels, who have any Ballances remaining out of the said Camp Necessary Account, after satisfying the expence of Camp Necessaries, to carry them to their own private Account, agreable to the Precedent of former Wars, which We likewise thinking reasonable under the particular circumstances of the last War are pleased to consent to; O. W. & P. therefore is that you do make such further deductions as shall be found wanting to ballance the respective deficiencies on the Camp Necessary accounts, and that an account of whatever sums shall be remaining, after satisfying all the above purposes, be, by you transmitted into the office of our Secretary at War, in order for the receiving our further directions for the Payment of them into the office of our Paymaster General, And for all these several disbursements and applications of the said Winter Stoppage, this shall be your sufficient Warrant, Authority and direction Given &c 20th day of June 1766 in the Sixth Year of our Reign.

By H M Command
Barrington

To: The Agents of our Regiments of Cavalry serving in Germany during the last War.

W.O. 26/27, pp. 285–287

125

Barrington to Lord Granby

[Copy]
War Office
17 July 1767

Since my Letter of 10th February last, in which I informed your Lordship of the very great Difficultys attending the carrying into Execution His Majesty's Regulation of 17th March 1761 for applying the Non-Effective Ballances, and beg'd your Assistance and that of your Military Friends in getting over those Difficultys I have turned my Thoughts to every possible Method of securing to the several Captains of Infantry such reasonable Allowances, as may come nearest to those designed by His Majesty's Warrant beforementioned. I have now the Honor of sending to your Lordship the annexed Proposal. [See Document 127] If it meets with your Approbation, I will transmit it to the Lords Commissioners of the Treasury, and, upon their Consent, will move

His Majesty, that a Warrant may be granted for its immediate Execution.

I think I am not mistaken in conceiving that Funds may be found for giving this Douceur to the Captains of Infantry, whom I am earnestly desirous of assisting, as well as the Captains of Cavalry, who got one of a similar kind last year.

[Added in the hand of another Clerk]: July 22d. Lord Granby this day at Court expressed to me his approbation of this Plan & desired it might be recommended to the Treasury. B.

W.O. 4/82, p. 188

126

Barrington to Sir Grey Cooper

[Copy]   War Office
                                                    19 August 1767

His late Majesty, by a Regulation in 1753, was pleased to order, that the Non effective Accounts of the several Regts. of Infantry should be annually stated on the 24th day of June, and that whatever Ballance remained (after deducting £5 for every Man wanting to compleat to be carried to the Credit of the succeeding Account) should be divided among the Captains, partly in Aid of their extraordinary Expences, and partly as a reward of their Care and diligence in compleating their Companies; but, as the difficulty of recruiting during the last War, arising from a scarcity of Men, made it impracticable to compleat the said Regts. the Ballances of their Non effective Funds increased to a very considerable Amount, for which reason it was thought proper from time to time to suspend the distribution thereof among the Captains, a regulation very beneficial to the Public at their Expence. It being afterwards represented to His Majesty, that the said Ballances since 24th June 1757 were still undistributed, He was most graciously pleased by His Warrant dated 17th March 1761 to direct certain Allowances out of the said Ballances to be made to the Captains of the several Corps of Infantry.

This Warrant was my last Work, before I quitted the War Office in 1761. It has been sent to the Agents with strict injunctions of speedy and effectual execution, but it has been found, that thro' many unforeseen Accidents very few Regts. can avail themselves of His Majesty's just and gracious intentions, under the terms of the Warrant.

The Interest, which, from my situation, I must necessarily take in everything that concerns the Army, joined to the strongest Sense of their great Services, makes me particularly regret, that a Plan, proposed for the equitable benefit of the Infantry, should after a delay of several Years prove so inadequate to His Majesty's most gracious purpose, tho' His Royal Bounty has already been amply extended to another part of the Army by the Allowances granted to the Captains of many Regts. of Cavalry. But my utmost endeavours to carry this Warrant into execution having been ineffectual, My Duty, as well as my Zeal required that I should search after some other method, which might secure to the Captains of Infantry Allowances in some degree equivalent to those designed by the Warrant. On mature consideration the annexed Proposal seems to be the most probable means of producing that effect.

To execute this plan a considerable Sum will be required, for it takes in a larger Field, than that, which was the Object of His Majesty's Warrant of 1761, comprehending not only all the Regts. that existed in the Years 1758, 1759, 1760 (the Period, to which that Warrant was confined) but also all the Corps raised after that time, to the end of the War. These had an equal Claim under the regulation of 1743, and must therefore have been the Objects of a future Warrant, had that of 1761 been carried into execution, an Indulgence which could not have been denied to them, as all Captains of Infantry now existing, enjoy annually, a similar Allowance by the late regulations in 1766. I flatter myself, without any new grant of Parliament, a sufficient Fund may be found for this purpose out of the Non effective Money of the Army, a very large part of which has already been voted, and applyed to the Public Service, but the remainder in the hands of the Agents, left there by the Treasury to answer this demand, together with the vacant Pay, appears by their Accounts transmitted to my office, to be sufficient for the carrying the annexed proposal into immediate execution.

I must therefore desire you to lay this letter, together with my Proposal before the Lords Commissioners of the His Majesty's Treasury for their Consideration, assuring them, that it appears to me equitable in the last degree.

You will also please to acquaint me, whether the Lords approve the Plan I have now recommended, that the Captains of Infantry may be informed, as soon as possible of their Lordships determination.

W.O. 4/82, pp. 208–211

127

Proposal enclosed with previous document

[Copy]

A Proposal for granting certain Sums to the Captains of the several Regiments of Infantry, to be considered as their full Allowance of Non effective money from 25th June 1757, to the 24th June 1765, both inclusive—

Allowance to the Captains in the several Regts. of Infantry raised before 24th June 1760, vizt.

To each Captain in Regts. that were abroad during the whole War £100.

To each Captain in Regts. that were partly abroad, and partly at home £80.

To each Captain in Regts. that were totally at home £60.

Allowances to the Captains in the several Corps of Infantry raised after 24th June 1760, vizt.

To each Captain in Corps that were totally abroad, from the time of raising to the end of the War £50.

To each Captain in Corps partly abroad and partly at home £40.

To each Captain in Corps totally at home £30.

The fund proposed for the above purpose, is the Non effective

Money remaining in the Agents hands, together with the vacant Pay of Commissioned Officers.

W.O. 4/82, p. 212

128
Warrant for regulating the non-effective fund of the several regiments of Infantry

[Copy]   Court of St James
                                            19 February 1766

WHEREAS We have judged it necessary for Our Service, to ascertain the Articles, which may be charged against the Non effective Fund of Our marching Regiments of Foot, excluding at the same time all other Articles whatever, in order that the said Fund may be kept apart for the purpose of Recruiting, and that the Ballance which shall remain after satisfying the Charges hereby admitted, may be applied to other public Military Uses; We have therefore thought fit to order and Direct that, for the future, no Charge shall be made against the said Non-effective fund, but what comes fairly & evidently under the following heads Viz:

The Levy Money and Expence of each Recruit, and also his Subsistence till he joins the Regiment.

Bounty Money to discharged Men to carry them home.

The Subsistence of Invalids discharged and recommended to Our Royal Bounty of Chelsea Hospital, from the day to which they are Subsisted by the Regiment, to that on which they are admitted on the Pension, or rejected by the Board.

Expences of Beating Orders, and Attested Copies thereof.
Expences of Debenture Warrants.
Expences relating to Deserters.
Expence of the passage of Recruiting parties and Recruits by Sea, from and to the Regiment.

AND WHEREAS Our late Royal Grand-father of glorious Memory was pleased to direct, by a Regulation in 1743 that the Non-effective Accounts of the several Regiments of Infantry should be annually stated on the 24th of June, and that whatever Ballance remained, (after deducting £5 for every Man wanting to compleat, to be carried to the Credit of the succeeding Account) should be divided among the Captains, partly in aid of their extraordinary Expences, and partly as as a Reward of their care and diligence in compleating their Companies; Which Regulation Our said late Royal Grand-father was pleased to suspend during the late War; AND WHEREAS We have judged that it will be more for the benefit of Our Service, that the Allowance made to the Captains should be limited, We are pleased to direct, that for the future, the Non-effective Accounts shall continue to be settled annually to the 24th of June, when £5 shall be set apart for each Man wanting to compleat at the preceeding Spring Review, and carried to the Credit of the succeeding Account; after which the Ballance which shall remain, shall be divided among the Captains, provided it shall not exceed £20 to each Captain. And We are pleased to direct that the Sums so paid to the Captains, shall be entered as the Cash Charge in the Non-effective Account of each Regiment. AND OUR FURTHER WILL AND PLEASURE IS, that in case any Surplus shall remain on Ballance of the Non-effective Fund, annually stated on the 24th of June, after deducting £5 for every Man wanting to compleat (which must be carried to the Credit of the succeeding Account as aforesaid) and after paying to each Captain their entire Allowance of £20, that Ballance shall be carried to the Credit of the succeeding Years Account. And the several Agents are hereby directed to acquaint our Secretary at war, upon the settling of each Years Accounts, with the Amount of this Surplus or Ballance for Our Information.

And We do hereby direct that all other Charges and Expences whatever incurred by Our Marching Regiments of Foot, and which have been usually allowed, shall for the future, be inserted in the General Half Yearly Contingent Bill ordered to be transmitted to Our Secretary at War by his Letter bearing date the 26th day of Novemr. 1765.

OUR FURTHER WILL AND PLEASURE IS that in the keeping and making up of the Non effective Accounts of each of Our said Regiments, the following Directions be for the future strictly observed.

That no more than three Guineas & a half shall be allowed to any Recruiting Officer for each Man recruited by him; out of which Sum no more than one Guinea and a half shall be given to each Recruit, according to Our Directions signified by Our Secretary at War bearing date the 17th of December 1765. But no Charge whatever is to be admitted on Account of Recruits who may desert before they join the Regiment.

No Recruiting Officer shall be allowed Credit for the Levy Money of any such Recruits as shall not be approved of by the Commanding Officer of each Regimt. respectively; but their Subsistence shall be allowed.

The Non-effective fund shall be charged with the real Expence of all the Recruits, who may die before they join the Regiment, provided the day of their Death and the exact Bounty Money given them be certified by the Recruiting Officer on the back of the Attestation. All subsistence given to Recruits before they join the Regiment shall be charged separately from the Levy Money.

The Accounts of all Recruiting Officers are to be stated and settled on or before the 24th of June.

In Regiments stationed in Great Britain, the Recruiting Accounts are to be signed by the Recruiting Officer himself, and by the Field Officer Commanding at Quarters; in Regiments stationed abroad, the said Accounts are to be signed by the Recruiting Officer, and by the Colonel, or one of the Field Officers, if either of them shall be in Great Britain.

AND OUR PLEASURE IS that the above Account so signed shall be good and sufficient Vouchers to the Agent, for the Credit given by him to each Recruiting Officer, on the head of Recruiting.

That in all future States of the Regimental Accounts given to the Reviewing Generals, the Number of Recruits for which Levy Money and Subsistence are charged, shall be particularly and separately specified.

AND WHEREAS it has been the practice in some of Our Marching Regts. of foot, to allow the Captain without Accot. the Subsistence of the Vacant Men in their respective Companies, arisen from Vacancies which happen between the days whereon each Captain usually receives the Subsistence of his Company: It is Our express Order that for the future, the Captains shall account for the vacant Subsistence of each Man who shall die, desert, or be discharged, between the above mentioned periods, from the date of such death, desertion, or discharge, and that the Non-effective Fund shall have Credit for the Vacant Subsistence of every Man, from the day on which he is no longer entitled to Subsistence.

We are further pleased to direct that every Colonel shall himself carefully examine the Non-effective Account previous to its being laid before the Reviewing General. He is likewise to certify under his hand, that he believes it to be fair and exact. And the Reviewing General shall report to Us any Articles which shall appear to him to be charged contrary to these Our Orders; As likewise whether proper Credit be given to the Non-effective Fund for the whole Vacant Subsistence.

All the aforesaid Orders, Regulations, and Directions, We strictly charge and command all Reviewing Generals, Colonels, Commanding Officers, and Agents of Our Regiments of Infantry and all others whom they may concern, to follow & obey, under pain of Our highest Displeasure. Given at Our Court at St. James's this 19th day of February 1766, in the Sixth Year of Our Reign.

By H.M.'s Command
Barrington

W.O. 26/27, pp. 224–231

129

Warrant for regulating the stock-purse fund of the Regiments of Dragoon Guards and Dragoons

[Copy]   Court of St James
19 February 1766

WHEREAS We have judged it necessary for Our Service to ascertain the Articles which may be charged against the Stock-purse fund of Our Regiments of Dragoon Guards and Dragoons, excluding at the same time all other articles whatever, in order that the said Fund may be kept apart for the purpose of Recruiting, and that the Ballance which shall remain after satisfying the Charges hereby admitted, may be applied to other public Military Uses; We have therefore thought fit to order and direct, that, for the future, no Charge shall be made against the said Stock purse fund, but what comes fairly and evidently under the following heads Viz:

The Levy Money and Expence of each Recruit, and also his Subsistence till he joins the Regiment.

Bounty Money to discharged Men to carry them home.

The Subsistence of Invalids discharged and recommended to Our Royal Bounty of Chelsea Hospital, from the day to which they are subsisted by the Regiment to that on which they are admitted on the Pension or rejected by the Board.

Expences of Beating Orders, and attested Copies thereof.
Expences of Debenture Warrants.
Expences relating to Deserters.

AND WHEREAS Our late Royal Grandfather of glorious Memory, was pleased to direct during the last peace, that each of the Captains of Our Regiments of Dragoons, should be allowed £25 yearly, to enable them to bear the contingent Expences of their respective Troops, which Sum was during the late War encreased to £35 AND WHEREAS it is highly proper that the said Allowance should be now fixed by Us; We taking into Our Royal Consideration various Expences, which have from different Circumstances become an Additional Charge on the Captains of Dragoons since the aforesaid Regulation of Our late Royal Grandfather at £25 p Annum, Are pleased to direct, that, for the future, the stock purse Accounts of Our Regiments of Dragoons shall be settled annually to the 24th of June, when £5 shall be set apart for each Man, and twenty Guineas for each Horse wanting to compleat on the 1st of February, and be carried to the Credit of the succeeding Account, after which the Sum of £30 shall be given out of the said Fund to each of the Captains. And We are pleased to direct that the Sums so paid to the Captains, shall be entered as the last Charge in the Stock purse Account of each Regiment of Dragoons.

AND OUR FURTHER WILL AND PLEASURE IS that in case any Surplus shall remain on Ballance of the Stock purse fund annually stated on the 24th day of June after deducting the aforesaid Sums for recruiting and remounting, (which must be carried to the Credit of the Succeeding Account) and after paying to each Captain their entire Allowance of £30, that Ballance shall be carried to the Credit of the succeeding Years Account. And the several Agents are hereby directed to acquaint Our Secretary at War, upon the settling of each Years Accounts, with the Amount of this Surplus or Ballance for Our Information.

And We do hereby direct that all other Charges and Expences whatever incurred by Our Regiments of Dragoon Guards and Dragoons, and which have been usually allowed, shall for the future be inserted in the General Half Yearly Contingent Bill ordered to be transmitted to Our Secretary at War, by his Letter bearing date the 26th day of November 1765.

OUR FURTHER WILL AND PLEASURE IS that in the keeping and making up the Stock purse Accounts of each of Our said Regiments, the following Directions be, for the future, strictly observed.

That no more than three pounds eight shillings shall be allowed to any Recruiting Officer for each Man recruited by him, out of which Sum no more than One Guinea and a Crown shall be given to the Recruit, according to Our Directions signified by Our Secretary at War bearing date the 24th day of Decemr. 1765. But no Charge whatever is to be admitted on Account of Recruits, who may desert before they join the Regiment.

That no Recruiting Officer shall be allowed Credit for the Levy Money of any such Recruits as shall not be approved of by the Commanding Officer of each Regiment respectively: but their Subsistence shall be allowed. The Stock Purse Fund shall be charged with the Real Expence of all the Recruits, who may die before they join the Regiment; provided the day of their death, and the exact Bounty Money given them be certified by the Commanding Officer on the back of the Attestation.

That all Subsistence issued to Recruits before they join the Regiment, shall be charged separately from the Levy Money.

The Accounts of all the Recruiting Officers are to be stated and settled on or before the 24th day of June.

The Recruiting Accounts are to be signed by the Recruiting Officer himself, and by the Field-Officer Commanding at Quarters; And Our Pleasure is, that those Accounts so signed, shall be good and sufficient Vouchers to the Agent for the Credit given by him to each Recruiting Officer on the head of Recruiting.

That in all future States of the Regimental Accounts given in to the Reviewing Generals, the Number of Recruits, for which Levy Money and Subsistence are charged, shall be particularly and separately specified.

That no more than Twenty Guineas shall be given for each Horse.

That the travelling Expences incurred until the Horses join the Regiment shall be charged in a separate Article, and the Charges on that Account particularly specified and vouched.

That the Captains shall account for the Subsistence of the vacant Men & Horses in their respective Troops arisen from Vacancies which happen between the days whereon each Captain usually receives the Subsistence of his Troop, and that the Stock purse fund shall have Credit for the vacant Subsistence of every Man who shall die, desert, or be discharged, and of every Horse that shall die; or be cast between the above mentioned periods, from the day on which they are no longer entitled to Subsistence.

That the Stock Purse Fund shall also have Credit for the Sums for which the Horses that shall be cast from time to time shall be sold.

We are further pleased to direct, that every Colonel shall himself carefully examine the Stock purse Account previous to its being laid before the Reviewing General. He is likewise to certify under his hand, that he believes it to be fair and exact. And the Reviewing General shall report to Us, any Articles which shall appear to him to be charged contrary to these Our Orders. As likewise whether proper Credit be given to the Stock purse fund for the whole Vacant Subsistence of Men and Horses, and for the price of the cast Horses.

All the aforesaid Orders, Regulations and Directions, We

strictly charge and command all Reviewing Generals, Colonels, Commanding Officers, and Agents of Our Regiments of Dragoon Guards & Dragoons, and all others whom this may concern, to follow and obey under pain of Our highest Displeasure. Given at Our Court at St. James's this 19th day of February 1766 in this Sixth Year of Our Reign.

By H.M.'s Command
Barrington

W.O. 26/27, pp. 232–239

130

'Memorandums given to the Secretary at War 8 Octor. 1765'

[Copy]

For consideration. Officers selling out (Having a Brevet of superior Rank to the Commission he sells) of Pretensions to . . . . Rank in the Army, at any future time, from the Pretensions of the Brevet?

Prices of Commissions to be fixed . . .

Colonel of the Regiment to Recommend the Successor, at the Price Ordered;

Q . . . If those Officers who may have given a Higher Price than what may be fixed for the Future, is to be Entitled to the Price he Gave, or to the fixed one?

Detriment to the Recruiting Service; by Recruiting Parties Overbidding each other, which is now much practised. A limited Sum to Beat up att being Ordered, will prevent it, both Dragoons and Foot.

The Order to Extend to all Parties which may Recruit in England . . . . Either from the Regiments in Great Britain, Ireland, or America.

A Limitted Price to be given by Regiments of Dragoons for each Horse, is Necessary to be fixed—as some Regiments have exceeded 20 Guineas as formerly Ordered.

The Stock Purse of the Several Regiments of Cavalry which were in Germany want Regulation.

A Memorial was given in for His Majesty signed by the General Officers of Cavalry, with proposals for that Purpose.

The Reviewing Generals (as the Accounts of the Stock Purses, and Non Effective Funds are Delivered to them at the Review) to Examine the several Particular Charges, If they exceed, or are Contrary to the Regulation, and make their Report Accordingly.

The Returns of the Invalids—Exceedingly Erroneous as to Numbers.

Particulars are given in . . . . . .

Officers having Brevets of Superiour Rank to the Regimental Commission . . .

No Pretensions to be Excused from Regimental Duty.

W.O. 4/1044, pp. 27–28

5

The Army and the Public

The unpopularity of the army in the eighteenth century was an aspect of a more comprehensive attitude of public suspicion of the executive. It showed itself in constant complaints, either literary and rhetorical in pamphlets and newspapers, or plain and to the point in the form of letters from hostile members of the public. The former expressed fears for a constitution in danger; the latter called for immediate practical remedies for some new outrage on the part of soldiers. The suspicion of a standing army persisted throughout the century, but particularly in the first half, when attacks upon it could always raise atavistic growls from the benches. It had been touch and go for the constitution in the seventeenth century and could be so again, ran the argument. The Rockingham Whigs took up anti-army arguments at the end of the 1760s and made them a part of their programme. By this date it had become perhaps a little unreal to suggest, as had been done in the 1690s, that the army should be disbanded at the end of every war, but Burke and his friends were determined to scrutinize very carefully the non-military uses to which the army might be put, particularly police-work. The general public, irritated by having soldiers living amongst them, were friendly towards the idea of the army being closely watched, especially in politically-conscious areas like the City of London. And it was to the Secretary at War that the task fell of writing soothing letters to angry individuals and corporations, and of apologizing in Parliament for the public behaviour of the army. Certain parts of his executive role at the War Office increased the political risks for him. One of his main tasks was that of marching and quartering soldiers in England. There was almost no barrack-accommodation outside London, and the regiments lived scattered in public-houses and in their adjacent stable-lofts, outhouses and similar unsuitable places.[1] This circumstance gave rise to endless friction between the people and the government. Worse, because of its management of the movements of the army at home, the

War Office had acquired the principal role in the maintaining of public order.[2] Barrington was always uneasy about being responsible for this, and did all he could to ensure that the troops should not be involved except as a last resort. The documents clearly show how distasteful to him were the frequent appeals of magistrates who properly had the responsibility of keeping order. In spite of this the popular image of him, encouraged by Burke's attacks in Parliament after the St George's Field's riot in 1768, was of a stern oppressor of public liberty.

* * *

Orders for marching and quartering (131) proceeded almost daily from the War Office and occupied a separate series of letter books (W.O. 5). The regiments, already suffering the inconvenience of being scattered piecemeal throughout the towns and villages of the country, were not even allowed to stay long in one place, for a number of reasons, very few of which had any real military content.[3] It was obviously prudent to remove troops from towns where fairs (132), horse-races or circuses were to take place. Further, an act of Parliament of 1735[4] laid a duty upon the Secretary at War, under threat of being dismissed from his office, to remove troops from places where elections were to be held.[5] No legislation required similar precautions upon the visit of assize judges, but they were nevertheless always taken, sometimes at some inconvenience (133). The interference of soldiers in the judicial process was an unlikely event, but it was better to be prudent.

Since the days when Walpole had been at the War Office ways had been sought to ease the burden of quartering without removing troops from an area. In wartime when the army might quadruple in size, there was not much scope for this, but existing quarters could be enlarged so as to include the surrounding villages (134). The discipline, cohesion and training programme of regiments suffered severely as a result of these unsatisfactory arrangements.[6] But there seemed no alternative. The army was suffered to exist, but the view was that it must not cost the country more than a bare minimum. A programme of building barracks would have been thought impracticable because of its extravagance.[7] If a ministry with a responsibility for military policy had been allowed to develop it might have attempted such a programme, but that was no more likely to be acceptable either. The best that Barrington could do was to be efficient in administering the system of troop movement as he found it, and to be tactful and apologetic when outcries arose. Much of his correspondence was with innkeepers or with those representing their interests.[8] He did not always comply with their demands, but in some cases the distress was genuine (135, 136, 137), and the danger always existed that they would relinquish their licenses and cease to trade if soldiers were quartered upon them in excessive numbers or for extended periods of time. One of Barrington's earlier actions on becoming Secretary at War was to call upon the Excise, the only agency with the necessary minute knowledge of localities, to draw up a survey of all inns, beds and stable-accommodation in England: this formed the basis for quartering for many years (138, 139, 140), when the Seven Years' War and the war with America increased a loading which had to be more equitably distributed. The prejudice against barracks, quoted with approval and perhaps exaggerated by Whiggish writers in the past,[9] began to break down. In 1759 the inhabitants of Guildford were so maddened by the constant quartering of soldiers upon them that they actually suggested the building of barracks in the area. They noted that public ovens for baking bread for the army had been built outside the town. Guildford had grown in importance during the century. It was centrally-placed between London, Portsmouth and Chatham, and a permanent stream of soldiers, marines, sailors, women, children, sick and wounded passed through it. Of the twenty-seven publicans in the town fifteen had failed and gone out of business in the previous three or four years.[10]

Innkeepers in the south of England were no better disposed towards foreign troops billeted in Britain (141, 142). The money paid for the subsistence of soldiers quartered in inns and alehouses had always been insufficient, and it became more so as prices began to rise after the middle years of the century. What made matters worse was the behaviour of the soldiers. The swaggering and bullying habits of the soldier of the late seventeenth century had probably been tempered a little, but his off-duty amusements did little to endear him to innkeepers and inhabitants. Drunken fights, riots, damage to property (143), poaching (144) and involvement in more serious crimes were not uncommon. Luring young men into the army by tricks did not add to the popularity of the army. Such recruits, if the matter came to light, were nearly always set at liberty, as also were young apprentices similarly entrapped (145, 146, 147, 148, 149). The above examples of day-to-day friction were punctuated by graver cases of bad military-civil relations.

The complaints of innkeepers and improperly-enlisted youths were unlikely to make much noise with press and Parliament. Others had to be taken more seriously. The magistrates of Plymouth, Barrington's own constituency town, became seriously alarmed at the beginning of the Seven Years' War when the Earl of Home, whose regiment was quartered in the town, began to behave like a military governor. Barrington reminded the earl that in disputes between magistrates and the military the latter would nearly always have to give way (150). The march of the Guards through the City of London one day in December 1769, conducted, it was alleged by Lord Mayor Beckford, in an ostentatious and offensive manner, brought a complete apology and reassurance from Barrington[11] (151). And the extraordinary case of General Gansell, who was rescued from the custody of sheriff's officers by soldiers of the Foot Guards, probably gave Barrington the worst fright of all (152, 153, 154, 155). Newspapers had grown a good deal in importance in Barrington's lifetime, and incidents with a constitutional dimension such as the Guards' march in the City, the St George's Fields riot (see below p. 258) and the Gansell case, all happening in London within a space of two years, were taken up by the press and discussed at length and in detail to the embarrassment of the Secretary at War.

* * *

Public order problems engrossed a great deal of Barrington's attention,[12] particularly in times of great risings of the people, when government thought that real rebellion was imminent. The food riots of 1756, 1757, 1766 and 1773 were in places remote from the capital, and gave rise to complex strategic problems for the War Office. In 1766 alone serious riots, involving the burning of mills, clashes with soldiers, and several deaths, took place in sixty-eight towns in twenty counties. The London riots of 1765 and 1768 were near to the centres of control but, for other reasons discussed below, were equally as intractable. The official procedure upon the outbreak of a riot was inhibited and cautious. It was not permissible for a magistrate to apply to the officer commanding the nearest troops and request help in suppressing disorder. By the middle of the century officers had become very cautious. The correct course was for a magistrate, even though living some hundreds of miles from the capital, to apply for help to the office of the Secretary of State in London. A riot was a point of civil government and the army at home should only be ordered into action by civil governors.

Only when the Secretary of State had satisfied himself as to the seriousness of the situation would he write to the Secretary at War asking him to order troops to march and assist. Many riots went unchecked as a result of this proper but cumbersome procedure, although the more long-lived riots associated with prices and food-shortages persisted for weeks.[13] As the scale of rioting increased in the middle of the century magistrates began to write directly to the War Office, and after a brief protest from the Secretary of State, Lord Holdernesse, Barrington was able to take the undivided task upon himself and develop some lines of conduct. The riots which broke out in the Midlands in August 1756 gave him opportunities to do this. He knew that a riot about provisions having arisen in one place was often quickly followed by others nearby, as a result of an organized march of rioters from one town to another. He also knew that officers uneasy about their legal powers might conceive that orders to suppress a riot in one named place might not entitle them to do so in a neighbouring place not mentioned in the orders. The authority to Lieutenant-Colonel Harvey of the Inniskilling Dragoons was therefore drafted more widely than usual (156), and he was asked to send back to London frequent accounts of his operations.[14] No previous Secretary at War had troubled to draw up flexible orders or to call for the gathering of intelligence. From this date the police-work of the War Office became more sophisticated.

A more serious outbreak of rioting at Nottingham caused Harvey's force to be moved there from Leicester (157, 158). Barrington at this stage in his career was much more concerned to have the approbation of the Duke of Cumberland, who returned from Windsor after several days and proceeded to reinforce the Midland area (159, 160, 163). But Barrington was always interested in the possibilities of the civil power exerting itself, and was pleased to receive support for this from Sir John Willes, the Lord Chief Justice, who was sitting at the Warwick Assizes (161, 162). Willes rallied the local magistrates and did much to quieten the area, but not before a dramatic confrontation between soldiers and rioters had taken place at Nottingham (164).

Although rioting was endemic in England at this date no serious widespread riots took place for some time after 1757. Not long after Barrington returned to office what was probably the greatest series of food riots of the century took place. By this date he was cautiously prepared to try more experiments to improve efficiency, although to the end of his career he continued to enjoin caution upon magistrates and Lords Lieutenant in the hope of keeping troops out of the matter (165, 166). He was aware that 1766 would be a difficult year. Prices were already high in 1765, and if the harvest of 1766 failed disorder was inevitable. In January 1766 he sent out secret orders to a number of cavalry and infantry units in well-known trouble spots to intervene in response to appeals from magistrates when the anticipated riots should begin. He urged the officers to keep the orders secret—for ever, if the riots did not occur—and took care that the copy orders in the War Office were not entered in the usual books. If Parliament called for the letter-books no evidence of these risky expedients would be found (167, 168). This might have been an excellent scheme and the delays in applying to a distant capital for a local sanction could have been avoided. But Barrington's well-meant prudence caused it to fail. The magistrates had not been informed, and they were by now well-schooled to refrain from making direct appeals to local commanders. When the riots began in August all the usual delays occurred, and he again issued general orders to intervene at the request of magistrates, although not troubling this time to keep them secret, as the emergency had now arisen (169). His next venture was to place the now-numerous units in the West Country under one local commander, giving him a fairly free hand (170, 171, 172). By this time every last reserve was used up (173) and Barrington had to tell the Revenue service that they could expect no help from soldiers.[15] The riots died away in October after a number of clashes. Altogether eighty-one orders had issued from the War Office in connection with these riots: the preambles to them indicated the type of riot as well as the instruction to act (174, 175, 176, 177). After the disorders had ended Barrington interested himself in the retributive side of the aftermath (178).

Tactics in 1766 as in many other police operations of this century, were less successful. The training of officers and men was however outside Barrington's brief, and he was always embarrassed and evasive when officers asked him for guidance about the legality or efficacy of tactical techniques.[16] It was perhaps not fair to ask him. He was not a lawyer or a military man. But he was concerned to find that his political masters showed no inclination to give guidance. Two years later he recommended that the trial of the magistrate who gave the order to fire on the crowd in St George's Fields should be published, as the judgement contained a clear statement of the law of military aid to the civil power (184).

The Wilkes riots of 1768 have received a good deal of attention from historians[17] but need to be briefly mentioned here because of their importance in Barrington's career (see Section 1). It was a bad time for him. In terms of strategy the clock was put back to 1756, with the overall control exercised by Lord Weymouth. It was galling for a Secretary at War who had developed good techniques to be reduced to a secondary role by an ineffective Secretary of State. Barrington took care to move a regiment of infantry and six regiments of cavalry into strategic points just outside London, but in spite of all his precautions the capital was increasingly given over to a victorious mob in the spring of 1768. The supineness of the magistrates and the wretched position of officers left unattended by the civil power particularly enraged him (179, 180, 181, 182). He did all he could to maintain a record of effectiveness tempered with humanity, but events were too strong for him, and the popular perception of him was as ineffective and harsh. In the debate on the address on the King's Proclamation to suppress riots he was stung by the implication of inefficiency, which he rightly considered should more precisely have been aimed at Lord Weymouth, saying 'I rise as an evidence, to assert that one department has done its duty.'[18] As for his reputation of harshness, this was added to by the publication in the newspapers of his well-known letter of support to the Guards after the killings in St George's Fields (183). This gave Burke his opening for a great attack on Barrington upon the whole question of the employment of troops against crowds (see above, p. 12) and Barrington had to defend himself more than once in the House of Commons. Many years later when Shute Barrington and Sir Thomas Bernard were preparing the manuscript of the *Life* of Barrington their uneasiness showed in their treatment of the St George's Fields riot.[19]

* * *

During the invasion scare of 1779 Barrington, by now retired from the War Office, went to much trouble to use his local influence in Berkshire to promote an association of propertied men for mutual defence against the risings of the people that many people expected would happen if the French invaded. In spite of years of organizing a system of policing by soldiers he still believed in the civil power and in self-help. At first local magnates and his brother the Bishop of Llandaff and Sir William Blackstone gave support, and some training went on of civilians in the musket exercise. But an uneasiness grew up that it might arouse rather than allay alarm, and with the decline of the invasion danger it was quietly dropped (185, 186, 187, 188, 189).

* * *

The smuggling service engrossed even more of the army's time than did maintaining public order.[20] Riots flared up and declined, but smuggling in England was a way of life. War Office documents speak of 'numerous daring and desperate smuglers and owlers', and of murderous struggles between revenue men and large gangs. Riding officers often lived an unhappy and alienated existence amidst a local population the major part of which might be involved in the smuggling interest. Nothing effective could be done in such a situation without soldiers.[21] This was particularly true in Sussex where for long periods the King's writ ran rather uncertainly. Serious rioting promoted to cover smuggling operations took place in 1766. The fears of the local revenue officers grew. They objected to the troops at Rye and Hastings being removed for a review, and they alleged that the innkeepers at Hailsham only objected to quartering soldiers because they were in league with the smugglers.[22] In the summer of the following year the revenue men made a great effort and arrested the local ring-leader in the area, Stephen Bourner, only to lose him to a determined rescue-party, a common feature of the smuggling war (190, 191, 192). Barrington gave orders to the nearest cavalry regiment in the usual form to intervene (193, 194); no doubt most of its horses were at grass. The intervention came too late to be effective, and the soldiers could do no more than exercise a controlling effect on the area. There would never be enough soldiers for this or indeed any other police action in the eighteenth century.

131

Christopher D'Oyly to Colonel Fletcher Campbell or officer commanding the 35th Regiment at Chatham Barracks

[Copy]   War Office
                                                          4 July 1767

In the Absence of the Secretary at War, who is gone out of Town for a few days, I have the honor to send you the enclosed Order for the march of the 35th Regt. under your Command to their Quars. in the Neighbourhood of London on Accot. of the Review, & for their proceeding, after the Review, to their destined Quars; I am at the same time to acquaint you, that the 22d. Regt. of Foot, is directed to march to Exeter & Tiverton, as the 22d. Regt. is to march on the same day with the 35th, I desire you will concert with the Officer commanding the 22d. Regt. so as to prevent the Divisions of the two Regts. interfering with one another on their March.

W.O. 4/82, p. 160

132

Barrington to Lt.-Colonel Pitt

[Copy]   War Office
                                                          8 May 1756

Mr Wright at the request of the Mayor & Corporation of Leicester having applied to me to move the Troops quartered in the Town during the Time of the Fair, and as it has always been Customary to comply with these requests & your Regt. being a Young One & undisciplined the removing them during the Fair time will I hope prevent accidents which probably would otherwise happen from Riotts & Drunkenness Generally attending Fairs. I therefore enclose the usual order for your removal.

W.O. 4/51, p. 452

133

Thomas Tyrwhitt to the Mayor of Winchester

[Copy]   War Office
                                                      1 July 1760

In the absence of the Secry. at War, I send you herewith an Order
for the removal of the Regt. Troop, Company, or any Detachment
or Recruiting Parties of His Majesty's Forces from Winchester,
to the next adjacent place or places, during the Assizes, where
they are to remain until they are over; But if you think it necessary,
on Account of the French Prisoners, that such part of the Militia
Forces that are not quarter'd in the Barracks, should continue at
Winchester, you will be pleased not to deliver the enclosed Order
to the commanding Officer, & to acquaint the Judges upon their
Arrival that the Troops not being moved as usual in like Cases,
is, at the request of the Corporation, for the reason above
mentioned; and likewise acquaint the Commanding Officer
therewith, that he may not be at a loss on this Occasion.

W.O. 4/61, p. 353

134

Barrington to Lt.-General Conway, or officer
commanding the 1st Dragoons

[Copy]   War Office
                                                      10 November 1759

I am to signify to You His Majesty's Pleasure that you consider in
what manner the quarters of the Regt. under your Command; can
be enlarged, so as to give most ease to the Country, without harm
to the service. For this purpose you will consult with the Civil
Magistrates, or other proper persons in the Neighbourhood, &
report your opinion to me, for His Majesty's information.

If the Head Quarters are eased during the Autumn & Winter, it
will be the less inconvenient or burthensome to bring the Corps

nearer together in the Spring, when discipline shall make it requisite so to do.

[Same letter to officers commanding twelve detachments of cavalry and twenty two detachments of infantry in Britain]

W.O. 4/59, p. 249

135

Barrington to John Dalston

[Copy]   War Office
5 March 1756

I return herewith the Petition which you did me the Honour to put into my Hands from the Inkeepers & Alehouse keepers of Burton; and cannot but observe, that as no Troops have been for great many Years or are likely to be Quartered for a time, upon that Town, I therefore think you'l be of opinion the Petitioners have little reason to complain of their being subjected a few times in a Year to have three or four Companies lie a Night or perhaps Two Nights in the Road to or from Scotland, and that the Complying with this Request would be a great hardship upon the troops by obliging them to March upwards of twenty miles a day and be an encouragement for other small Towns on that Road to make the same request.

W.O. 4/51, p. 237

136

Barrington to Earl of Darlington (at Raby Castle)

[Copy]   War Office
10 December 1765

I have the honor to acknowledge the receipt of the Favor of your letter of the 6th. instant with the Petition of several Innkeepers of the City of Durham desiring on accot. of the great price paid for hay & straw in that Neighbourhood, that H.M.'s Troops at present quartered there may be removed.

Your Lordship, I trust, is well satisfied that I should have great pleasure in granting instantly any request of your's, but as these Troops were, upon the earnest application of the Civil Magistrates, sent to Durham in order to assist in quelling & preventing the disorders apprehended from the Colliers, I dare say your Lordship will not disapprove of my sending a Copy of the Petition to Sir Walter Blacket, that he may communicate the same to the Magistrates in the Neighbourhood of Durham, in order that I may receive their concurrence for the removal of the Troops before I issue any Orders for that purpose, as soon as I receive His answer, I shall take the first opportunity of writing to your Lordship again.

W.O. 4/78, p. 168

137

Barrington to William Hawks
(Innkeeper of Brentford, Middlesex)

[Copy]   War Office
                                                         9 July 1777

I have received the Petition signed by you and other Innkeepers of Brentford, and wish it was in my power to give you the relief you request, but no alteration can be made in the present disposition of the King's Light Dragoons. Next year Richmond shall have the whole Detachment.

W.O. 4/100, p. 246

138

Barrington to the Commissioners of Excise

[Copy]   War Office
                                                10 May 1756

I have His Majesty's Commands to signify to you, His Majesty's
Pleasure you forthwith give the proper Directions to all Excise
Men in the several Market Towns and great Villages throughout
all England, that they render You an Account (with all possible
Exactness) of the Number of Beds, and Stable Room for Horses,
which the Publick Houses and Inns, within their Sundry Districts, can and usually do, accommodate Guests withall, and that
you do transmit the said account to this Office, for the Use of His
Majesty's Secretary at War, by which Means, the Troops may be
more commodiously Quarterd, and the Subjects bear a more
equal Proportion of that Burthen.

W.O. 4/51, p. 454

139

Commissioners of Excise to Barrington

[In Clerk's hand, signed by 5 Commissioners]   Excise Office
                                                6 August 1756

In pursuance of your Lordship's Letter of the 10th May last, We
take the liberty to transmit to you the returns We have received
relating to the number of beds and standings for Horses in the
several Collections in England. If any difficulties should arise
from the accounts not being drawn upon in the same Method,
Our Officers in the several places will be able to explain them to
the Satisfaction of the Officers of the Army quartered in that
neighbourhood.

W.O. 30/49, f. 2

Enclosure with Document 139

'A List of the Inns &c. No of Beds & Stable Room for Horses in Bucks Collection'

Stony Stratford Division

	Inns etc	No of Beds	Stable Room for Horses
Winslow Division	14	30	74
D O Ride	14	20	40
Bucks Division	35	98	250
Do 1st O Ride	13	14	67
Do 2d O Ride	15	27	35
Stony Stratford Division	26	127	276
Do 1st O Ride	19	42	52
Do 2d O Ride	25	24	49
Olney Division	18	43	73
Do O Ride	13	25	44
Newport Division*	29	83	107
Do 1st O Ride	26	53	79
Do 2d O Ride	20	38	41

*Philip Thompson at the Saracen's Head, one of ye principal Inns in Newport Dn. refuses to give an Account of his Beds or Stable Room.

Aylesbury 1st Division	14	55	126
Do 2nd Division	17	38	37
Do 1st O Ride	7	11	32
Do 2nd O Ride	12	12	25
Do 3rd O Ride	12	23	83
Risboro' Division	13	16	30
Wendover Division	17	36	71
Do O Ride	3	19	25
Amersham Dn	20	44	71
Chesham Dn		60	110
Tring Division	17	37	105

THE ARMY AND THE PUBLIC

Do O Ride	5	6	7
Berkhamsted Dn		40	46

Leighton District

Fenny Stratford Dn	29	66	79
Do O Ride	37	54	55
Leighton Division	29	107	325
Do O Ride	27	8	10
Ivinghoe Divn.	22	28	57
Dunstable Division		97	110
Do O Ride		10	30
Toddington Dn	22	99	186
Ampthill Dn		50	100
Do O Ride		20	24
Wobourn Divisn		75	179
D.O. Ride	13	19	39
Total	538	1654	3153

W.O. 30/49, f.8

141

William Murray to Barrington

[Holograph]   N.p.
13 October 1756

I have this Morning heard by Accident that Cases are laid before
Council for Opinion as to billeting the Hanoverian Soldiers in
Kent. The Inn Keepers are determined to resist & to bring
Actions. I give you this Hint by way of Caution, that you may have
the thing very deliberately & Ministerially considered. Talk with
the Speaker as from yr self. It is certain that these Soldiers cannot
be within the other parts of the Mutiny Bill. If they cannot be
billeted, unless You find Barracks in time It is impossible for them
to stay. The present Temper & Disposition makes evry Caution
necessary. I knew the Fact to be true as to the Cases laid for
opinion.

Ipswich 3a, no. 61

225

142

J. Knowles: Statement of Case

[Holograph]   N.p.
                                              13 October 1756

The Hanoverian Troops now encamped at Cocksheath are very soon to remove into Winter Quarters The Mayor and Constable of Maidstone have been called upon to provide Billets for some Hundreds of them at Maidstone in the same manner his Majesties British Forces are Quartered under the Mutiny Act Several of the Alehouse Keepers (Apprehending that the Mutiny Act does not empower the Mayor or Constable to Billet those foreign Troops in the same Manner as our own) declare that they will not Receive them and threaten to Commence Actions against the Mayor and Constable in Case they take upon them to send Billets as for our own Soldiers The Mayor and Constable are ready and willing to Billet the said Foreign Troops if they can Legally and safely Do it and to lend All the Assistance in their Power towards providing proper Quarters for them therefore

Q. . . . Whether the Mayor or Constable by virtue of the Mutiny Act or otherwise are empowered to Billet those Foreign Troops in Inns Alehouses &c in the same manner the British forces are Billetted; Will they be liable to any Action for so doing? in what manner can they compel the Alehouse keepers &c to receive them and upon the whole in what manner is it most Advisable for them to act on this Occasion. Upon reading the Act for punishing Mutiny and desertion and considering the Law as it stood before the making that Act it seems to me the Mayor and Constable of Maidstone have no Authority to Billet foreign Forces in Inns Alehouses &c in the same manner the National Forces are Billetted for the subject of the Act is his Majesties Forces, and no forces can with propriety in my apprehension be deemed his Majesties Forces but such Forces as are Commissioned by his Majesty as King of Great Britain but the foreign Forces now in England are rendered incapable of every Military Commission from the Crown of Great Britain by the Act of Settlement and therefore can be considered only as Auxiliaries or Mercenaries for the billetting of which there is no provision in the Act and as I think the Act does not extend to foreign Forces the Mayor and Constable cannot Billet them without being Liable to an Action for so doing neither do I know of any compulsory means which can be used to compell the Innkeepers and Alehouse keepers to receive them. I should think it most Adviseable for the Mayor and Constable to endeavour to prevail on ye persons who are liable to have Soldiers billetted on them to receive them into their Houses upon the Terms they received them before rather than to take rigorous Measures lest the Publick Service should suffer.

Ipswich 3a, no. 59

143

Thomas Sherwin to George Stone
(Innkeeper of Cobham, Surrey)

[Copy]   War Office
                                                  18 November 1756

I am directed by the Secry at War to acquaint you that a Warrant is obtained for Forty Seven pounds to make good the loss you Sustained by having your apartment blown up by the Light Dragoon, which you may receive by applying at this Office.

W.O. 4/52, p. 403

144

H.B. Legge to Barrington

[Holograph]   Holt Forest
                                                  1 September 1758

My dear Lord
    I have a complaint to make to you as Secretary at War in which your speedy & effectual interposition will give great pleasure as

well as be of signal Service to yr. humble servant, & save me the trouble of civil Process against the Offenders. One John Mills, a recruiting Serjeant in General Bockland's Regimt attended by his Drum, whose name I don't know has of late frequented this Country & been quartered at an Inn upon Bentley Green within less than two miles of me & very near a trout stream the Royalty of which is mine as Lord of the Manor.

Two or three days ago He and his Drum betook themselves to fishing & with so good success that they presently caught 3½ brace of fine trouts besides other fish. Upon returning to his Inn, where they were dress'd, he was told by the people of the House that the stream belong'd to me & that I did not suffer anybody to poach it &c &c. To all which he reply'd, with the military grace of a round oath that he was the King's Servant & I was no more & that he would go a fishing & sporting wherever he pleas'd for all me. That he was to go away yesterday (which he has done accordingly) but should return again very soon with Recruits & liked the sport so well that he should certainly repeat it as often as he came into this Country. Now tho' it is a very proper thing to want raw Recruits well flesh'd I don't conceive it will answer any good military purpose to have them well fish'd, & therefore must beg the favour of You that Mr. Mills & his Drum may be made sensible that they have clearly exceeded the bounds of their Duty & that it will be still much worse for them if they persist in their sportly intentions. If an Affidavit of the fact be requisite I will send you one in due form upon the first notice, or if you should think it proper that I wrote to General Bockland who is my old acquaintance, I will do it as soon as I know where he is to be found.

* * *

Ipswich 112, no. 83

145

Barrington to Lt. Sharpe of Lord George Beauclerk's Regiment
(at Gainsborough, Lincs.)

[Copy]
War Office
21 January 1756

I have your letter of 17th together with one of the same date from Chancellor Reynolds concerning the Inlisting Joseph Roberts at Gainsborough, and cannot but observe that your Serjeants giving Roberts a Shilling more than his Change in order to Inlist him (which I do not find is contradicted by anybody) was an unfair way of proceeding and he having accepted the Twenty Shillings Smart Money which Roberts immediately threw down; I am to desire you will give no further molestation to the said Roberts, as it may greatly hurt the Service.

W.O. 4/51, p. 145

146

Barrington to Colonel Fletcher of the 35th Regiment

[Copy]
War Office
11 July 1766

I have the honor to send you enclosed a Copy of a Letter I have received from Lord Strange Colonel of the Lancashire Militia, together wt. Copy of a Beating Order produced by a Serjeant of your Regt., recruiting near the place of Exercise of the said Militia, and am to desire you will make Enquiry into this Matter, and give such Orders as you may judge necessary to prevent these irregularities for the future; and that you will be pleased to make a proper Example of Serjeant Surman for presuming to alter the date of H. M's. Order for Recruiting.

W.O. 4/80, p. 67

147

Lord Strange to Barrington, enclosed with Document 146

[Copy]   Aughton Camp near Ormskirk
                                                        4 July 1766

I am sorry to be obliged to trouble you with a Complaint, but some Recruiting Parties having made unfair Attempts to trepan some of Our Men even in the Camp, I called to one of the Serjeants for his Beating Order which he produced, and a manifest Forgery appearing upon the face of it, I thought it my duty to transmit it to your Lordship, who will I doubt not do yours. You will be pleased to observe that the Forgery is in the Date which has been altered to 1766, and the figure for the year of H.M's. Reign, is also changed into a 6. As the Order is countersigned by Mr. Ellis who was not Secretary at War in May last, the Fraud is apparent. The Serjeant's Name is Thomas Surman, and he says he belongs to the 35th Regt., and had no other Beating Order but the enclosed. I need not take Notice to your Lordship of the Dangers that may arise from such practices, especially where the Instrument carries H.M's. Sign Manual.

As the Clause relative to Recruiting was put into the last Pay Bill to prevent the Officers of the Army being cheated by enlisting Militia Men unknowingly; I hope the War Office will not suffer it to be made Use of to enable them to enlist such Persons as they must know are in the Militia by seeing them in their Regimentals, and performing their Duty at the place appointed for annual Exercise.

* * *

The time of Exercise will expire to Morrow Se'en-night when I shall go to Knowsley.

W.O. 4/80, pp. 68–69

148

Barrington to officer commanding troops at Chatham Barracks

[Copy]   War Office
                                          21 January 1777

It having been represented that John Milward, a private Man with the Party of the 44th Regiment of Foot under your Command, in Chatham Barracks, is the Apprentice of Mr. Dring of Birmingham, Bridle Cutter, I am to desire you will be pleased to discharge this Man, his Indentures having been produced at this Office.

W.O. 4/99, p. 51

149

Barrington to Colonel Montague (at Leicester)

[Copy]   War Office
                                          14 April 1756

I have your favour of the 12th relating to the two Apprentices in your Regiment being demanded by their Masters, and desiring to know how to act in this Affair; I am thereupon to Acquaint you, that if upon Strict Examination, you find the Men to be regularly indented, and not out of their Time, You do Acquiesce; Acquainting, at the same time, the Young Men, that when their respective Apprenticeships are Expired they are to join the Regiment, or they will be proceeded against as deserters.

W.O. 4/51, p. 38

150

Barrington to Maj.-General the Earl of Home

[Copy]   War Office
                                              28 September 1756

I have had the Honour to lay before the Duke several Letters from
your Lordship, and the Magistrates of Plymouth relating to a
Dispute about Patroles Ordered by You in the Night time, and am
to intimate to your Lordship that your Order for Patrolling to
prevent Desertion, and the escape of French Prisoners, a great
number of whom you represent to be at large in that Town, is very
proper, but I wish it had been done with the Knowledge and
Approbation of the Magistrates as it was within their jurisdiction,
and that your Lordship had left out of the said Order what relates
to stopping or taking up the Inhabitants, which gives the Corporation Offence, and makes them apprehend that the Liberties of
the Town, and Jurisdiction of the Civil Magistrates in particular,
are Invaded.

I shall transmit that part of your Lordships Letter relating to a
Number of French Prisoners being at large in the Town of
Plymouth to the Lords Commissioners of the Admiralty, that
their Lordships may give the proper Directions thereon.

Your Lordship for the future will please to confine your Orders
to the Forces under your Command, & the Prisoners of War,
unless the Civil Magistrates shou'd require the Assistance of the
Military Power.

I need not hint to you how fatal any Want of Concert with the
Magistrates, or Misunderstandings between the King's Officers,
military and Civil must be, particularly at this juncture, & I beg
leave to repeat what I mentioned in a former Letter, that from the
Nature of Our Constitution the Civil Power will always in
Disputes (unless on very extraordinary Occasions) have the
Advantage of the Military.

I have strongly recommended to the Magistrates an amicable
Correspondence with your Lordship, of whose Zeal for the
King's Service they can have no doubt, and whose Person they

must respect. I flatter myself there will be the utmost Cordiality for the future at Plymouth among all those who are intrusted with the Preservation of the public tranquillity.

W.O. 4/52, pp. 265–266

151

Barrington to William Beckford, Lord Mayor of London

[Copy]   War Office
                                                19 December 1769

I received your Lordship's Letter of yesterday, informing me that on Saturday last, a relieved Detachment of Soldiers from Spital-Fields, without any previous Notice given to You, marched, on their Return, before the Mansion House, and through the Heart of the City, with Drums beating and Fifes playing.

Your Lordship desires I will inform you, whether this was occasioned by me, or the Order of any Commissioned Officer. The Detachment from the Foot Guards, relieved every twenty four Hours, which has for some Time past done Duty in Spital-Fields, at the Requisition of the worthy Magistrates acting there, in order to secure the Public Peace, went by Order from hence; but no particular Directions were given as to the Manner in which they should march, which was left, as usual, to the Discretion of the Commanding Officer.

I am very clear in Opinion, that no Troops should march through the City of London in the Manner described by your Lordship (though I find, on enquiry, it is sometimes done) without previous Notice given to the Lord Mayor; and I shall take care that the Officer who commands the Detachment which returned from Spital-Fields last Saturday, shall know my opinion. I will also take such Measures as shall, I trust, for the future, prevent any just Offence being given to the City or its Chief Magistrate.

W.O. 4/86, p. 151

152

Barrington to Lord Chief Justice Mansfield

[Copy] War Office
21 September 1769

Having heard accidentally that Major General Gansel was this day rescued out of the Hands of the Sheriff's Officers by a Party of the Guards, I immediately sent for Captain Garth who was on Duty; & enquired what had happened. He acquainted me that he was not on the Spot at that Instant, but that he believed the Fact was true as represented to Me, and that Serjeant Bacon of the 1st. Regiment was the Commanding Officer present. I have ordered that the said Serjeant shall be secured so as to be forthcoming, to answer any civil Process which shall commence against him.

I thank God there never was an Instance before of the Law being resisted by the Soldiery. I trust it will never happen again. I am without Precedent for my Conduct but I think I cannot do wrong in acquainting the Chief Justice of England that the Person who appears chiefly responsible for this atrocious Act is in safe Custody, to abide the Judgement of the Courts of Justice.

W.O. 4/85, p. 492

153

Barrington to Maj.-General Clavering, Maj.-General Cary and Maj.-General Carpenter

[Copy] War Office
3 March 1770

In the Month of September last, Major Genl. Gansell, who had been arrested by the Officers of the Sheriff of London and Middlesex, was rescued by some Soldiers on duty at the Tilt Yard Guard, who together with a Serjeant then present, were taken into Custody. The Sheriffs were by me acquainted with this Event, and the prisoners delivered over to the Civil Power, but discharged after Examination before a Magistrate. An Indictment was however brought against Major General Gansel, Captain Dodd, & a Serjeant of the Coldstream Regiment of Guards; —neither of the two last on duty that day. I am informed these prosecutions have been ended without any Trial, by which it might appear how the Defendants had conducted themselves in this Business.

While Civil Process was going on, any Military Enquiry would have been highly improper, but that being over without any decision, it is expedient the King should be fully informed how any Person (particularly an Officer of Rank in his Service) comes to be rescued out of the hands of Justice, upon the Public Parade, in broad day. I am therefore to signify to you His Majesty's Commands that you do fully enquire into the whole of this Matter, and report to me the Result of your Examination, that I may receive His Majesty's farther pleasure thereupon.

I send you herewith a Copy of the Report of the Officer who had the Command of the Tilt Yard Guard at the Time in Question; to which I need only add that John Smith Esquire of Austin Friars, one of the under Sherriffs of London and Middlesex, together with the Bailiffs who arrested Major General Gansel, and whom Mr. Smith will point out to you, will probably be able to furnish you with farther Information. I also presume the Examination taken by Sir John Fielding may be of some use to you.

W.O. 4/86, pp. 327–328

154

Barrington to field officer in staff waiting for the three Regiments of Foot Guards

[Copy]   War Office
                                                    18 April 1770

I need not inform you that Major General Gansel was rescued by Soldiers in the Month of September last on the Parade, from some Sheriffs Officers who had arrested him: The Transaction was publick, and justly occasioned much Scandal.

As the Major General and others were prosecuted by the Sheriffs, it was improper to begin any military Enquiry while the Civil Process was going on. It ended in the Month of February last, in a way that threw no light on the Transaction, and therefore a military Enquiry became expedient. Major Generals Clavering, Cary, & Carpenter were appointed by the King for that Purpose, and they lately made their Report to His Majesty, by what it appears clearly that Major General Gansel was rescued by Soldiers on Duty, and particularly by Serjeant Bacon, Joseph Powell, William Hart, James Potter, and Joseph Collins of the First Regt. of Guards. The Generals in their Report, while they condemn the violent Part taken by these Military Men, in Contempt of Civil Authority, are of Opinion they were induced to it by Compassion for a General Officer who had long served in the Guards who had thrown himself on their Protection, and who professed he was in Danger of being murdered. There appears no Proof that the Soldiers knew at first the General was in the Hands of Bailiffs, and when they did know it, they conceived he had been arrested in the Park. Captain Dodd an Officer in the same Regt. (tho' not on Duty that Day) going accidentally by, and alarmed by the Cries of Murder from the Midst of the Crowd, called out the Guards to give assistance. These Circumstances in the Opinion of the three Major Generals tend much to extenuate the Guilt of the Soldiers, and likewise induce the King to hope they were not intentionally Perpetrators of this atrocious Offence. However it is His Majesty's Pleasure that you reprimand them severely; as likewise Serjeant Parker of the Coldstream, who, tho' not on Duty that Day, had too great a Share in this Business.

The King is willing to believe that Captain Dodd at first knew nothing of the Arrest, and that he ordered the Soldiers back into the Guard Room the Moment he heard of it; Circumstances which he positively avers, and which no Evidence contradicts; but His Majesty expects you will make him sensible how improper and unmilitary it was for him to give Orders to the Guard, without the Knowledge of the Officer who commanded it.

The Generals farther Report that Captain Garth who commanded the Tilt Yard Guard that Day, acknowledges that he was near, heard a Noise, saw a Mob, and in it one or two Soldiers with

Arms, enquired the Occasion, was told it arose from General Gansel's being arrested, and yet did not interfere. The Generals do by no means approve Capt. Garth's Excuse, viz. that he was not to stir in such a Case without the Requisition of a Civil Magistrate; but they do not suppose it possible he could be privy to the Assistance his Guard gave on this Occasion.

The King not less inclinable than his Generals to judge favourably of Captain Garth's Motives, agrees with them in censuring his Remissness: His Majesty directs you to reprimand him for suffering any of his Men to take Part in a Riot, especially so near his Guard Room.

This very atrocious Transaction has given the King much Concern. It is the first of the kind, and with a View that it may be the last, His Majesty directs that you do inform the Non-Commissioned Officers and Private Men of the three Regts. of Guards, in the way that will make it most clearly & universally known, that they must never presume to interfere with Bailiffs or Arrests, on any Account or Pretence whatsoever.

I am commanded to send you herewith a Copy of a Letter, which I have wrote by the King's Order, to Major General Gansel; that the Guards who are well informed of his Conduct on this Matter may be likewise acquainted with His Majesty's thorough Disapprobation of it.

W.O. 4/86, pp. 482–484

155

Barrington to Maj.-General Gansell

[Copy]   War Office
                                                  18 April 1770

I have laid before the King the Report of Major Generals Clavering, Cary and Carpenter, made in Consequence of His Majesty's Command, directing them to enquire how you came to be rescued in September last, on the Parade, and by Military Men, from the Officers of the Sheriffs of London & Middlesex.

It clearly appears by this Report that you solicited, first Serjeant Parkes of the Coldstream, & afterwards the Soldiers on Duty, to deliver you from the Consequences of your Arrest.

The King is equally surprized, concerned, & displeased, that a Major General in His Service, should in so material a Circumstance act directly contrary to his Duty, both as an Officer & a Subject.

It is of no Consequence how or where you were arrested: If you were injured the Courts of Justice were open, and the Laws were your Defence. To these you should have appealed, and not attempted to right yourself by Violence.

Your Misconduct is highly aggravated by seducing Soldiers (some of them on Duty) to be your Accomplices: Soldiers, who in this free and well governed Country, are never to interfere with Civil Transactions, except in Cases of Necessity at the Requisition of the Civil Magistrate. If on any Occasion they attempt to do otherwise, their Officers should strenuously endeavour to restrain them: But these Men were innocent till your Solicitation made them criminals. Such a Conduct is the more unjustifiable in you, Sir, because being a Gentleman by Descent and possessing Lands by Inheritance (Circumstances which in a Country like this render you the more proper for military Rank & Command) the sacred Rights of Magistracy & of Property should in a peculiar Manner be present to your Mind.

If the King only considered what strict Justice suggests on this Subject, he would immediately dismiss you from his Service: But recollecting how long you have been in the Army, & without Reproach, he is unwilling that the Misconduct of a Moment, on a sudden Occasion, should deprive you of what was earned by many years good Behaviour. His Majesty has therefore recommended me to write you this Letter of severe Reprehension in his Name. He expects that following his Example, you make the Laws of the Land the Rule of your Actions; and trusts that His Royal Lenity at this Time will have the proper Effect on your future Conduct.

W.O. 4/86, pp. 485–486

156

Barrington to Lt.–Colonel Harvey of the Inniskilling Dragoons

[Copy]   War Office
                                                        24 August 1756

Mr Wright Recorder of Leicester having transmitted to Mr. Fox One of His Majesty's Secretaries of State an Affidavit made before him on the 19th. instant, Setting forth that a Number of near Three Hundred Persons had Assembled and done great Mischief in pulling down Meeting Houses, Destroying Stacks of Corn, Water Mills and other Outrages at several Places in the Counties of Warwick and Leicester, and that they intended to proceed to Leicester: and the said Recorder Expressing his Apprehensions of the Consequences which might happen unless timely prevented; It is therefore His Majesty's Pleasure that you cause Three of the Six Troops of Lieut. General Cholmondeley's Regiment, to March under your Command with all possible Expedition to Leicester, or to any other Place or Places, as you shall be informed the Rioters may be at, or should the said Rioters disperse themselves into Parties, You make such Detachments as you shall think proper and be Aiding and Assisting to the Civil Magistrates in Suppressing any Riots and Disturbances that may happen, and in apprehending the said Rioters; for which purpose It is His Majesty's further Pleasure that the said Troops shall be Quartered in such Place or Places as you shall think convenient from time to time for the more Effectually Answering the Purposes aforesaid; But not to repell Force with Force, unless in case of Necessity, or being thereunto required by the Civil Magistrates, Wherein the Civil Magistrates and all Others Concerned are to be Assisting in providing Quarters, Impressing Carriages and otherwise as there shall be Occasion. Given at the War Office this 24th day of August 1766.

By His Majesty's Command
Barrington

Ipswich 3a, no. 69

157

Lord Holdernesse to Barrington

[In Clerk's hand, signed by Holdernesse]

Whitehall
26 August 1756

I herewith send your Lordship a Copy of a Letter I have received from The Mayor and Aldermen of the Town of Nottingham, giving an Account of a Tumult that has happen'd there, and which seems to be too great to be suppress'd by the Civil Magistrate; And, having laid the said Letter before the The King, His Majesty has commanded me to signify to your Lordship His Pleasure, That you should, immediately, send Orders for such a Number of His Forces as may be sufficient for that Purpose, and are nearest at Hand, to march to Nottingham, and assist, as far as They may, according to Law, in putting an effectual Stop to the Disorder abovementioned, and in Preserving the Publick Peace; and your Lordship will, upon this Occasion send Instructions to the Officers who command those Troops to Act according to the Directions they shall receive from the Magistrates of Nottingham.

Ipswich 3a, no. 71

158

Samuel Fellows (Mayor), John Burton and H. Butler (Aldermen) to Holdernesse

[Copy]

Nottingham
25 August 1756

We the Subscribers being His Majesty's Justices of the Peace for the Town of Nottingham, think it Our Duty to signify to your Lordship, that about 9 o'Clock this morning, a great Number of Colliers & other Persons, entered this Town armed with Stakes Hatchets & Pix-Axes shouting and making a great Noise, upon which the Proclamation against Rioters was read, & three Persons were seized & carried into the Guild Hall, to witt Thomas Johnson & William Johnson of Cossall, and William Waplington of Frowel, all in Nottinghamshire, being three of the Colliers employed to work Lord Middleton's Coalpits at Woolaton in the County of Nottingham. Before any Examination could be taken, the Mob encreased to a very large Number, demanding to have these men released, & beginning to grow desperate, several of the Foremost were admitted to a Conference, & promised to quit the Town, & go Home quietly, if the Three Men might be set at Liberty. And as no real Mischief was then done, & finding that the Men would be rescued, & that probably the Town Hall would be pulled down over Our Heads, We set the Men at Liberty, & the Mob was actualy about to leave the Town, but a Number of Women, (of this Town as 'tis supposed) gave them Mony to come back, & shewed them to a Windmill within Our Limits, belonging to One Mr. Foulds, having French Stones, these Mill-Stones they demolished, & did other Damage to the Mill, & soon after the same Mob, demolished the French Stones, & did other Damage to a Waterborn Mill in this Town, & they are going on still doing Damage to the Corn Mills in the Neighbourhood, & Nobody knows when or where they will stop, they are a powerfull Body, & seem to have been set on by Persons that don't appear with them, & We give it as Our humble Opinion, that if they are suffered to get a Head for any Time, & they are already superior to the civil Power, it will not be very easy for the Military Power to subdue them.

Ipswich 3a, no. 70

159

Barrington to the Duke of Cumberland

[Copy]   Cavendish Square
                                                      27 August 1756

Late last night I received from Lord Holdernesse the papers which I have the Honour to transmit herewith to your R.H. and early this Morning I went to Kensington to receive your Commands upon the Subject of them. Finding your R.H. gone to Windsor I thought it best to lose no time in sending an order by Express to Colo. Hervey which will overtake him by the time he gets to Northampton so the order of yesterday will occasion no delay. I venture to trouble you with a Copy of my order grounded on Lord Holdernesse's Letter in which your R.H. will please to observe the latter part which I thought necessary to add because it is not improbable the Rioters may have left Notingham before the Troops arrive there, and perhaps be at Leicester while they are passing.

I humbly hope the steps I have taken are such as your R.H. does not disapprove and I wait your farther Pleasure.

Ipswich 3a, no. 72

160

Barrington to Lt.-Colonel Harvey

[Copy]   War Office
27 August 1756

It is His Majesty's Pleasure, that, former orders to the Contrary notwithstanding, you do cause the Three Troops of Lieu. Genl. Cholmondeley's Regiment now with you and under your Command to March with all possible Expedition to Notingham, there to be aiding and assisting to the Civil Magistrates in suppressing any Riots or disturbances which may happen and in apprehending the Rioters and preserving the Public Peace But not to Repel Force with Force until in case of absolute necessity or being thereupon required by the Civil Magistrates. If in your March thither, or after your arrival there you shall find that the Rioters have removed to any other place or places, in such Case It is His Majesty's further Pleasure that you follow the directions of the order dated the 24th. Instant. Wherein &c

Ipswich 3a, no. 72

161

Barrington to Sir John Willes, Lord Chief Justice

[Rough draft in Barrington's hand: crossings-out omitted]

Cavendish Square
27 August 1756

The Duke of Newcastle having done me the honour to shew me your Lordships Letter and his answer to it, I beg leave in addition to inform you more precisely of the Orders under which Col. Hervey (who commands the three troops of Dragoons order'd to Notingham) now acts.

He is directed to march thither in consequence of the requisition made by the Magistrates of that place and to assist them in preserving the publick Peace: but in case after his arrival there or during his March thither he shall find that the rioters (who are of a very ambulatory Nature) shall have removed to any other place or shall have dispersed themselves into Parties he is to make such Detachments as he shall think proper & to be aiding and assisting to the civil Magistrates in suppressing any Riots and disturbances which may happen & in apprehending the Rioters; with the usual direction not to repell force by force unless in case of Necessity or being thereunto required by the civil Magistrate.

I thought it right to give a certain degree of Latitude as to the places where the troops shd. be disposed in order to their being at hand when their assistance shall be necessary; but as this matter is left to the direction of Col. Hervey (who is very much a man of Sense) the least hint of advice from your Lordship will keep him from or bring him to any place where you think either his absence or his presence expedient.

Besides acquainting your Lordship with these particulars from which you may possibly receive assistance and information I have a farther view personally to my self, depending on your free Sentiments with relation to my orders in case you shall find any occasion for an addition to or alteration of them.

I cannot conclude without returning my grateful acknowledgements to your Lordship as Ld. Barrington for the spirited manner in which you have enforced the civil authority, and as Secretary at War, for having discouraged the unnecessary requisition of Troops the sending of which on these Services is the most disagreeable part of my office.

Ipswich 3a, no. 74

162

Sir John Willes to Barrington

[Holograph] Astrop
29 August 1756

I had ye Favour of yr Lordship's Letter of ye 27th, and am glad yt you think yt I have acted right, and It has had ye Desired Effect, for ye Rioters in Warwickshire are all dispersed, and the County is now in Perfect Peace & Quiet.

I am sorry yt ye Magistrates in Nottingham have thought it necessary to send for ye assistance of a military force; For I am satisfyed yt if they would have done their Duty with that Resolution that they ought, This application would have been unnecessary. I doubt not but yt the Civil Magistrates are most of them well affected, & thoroughly attached to his present Majesty; but I wish tht I coud inspire a little more Courage into them. as they applyed for Soldiers, To be sure it was very right to send some to them immediatly, and the orders which yr Lordship has given them, are very Prudent & proper, & to which I can add nothing, But my hearty Wishes yt there may be no Bloodshed, ffor it makes more noise in the Country, to have one Man killed by Soldiers, than to have ten hanged, that are tryed by a Judge & a Jury.

I am heartily glad yt ye Conduct of this affair is intrusted to a Man of such Good Sense as Colonel Harvey, and doubt not but yt he will act both with Discretion & Courage.

To be sure, This is a very Critical Juncture, and it is absolutely necessary for ye ffriends of ye Government to act with Great Prudence as well as Great Resolution.

I shall be always glad, & think my self sufficiently rewarded, If my poor Services, can any wayes contribute to promote his Majestie's Interest, & to preserve the Peace of this Country.

Ipswich 3a, no. 75

163

Barrington to Lt.-Colonel Harvey (at Nottingham)

[Copy]   War Office
                                                    4 September 1756

The Duke being desirous to prevent any future Riots, and that the Troops may be at hand to assist the Civil Magistrates, His Royal Highness has been pleased to order a Squadron of the Earl of Albemarle's Regiment of Dragoons from Henley to Coventry; and another Squadron of that Regiment from Reading to North-ampton with the same powers and directions as were given to Major Hepburne, a Copy of which I enclosed to you in my letter of the 31st of last month. Major Hepburne is directed to march with his Three Troops on the arrival of Lord Albermarle's from Coventry* to Derby there to follow the directions of the before mentioned order of the 31st of last Month.

I have the honour of your Letters, and it gives me great pleasure to acquaint you that your Conduct & proceedings are much approved of.

P.S. *Or from Northampton on the arrival of the Squadron of the Earl of Albemarle's Regt. (should the Major not be removed from thence to Coventry) in both which cases Major Hepburne is directed to follow your orders.

Ipswich 3a, no. 77

164

Lt.-Colonel Harvey to Barrington

[Holograph]   Nottingham
                                    7 September 1756

I am sorry to trouble your Lordship so often, but take the Liberty
of Informing you what Happen'd yesterday. In several Places
about four miles from the Town the Colliers assembled in party's,
and came toward the Town about twelve o'clock.

By the Magistrates request I had the Troops under arms. from
that time to about five they kept att a distance, but then in a body
came within a quarter of a mile of the Town. The number I think
by their appearance under two Hundred; Severall of them armed
with Scythes, Pitchforks, Pickaxes, &c: They Halted there and
stayd sometime. Their cry was that they wou'd Immediately come
to the Jail and Either Rescue the Prisoners or die. After they had
been there a little while, I Rode towards them, leaving the Troops
in the market place, and sent that I Desired they wou'd let me
speak with them. They agreed and on my coming to them and
asking what their Intentions were, they all said to have their
Comrades or die.

One of their chiefs proclaimed Silence, and we had a long
Parley. I declared to them my positive orders from the Magistrates to fire on them, and Endeavoured by persuasion to disperse
them, or otherwise on the Instant of any numbers Entring the
Town to forward their attempt, a fire would Ensue. Reason had
no Effect and the chief orator declared as their finall resolution
that they wou'd either succeed in the attempt or die. They lett me
argue with them very quietly, but finding I cou'd do no good by
words, I returned to my party.

I Imagined they Expected to have been joined by the mob of the
Town. To prevent their Intentions I Had my men near the Jail all
night; They thought better of it, and attempted nothing. They are
now about their Colliery's.

The Populace Encourages me much, I can't say that It appears
to me that the Gentlemen of the Country in the Commission of

246

peace assemble to consider of means to prevent these Riots, the Colliers within twelve miles of this Town very numerous, The whole poor people Enraged by the dearness of Corn, all these things together rather persuade me that their Rashness will not be stopped as to attempting the Jail till force is used against them. We are obliged constantly to be under arms, as in two hours time they may collect Near three Hundred & come into the Town. By the Detachments That the Duke of Devonshire, the Mayor of Derby, and other Justices here Required I Have Sixty men in this Town. On the Majors coming to Derby I shall have Sufficient for the Troops sometimes to be relieved, which for three days & nights has not Happ'ned.

These alarms here and att Derby are likely to continue, and I Hear the Magistrates have Intentions of applying for an Immediate Example on some of the Prisoners now in custody.

If they lye till the next assizes I think I can foresee that some mischief must Ensue, as they are not properly checked from their Intentions of Rescuing.

I beg pardon for troubling your Lordship so long.

* * *

I have Inclosed to your Lordship
a copy of my Directions from the
Magistrates By which you'll see they are a good deal alarmed.

Ipswich 3a, no. 79

165

Barrington to the Rev. Dr Parry J.P.
(of Market Harborough, Leics.)

[Copy]   War Office
                                              17 February 1773

I am to acknowledge the rect. of your letter of the 11th. instant. In a Matter of so much Importance as the question stated by you, I have always thought it my Duty to follow the constant practice of my predecessors in Office. Whenever disturbances have happened, and the Magistrates have found Military Aid absolutely necessary, it has been usual to state this to the Secretary at War, applying for the assistance of a Military force, which is generally complyed with. When Orders are issued for any Part of the Troops to be aiding upon Requisition made by the Civil Magistrate, it had been thought proper to remind the Magistrates of not calling upon H.M. Forces for their Aid till every effort of the Civil Authority had been exerted, and found ineffectual. The Military on their part have seldom judged themselves authorized, without Orders from hence, to march out of their Quarters upon the Requisition of the Magistrate. Your Opinion may probably be well founded as to the Right the Magistrates has to call upon every individual for his Assistance in preserving the Peace, but I am rather inclined to think that the mode now in use tends as much to the secure guidance of the Magistrate as of the Military, who must at all times be under strict government, so essential to the being of an army in this country.

W.O. 4/90, pp. 402–403

166

Barrington to Lord Burgersh

[Copy]   War Office
25 January 1765 [sic, in fact 1766]

I have the Honor of your Lordship's Letter of the 24th instant, inclosing two Papers, relative to Disturbances apprehended by the Inhabitants of Lynne, which I have carefully considered; and, in Answer to the Application made by the Inhabitants for two companies of Foot, must beg Leave to inform your Lordship, that I have always considered the Interposition of a Military Force as a Resource only to be made use of in the last Extremity, when the Civil Magistrate has already exerted the utmost Authority of the Law, and of that Force, with which the Law has intrusted him. Your Lordship will easily perceive how inconsistent it would be with this Principle, for me to order the March of Troops upon the bare Apprehension of Dangers, which may never exist, and that too upon Informations which, I confess, appear to me to be very uncertain. I should be very happy in obliging your Lordship, and Mr. Fane, but cannot think I should be justified, in the present Case, if I complied with the Request of the Inhabitants of Lynne, without a Certainty that some Acts of Violence, such as are expected, have been committed, or some more authentick Evidence of their being really intended.

W.O. 4/78, p. 337

167

Barrington to Lt.-Colonel Warde of the 4th Dragoons [at Manchester]

[Copy in clerks hand]   Cavendish Square
(Private)   22 January 1766

The present State of Things makes it apprehended that many Manufacturers must soon be discharged in many Parts of the Kingdom. Poor Men out of Employment especially when they are in large Numbers, generally grow riotous, and too often are above the Management of the Civil Magistrate, unassisted by Military Force. The safe & usual Method of the War Office has been to defer any Orders till Application should be made to it, in form, but there are Occasions when Men in Public Employment should venture for the Public Good, & prevent Delays when Delays might be dangerous.

I have therefore unasked, but not uninformed of the present State of your Neighbourhood, sent you an Order herewith enclosed, which I desire you will keep entirely to yourself, till the Civil Magistrate shall apply to you for Assistance. If that never happens, the Order had better never be known, & therefore it is not yet entered in my Books, or communicated to more than one or two in my Office.

I trust safely to your good Sense and Discretion.
[Also sent to officers commanding troops of 1st Dragoons Guards (York), 1st Dragoons (Wells), 2nd Dragoons (Lichfield and

Bromsgrove), 3rd Dragoons (Warwick), 4th Dragoons (Warrington), 10th Dragoons (Leicester), and companies of 4th Foot (Tiverton and Exeter), and of 23rd Foot (Gloucester)].

W.O. 40/17 [unnumbered]

168

Secret orders, enclosed with Document 167

[Copy in clerk's hand]   War Office
                                                        22 January 1766

It is His Majesty's Pleasure, that in case of any Riots or Disturbances that may happen at or in the Neighbourhood of your Quarters, upon Application being made to you by the Civil Magistrates there, or in the Neighbourhood thereof, you cause such Detachments as may be judged necessary to be made from the Troops of the 4th: Regimt. of Dragoons under your Command at Manchester and march from their present Quarters, acquainting this Office with the Receipt of this Order, to such Place or Places as may be judged most expedient, where they are to be quartered, & be aiding & assisting to the Civil Magistrates at their Requisition, in quelling any Riots or Disturbances that may happen at the said Places or in the Neighbourhood thereof, in preserving the Public Peace & in securing the Offenders, but not to repell force with force unless in case of absolute Necessity, or being thereunto required by the Civil Magistrates. Wherein &c. Given at the War Office, 22:d January 1766.

By His Majesty's Command

                                                            Barrington

W.O. 40/17 [unnumbered]

169

Barrington to Lt.-Colonel Kellet of the Royal Regiment of Horse Guards (at York)

[Copy]   War Office
                                               24 September 1766

The present riotous Assemblings on Account of the high prices of corn and provisions in many parts of the Kingdom, having made it necessary for the Magistrates to call in a Military Force to their assistance, and there being Reason to apprehend that the same Disorders may continue and spread farther, I think it proper to send you enclosed an Order for aiding & assisting the Civil Magistrates in the Neighbourhood of your Quarters, in case they should have occasion upon any Riots or Disturbances to apply to you; and upon Receipt of this, you will be pleased to wait on the Magistrates of the Neighbourhood, and give them information of the Directions you have received for the more early prevention of these Disturbances.

I am persuaded there is no occasion for me to caution you to take great care that the Troops under your Command do not at all interfere in any of these things, but at the such times as they shall be required by the Civil Magistrates, who best will judge when they stand in need of Military Assistance.

[Same letter to officers commanding 2nd Dragoon Guards (Colchester), 3rd Dragoon Guards (Manchester), 1st Dragoons (Canterbury), 2nd Dragoons (Lewes), 3rd Dragoons (Blandford), 4th Dragoons (Worcester), 6th Dragoons (Coventry), 7th Dragoons (Northampton), 10th Dragoons (Leeds), 11th Dragoons (Stamford), 1st Light Dragoons (Bridgnorth), 2nd Light Dragoons (Epsom), 4th Foot (Plymouth), 13th Foot (Salisbury), 22nd Foot (Dover Castle), Companies of 23rd Foot (Carlisle, Whitehaven, Newcastle, Berwick), 43rd Foot (Winchester) and Troops at Chatham]·

W.O. 4/80, p. 319

170

Barrington to Lt.-Colonel Warde of the 4th Dragoons [at Winchester]

[Copy]   War Office
3 October 1766

The continued disturbances, which have happened in the Western Counties, having made it necessary to station a number of detachments both of Dragoons and Foot at different places in those Counties, it is thought highly expedient that they should all be under the Command of one Officer of Judgement & Experience; & I am to acquaint you that the King has appointed you to take the care of this Service. It is H.M.P. that you shou'd immediately repair to the Devizes, which is the most Centrical Place, with respect to the different Quarters of the Troops, as you will see by the disposition which I send you inclosed, & take upon you the Command of the Troops specified therein. You are at liberty to make any alteration that you shall judge necessary in the present disposition, for preserving the Public Peace & to remove yourself to any other Quarters as occasion may require.

You will be so good as to inform me from time to time, of any thing of consequence that may happen.

* * *

P.S.
It is unnecessary for me to add that the Troops are never to be employed but in the usual manner upon requisition made by the Civil Magistrates & for their Assistance.

W.O. 4/80, p. 384

171

Enclosure with Document 170

'Disposition of the Troops destined for the Western Counties that are to be under the Command of Lieut. Col. Warde'

	Troops
Albemarles Dragoons	2 Blandford
	2 Columpton Ottery St. Mary &c
	2 Frome
	Detachmt.—Marlborough
Rich's Dragoons	2 Gloucester
	1 Strode Hampton & Painswick
	2 Devizes
	1 Bradford
	Comps
Duke of Gloster's Foot	3 Salisbury—2 Devizes
	2 Troubridge 1 Calne
	1 Chippenham
Cary's	3 Marlborough
	2 Winchester
	2 Glocester

W.O. 4/80, p. 385

172

William Dallaway, High Sheriff of Gloucester
to Henry Seymour Conway

[Copy extract in hand of clerk in office of Secretary of State]

Brimscourt near Hampton
23 November 1766

After having depended upon the following Paragraph with which
your last Favor concluded, Vizt. 'I will not fail to represent to the
Secretary at War the necessity there is of letting the Dragoons
remain where they now are, and I can assure you that there has
not hitherto been any Intention to remove them'. and also one to
the same Purpose from Lord Barrington of a Prior Date; and after
having in consequence assured our Neighbouring Magistrates
that the Dragoons would not be removed from their present
Quarters 'till after the Assizes, nor then without their Consent &

Approbation. I was greatly surprized this Afternoon to receive a Letter from Col. Warde dated at Gloucester the present Instant which begins thus. 'I beg leave to inform you, that I have Orders to march Three Troops of the Regiment under my Command to Worcester, & to Quarter the other Three all in this Town.' There never has been any Objection to the Departure of one Squadron of the Dragoons out of the County, but the same Opinion still prevails, & the same Reasons still subsist for the necessity of the other Squadron remaining in it, & the Parties thereof to continue quartered in the Towns of this Neighbourhood. And I cannot help concluding that Magistrates & others who live here upon the Spot are the best Judges of the necessity, & are certainly more capable of Judging than those who live at a Distance, or who are now in Town, & may have given contrary Advice.

It is very disagreable to me to have a second Time an Occasion to mention a Circumstance of this Kind to you, nor if I did not apprehend a Necessity of their remaining I would not have troubled you with this but I can assure you, that if no other Consequence arises from their Departure, it will greatly abate the zeal for Publick Justice, which at this time is required to prevent future Insurrections.

W.O. 1/873, no. 497

173

Barrington to Earl of Suffolk

[Copy]   Cavendish Square
                                             1 October 1766

I have heard a great deal too much of the Riots in your Lops neighbourhood, as well as many other places; but I am particularly concern'd to find that they are got so near to your residence. I would immediately send Troops to your assistance if every spare Soldier in the Kingdom were not already so dispos'd of at the requisition of the Civil Magistrate that there is not a Troop or

Company which can be employ'd without endangering the public tranquillity in others. In this very disagreeable & helpless situation I can only acquaint your Lop that there are 2 Troops of Dragoons at Bradford, 2 Companies of foot at Devizes, 1 at Calne, 1 at Chippenham & 2 at Troubridge (all in your County) employ'd to prevent Riots there and in the *neighbourhood*: As this last word [*i.e.* would] comprehend Malmesbury any Justice of the Peace may require such Military Assistance as can be spared without abandoning the same objects elsewhere. All these Troops are under the command of Major Hill of the 13th Regt. whose headquarters are at Devizes; & I have writen to him to give all possible attention to your Lops applications. I am very glad for the public benefit that you are at Charleton at this juncture, knowing how much a person of your quality, talents, prudence and spirit may do in your neighbourhood at a time when there is so great a need of them all. I entreat your Lop to believe that I shall on all occasions be happy to receive and obey your Commands.

Ipswich 107

174

Preamble to a marching order: Barrington to officer commanding the Troop of 3rd Dragoons (at Dorchester)

[Copy]   War Office
                                    1 August 1766

It having been represented that a Mob of about 500 people at Ottery St. Mary, in the County of Devon, demolis'd two Flour Mills & from there proceeded to Sidbury & demolish'd another & compell'd the Farmers to sell their provisions at a fixed price & that they threatened to demolish the starch Mill at Lyme; and a Military force having been requested as necessary to prevent & put a stop to such illegal proceedings . . .

*   *   *

W.O. 5/54, p. 270

175

Preamble to a marching order: Barrington to officer commanding the 16th (or 2nd) Light Dragoons (at Epsom)

[Copy]   War Office
                                                    8 August 1766

Whereas it has been represented that a numerous & riotous Mob has assembled at Newbury, where they had broken the Windows of several Mealmen, taken away Part of their Effects, and seemed disposed to do farther Mischief, and a Military force having been requested as necessary to put a Stop to and prevent such illegal Proceedings . . .

* * *

W.O. 5/54, p. 278

176

Preamble to a marching order: Barrington to officer commanding the Troop of the 3rd Dragoons on arrival at Collumpton and Ottery St. Mary

[Copy]   War Office
                                                    6 September 1766

It having been represented that a dangerous and riotous Mob has for some time disturbed the course of the Markets at Columbton & Ottery St. Mary in the County of Devon, & in the neighbour-hood thereof and proceeding to Acts of Violence have destroyed most of the Bolting Mills for twenty miles around, and done other damages throughout the Country & a Military force having been requested as necessary to prevent & put a stop to such illegal proceedings . . .

* * *

W.O. 5/54, p. 294

177

Preamble to a marching order: Barrington to officer commanding Troops of 3rd Dragoons on arrival at Dorchester

[Copy]   6 Setember 1766

It having been represented that a dangerous & riotous Mob has for some time disturbed the course of the markets at Columpton & Ottery St. Mary in the County of Devon & proceeding to acts of violence, have destroyed most of the Boulting Mills for twenty miles round & done other damages throughout the Country & a Military Force having been requested to put a stop to such illegal proceedings . . .

* * *

W.O. 5/54, p. 295

178

Barrington to Thomas Nuttall, Treasury Solicitor

[Copy]   Cavendish Square
                                          31 October 1766

I have made application to My Lord Chancellor & to Lord Shelburne that Berkshire may be one of the Counties to which a Judge shall be sent with a Special Commission for the trial of Rioters. They have inform'd me that for this purpose some Examinations taken in the Country should be sent to you who know what is to be done with them. I accordingly transmit to you herewith some examinations taken by myself and other Justices who attended the late Quarter Sessions at Abingdon. We issued Warrants in consequence, & several very notorious offenders have been taken up by these Warrants, & are now in the County Goal. If the attested Copies of these Examinations are not sufficient, I desire you will acquaint me, & you shall immediately have the Originals; and if necessary I could produce a great many more. What I now send you relates only to the Offenders in the neighbourhood of Abingdon; but there are many others in the County Goal sent thither from Maidenhead, Reading, Walling-ford & other places. It is of the utmost consequence that they should be tried as soon as possible; and therefore if anything more than what I have furnish'd you with be necessary in order to have Berkshire inserted in the Special Commission, I beg I may know it from you as soon as possible, that I may procure other Examina-tions from different parts without loss of time. I am authorized by Lord Shelburne to recommend this Business in his name very particularly to your speedy consideration.

* * *

P.S. If it be not improper I wish this
Letter may be laid before the Attorney
& Solicitor General together with the
Examination.

Ipswich 107

179

Lt.-Colonel Rainsford commanding detachment of Foot Guards to Barrington

[Holograph]   Kings Bench Prison
                                          23 May 1768

I am very sorry to trouble you Your Lordship though with a very necessary Complaint, & there being no Civil Magistrate attend-ing upon the Guards I have the Honor of commanding at the King's Bench Prison after several repeated Applications. Your Lordship knows how very ineffectual our Force must be without a justice of the Peace to direct us, and this being Holy day time we have Reason to expect a great Assembly of People in the Evening. Those Gentlemen are in general very unwilling to attend, and shew'd a great Dislike to it when they were applied to this morning at their Meeting on St Margaret's Hill. It is now past three o'Clock; and none of them have appear'd. I could do no less than represent this to Your Lordship, who know the Difficulties the Military are subject to in Cases of Riot, when not supported by the civil Authority.

* * *

P.S. The Place of Meeting at St Margarets Hill is a Mile at least from this Place & much Mischief might be done before a Justice of Peace could arrive, if the Mob would give him Leave which has happened as the Marshal now desires me to inform Your Lordship of.

W.O. 1/874, p. 85

180

Barrington to Lt.-Colonel Rainsford

[Copy]   War Office
23 May 1768

It is with the greatest Concern, I learn from your favor that there is no Civil Magistrate attending with the Detachment of the Guards at the King's Bench Prison; I have sent your letter to Lord Weymouth, and I beg leave to assure you that I rely on your Prudence, and firmness that the Guards will not be permitted to Act but in the Presence of, and by the direction of the Civil Magistrate.

W.O. 1/874, p. 95

181

Robert Wood (Lord Weymouth's secretary) to Barrington

[Holograph]   St James's
23 May 1768

Mr Wood presents his Complimts to Lord Barrington & begs to inform His Lordship that he has laid his note before Lord Weymouth, & that His Lordship has wrote to desire that a Civil

259

Magistrate may attend at the King's Bench Prison as long as any Detachment of the troops does duty there.

W.O. 1/874, p. 89

182

War Office attendance note

[Copy in clerk's hand] War Office
24 May 1768

Lt.Colo. Rainsford called at the War Office to acquaint Lord B. that he came this morning off Guard from the King's Bench Prison, that no Justice of the Peace appeared till 10 o'clock last Night, when Mr Ponton and Mr Capel came, and said they were ready to head the Military by day, or Night if Occasion requir'd, but that the other justices at St Margarets Hill Meeting shewed a Backwardness, and unwillingness (as they said) to meet danger. Colo. Rainsford says that everything was very quiet last Night excepting a small Mob which assembled about Wilk's Window, to look at him as they would at a Bear, (to use the Colonel's Expression) and to give him a Holloo.

The above two justices are gone this Morning to wait on Lord Weymouth and to represent to his Lordship that it is their Opinion; as well as the Marshals, that a force of a Serjeant, and 18 Men is sufficient at present to suppress any Riot which may happen.

Colo. Rainsford seemed desirous that Mr Ponton & Mr Capel might be distinguish'd from the other Justices for their Zeal and Activity, as the only Magistrates that did not seem to *Throw cold Water* on the Cause.

W.O. 1/874, pp. 105–106

183

Barrington to Gold Stick in Waiting

[Copy]   War Office
                                                        11 May 1768

Having this day had the Honor of mentioning to the King the
behavior of the Detachments of the Troops of Horse and Grenadier Guards which have been employed yesterday & the day
before in assisting the Civil Magistrates and preserving the
publick Peace, I have great pleasure in Informing Your Lordship
that His Majesty highly approves of the Conduct both of the
Officers and Men, and means that His Gracious approbation
should be communicated to them through you.

Employing the Troops on so disagreable a Service always gives
me pain; The present unhappy Riots makes it necessary. I am
persuaded they see that Necessity, and will continue as they have
done to do their duty with Alacrity. I beg you will be pleased to
assure them that every possible regard shall be shewn to them;
Their Zeal and good behaviour upon this Occasion deserve it,
and in Case any disagreable Circumstance should happen in the
Execution of their duty, they shall have every defence and
protection that the Law can authorize and this Office can give.
[Same letter to Field Officer in Staff Waiting for the three
regiments of Foot Guards].

W.O. 4/83, pp. 379–380

184

Barrington to Thomas Bradshaw

[Copy]   Beckett
                                                    12 October 1768

The long walks which you know I take by myself every day,
naturally produce contemplation in me. Among other Subjects of
the political kind the following have occurred to my thoughts.

Notwithstanding the shameful dangers and inconveniences which arose last Summer from a want of good Middlesex Justices, there has been no new Commission of the Peace for that County, appointing men on whose ability & Spirit Government can rely. If persons properly qualified will not serve gratis they should be paid in some shape or other. The Peace & Order of such a Capital of such a Kingdom cannot be purchased too dear.

Justice Gillam, who acted a most worthy part in a neighbouring County, who received publickly the Commendation of three Judges, who in reality put an end to the dangerous Riots in favour of Wilkes, who by his meritorious zeal and Spirit has drawn on himself the resentment of a most profligate and vindictive faction thro' whose machinations he was tried for his Life, has not yet received the least mark of the King's favor and approbation.

The trial of the said Justice Gillam was taken in shorthand; its publication with the opinions given by Three Judges on the point of calling in and employing Military Aid is material to the last degree, both as a record of these opinions, and as information to the Magistrates in all parts of the King's Dominions: And yet the Trial remains unpublish'd to this moment.

Several Witnesses swore that Allen was murder'd by the Soldier, whose acquittal at Guildford shew'd they were perjured; & yet none of them have been prosecuted for perjury.

* * *

I need not tell you that in times like these I am a friend to Administration in general & that I am personally a friend to some of the principal Ministers now in the Service of the Crown; Ministers cannot remember all they might do for their Country: I do not regard being thought troublesome or officious when I am endeavouring to do good; and therefore I always give hints which I conceive may be useful. I should not scruple writing this letter to the Duke of Grafton, but I think on the whole I had better send it to You who have the means of knowing when such matters can be mentioned with effect; & who will save his Grace the trouble of hearing them at all if you find they will not be effectual.

* * *

Ipswich 107

185

Shute Barrington, Bishop of Llandaff, to Barrington

[Holograph]   Mongewell
                                                 9 July 1779

In consequence of the freedom you so earnestly recommend, Sir William Blackstone & I have considered your papers with the attention they require. In that marked (A) all those parts included within asteriscs, with lines drawn under them, in the most decided opinion of Sir Wm. in which I intirely concur, should be omitted. The grounds of his opinion are, that if left to stand, the idea of apprehension would be conveyed, though meant to be concealed; & much of the spirit diminished which declaration of this Kind should always breathe. We conceive the paper marked (B) to be superfluous; as (A) will better answer every purpose. Sir William B. advises the printing the declaration as soon as agreed to & signed; together with the names of the Subscribers at The Assizes, which may be done that evening or early the next morning at Oxford; & the circulating copies to the different Market & considerable towns of The County; in each of which some proper person should be instructed & desired to explain & enforce the association to Farmers & others. The measure itself meets with my neighbour's highest approbation. I have Kept a copy of the declaration. Perhaps you may think it expedient to order Clinton to continue the advertisement till the middle of next week that it may not be forgot in the distant counties before their respective Assizes.

With regard to what should be done in Oxfordshire, the proposition & the person to move it must necessarily depend upon your success, & what Gentlemen are present at our Assizes. Our members are not ably qualified for such a task; Norton, who when resident at Tackley, was always Chairman of the Quarter Sessions, would be the fittest who occurs to my mind. Have you any objection to writing to him upon the subject? I propose dining with The Bishop of Oxford to day, & as his appearance will give countenance & propriety to mine I mean to open the plan to him in strict confidence as far as is necessary, & desire him to hold himself in readiness to attend at the Assizes on Thursday morning on my summons. You will either in person, or by letter acquaint me on Wednesday Evening with what has passed at Abingdon.

Ipswich 7, no. 8

186

Barrington's Plan of Association:
returned with Document 185

[Holograph: written columnwise with blank margin to left]

July 1779

If an enemy should land in any part of England the whole Kingdom would be thrown into confusion and alarm which always produce disorders.

The War with Spain will lessen our manufactures especially if the numerous fleets of the Enemy should prevent exportation tho for a short time only: Many hands will become unemploy'd, idle Manufacturers are always disorderly, and having neither money nor food will prey on the publick. Other probable causes of riot at this juncture might be suggested. The Civil power is now peculiarly weak because it cannot be help'd by the military. Magistrates tho by law entitled to aid and assistance from the subject can seldom be obey'd when they call for it, because no man knows that he shall be supported by another: For the same reason a man whose property is attack'd by violence often submits to injury thro' fear: He would stand on his defence if he was certain of a numerous and vigorous support.

Suppose a hundred dissolute fellows wandering about a County and plundering Mills farms &c; the Millers and farmers are frightened and run away, their goods are seized or spoilt; but they would oppose these invaders and save their effects if the inhabitants of their parish or of neighbouring parishes had formed an association to assist in defending their joint properties. The Magistrate would also be encouraged to act his part with spirit, when he thought he should be properly supported by such an association.

On this ground there is an Idea of moving the Grand Jury at Abingdon Assizes to sign a paper herewith inclosed marked (A). If they approve the contents it shd. be first laid before the High Sherif for his signature, then be signed by them, and afterwards by such gentlemen &c of the County as attend the assizes. The Mayor and Corporation of Abingdon shd. be invited to sign the Paper marked (B) and to advise the Inhabitants of the Town to do the same. Different Copies of the Paper (B) should be sent to every parish in the County, and put in to the hands of some leading man likely to prevail on the Parishioners to sign it. All these Papers when signed, should finally be sent to the Clerk of the Peace and then a well digested list might be easily formed of the associaters to preserve the peace and support the civil Magistrates in the discharge of their duty. Copies of the Association (A) should be sent to London to be immediately printed in the Evening Papers soon enough to be read in the Country before many assizes are over and a Copy should be communicated to the High Sherif and Grand Jury at Oxford (the next assize Town on the Circuit) with an invitation to accede to it. Some Counties might immediately adopt the measure; all would have a plan to pursue when they find it expedient.

At the meeting of the Quarter Sessions at Abingdon a week after the assizes, the proceedings in this matter should be laid before the Justices, who if they approve the measure may give the most proper directions for making the Association general throughout the county, and putting it to the best Uses.

Ipswich 7, no. 18

187

Proposed Declaration of Association

[Holograph: this is the second of two drafts amended by the Bishop]

[July 1779]

(A) We the high Sheriff and grand jury of the County of Berks together with others assembled at the assizes holden at Abingdon on tuesday the 13 July, are determined to take every proper measure which may contribute to the internal defence & peace of this County; knowing what we owe to our King and Country, and thinking it base in the highest degree to suffer the families or properties of our county militia to be exposed to injury or danger at home, while they are employ'd jointly with his Majesty's regular forces in the defence of this Island against the united powers of France and Spain. And we conceive it will be *highly* [greatly, *added in the Bishop's hand*] conducive to this good purpose, that we should engage ourselves, as we now do, to be always ready with our own persons and with those over whom we have influence or authority, to aid and assist the civil Magistrates of this County with the utmost zeal in case we should be calld upon [in any unexpected emergency, *added in the Bishop's hand*] *at any time* to obey their lawful commands for the preservation of peace and good order. We likewise recommend in the strongest manner to all other well disposed persons to join with us by entering into *a like* [this, *added as before*] engagement:

   * *But least this measure should be misunderstood and thereby convey alarm as if we expected internal commotions at this time, we declare that we have no ground for such apprehension: on the contrary we believe as well as hope** [being firmly persuaded *added by the Bishop, as also the underlining between the asterisks above. See Document 185*] that all ranks & conditions among us are zealously united for the defence of our Religion, Liberty, Constitution, Laws and every other thing dear to us, against the Enemies of our [King & *added by Bishop, also underlining below as before*] Country. **Yet as unexpected emergencies some-*

266

times arise suddenly, we think it right to be prepared against them at this juncture; and to declare that we will zealously perform the duty which we at all times owe, by aiding and assisting lawful authority for the preservation of the publick Peace* Given under our hands this day of July 1779.

Ipswich 7, no. 4

188

Shute Barrington to Barrington

[Holograph]   Mongewell
                                                                 July 16 1779

The first discussion of yesterday's meeting at Oxford was the volunteer companies. Should an insufficient number of officers offer by friday the 23d, a second meeting will be summoned to consider to what purpose the subscription shall be applied. The prevailing idea seemed to be the raising, if our fund be adequate, a corps to be Officered by The Crown; otherwise, bounties to be given to men enlisting in any of the regulars. The sums subscribed when I left the room, were, Duke of Marlbrough £500, Ld. Macclesfield £250, Lord Charles Spencer £100, Myself £40, as I understood that The Gentlemen of better property meant to be responsible for £30.

When this matter was settled, having previously sounded some of The Principal Gentlemen, I proposed The Berkshire Association as worthy of being imitated; explaining the plan as far as was proper, & stating it's beneficial consequences. It was well relished by The Sheriff & the larger part of The Company: Ld. Macclesfield only doubting of alarm, & of the expressions which imply the civil power to want assistance beyond that which it can legally demand. Upon my readiness to qualify these expressions he was satisfied, & I thought the scheme to be on the point of succeeding when it was objected to by a Mr Willoughby of Baldwin, formerly a Lawyer & foreman of The Grand Jury. I endeavoured to obviate all his objections, & flatter myself to the conviction of others. He however persevered, called his brethren aside, & then publickly declared the dissent of some of them. As the question could not therefore be carried unanimously, it was not worth carrying at all, & I gave it up. Thoroughly persuaded of the utility of the plan I feel hurt at its' not having succeeded.

Ipswich 7, no. 11

189

Charles Jenkinson to Barrington

[In clerk's hand, signed by Jenkinson]   Addescombe Place
9 October 1779

I have had the honour of your Letter of the 4th, in which you give me an Account of the manner in which some of the Gentry Clergy & Comonalty of Berkshire are at present learning the use of arms; & you desire my Opinion, whether it is necessary, that such an *arming* should be authorized by Government; Though I am no Lawyer, & it is very difficult, as you know, to find one to consult at this Season of the year, I am clearly of Opinion, that all your Lordship & your Friends are doing, according to the account you give me of it, is perfectly legal, without having any authority from Government; The People of this Country have a right to the use of Arms; They may learn with them any Exercise they think proper; but under this Pretence no one can exercise any Command or Authority over another, unless what He derives from Government; Provided it be voluntary, the whole is to be considered as play & amusement, & is meritorious or not according to the Intention, with which it is done. I am perswaded that what your Lordship & your Friends have done has this Title to merit; for I am sure you have all of you acted with the very best Intention; but I am very doubtful, whether it would be wise in Government to encourage Proceedings of this sort, as they tend to arm & discipline men, who are not under the command of the Crown; & who might on some occasions make an ill use of the Arms with which they will under this pretence provide themselves, & of the discipline they may have learnt; We have in this moment melan-

268

choly accounts of the proceedings of a great number of Rioters, partly armed with Firelocks, in Lancashire; where they have done a great deal of mischief, & some of the Master Manufacturers are said to have encouraged them in it. We have order'd a great number of Troops to March from a distance to quell these Riots; I am of Opinion however that in any Place where the people have begun to learn the Military Exercise in this manner, it should be suffer'd to continue, as the putting an end to it, or even the discouraging of it, would imply a Jealousy very ill founded in that particular instance, & might create disgust.

Ipswich 7, no. 20

190

Commissioners of Excise to Barrington

[In clerk's hand signed by 5 commissioners]

Excise Office, London
17 July 1767

We have received a Letter of the 6th. Instt. from George Taylor our Supervisor of Battle in Sussex, and also one of the 30th past from John Buckly, Excise Officer of Hastings, representing to us that a very great Riot had been committed by the Smugglers at Hastings armed with Pistols, wherein Stephen Bourner, who had been arrested and carried to the Excise Office, was rescued out of the hands of the said Buckley by the said Smugglers; And the said Buckley having further represented to us that when the Mob first assembled The Lieutenant of Dragoons, Mr Robert Keily told the Serjeant that the Soldiers had no Business there, that he the Serjeant should order the other Soldiers from the assistance of Mr Buckley, and that he should be confined if he assisted any longer, whereby the Mob were encouraged to continue the Riot, and the Smugglers enabled to carry off the Prisoner, which they did in Triumph firing several Pistols as they went along; and our said Supervisor having represented to us, that, while he was at Hastings, Stephen Bourner who had been rescued, together with

30 more Smugglers went in Triumph on Board a Cutter and set sail for France; that it was confidently reported that they carried seven hundred pounds for a Cargo of Tea Brandy &c. That Mr. Milward the Mayor of Hastings had desired him to represent to us that the safest Way to take them is to send a King's Cutter well armed and manned as they may in the Day time lay on board the Cutter about a Mile from Hastings; We beg Leave to trouble your Lordship with Copies of the said Letters, and also to acquaint Your Lordship that upon an Application to the Lords Commissioners of the Admiralty their Lordships have been pleased to order an armed Cutter forthwith to proceed upon this Service, and as it may happen that the Assistance of the Military quartered in and about Hastings may be necessary to secure this dangerous Gang of Smugglers we request that such orders may be sent to Captn Keily and the Officers commanding in and about Hastings as shall appear to your Lordship to be proper for defending the Officers of the Revenue against the Smugglers.

W.O. 1/989, no. 401

191

John Buckley to Commissioners of Excise

[Copy in clerk's hand]   Hastings
                                                        30 June 1767

By Virtue of a Warrant from Mr. Poole Sollicitor I arrested Stephen Bourner and took him to the Excise Office till Bail could be procured. I had five Soldiers to assist that he should not make his Escape; as soon as I had secured him I searched and found in the Inside of his Waistcoat Lining a double barrelled pistol loaded with Balls and primed, which I took from him. I then dispatched Mr. Lidwell Expectant to Battel for Mr. Taylor Supervisor to come and assist, about an hour after Mr Lidwell was gone a Mob of upwards of two hundred People assembled before the Excise Offrice, and ten or twelve of the Ringleaders with Pistols in their hands, swore that they would die every man but the Prisoner should be set at Liberty, nor a man should not be taken out of the Town or any Bond given. Robert Bourner came into the Room & pretended to be bound for Stephen Bourner, he would not execute the Bond I had got ready, but swore that if ever I met him with any Goods and attempted to seize the said goods he would kill me on the Place. When the Mob first assembled Mr. Robert Keily the Lieutenant of Dragoons came and told the Serjeant that the Soldiers had no business there, and that he the Serjeant should order the other Soldiers from the assistance of Mr. Buckley, and that he should be confined if he assisted any longer. The Mob hearing this gave them Encouragement and came upstairs with Pistols in their hands pointed at the Soldiers and swore they would blow their Brains out if Bourner was not released. I opened the Door to speak to the Rioters, William Geery one of the Leaders presented a pistol at me and swore that what the pistol was loaded with should go through my Body if I did not let Stephen Bourner go, and also threatens my Life for taking him up, at the same time three or four more with Pistols in their hands pointed at me and the Soldiers and swore that I or anyone that assisted should not live an hour longer. I saw by all appearance that murder would be committed to prevent which I let the Prisoners go, they all went off in Triumph and fired several Pistols as they went along.

W.O. 1/989, no. 397

192

George Taylor to Commissioners of Excise

[Copy in clerk's hand]   Battle
                                                    6 July 1767

I got to Hastings the 30th Evening and found that Stephen Bourner was rescued; I have examined the particulars of Mr Buckley's Report and find by several Witnesses to be true. July the 1st. I went to the Mayor's house but he was gone a Journey, I then waited on Thos. Evitt Esq. Deputy and told him that Bourner might then be taken and desired his Assistance. He answered that they was a set of desperate Fellows, and that he would have nothing to do with them, he also said that on the 30th. he saw 10 or 12 of the Mob with Pistols & that he took a Pistol out of one of their hands examined and found it was loaded; Mr. Evitt knows most of the Men's names that were armed, but I believe is afraid to impeach any of them, whilst I was with Mr. Evitt Stephen Bourner and 30 more Smugglers went in Triumph on Board a Cutter and set Sail for France; it was confidently reported they carried £700 for a Cargo of Tea Brandy &c.

I went to Hastings the 3rd of July Edward Milward Esq. the Mayor was at home, I waited on him, he said he was sorry he was not at home at the Time of the Mob, but said they were a set of Villains & that the Town would be glad if they were all transported. Mr. Milward desired me to make use of his name to Your Honours that the safest way to take them is to send a armed King's Cutter, or the Dover Excise Boat well armed and manned and they might be taken in a Week's time as they mostly in the Day time lay on Board the Cutter about a Mile at sea from Hastings. After taken not to let them come on Shore but carry them to Dover Castle immediately, and he is very ready to sign their mittimus at any time. I most humbly pray some method may be taken to punish these Villains.

W.O. 1/989, no. 393

193

Barrington to officer commanding the troop of the 3rd Dragoons at Hastings

[Copy]   War Office
                                                         21 July 1767

I send you herewith an Order for giving assistance to the Civil Magistrates in case of any Riots or disturbances which may happen at Hastings and for assisting the Officers of the Revenue in preventing Smuggling and securing the Offenders.

For your better information on this head I transmit to you copies of the Representations made to me relative to the late behaviour of the Smuglers at Hastings and that neighbourhood.

W.O. 4/82, p. 196

194

Barrington to Commissioners of Excise

[Copy] War Office
21 July 1767

I have received the favor of your letter of the 17th instant together with the papers relative to the late disorderly proceedings at Hastings, and I have this day sent Orders to the Commanding Officer of the Troop of the 3rd Regiment of Dragoons stationed at that place to give the proper assistance to the Civil Power in case of any riots or disturbances which may happen there or in the neighbourhood of Hastings, and for assisting the Officers of the Revenue in the prevention of Smugling.

Enclosed I send you for your better information a Copy of the said Orders.

I apprehend Lieut Keily behaved very properly in calling off the men and not suffering them to interfere in the disturbances as they had then no order for that purpose, and could not properly be called upon, after receiving their Orders, but by some Civil Magistrate.

W.O. 4/82, p. 197

6

Patronage and the Purchase System

Throughout the eighteenth century the Secretary at War was in constant touch with the officers of the army, hearing their complaints and solicitations, composing their quarrels, and regulating and recording their promotions. During the long periods when there was no Commander-in-Chief, he also administered patronage, either that of powerful senior colleagues in government, or in some cases originating from his own prerogative. These tasks probably gave Barrington more personal embarrassment than any other single part of his role, and certainly caused him to acquire more odium. It could not be otherwise. The eighteenth century was an important stage—and the Secretary at War was an important agent—in the process of change from a medieval to a modern state-controlled army. The privileged class had always regarded the army as a suitable and honourable haven for their sons and clients, often irrespective of merit. It was necessary to show them that they joined on the State's terms, not their own. George II was proud of his army and of his knowledge of it. Both he and George III kept a book of officers' names, descriptions and pretensions. The theory was gaining ground that the army should not be used for the private advantage of individuals in quite the same way as some officers and their patrons would have wished. To their dismay they found that professional competence might be at least as important as being 'a firm friend of administration', or 'essential to my interest in Devonshire'.

But the weight of carrying out this policy and of confronting aggrieved and sometimes aggressive officers and would-be patrons fell upon the Secretary at War. Between them and a man like Barrington, public-spirited and, it must be admitted, a little priggish, who wished to preserve standards, antagonism was bound to occur. He seems to have had a vision of a fairer world in which there could exist a better type of officer, more efficient and committed to his career, perhaps sometimes of humbler origins. Such a man could be helped by disinterested public intervention to overcome lack of funds and to compete with those whom private patronage and means had placed in positions that were sometimes unsuitably advanced. But writing disapproving lectures to influential people who wished to exert improper pressure did a good deal to create an image of moral rectitude which contemporaries found it difficult to like. It was a pity that Barrington demanded that his righteousness be noticed, for there seems no reason to doubt his genuine feelings in the matter. He simply did not enjoy, as the Duke of Newcastle clearly did, the administering of patronage. 'I have hated patronage all my life,' he wrote to Lord Townshend in 1771.[1] Aside from considerations of public interest, it was troublesome and could make him appear disobliging, sometimes to old friends. During his first period at the War Office he gladly left the most valuable part of it to Cumberland and then to Ligonier. During his second term after 1765 he surrendered most of the initiative to Lord Granby. But his attitude was not entirely simple. He carefully guarded the small amount of 'efficient patronage' retained by the War Office over staff appointments in regiments—the surgeon, the quartermaster, the adjutant, the paymaster and the chaplain[2] (212)—but at the same time succeeded in reducing, though not entirely extinguishing, the extent to which these posts, requiring as they did some degree of expert knowledge, were bought and sold. And he was prepared to help close friends and family, offering to get Governor Bernard's son into the army[3] and to recommend a cousin to a minor office in Ireland.[4] Also his objections to patronage tended to abate when high degree and political support were joined with at least some degree of merit. But in these cases he was usually in the position of acquiescing in the actions of others—the King, the Commander-in-Chief, the First Lord of the Treasury—rather than being ambitious for the role of patron himself. His main purpose was to keep out of confrontation. But although others might have the credit and the blame of patronage Barrington nevertheless ran into criticism because of his determination to regulate appointments. He may not have wanted his own patronage, but he did wish to retain the right to object to patronage improperly used by others. Here the dual nature of his position could be used to advantage. One aspect of it was formal and official, consisting in registering and publishing appointments, the other unofficial and much more sensitive, that of patronage and influence, which involved choice. The connection between the two was too close for him to escape difficulties, and as will appear below, Barrington's method of avoiding pressure was to devise a screen behind which he could shelter. This screen consisted of a steadily-growing body of rules, some inherited, others devised by himself and settled after consulting with the King and the Adjutant-General, by which the operation of patronage could be guided, tempered and sometimes nullified altogether.

In spite of this he could not evade solicitations, sometimes from people he could not afford to offend. At times he agreed, rather wearily, at others he was evasive, at others he was deliberately obstructive when he considered that right was on his side (195). Many of the applications in the period 1755–1761 were unashamedly political and marked by an indifference, which Barrington found offensive, to the military merit of the protégés (196, 197, 198, 199), for example, one request for an ensign's commission in a marching regiment of foot included a post-script 'I must beg it may be done before the Election.'[5] In certain cases merit did occupy some place in the writers' minds (200, 201, 202). In at least one startling case straightforward bribery was attempted, a situation from which Barrington extricated himself with tactful good humour (203). For cases of commission-broking however he had only contempt (204, 205).

His first term of office taught him a good deal in this as in other areas, and he became determined to bring some system into promotions. The climax of this was the publication of the 1766 regulations about purchase (see below, p. 297). Armed with these he hoped to avoid in his second term the uneasiness and pressure of the first. But even during the first term he made steps in this direction. The first stage was to develop the practice already used of keeping lists[6], in concert with the Commander-in-Chief and the King. These lists contained the names of aspirant officers and of their patrons, their length of service and some frank descriptions. Comments and annotations which might improve a man's chances were sometimes added later, for example 'Col. Mordaunt recommends him earnestly. Lord Barrington knows him and wishes him well,' or 'A whig gentleman & his family always in the Government Interest.' Lieutenant Bosomworth was described as 'perfectly acquainted with the manner of Wood Fighting'. John Playters's grandfather was 'the first baronet in Suffolk', and he was recommended by 'Mr Horace Walpole of the Cockpit, attends his duty and is of sound principles.' Other more formal methods were resorted to. Barrington's advertisement in the *London Gazette* in 1759 was an attempt to remind officers that the Crown and the War Office needed to be involved at the beginning and not the end of a commission-transaction (206). By that stage in the war there was a brisk trade in commissions, and he had become irritated by the extent to which officers treated clandestinely and settled their bargains, at length revealing them for registration at the War Office as *faits accomplis*. A year later he wrote to all regimental agents asking for a list of all officers who had purchased their present or earlier commissions.[7] The ground was being cleared for tighter control.

In 1765 on his return to the War Office he was able to provide the King with a list of procedures which could by then safely be called customary (207). More certainty was needed, however, about prices to be given for commissions. Attempts to regulate prices had been made in the time of George I,[8] but the list settled then was out of date in relation to the market that had since developed. In October 1765 the Judge Advocate General was asked to take the opinion of the Board of General Officers about prices (208), and in November agents were urged to provide more information when commission bargains were being proposed (209). Early in 1766 the Board reported their recommendations,[9] including the revised list of prices, which the King approved.[10] No attempt was made to suggest a figure for colonelcies, the sale of which had by 1766 been stopped. To be a lieutenant-colonel in the different sorts of cavalry regiment cost from £4,700 to £5,500, in a marching regiment of foot £3,500. The highest sum was for a lieutenant-colonelcy in the Foot Guards, at £6,700. But for the greater part of the officer class, who first of all wanted to get into the army, and then to acquire their own company, the most interesting information in the new list was that an ensigncy in the infantry would now cost £400, and a company £1,500. Having completed this exercise Barrington wrote at length on the subject to the Judge Advocate General; this interesting letter was clearly the result of a long period of thought and experience (210).[11]

Armed with these new safeguards he faced the solicitations of the great and powerful, as well as of the needy and friendless, for another thirteen years. His position was difficult because the army had been considerably reduced after the peace of 1763 and the flow of promotions had dried to a trickle. In such a season Barrington was glad to leave most matters to Lord Granby, the Commander-in-Chief from 1766 (211), although there were clashes when he considered that Granby's influence was being wrongly exerted (212). After Granby's resignation[12] in January 1770 the full weight of the patronage and the obloquy that went with it descended upon Barrington, to remain for the rest of his career. At times his friendly civility created extra difficulties. As with many insecure men in public life his manner remained urbane and obliging even when he was irritable or frightened. Applicants who considered that they had made good progress in a personal interview with him were often angry at receiving a refusal the following day (213, 214). His comfort was that he could sometimes use the Crown, and sometimes the rules he had established, to veto certain bargains proposed by powerful patrons, but the reproach still clung to him, and the impression of improper Closet influence was increased. Amid increasing unpopularity Barrington battled on, facing up firmly to many forms of influence, sometimes insinuating, sometimes bullying. The once-powerful Earl of Bute, whom Barrington had obliged in 1760[13], was in 1771 informed that a relative could not have a troop of dragoons, and James Grenville was lectured about a promotion for his son which Barrington frankly admitted he had tried hard to prevent[14] (215, 216). At other times he bowed to decisions made by the King (217), or where the candidates appeared to have some merit, and obliged old political associates as different as Holland and Chatham (218, 219, 220, 221). But a good many men lacking influence (222, 223), or sufficient influence, or even in some strange cases possessing the wrong sort of influence,[15] were sent away empty-handed. He received numerous letters containing sad recitals of long service, battle-experience, wounds, lonely duty in distant garrisons, and decline of health, mixed with peevish remarks about the promotion of much younger men. Piteous phrases recur in this correspondence[16]: 'Nothing but my being reduced to the last pitch of human Misery shoud make me thus presume trespassing on your Lordship's patience in hearing a repetition of my sad story,' or 'Could my Sorrows and inexpressible distress admit of an addition it would be least my presumptious Liberty in again troubling your Lordship might in the smallest degree offend.' To all these appeals Barrington returned unfailingly polite but unhelpful replies. There were simply not enough posts in the reduced army of peace-time, and the most deserving cases on the half-pay list had to come first.

A natural result of the shortage of commissions on the market was a steep rise in the perceived value of them. Reports began to circulate of secret bargains involving extra payments. In July 1772 the price of a Captain-lieutenancy in the foot was officially raised by £450,[17] and in November agents were reminded that price-levels must be strictly adhered to (224). A further regulation in 1775 was also aimed at secret transactions (225). By that date the augmentations of the American War were easing the situation for aspirant officers, but for the years 1763 to 1774 the trade was almost at a standstill, and a man needed to be well connected, moneyed and meritorious to receive much encouragement from the Secretary at War. The unfortunate Captain Singleton pursued Barrington for years in the hope of preferment, but had nothing to offer in support of his claim but length of service (226). At length he was permitted to exchange into the lieutenant-governorship of Landguard Fort garrisoned by a company of invalids, where he remained for over three decades.[18] Some men lost their tempers and returned rude replies, some even lost their reason: there exist several sad and embarrassing letters addressed to Barrington more than ten years after he had quitted the War Office by elderly crazed officers desperately seeking remedies for their lack of professional advancement.[19] Sometimes applicants presented very detailed schedules of what they considered was owed to them (227, 228, 229). Schemes of arrangement between more than one officer, sometimes between all the officers of a regiment, were also presented for adjudication: they had a much better chance of success in wartime (230). But always Barrington strove to keep before patrons and officers the rules of preferment: that babes-in-arms and schoolboys should not get commissions (231), that the colonel's recommendation was important in a promotion (232), that anyone fortunate enough to get a commission in an invalid company—looked upon as a sort of pension—could not thereafter expect to be promoted[20] (233), and that posts on the staff within the legitimate patronage of the War Office (234, 212 above) should not be sold (235, 236). Most important he tried to stamp out irregularities in sale and purchase. If there had been no purchase there could be no sale (237). This rule on the face of it appeared excellent. An officer without means who had been promoted without purchase, during wartime expansion, had thus avoided a notable disadvantage, perhaps at a critical time in his career. Why should he also be allowed to sell what he had not bought? The case often looked different twenty years later in a career, when the officer, worn out by work, wounds or service in an unhealthy climate, was forbidden to sell to provide for his old age. Was a worthy, perhaps a brilliant, career to have no weight? Barrington was less generous than Granby in this respect, being afraid of setting precedents, but allowed himself to be over-persuaded on occasion (238). But he was determined to make such occasions very unusual, and most requests, however ingeniously distinguished in point of detail, were rejected.[21]

At other times he was outmanoeuvred. He carefully set forth his views on exchanges in a letter to General Elliot (239). Exchanges, although a more practicable mode of advancement in the peacetime army, still required careful regulation. Barrington had inherited and continued to administer a rule originating in the War Office earlier in the century, that all such arrangements should be on equal terms.[22] Elliot got his son into a cavalry regiment by making another application, this time to the Commander-in-Chief. In giving him news of his success Barrington could not resist adding 'I must frankly acknowledge that the whole transaction was settled between the King and Lord Granby.'[23] After Granby's resignation he was in a stronger position to make his opinion felt in the Closet, and was therefore able to stand up to General Elliot when in 1773 he made another application (240), although Elliot was able to prevail when a mode of achieving equality between the parties was discovered.[24]

The strain of administering this part of War Office business and of adhering to rules which others, who should have known better, conspired to break told heavily on Barrington. Amongst the trail of aggrieved suppliants already mentioned the occasional powerful enemy was found, such as Isaac Barré. His impression that he had been churlishly treated by government in general, and by Barrington in particular, did much to push Barré into the ranks of political opposition. A man of great military ambition, he returned from America in 1760 with a considerable sense of his own achievements, and demanded promotion. The content of Barrington's letter to his commanding officer, General Amherst, serves to show that he was not an enemy to Barré's promotion (241, 242), but even the check of a slight delay in obtaining what he wanted exasperated Barré. While letters were exchanged between the War Office and America he complained of his treatment to Pitt and Lord Bute,[25] and did not seem much mollified at the end of January 1761 to get the post of

Deputy Adjutant General in North America, with the rank of Lieutenant-Colonel. After a short period of prosperity in the army Barré fell into disfavour and in revenge pursued Barrington with relentless sarcasm for the next fifteen years, taunting him with being 'the servile representative of the patronage system'.[26] This did not prevent him from trying to secure fresh preferment from that system: he got little sympathy in his attempts from Barrington or the King (243). At length in 1773 Barré received 'His Majesty's permission to retire from the service'.[27]

A more short-lived but for a time more alarming foe was the Scottish judge Sir John Dalrymple, who published an insulting series of letters setting forth the manner in which he believed the Secretary at War had injured the prospects of his brothers in the army. Barrington had had at least one narrow escape from a duel[28] with an angry officer; now he issued his own challenge. Dalrymple declined to fight, at least on British soil—'the King's Judges do not fight duels'—but he would defend himself if attacked.[29] He offered some barely-satisfactory words of explanation and Barrington allowed the affair to lapse, at length wondering if Dalrymple was in his right mind.

In all the circumstances it is not surprising that the latter years of Barrington's office were marked by trouble and weariness. His opposition to the mode of carrying on the American war was a major factor in this (see Section 1). To this must be added the strain of keeping up a polite front, and of adhering to 'good general rules' in officer preferment, with the knowledge of widespread enmity which isolated him officially and personally (244). But he stuck firmly to his self-appointed principles, and as with his reforms in other areas, his lines of conduct in this remained after his retirement as authoritative precedents for his successors.[30]

195

Barrington
to the Duke of Newcastle

[Holograph]   Beckett
                                             12 September 1757

I am honour'd by a letter from your Grace recommending
strongly a request of Sir William Owen's, in favour of his Brother
a Lieutenant Colonel on the Irish Establishment, and now getting
towards the head of the List. I have already presented Memorials
from him both to the King and the Duke, and he cannot be
overlook'd when Regiments are given away; but I beg leave to
observe to your Grace that besides some Lieutenant Colonels
already superseded who may possibly get rank hcrcafter, there are
a few officers of Service & Merit still before Mr Owen. I shall not
fail to take every proper occasion of mentioning him, in the way I
think most likely to serve him & thereby to shew my obedience to
your Grace's Commands.

Add. MSS. 32874, f. 13.

196

Lord Powis to Barrington

[Holograph]   Albemarle Street
                                                    1 March 1761

In respect to the Application for Ensign Browne of Genl. Guise's
Regiment, That he may be made a Lieutenant in any other Corps,
I am so much pressed (as the Application has been depending
since Febry 1760) that I cannot avoid giving Your Lordship this
trouble. Your Lordship's Goodness I have experienced, and
doubt it not;—but as This is, in many respects, a critical Season
with me it woud be doubly agreeable, if the Affair coud be soon
dispatched. Of this, whether it be practicable Your Lordship can

judge best: And to this, I will therefore add only that I have the Honour to be with great regard [etc]

Ipswich 3b, no. 118

197

Sir Edward Walpole to Barrington

[Holograph]   Pall Mall
                                               5 February 1760

Not being well enough to pay my respects to you, I hope yr Lordship will suffer this Application by letter in favour of an Old Soldier who is now a Serjeant in the First Troop of Horse-Grenadiers Guards, and wants an Ensigncy in the Invalids. Having faild in some of my little Attempts with yr Lordship, I shall take it very kindly if you will do this for me, as it is to oblige some of my Yarmouth Constituents, one of whom the bearer Serjeant Bowles is, and a very worthy man.

Ipswich 3b, no. 101

198

Sergeant Robert Bowles to Barrington

[Holograph]   N.p.
                                               22 August 1760

Acording to your Lordships Desire, I have Sent this Letter to acquaint your Lordship that Ensign Mathew Hall, of Genl. Parsons's Regiment of Invalids at Portsmouth is Dead I beg your Lordship will be pleased to recommend me to that Ensigncy [ps] Sir

    I was recommend to your Lordship by Sir Edwd. Walpole

Ipswich 3b, no. 100

199

Duke of Marlborough to Barrington

[Holograph]   London
29 February 1760

After having troubled you so lately about Capt. Lloyd, you will
think me very impertinent to give you this fresh trouble about
another Person; however, my Lord, as I hope you will tell me, if
what I am going to ask, is disagreeable to you; I will venture to lay
it before you. What I would wish then, my Lord, is a troop of
Dragoons; or a Company in an old Regt. for a Gentleman's whose
name is Travell; his Father was a very zealous friend to us in the
late Oxford-Shire Election—which makes me interest myself for
his Son,—who has really an unblamable Character—he bought a
Cornecy of Dragoons about 6 or 7 years ago—and has been
sometime Lieutenant in the Regt. late Lord G. Sackvilles; where
he may stick some time unless your Lordship will favor him with
your interest to get him promoted.
[p.s.]
Capt. Travell now is past thirty

Ipswich 3b, no. 88

200

Endorsed 'Lord Hillsborough's Recommendations'

[Holograph]   n.d.[1760 or 1761]

List of what the Ld. Vt. Barrington may if he pleases do for the
Gratification of his Obedt. Servt. all or part or if inconvenient
none.
   One Captn. Fish ordered to Gaudalupe has fds. [friends] who
plague me to write to get him some exchange to save him from
going, to make him a Major, or get him a Company in another
Regiment, or procure him leave of absence, are they think as easy
for Ld. H. as to take a pinch of Snuff. If Ld. B. wd write an

ostensible Ld. H wd be much obliged in which Majority & exchange shd be mentioned.

If My Lord is encumbered with Ensigns Commissions they might be filled with the following names—

Jaspar Waring, eldest son of Mr Thomas Waring Minister of the Church of England, who is a younger Brother of Mr Waring of Waringston, a good family with £1200 p An.—The young Man 6 feet high 20 years of Age.

Alexander Colvill son of Doctor Colvill a presbyterian Parson; he is a private Man in Ld Loudons Regiment, & Ld Barrington said he liked to promote such a person, if his Character justified it, for which Ld Loudon is referred to.

There is one Savage who is a Brother to two that you have provided for already, one of his brothers in General Barrington's Regiment; this is a pretty young fellow, & fit for the Service. There is also one Johnston a young Gentleman of a good Family who would gladly carry Colours. If your Lordship is distressed & wishes I should mention any more, I will do it.

Ipswich 3b, no. 126

201

Lord Tyrawley to Barrington

[Holograph]   Bath
                                        16 October 1758

One should have better grounds to write to a Secretary at War, than to report: Nevertheless as report is sometimes true, as well as false, pray pardon the trouble of this letter, let my intelligence be what it will; Which is—that Major General Noel is to have a Regiment and that Colonel Blaney is to raise One: In this Case two Ensigns will be Vacant in the Coldstream, which I claim your Lordship's kind promise upon these Occasions to give Mr Fisher time, to lay before you such Names, as he will give you, by my directions.

If Preferments go in the Regiment, I cannot but in Justice, take

Notice to your Lordship, that tho' you will find Sr William
Wiseman eldest Lieutenant in it, yet Captain Clarke, and Captain
Rainesford [ie, Rainsford] was so, and Clark first, and Rainesford
next and that Sr Wm bought his Lieutenancie Over their Heads,
as they had not Money to purchase. This Retrospect, into
Seniority of Commissions has often and very Equitably been
considered in futur preferments. Otherwise he that has Most
Money, must soon Outstrip all his brother Officers. And I am of
oppinion that Clarke has the undoubted right to the Captain
Lieutenancie, Notwithstanding Sr Williams purchased Seniority,
and I do recommend him as Such, and Rainsford Next upon any
Promotions in the Regiment.

The Vacant Ensigns I hope your Lordship will get me, at least
to Gild a Pill, that I as well as all the Old Lieutenant Generals in
the Army have had lately Crouded down their Throats, by the
Duke of Marlbro's Commission of General of the Foot, which
Rank I cannot persuade my Self, The Kings Justice, or the known
Custome of all Armies can permit to be to Our prejudice. Permit
me My Dear Lord, to say Many Among us of far greater Service
than his Grace.

Ipswich 3b, no. 62

202

Lord George Sackville to Barrington

Camp at Anruchte
[i.e. Anröchte near Lippstadt]
[Holograph]   14 June 1759

I have been prevented writing to your Lordship, by having lately
been much out of order. I am now so well recover'd as to be able to
attend my Duty as usual.

I am sorry it so happens that I cannot recommend Lt Bland to
succeed to the Troop, his being the Generals nephew is an
unlucky circumstance, as it hurts me to be obliged to state
objections which must be disagreeable to the good old General,
for whom I always had the greatest regard.

The Truth is that the Lieutenant Colonel, the Major and all the Captains agree that Lt Bland is not fit to be rais'd to the rank of Captain or to be trusted with the Command of a Troop, and this opinion of theirs is confirm'd by the Major General of the Brigade, under these circumstances your Lordship perceives I should ill discharge my Duty to His Majesty if I did not lay before your Lordship my real sentiments upon this occasion, and I hope you will recommend Lt. Lovibond for the purchase of the Troop as I am told, (tho' I have little or no personal acquaintance with him) that he is a very diligent and an intelligent officer.

Lt Bland has not been long in his present rank is but nineteen years of age, and he may hereafter reflect upon his past Conduct and endeavour to deserve the good opinion and approbation of the officers of the Regiment. Col: Sloper acquainted Genl. Bland with the Steps he had taken, and Capt. Hamilton, in whom the Genl chiefly confides has wrote to the same purpose.

I would not have troubled your Lordship so particularly upon such a subject had I not been desirous of Convincing you that I did not upon slight grounds make objections to the natural Course of Promotions, and I am glad in this case it happens that Lt Lovibond is barely known to me, all I insisted upon was to have an Elder Lieutenant than Mr Bland that the general might feel less how undeserving his nephew was.

* * *

Ipswich 3b, no. 82.

203

Barrington to Lt.-Colonel Hector Monroe

[Copy]   War Office
                                          12 October 1765

I have the pleasure to acquaint you, that the King has promoted You to the Rank of Lieutenant Colonel, in consideration of your meritorious Conduct in India & distinguish'd Services to His Majesty & the Publick.

A Step of this sort, given after important Successes, to the Eldest Major in the Army who has any expectation of advancement & which has been invariably bestow'd on every Major who like you has had the Command of a Regiment in India, during the late War; may not appear any extraordinary favor to those who left England before the Peace: but things are much changed since that time. Promotion is grown so difficult, the objections to Brevets are so well founded and the King's intentions & declarations that Rank shall not be given in that way are so well known; that nothing less than the Circumstances before mentioned, joined to your very extraordinary merit acknowledg'd by all the World and highly extoll'd in some Letters received lately from General Lawrence your Commander in Chief, cou'd have excepted you out of the general Rule, and produced this unusual & unsolicited Mark of Royal approbation. I am certain you will receive it with all proper gratitude; & shew how much you deserve it, by the correspondency of your future conduct to the past.

I feel very particular satisfaction that you have had this mark of favor since my Return to the War Office, but wou'd have laid me under great difficulties, if I had not long since disposed of the noble present you sent me for your profit and advantage, as I informed you by a letter written last year.

W.O. 4/78, p. 109

204

Barrington to Charles Townshend

[Copy in Barrington's hand]
Cavendish Square
24 April 1762

I was informed last week, that a Subaltern, late of the 5th Regiment, named Gillingham, had obtained leave to sell out of the Army, on his assertion that he bought his Commissions, particularly that of Ensign. It has I find been since recollected, that he signed the usual Paper, declaring on his honor, that neither he, nor any other person to the best of his knowlege, had given any thing for the Ensigncy: And it appears (by what is commonly called the *private* Notification Book, which I left for public inspection when I quitted the Office) that he was recommended by Monsieur Mello the Minister of Portugal.

I took the first opportunity of speaking to General Hodgson on this Subject, who confirm'd the story; & at my desire sent me Gillingham's father who is a Master Brickmaker & Surveyor, & a man, as the General has been inform'd, of very good character; which information his behaviour to me confirm'd: he gave me the following account with the utmost frankness.

He intended to breed up his son to his own business, but the young man would not be satisfied without going into the Army. Being shewed an Advertisement in the News Papers of a Commission to be sold, he was prevailed on to meet the Advertiser who said his name was De Marville; that he taught French and Geography, and was employed by the Minister of Portugal, to sell a Commission for his benefit. Gillingham deposited 300 Guineas at Childs', to be delivered when the Commission should be obtained for his son; and wch accordingly was afterwards paid to Monsieur De Marville. Young Gillingham was twice carried by De Marville to Monsr Mello, and also to a woman who he was told was that Minister's Mistress, & lived in Leicesterfields; to whose Maid Servant 2 guineas were given, 3 more to a man whom Gillingham senior does not know, and 12 Guineas to De Marville himself for his trouble; he protesting that all the purchase money was for the sole use of Monsieur Mello. The young man, when the Commission was out, went with De Marville to Lord Geo. Bentinck then Colonel of the Regiment, by whom he was approved: but the father seemed surprised, and much concerned when I acquainted him with the Declaration his son had given, which said he, 'I would never have suffered, had I been made acquainted with it; for my son knew it was untrue'. These particulars, Mr Gillingham protested, were all he knew of the transaction.

I saw Monsieur Mello the same day & asked him if he recollected his having recommended a person to me, for an Ensigncy, about three years since; which he did recollect. I then desired to know, at whose request he had given himself that trouble; to which he answered that a French Master, one De Marville who had been recommended to him for his improvement in the French Language soon after his arrival in England, had begg'd of him to do this good Office for a friend of his own; and De Marville having behaved much to his satisfaction, he had been prevailed on to mention the request to me.

Monsieur Mello said he had sent for the young man, on my requiring to be satisfied that he was of an age and figure proper for the Commission desired; and that he had also spoke very seriously to De Marville, in consequence of my caution about the particular care necessary to prevent money or other gratification being clandestinely paid on that account; whereupon De Marville had given him the most satisfactory assurances; and added that every such corruption was become impracticable, by reason of an Oath which all Ensigns were obliged to take at the War Office.

Monsieur Mello declared the utmost ignorance as to all that Mr Gillingham had told me concerning the Woman in Leicesterfields; & he denied being acquainted with any Woman so described: he was greatly concerned at his facility in recommending De Marville's request to me & express'd great indignation at the manner in which this imposition had been put upon him.

I need not add, that in this transaction I have not the least suspicion injurious to the honor of the Portugueze Minister: I well remember all that has before been stated to have past between him & me; & that the late King willingly consented to Gillingham's having a Commission in an old Regiment, on being told that it was desired by Monsr. Mello.

I sent a person to inspect the Books at Mr Child's Shop, & he finds that 300 Guineas were paid in by Gillingham, & paid out to De Marville in the manner beforementioned.

Having thus track'd to it's source, an iniquity which happened while I was Secretary at War, I think it incumbent on me to lay my discoveries before you; not doubting but you will take every possible measure, to find out & punish all who have been concerned in so infamous a transaction.

P.S. I forgot to mention a circumstance which shews that De Marville continues to transact the Sale of Commissions. Mr

Gillingham told me that a person came to him lately, & enquired how De Marville had used him in the business of the Commission bought by his son. The person said the motive of his enquiry was that De Marville was negociating a purchase of the same kind for a friend of his.

Ipswich 3b, no. 222

205

Charles Townshend to Barrington

[Holograph]   Grosvenor Square
                                                 Sunday, 5 o'clock

I have this moment received your Lordship's representation of the circumstances attending the sale of Lieutenant Gillingham's commission. Your Lordship may be assured that I will pursue the most effectual measures the Law directs for the full discovery and adequate punishment of Those, who have evaded all the prudent restrictions you so wisely established at the War-Office, and been accomplices in so infamous a transaction. I have already ordered a letter to be wrote to Mr Webb, ordering him, without delay, to take the method he thinks most expeditious of bringing the Matter itself to Trial, and the Parties to Justice.

Ipswich 3b, no. 217

206

Notice on purchase of commissions

[Printed]   24–27 February 1759

This is to give Notice, that, for the Future, whoever intends to purchase a Commission in the Army, should first inform himself at the War Office, whether the Commission, for which he is in Treaty, may be sold with the King's Leave. And in all Instances, where it shall be found that any Money, or other Consideration, has been given for a Commission, not openly sold with the Leave of His Majesty, the Person obtaining such Commission will be superseded.

By His Majesty's Command
Barrington

London Gazette, No 9873, and six subsequent issues

207

List of rules of service and preferment for officers, for the use of the King

[Copy in Barrington's hand]   n.d. [1765]

Your Majesty having been pleased to direct that I should reduce into writing such General Rules relative to the Army, as you have thought fit to be observ'd, but which however do not appear in the Books of the War Office. In obedience to your Majesty's said Command, I most humbly represent

1st That your Majesty does not permit Officers to sell any Commissions in the Army which they did not purchase; and that you confine buying and selling to Regimental Commissions only. Commissions in the Invalids are never bought or sold.

2nd That your Majesty directs when Commissions are sold, that the Commanding Officer of the Regiments shall always recommend the Purchasers whether in or out of the Corps.

3rd That your Majesty does not allow Officers to go out on their Pay, on any occasion whatever.

4th That no Warrants for Leave of Absence are to be brought to your Majesty to be signed, unless such Leave be recommended by the Commanding Officer of the Corps, And that such recommendation be always stated in the said Warrants.

5th That unless on very extraordinary occasions all the Regimental Vacancies shall be filled from the Half Pay; and that Half Pay Officers be always replac'd according to the rank in which they were reduced.

6th That no Exchange between Officers on Half and whole Pay shall be allowed, unless when both are of the same rank.

7th That no Exchange between Officers of different Corps shall be allow'd except when their rank is the same, when each Colonel consents, and when both parties have given their honour that no pecuniary consideration is, or shall be given or received.

All which is most humbly submitted.

Ipswich 3b, no. 379

208

Barrington to Charles Gould, Judge Advocate General

[Copy] War Office
30 October 1765

Certain Commissions in the Army are sometimes allowed to be sold, altho' the King in general be very much averse to a practice injurious to Officers of merit who have no money; but it is highly proper when any Commissions are sold that their Price should be fixed, determined & known: Without some Regulation of that kind, a practice exceptionable at best, may be rendered very hurtful to the Army.

Before the King declares H.P. on this Subject He wishes to know the opinion of his General Officers what Sum is proper to be given for each of the following Commissions.

Horseguards
1st & 2nd Lieutenant & Lieutenant Colonel
Cornet & Major
Guidon & Major
Exempt & Captain
Brigadier & Lieutenant
Adjutant & Lieutenant
Sub Brigadier & Cornet

Grenadier Guards
Lieutenant & Lieutenant Colonel

Major
Lieutenant & Captain
Guidon & Captain
Sub Lieutenant
Adjutant & Sub Lieutenant

Horse
Lieutenant Colonel
Major
Captain
Capt. Lieutenant
Lieutenant
Cornet

Dragoon Guards & Dragoons
Lieutenant Colonel
Major
Captain
Captain Lieutenant
Lieutenant
Cornet

Foot Guards
Lieutenant Colonel
1st Major
2nd Major
3rd Major
Captain
Captain Lieutenant
Lieutenant
Ensign

Marching Regiments of Foot
Lieutenant Colonel
Major
Captain
Captain Lieutenant
Lieutenant
Ensign or 2 Lieutenant

It is therefore His Majesty's Pleasure that you do Summon the Board of General Officers who are to consider the Matter aforesaid, and you will transmit to me their opinions thereon to be laid before His Majesty. And it is His Majesty's further Pleasure that they also take into their consideration whether any difference should be made between the price of Commissions in Regiments serving in and out of Europe, and if any to specify what difference.

W.O. 4/77, pp. 484–486

209

Barrington to Messrs Cox & Drummond and other agents (see below)

[Copy]   War Office
16 November 1765

I desire that for the future, whenever You recommend to me in the Colonel's Name, that any Officer shall be allowed to dispose of his Commission, You will always apprize me for the King's information, what Commissions that Officer bought, in what Regiments, and at what price, I likewise desire that You will always send all recommendations whatever for Commissions and for Leaves of Absence to my House in Cavendish Square.

Like Letters of same date to the following Agents, Viz.

Messrs. Bishop & Kidgell	George Ross Esqr.
Messrs. Meyrick & Porter	John Richardson Esqr.
Ireland Esqr.	David Roberts Esqr.
John Loumies Esqr.	Augustin Oldham Esqr.
Vincent Mathias Esqr.	James Fitter Esqr.
Blunt Esqr.	Thos. Fisher Esqr.
Sir Thomas Wilson	James Baird Esqr.
John Winter Esqr.	
Henry Bullock Esqr.	
John Lamb Esqr.	

W.O. 4/78, p. 80

Barrington to Charles Gould, Judge Advocate General

[Copy]   War Office
                                                 8 February 1766

I have laid before the king, your letter of the 31st day of January, containing a Report of the Board of General Officers on a matter referr'd to them by His Majesty in my Letter of the 3rd day of October last, touching the different prices to be given for Commissions in the Army, in cases where He shall please to allow them to be sold. The King entirely approves the said Report, and every particular therein contained. His Majesty Commands me to express his perfect satisfaction to the Officers who have signed it; and to acquaint them that He will Order what they recommend to be invariably observ'd for the future, under pain of His highest Displeasure.

Having now finish'd what I am Commanded by the King to communicate to the Board, I take this opportunity of conveying thro' you, Sir, to the Generals who compose it, some thoughts on a matter of great importance to the Regiments they Command, and indeed to the whole Army.

Colonels frequently recommend that Officers in their respective Corps should sell Commissions which they did not buy: Long and faithful Service has worn them out, they have families, the Eldest in each Rank are able and willing to purchase, they all deserve preferment which in time of Peace can scarcely be obtained any other way; In short the good of the Corps, merit and humanity all strongly plead for the indulgence which is Recommended. It is no wonder that these Arguments have so frequently succeeded, when any one of them would be sufficient inducement, if there were not another side of the Question.

Officers who buy are permitted to Sell; Men who find themselves growing old or infirm dispose of their Commissions which are purchased by the Young and the healthy; and thus what has been once bought continues for ever at Sale, especially in time of Peace, except now and then in a case of sudden or unexpected death. The Consequence often is, that Men who come in to the

Army with the warmest dispositions to the Service, whose Business becomes their pleasure, who distinguish themselves on every occasion that offers, are kept all their lives in the lowest ranks because they are poor. These meritorious Officers have often the cruel mortification of seeing themselves Commanded by Young Men of opulent families, who came much later into the Service; and whose fortunes have enabled them to amuse themselves frequently elsewhere, while the others continually at Quarters, have done the duty of those Gentlemen and have learnt their own.

Flagrant abuses seldom grow up at once, but arise from circumstances whose Consequences were not foreseen. The first time a Commission is sold, it is almost always bought by a Good Officer the next in Succession; he afterwards asks to sell; the Corps is chang'd, the senior officers have merit and long Service, but they have no money. This circumstance does not prevent the transaction; and the Commission is purchas'd perhaps by the Youngest, least steady & least experienced of that Corps or of some other, to the infinite distress of many deserving Men, and to the great scandal and Detriment of the Service. Like circumstances happen more or less every change, and bring with them the same distress and mischief: Each fresh Commission brought to Market multiplies both, and therefore instead of encreasing purchases, they cannot be too much lessen'd, so far as is consistent with the invariable practice of the Army.

That Colonels of Regiments should not attend to these consequences is not matter either of Wonder or blame: their care is extended no farther than to their own Corps, & while they command it; but the Officer of the Crown who is entrusted with the important Charge of the whole Army, a Body whose probable duration infinitely exceeds the short Space allotted to Individuals, cannot be too vigilant, least confin'd temporary convenience or Compassion, should produce general permanent mischief or distress. To be firm in preventing future evil by immediate refusal, is not the least difficult part of his Duty: He must withstand the feelings of humanity and the desire to please; he must expect the uncandid interpretation of the prejudic'd, the hasty judgment of the ignorant, and the malignant conclusion of the disappointed; Arrows shot in the Dark, against which a good conscience is an insufficient defence: He must often contradict the passions & Interests of the powerful; and even disappoint the wishes and expectations of the deserving: He must acquire a great many Enemies, and lose a great many friends; and yet he had better suffer all this than do wrong.

It is of consequence that the Army should know the Rules of the Service, and see the reason of them. That Officers should sell what they bought and no more, has long been a Rule, and perhaps this Letter will tend to explain the grounds on which it was Establish'd. If that Rule be good, can it be too invariably observed? Specious distinctions will be made; they should never be admitted, for every deviation tends to disuse. Nothing can be more fatal for the Army in general, than occasional exceptions from good regulations; or give more advantage to the unjust attempts of the importunate & of the Great. It is frequently ask'd what can be done with an Officer who is become useless to his Corps thro' Age, Wounds, or infirmities? It must be owned there are too few comfortable Retreats from active service in this Country, however Our Establishment affords some. The Commissions in the Invalids, small Government and other Garrison Employments always properly bestowed, would go a great way; 'till there can be a more ample provision, the Young & healthy must do the duty of the old and infirm; and they can sufficiently do it in time of Peace, hereafter in their turn, they may receive the like benefit themselves; and in the mean time escape a thousand mortifications to which indigent merit is too often expos'd. It frequently happens in the Army, as elsewhere, that want of money is also accompanyed by a want of assisting friends: but the poor, tho' deserving Officer should always find at the War Office, a constant assertor of his rights, and faithful Guardian of his Interests.

W.O. 4/78, pp. 373–377

211

Barrington to Lord Conyngham

[Copy]
Cavendish Square,
31 October 1768

Ever since Lord Granby was appointed Commander in Chief, he has at my desire recommended to all Vacancies in the Army, & I have not recommended to one. I have had continual occasion to approve of this arrangement, but I am now and then sorry (as in the present instance) that it prevents my obliging persons whom I respect.

Ipswich 107

212

Barrington to Lord Granby, Commander-in-Chief

[Copy]
Cavendish Square
17 June 1767

I was in hopes of meeting you at Court today; if I had seen you there I could have saved you the trouble of a Letter.

All your recommendations are agreed to, except that of Lieut. Smith to be Judge Advocate at Minorca. I flatter myself you will approve my reasons for not proposing it to the King.

It comes recommended to you from Colonel Johnstone, which I know because the same came recommended by him to me. I think the Military Officers in Regts should not have Civil Employments which require permanent residence in Garrisons. It is sometimes the Case, but in my opinion always wrong.

I know, my Dear Lord, that you will not be displeas'd with my informing you that neither the Duke of Cumberland or Lord Ligonier ever interfered with the War Office in the disposal of those Employments belonging to the Army which can be held and executed by Civil Men. This patronage always belonged to the Secretary at War and is all that the present Secretary, your affectionate humble Servant has kept, or wishes to enjoy.

If I had recommended a friend, Voter, or Relation of my own to such an Employment, no body could have blamed me: but I have recommended for it, & the office of Commissary of the Musters which always went with it, a man whom I only know from his distresses. He was a captain in the Army, is too infirm to return to active Service, & tho' he serv'd long and unexceptionably yet he had not so good pretensions to Invalids as Men without Legs & Arms, of which your Lordship & I know more than can be provided for. He is in short, very poor, very well born, & well qualified to fill the Civil Offices enjoy'd by Zachary Moore; Both of them will give him 10s a day, & save 5s a day which is his half Pay to the Publick.

P.S. I will fully explain all this to Johnstone, & take the failure of this recommendation entirely on myself.

Ipswich 107

213

Duke of Argyle to Barrington

[Holograph]   Argyle House
                                                4 May 1774

From the manner in which Your Lordship receivd my Application in favour of Lt Patrick Campbell, I did not think you woud have examined so narrowly in order to find out an objection to him, which however I cannot say seems to me to have any Foundation. Tho he might have been a boy at School when he got his Commission, he was perhaps sixteen years of age. If he did not join his Regiment, his Colonel or the Secretary at War I suppose had their reasons for allowing him to be absent, And most probably he was employed in recruiting, having I believe obtaind his Commission on account of being able to raise a considerable number of men, which however was only to be done at a great expence, & indeed in many cases was equal to purchasing a Commission. As to his being preferred to other Candidates for the same favour, Your Lordship well knows that the number of them lies within a very small compass, & if all their pretensions were to be scrutinized without favour, I scarcely think there would be any who would have a better right. I therefore hope your Lordship will not set him aside after having given me such assurances that my request should be complied with in consequence of which I have pledged my Credit and interest to his relations who are persons of great consequence to me, that he should very soon be provided for. I am to set out to morrow at noon for Scotland, & therefore beg to have your Lordship's answer which I flatter myself will not bring a disappointment to me, and the friends of this young Gentleman whom I shall meet with immediately on my Arrival.

Ipswich 6a2, no. 443.

214

Barrington to the Duke of Argyle

[Holograph]   Cavendish Square
5 May 1774

On my return home last night I found myself honour'd by your Grace's Letter of yesterday. I shall not trouble your Grace by a repetition of the facts on which I have formed my opinion of Lt. P. Campbell's pretensions: I will only observe that I stated that opinion the day after I learned those facts from Col. Oswald; & till then I could only express that general desire to assist your Grace's wishes which I shall always feel on every occasion that offers.

When I returned to the War Office in the year 1765 in order to do fair justice to the Officers of half pay I establish'd the following method of conveying their applications & pretensions to the Crown. Two Books were prepared with a number of Columns in which, (according to their several ranks) the names, Seniority & respective Corps of such as applied for preferment were entered; Likewise abstracts of their Memorials, characters given by the Colonels under whom they had last served & the names of persons by whom they were recommended. One of these Books I keep myself; the other is always in the King's possession, except when he gives it to me that I may enter fresh applications. When a proper vacancy happens for a half pay Officer H.M. always

consults his Book & makes his choice which I guide no farther
than by submitting to his particular consideration such names as
from any circumstance seem to deserve it; but he never fails to
consider & weigh *every* application. I shall take care that Mr
Campbell's application, Col. Oswald's report with your Grace's
recommendation in your own name & the Duke of Athol's, as
likewise the recommendation of Lord Breadalbane shall be well
consider'd by the King. If powerful & respectable sollicitation
should ever prevail over merit & Service, it would be in the Case
which is the Subject of this Letter; but I ought to inform your
Grace that if any Lieut. like Mr Campbell has ever got employment (which I doubt) it has been only by Exchange recommended
by the Colonel of the Regt. into which he was brought.

I will only add that there are still unprovided for 21 Lieuts. who
after serving in that rank & likewise as Ensns during the late War
in Corps older than Sir Wm Drapers which was long employ'd in
India, have been long to their concern & mine languishing on
halfpay.

Ipswich 6a2, no. 444

215

Barrington to Lord Bute

[Copy]   Cavendish Square
                                          30 August 1771

In consequence of your Commands I have laid your Letter before
the King who orders me to state to your Lōp the real truth in
respect to your request that Mr Stuart may have a Troop of
Dragoons.

There are, My Lord, Many Captains of Cavalry who were
reduced to half pay at the conclusion of the last War, during
which, a number of them served with much honor & distinction:
With these only one set of Officers can come in competition, Vizt.
Those Captain Lieutenants of Dragoons who have served well
both before & since the Peace. In fact no vacant Troop has gone
otherwise than either to the one or the other. Justice argues

forcibly in their favor, & if Government were deaf to that Plea, it would not in those times dare to disregard their pretensions.

In two instances, & only in two, Young Men of Quality serving in the Infantry have been allowed to *buy* Troops. Your Lordship will permit me to state shortly the circumstances of those two transactions.

Lord Robert Kerr had a friend a Captain in the Inniskillin who having a right to sell would sell to no body but his Lordship. In these circumstances the Subalterns all thought it their interest that Lord Robert should buy the Troop, and General Cholmondley the Colonel therefore recommended it strongly.

Lord Thomas Clinton bought a Troop in Mostyns at the Strong recommendation of the General, who sollicited the King in person, & undertook that all his Subalterns should be pleased with his Lordship's getting over their heads. Notwithstanding that assertion, I frankly excused myself to the Duke of Newcastle from giving any assistance in this business, tho' I acknowledged my Obligations to his family, & shall always gratefully remember them.

The King directs me to assure your Lõp that He will not refuse to Mr Stuart what He has granted or would grant to any young Men of Quality in the Army.

May I venture, My Lord, to add from Myself that I shall be always happy to talk over with Mr Stuart, or any person employed by him, every Proposal which he thinks can be for his advantage, and he may depend on every friendly assistance that I would give to a Son of my own.

Ipswich 107

216

Barrington to James Grenville

[Copy]   Cavendish Square
4 April 1772

I can now inform you that your Son has a Company by purchase in the Coldstream Regt of Guards: & I may wish you joy of that event with a clear conscience, after having done my best that it should go in the Corps. He owes his promotion to the King's particular favour, and he is the more distinguished by it, as H.M. seldom allows any commissions (especially those which are purchased) to go out of the regular course. The King remembers that Lord Granby, (to whom Mr Grenville was so long Aid de Camp) often recommended him in the warmest manner, prevented his purchasing advancement some years ago, intending to propose him for a Company in the Guards; & was only prevented from executing that intention, by the want of a proper vacancy while he continued Commander in Chief. I think I may add that his father's very honourable & meritorious conduct has been no inconsiderable inducement. In short, Dear Sir, I congratulate you on this very unusual manner of a Royal favour, such as hath seldom happened & indeed ought seldom to happen to Captains in Marching Regts, however deserving.

Ipswich 107

217

The King to Barrington

[Holograph]   Queen's House
                                        7.35 p.m. 6 April 1774

Lord Barrington, having seen Your Coach at the War Office when I went to the Parliament House this day, I trust this will catch You yet in Town. I therefore send to acquaint You, that the Duke of Athol has this day sent a letter by which he resigns the Government of Upnor Castle in the name of his Uncle Colonel Murray, You will therefore notify his friend Captain Browne as Governor of Upnor Castle.

I have mentioned the idea of promoting General Mordaunt to Berwick and Lieut General Craig to Sheerness, to Lord Amherst who thinks no one can with reason blame my disposition on this occasion, I have seen a letter from Sir Edw. Hughes at the Cape which authentically mentions the death of Sir John Clavering.

Ipswich 111, no. 84

218

Lord Holland to Barrington

[Holograph]   Holland House, Middlesex
5 January 1773

I have found a Vacancy which Genl. Campbell dos expect your
Lordship will fill up, and will have no objection, to your filling it
up with My Son, all the Lieutenants except a very young one
refuses. My Son who is an Old Cornet of Dragoons will be very
glad of this Company of Foot, and I fancy, you will find the Gen[l].
nor any body else averse to it, I am sure My Dear Lord Barrington
will not. Harry is at Quarters and I believe very desirous to go on
in the profession, which he seems to set his heart upon more than
I would have had him done, when I wish'd him to be a Clergyman.
But thats over, and I hope he will find admission to this Company.
I think I can assure you he will stick extreamly to it, and I shall be
mighty glad to send for him to Town for the Purpose. Mr. Powell
will talk to your Lordship upon this subject and assure you that
he is big enough, & handsome enough, & Old enough. Let
me assure you that it would oblige My Lady Holland & me
exceedingly,

Ipswich 6a2, no. 5

219

Lord Chatham to Barrington

[Holograph]   Burton Pynsent
5 November 1773

The very obliging expressions with which your Lordship has
honourd Lord Pitt, in your answer to General Carleton on this
Subject, are too flattering towards the Son, and too kind towards
the father, to allow me to pass in silence such interesting marks of
friendship. After the many kind offices I have experienced, thro'
our long acquaintance I indulge, with pleasure, the hope that your

Lordship will not be unmindful of a young man, aspiring, with some impatience, to begin that Profession, which constitutes Him the immediate Client of your Lordship. Lord Pitt, (let me say by the way) is now pass't seventeen, he has indeed but just turned the corner, having been born in October, if happily, he arrives to the grey hair, he may not possibly, be *then* unwilling to sink a year in his register. at present, your Lordship will easily imagine, he counts his *seventeen* with no small pleasure. nothing can be kinder, my Dear Lord, than the thought of managing a vacancy for him in the 47th if such an arrangement cou'd (with the liking of All Parties concernd) take place, I shou'd feel myself highly indebted to your Lordship's friendship on so interesting an occasion, to my Son's ardour and to my own wishes for him.

Ipswich 6a2, no. 548

220

Barrington to Lord Chatham

[Copy]   Cavendish Square
                                                 November 5 1773

I should have acknowledged by last post the honour of your Lordship's most friendly and obliging Letter if I had not been desireous to convey some information concerning the matter entrusted to my care together with my thanks for the confidence you reposed in me. I am just come from Court where I received full powers to bring Lord Pitt into the Army in the way most advantagious for him. Your Lordship could not have chosen a better Corps than the 47th destined to Quebec where its Colonel is Governor. I sincerely wish there was a vacant Ensigncy in it; There is one in the 29th commanded by Major General Evelyn and returning to England which may possibly furnish an opening in the 47th. I shall immediately invest M General Carleton with the disposal of it. If it is acceptable to any of his Ensigns, your wish (and permit me to add mine) is compleated: If they decline it, I submit to your Lordship's consideration whether Lord Pitt might not take it himself: With leave of absence he might attend Genl.

Carleton to Quebec, ready there for the first open colours in the 47th. It may be two or three years before a vacancy happens in that Corps; and as he is seventeen, he should not remain one unnecessary day out of the Army. You see my Lord I am as impatient as Lord Pitt can be, and I hope he will beleive so. I am indeed eager to bring such a Recruit into the Service, and to assist the judicious plan you have formed for him: I hope it will succeed to the full extent of your wishes, and that he may attain every Glory and advantage which a military profession can furnish, adorned by every accomplishment and Virtue of civil life.

I am sorry My Dear Lord that I am not able in somewhat more material than this triffle, to shew the truth and affectionate respect with which I have been five and thirty years and shall be all my life,

Your Lordships
* * * &c

P.S.
I am so well acquainted with Lady Chatham's sentiments that I do not fear to offend her by endeavouring to send her son to America. I beg leave to add my respects to her Ladyship & Compliments to Lord Pitt.

Ipswich 6a2, no. 553

221

Lord Chatham to Barrington

[Holograph]   Burton Pynsent
                                                    10 November 1773

Tho' but just able to use a gouty hand, I can not defer a moment to return your Lordship abundance of very sincere thanks for the kind manner in which you have had the goodness to meet *all our* wishes for my Son. Lady Chatham, Lord Pitt, and your humble servant, *the whole House*, Root and Branch, have the justest Sense of your Lordship's most obliging Proceeding. Lady Chatham feels herself much honour'd by the flattering guess you make of

308

her maternal Sentiments, and has charged me with her particular Compliments to your Lordship, the future Ensign is more your obliged servant than I have words to say; and if making young minds, rightly disposed, happy be what I know it is to your Lordship, your goodness, on this occasion, is not in vain: the vacant Colours in the 29th, with the disposal of which General Carleton is invested, will probably produce the arrangements wish'd; and the kind facility your Lordship has suggested, in order to expedite our desires, fills up the measure of our obligations, keeping the kind and invariable tenour of *thirty five years* of friendly Offices, which you remember, in a manner so flattering to me.

The *full Powers* your Lordship receiv'd at the *high Place* you just came from, when you honoured me with your letter, cou'd not fail to penetrate my mind with the deepest and warmest Sentiments of Veneration, and most dutiful feelings of grateful Sensibility: and I have only to wish for my Son, that he may prove not unworthy of such gracious marks of Condescension and favour. if it be not improper your Lordship wou'd confer a great favour by laying, on any fit opportunity, these Sentiments of Duty at the King's feet.

it is now high time my Dear Lord, to release you: the Chapter of thanks, when the Heart is really interested is, you know, a long one and not easy to close. for this time, at least, I will close it by assuring you I am ever, my Dear Lord, [etc.]

Ipswich 6a2, no. 557

222

Captain P. Fancourt to Barrington

[Holograph]   Gibraltar
                                                    5 December 1774

Will your Lordship give an Old Officer leave to lay before you a few unadorned truths in regard to himself.

In the year 1756 on the breaking out of the French Warr, I purchased an Ensigncy in the 14th Regt. of foot then in Gibralter

& paid 360 Guineas for it; in January 1762 on the breaking out of the Spanish Warr I purchased my Company in the Regt. I am now in the (56th) when it was under embarking orders for Foreign service, and pay'd 1600 Guineas for it, besides being obliged to sell my Commission in the 13th Regt. at an under price; I was with the 56th Regt. at the Seige of the Havanna, saw several Lt. Colonels & Majors put in upon the Regt. there, & one Major while on the Irish Establishment, since that & on our embarking for this Garrison our present Major a Junior Captain & much younger Officer who purchased from half pay after our coming from the West Indies, has by paying a large Sum of mony got over my head.

I dont mean my Lord to plead any merit as I am conscious I have done no more than my duty; all that I request from your Lordship is (and which I hope you will think reasonable) that in case any further purchasing should be going on in the 56th Regt. by the present Majors purchasing a Lieut. Colloncy or otherwise, your Lordship will look on me as entitl'd to succeed according to the Kings regulation, and that I shall have a sufficient time given me to raise my mony.

I have neither high birth nor freinds of great interest to plead for me, nothing but the behaviour and character of a Gentleman, this my Lord are what must support me and what I glory in, the rest I must beg to sumitt to your Lordship, being satisfied that you will always do that justice, that you have so humanely promised in the conclusion of your letter of the 8th February 1766,

Ipswich 6a2, no. 541

223

Barrington to Captain P. Fancourt

[Rough draft]   Cavendish Square
                                               31 December 1774

I have recd yr Lr. of the 5th inst.: The transactions you mention in it, since you have been in the 56th Regt having happened either when I was not in the W.O. or while the Corps was in Ireland, did not come within my knowledge. My invariable rule in all matters of purchase is to wait for the Colonel's recomdn., & never to let any Officer suffer in his prefermt. for want of reasonable time to provide money for his advancement. I am also always very sorry when the Officer next in Succession is not promoted.

Ipswich 6a2, no. 542

224

Barrington to Messrs Ross and Gray, and to sixteen other agents

[Copy] War Office
17 November 1772

I am to acquaint you that for the future, it will not be required that Officers who purchase Commissions in the Army should sign Certificates that they have not given, and will not give more than the regulated price; but it is not to be understood that the King will permit the least Relaxation of his Orders expressed in a Warrant under his Royal Sign Manual, dated the 10th February 1766, and directing the Strict Observance of the price for Military Commissions settled by a Board of twenty Nine General Officers in that Year. Of this you will acquaint the Colonels of Regiments to which you are Agent, and that His Majesty expects they will take the utmost possible care, that no Commission in the Regiments under their Command shall be sold for more than the Regulated Price.

W.O. 4/90, p. 242

225

Regulation on Purchase

[Copy] War Office
23 December 1775

It is the King's Pleasure, that for the future whenever any Officer in the Army shall desire to sell his Commission, he shall sign a Memorial stating the grounds on which he forms his Expectations of being permitted to dispose of his Commission, and praying that he may be allowed to sell it at the regulated Price to any Person whom HM shall appoint.

If such Memorialist be with the Regiment, he shall deliver his Memorial to the Officer commanding at Quarters, who shall send the same to his Colonel, (if within the Realm) who must approve thereof, previous to its being laid before His Majesty. But in the Absence of the Colonel, if the Lieut. Colonel be not at Quarters, the Memorial shall be sent to him in order that he may transmit it to the War Office, certifying under his hand the truth of the facts therein contained, so far as his knowledge or belief may extend.

In North America these Memorials shall be transmitted, certified as aforesaid, to the Commander in Chief. In Gibraltar and Minorca to the Governor or Commandant for the time being in these Stations. But in the West Indies they may be sent directly to the War Office. It is however the King's Pleasure, that a Duplicate shall at the same time be always sent to the Colonels of the Regiments. Given at the War Office this 23d day of December 1775.

By HMC
Barrington

W.O. 26/29, p. 177

226

Captain A. Singleton to Barrington

[Holograph]   Landguard Fort
                                                1 July 1773

I am Honoured with your Lordship's letter; and am sorry to find my Situation is not deemed 'Sufficiently Single' to merit the Smallest Favour. That it is, notwithstanding, absolutely and altogether 'single', I am, myself, pretty confident.

When I can hear of an Officer who has served seven & twenty years with an unblameable and unblamed Character; That has *purchased all his Commissions, & that has been sent Home Express with a Recommendation from a Commander in Chief on a foreign Service* (which was my Case Eleven years ago) and that yet Continues In the same *Rank and with the Same Emoluments He then held*; I shall, I say, when that Happens, My Lord! begin to be content with my situation and to think that I have not been hardly used. Till then (which I believe will be for ever) I shall Rest your Lordships Most Obedient and Most Humble Servant [etc.]

Ipswich 6a2, no. 124

227

Schedule of proposals from Major Allan MacDonald to Barrington

[Holograph]   London
                                                   22 April 1773

1st   That I may have a regular Promotion, in Course of a long Service, & repeated Promises; being long ago, not only, the oldest Captain in the 59th, but also in the Army.

2dly That I have Leave to sell to the best advantage, having received my Company 18 years ago, in lieu of a Pension on the Scotch Exchequer of £200 a year without Fees; with repeated Promises of speedy Promotion.

3dly That I have Leave to sell at £1500, & be put on a Military Pension of 10s pr Day, during a short Life—*or on a Major's half Pay, with the Rank continued.

4thly That I receive some Lieut. Governmt of 10s pr Day, after selling my Compy, at £1500, or continuing my Company, as at present.

5thly That I have Leave to retire on my Pay, with £100 from each of the 4 succeeding officers, & be put on *Captain's half Pay; which only costs Government 5sh a Day, as a Reward for 28 years Service, & something more?

6thly That I have a Company of Invalids, in one of the best Quarters; with some little additional Support for my Family; such as His Majesty will think proper.

7thly That on Selling at £1500, I be allowed the Pay of Captain of the Guides, by my Warrant, justly due till General Bland's Death.

8thly Should the King on a fair Representation of my Case by the Minister at War, think of Civil Employments, for me & my Sons, genteely educated, any where, at Home or abroad, entirely and of the Army Department, where we have had no Chance, they would be gratefully acceptable.

* By the half Pay mentioned above is meant an equivalent Sum of his Majesty's gracious Bounty, as a military or civil Pension, not on the Army half pay list.

Ipswich 6a2, no. 71

228

Barrington to Major MacDonald

[Rough Draft, including corrections]   Cavendish Square
                                                        26 April 1773

I have carefully considered the Paper you sent to me, & I will very honestly frankly tell you my opinion of the Proposals therein contained. Some of them appear to me impracticable, others some improper to be done for anybody & those things which might perhaps be done for you when Vacancies happen may be also claimed by many good other Officers, who have as good or better pretensions to them. I may be mistaken, & whenever I find myself so I shall readily own it.

   I am always concerned when I cannot with propriety assist every any man's wishes; when I cannot but in that case, I fairly say so, & do not never deceive.

Ipswich 6a2, no. 72

229

Major MacDonald to Barrington

[Holograph] Downing Street
28 April 1773

It seems I misunderstood your Lordship, last week, when you was pleas'd, as I thought, to direct me to commit to writing what I then might judge practicable to be done for me and that your Lordship would take it into Consideration. In consequence of that favourable Countenance and of your Lordship's Answer to the Gentleman, who was so humane as to present my Letter, I did write what common Sense, some Experience and, possibly, self Interest dictated. If I exceeded the Bounds of Respect & Propriety, I am excessively sorry for it. I meant due Deference, Complacency and Distance; at the same Time my Heart was full of Gratitude for my Reception, & wrote from that sort of Gayety peculiar to an innocent Heart, when elated with a sure View of Success. Such was mine indeed, at the Time. I now received your Lordship's Letter, & with it a mortifying Blow, from which I can draw no favourable Conclusions. Notwithstanding, I'll hope for Leave, this once, to lay before your Lordship, that there is now in my Offer, in Conjunction with my Brother and a Brother in Law, a snug little Retirement in the West of Scotland, to which I would *retire* if in my Power. The Price at which my Company is fix'd, with £7 or 600 would put me in Possession of my Share, & put me forever out of the Way of the great world. I thought I might in some Respects claim this much, in the military Line, after the many Dissappointments I had, well known to your Lordship; to say nothing of a long & sometimes, a disagreeable Service. Alas, my Lord, I must think, & indeed so will many others, who know my History, that few Officers, at this instant, can lay stronger Claims to some little notice, than I can. £26 a year will be lost to my Wife and Children, if I sell at £1500. I should be ready to fall a Sacrifice, this Moment, should any certain Prospect open for them. My Heart is fallen to the opposite Extremity of last Wednesday's Elevation.

Ipswich 6a2, no. 84

230

Barrington to Colonel Parslow, or officer commanding the 7th Foot

[Copy] War Office
4 January 1760

Having laid before the King your request that Lieut. Colo. Vignoles of your Regt. may be permitted to retire from the Service, and your recommendation of the following Succession in the Regt. Vizt Major Robt. Pigot to be Lieut. Colo. Capt. Wm. Nesbitt to be Major, Capt. Lieut. John Fowle to be Capt., Lieut. Messinden Johnson to be Capt. Lieutenant, Ensign George Kinlock Lieutenant, and a new Ensign to be Appointed, on Condition of their disclaiming all title or pretence of any Consideration here after in Consequence of their Commissions so obtained by the retiring of Lt. Colo. Vignoles from the Service, I am to Acquaint You that His Majesty has been pleased to Consent that Lieut. Colo. Vignoles should retire and that the Officers recommended by you should Succeed in the Regiment upon the Conditions abovementioned At the same time I am to desire by His Majestys Directions that you will order this letter Containing the Conditions on which His Majesty has Consented to this promotion to be Entered in your Regimental Book that no doubt may Arise about them at any time hereafter.

W.O. 4/59, p. 669

231

Barrington to Lord North

[Copy] Cavendish Square
December 1771

I am not surprized that you are so anxious to oblige Sir Gilbert Eliott; You cannot love or esteem him more, you cannot rate his importance higher than I do; and yet I must not assist in getting a Company for his Son.

Two invariable & indispensable rules of the Army are that every man shall begin Military Life with the lowest Commission, and that he shall be at least 16 years of Age before he obtain any. The Duke of Richmond was older before he was an Ensign in the Guards, in which station he remained several years till he got a Company in some new Levies. Your Lõp must remember that you recommended the Son of an Earl for Colours in a Marching Regt. which he could not have till he was 16 compleat. The late Duke of Cumberland when he commanded in Chief, gave an Ensigncy to the Orphan Son of an officer who lost his life in the Service; but finding the Boy not to be of the proper age, recalled his Commission, educated and maintained him till he was turned of 16, & then gave him a new one in another Regt.

Mr. Elliot was not I believe ten years of age when he had a Commission of Lieutenant, & soon after he was most irregularly made a Captain. At the reduction of the Corps, he was not kept on any List, or put on half pay: I know Sir Gilbert was above receiving any, but his Son could not have been allowed either rank or emolument after the north Briton had published his Case. Other Boys who were known to be under age were struck off when their Regts. were reduced, of which I happen to be acquainted with one instance. Some Boy-Lieutenants & Ensigns escaped observation; & a few of them may possibly have exchanged by recommendation of Colonels with Oficers who wanted to retire on half Pay; If Mr Elliot had not unfortunately been appointed a Captain, he, like others, might have escaped notice, & have got advantagiously into the Service; I heartily wish he had, both for his sake & mine.

As to the Precedents mention'd to your Lõp, I know nothing of them; but I will inform myself by conversing with Sir Gilbert Elliott. I am certain nothing irregular has been done on this Establishment, since for my sins, Military Recommendation devolved on me: Precedents are only to be followed when they are good: when bad they are to be used no otherwise than as Light Houses are at Sea.

· Mr Steuart bought an Ensigncy some years ago in the 37th. Regt. and afterwards a Lieutenancy in the 7th. His Father, Lord Bute, has asked a Company for him of the King, thro' me, but he cannot have one till he shall be recommended by some Colonel of a Regt. where the Lieutenants of any standing cannot purchase. The Nephew of the present Secretary at War, bought a Cornetcy; Served six years till he was eldest in that rank, & then bought a Lieutenantcy: What shall I say to the friends of Mr Steuart, Mr Price, or many others, if Mr Elliot is a Captain before them? I shall be told with great truth that his former Commission is a Nullity tho' it still remains in his possession; The whole world will condemn me, & what is worst of all, I shall condemn myself.

Ipswich 107

232

Colonel J. La Faussille (66th Foot) to Barrington

[Holograph]   Sunderland
                                                  25 March 1759

I have lately received a letter forwarded to me by the Admiralty Office, from a Serjeant of the 66th Regt. of Foot under my Command, dated at Morocco where he is, or rather was Prisoner with another Serjeant one Drummer and twenty two private men of my regiment, (part of the Detachment belonging to it now at Senegal) the letter dated the 1st. Jany. last; he reports to me that the Somerset Transport on board of which a Party of my regiment was embarked, was cast away the 29th. Novr. last on the coast of Barbary, and that twenty five men of my regiment lost their lives on that Occasion; and that Lieut. Willm. Harrison of the aforesaid 66th. Regt. who Commanded the party of it on board the said transport after escaping the Shipwreck, dyed on their March to Morocco the 13th. December last: As the Serjeants hand writing is perfectly well known, and that there is no room to doubt the Authenticity of his Account and report; I beg leave to recommend to Your Lordship Eldest Ensign Willm. Gregory of the aforesaid Regt. who has served two years and seven months in it, and is a very well behaved Young gentleman, to succeed Lieut. Willm. Harrison; I also recommend Mr William Catherwood to succeed Ensign Gregory in case he succeeds to the Lieutcy. now vacant; Mr Catherwood is nephew to a Capt. of Invalids of the garrison of Plymouth of the same name, who served with me upwards of thirty years in the King's or 8th. Regt. of Foot, & during the whole course of the late war abroad & at home on Account of the rebellion, and was severely wounded at Laffeldt: he is the only support the young gentleman has, and I entreat Your Lordship's favourable recommendation of him to His Majesty for the said Vacancy or any (if you are engaged) at home or abroad whether East or West Indies the Land or Marine service he is a handsome youth able & willing to serve.

Ipswich 3b, no. 54

233

Barrington to Ensign Renwick (Invalids at Yarmouth)

[Copy]   War Office
                                                          18 February 1766

I have received your Letter of the 15th instant, desiring me to move His Majesty in your behalf for a Lieutenancy in the Invalids, which Request it is not in my Power to comply with, as in the Invalid Corps, Promotion is not to be expected, Commissions there being always given to Officers according to the Rank in which they have suffered during Service.

W.O. 4/78, p. 412

234

Description of War Office patronage
after Barrington's term

[Entry in Office Book]   N.d. [July 1782]

There being a General, commissioned to act as Comander in Chief, the King's Pleasure is taken by Him, on all appointments to Regiments, Governments, Staff Brevet & Regimental Successions. But the following Offices, borne on the Military

Establishment, are in the appointment of the Secretary at War—All Chaplains to Garrisons at Home & Abroad. All Commissioners & other civil Officers under the military Establishments, the Deputy Judge Advocate. The Deputy Comissary General & 7 Deputy Commissaries, The Former with £800 p An the latter £150 each. Persons supplying the Troops in Barracks with Coals & Candles worth £200 p An in War Time less in Time of Peace and may appoint a Deputy. And all other Civil Officers employed in the Establishment of the Army. With the Patronage of the Horse and Foot Guards.

W.O. 2/42, p. 10

235

Lieutenant Thomas Gaylord to Barrington

[Holograph]   Kilkenny
                                                        13 January 1758

As a report strongly prevails, that Genl. Handasyd's Regiment, in which I have the Honor to serve His Majesty as Lieutenant, is to go to America this year, I take the Liberty to acquaint Your Lordship that I was Quarter Master to the said Regiment from the 22nd March 1745/6 to the 4th of December 1748, when I was reduced at Stirling upon the Regiment being orderd to the Irish Establishment, and as the said Quarter Master's Commission cost me £300 without having received half pay or any Consideration for the said loss, I hope your Lordship will be so good as to use your Interest, if the Regiment serves abroad that I may be again Reinstated, and I flatter myself that your Lordship will excuse this my Application to you, and from your known befriending Character Assist me . . . .

[*Endorsed on back in Barrington's hand*]: I think Mr Gaylord's pretensions very reasonable, & if Genl. Handasyd's Regt should be order'd abroad, & he continuing desirous of the Quarter masters place he may remind me of this request.

W.O. 1/976, f. 543

236

Barrington to Lieutenant Basil Alves

[Copy]
War Office
17 December 1765

I have notified you for the Fort Majority and Lieutenancy of Edinburgh Castle, in the room of Mr Bredin who goes on your ½ pay. I do not like any transactions in regard to the Staff, or in Garrisons, but I have consented to this manner of Mr Bredin's retiring because he has a Claim to Sell having as he asserts bought the Employment. I do not in any degree admit of this Claim, but my Successors in Office possibly might think it good. I am therefore glad to prevent all further doubt or dispute by allowing the Exchange proposed to me. For greater certainty however, I apprize you before the Commissions are made out, that I do not conceive you have any Claim hereafter to receive any money either by Sale of even Exchange of your Commissions; And, if you have any objection to this Condition, you will let me know it in time that I may stop all further proceedings; I am anxious to keep every thing of the sort now under consideration, on such a footing that deserving Officers who have no money, may sometimes obtain a comfortable retirement from the Service, may keep it while they live, and be succeeded when they die by others like themselves.

W.O. 4/78, p. 202

237

Barrington to George Lewis
(formerly Captain in the 30th Foot)

[Copy]
Cavendish Square
7 September 1772

I am favoured by your Letter of the 30th of Augt. & can bear testimony to the truth, of what Mr Ellis told you, that the King did not approve of Officers selling what they did not buy. I found

H.M. in that disposition when I returned to the War Office in the year 1765: And my own opinion has always been against buying or selling; because that practice tho' attended with many conveniences in many instances has this radical fault, That it prevents Officers of merit who have no money, from getting that advancement which their Services deserve. When Lord Granby had the Command of the Army, he gave very different advice being of a different opinion, as well as almost all the Colonels of Regts. By his Lordship's influence a number of Officers were from time to time allowed to sell what they did not buy: and ever since his resignation, the same indulgence has been sometimes granted on the applications of Colonels of Regts. to Officers worn out by long meritorious Service, & who could retire no other way. On this ground Major Ramsay obtained in the year 1771, that permission which was refused in 1765.

As to the brevets of Major lately given, they have been confined entirely to old Captains actualy serving in Regts: Captains on half pay have not had any share in the promotion, much less those who sold out of the Army.

I have thus, Sir, given you the best account I am able of this matter, & shall be very glad if I have contributed to restore that philosophic calm which in my poor opinion no late transactions ought to interrupt.

Ipswich 107

238

Barrington to General Amherst

[Copy]   Cavendish Square
                                     23 September 1772

I have laid before the King your Letter to me of the 8th instant. H.M. has order'd that Capt McAlpin shall sell the Adjutancy of the 60th Regt., tho he did not buy it. This is the only instance of the kind which I remember; & I do not believe there will be another. But the King would not object to the disposal of a Commission in the way Sir Jy. Amherst recommends as Colonel, when it was formerly bestowed by him as Commander in Chief during the late War, solely from the merit of Service.

Ipswich 107

239

Barrington to Lt.-General Elliot

[Copy]   Cavendish Square
                                      25 November 1767

I have kept my promise to consider the proposal relative to your Son, & I have done it with the greatest disposition to oblige you. I am sorry that the result is an opinion that I ought to adhere to a rule never once broken by me, not to propose an Exchange where there is any money given or received.

When Exchanges are made on equal terms, they arise from such a mutual convenience as seldom happens & they should not be too frequent; but if pecuniary considerations are once introduc'd or allow'd, there will be scarce such a thing as an Officer contented with his Corps. Is a young man in disgrace with his Superiors on account of his conduct? instead of considering how he shall mend it, he looks out for another Regt. Is another in debt? instead of paying it by frugality, he looks out for somebody who will give him money to exchange Commissions. Does a Corps go abroad to a disagreable station? The Officers who have got or can raise any money, exchange with needy men, & shamefully stay at home. I might enumerate many more such probable cases. I am sensible that none of them exist in the present instance; but what is once done innocently, will be often repeated inconveniently, especially in a Country like this with some hundred unreasonable Parliament men, supported by unreasonable but powerful Patrons. Many years of my life have been spent in Warfare against these Gentlemen; And whenever I have success, it arises entirely from an invariable adherence to good general rules, without admitting one single exception. I do assure you nothing is more impossible than to make men comprehend or allow any distinctions which weigh against their desires.

I will also frankly confess that I fear to introduce a practice of bringing on this Establishment thro' the Irish, younger Captains than it would be thought expedient to promote here at the same age. A Troop or Company is a Command which requires experience & a cool head, especially in Quarters, and when employ'd at the requisition of the Civil Magistrate. I declare I should have a thorough confidence in your son's discretion, because he had been got & instructed by you, and therefore I should be happy to assist in bringing him hither by an Exchange without money, which would not often be propos'd: but requests to exchange with money once granted would soon become frequent; and as I said before, what is done for one man in this Country, cannot be denied to more.

If you do not believe these motives would operate on me equally in the case of the nearest relation or dearest friend I have in the world, you will not judge according to your usual justice & candour.

* * *

P.S. Exchanges between Officers on the two Establishments without money, sometimes are propos'd. I had a Proposal of that kind between two Captains of foot last week.

Ipswich 107

240

Barrington to Lt.-General Elliot

[Copy]

Cavendish Square
14 December 1773

I have recd your recommendation of an Exchange between Lord Ferrers & Captain Hamilton. If I do not mistake, this Proposal is exactly similar to one which regarded Capt. Elliott. My opinion on that matter was contained in a Letter to you, the Copy of which I have lately read. My Sentiments are not changed in the least. I have great regard for Lord Townshend my old acquaintance & friend; I have the greatest desire to accommodate Lord Ferrers who is a most amiable & hopeful young man, but these inducements, however weighty, must not prevail on me to advise what appears to me to be wrong; Allow me to add on this occasion that nothing could have induced me to object to your Son's coming into your Regt, but a thorough persuasion that the allowance of Exchanges, except of the most perfect equality without any difference in money, would introduce great inconveniences into the Service.

* * *

P.S. Some months ago an Exchange was propos'd between a Son of the Arch Bishop of York, then a Lieut in the 61st. Regt. & a Lieut of Dragoons; but it was refus'd by the King tho' earnestly requested by His Grace. Mr Drummond has since bought into Burgoynes.

Ipswich 107

241

Barrington to General Amherst

[Copy]   War Office
                                                  20 October 1760

Major Barré is very urgent to have a Commission from the King, as Deputy Adjutant General in North America with the Rank of Lieutenant Colonel usually annexed to it. This Claim lays me under great difficulty. On the one hand, I should be extremely sorry to hinder or retard the Promotion to which a good and brave Officer has a reasonable Claim. On the other hand, to forward any American preferment without your *express* Recommendation would be contrary to the Respect due to you as Commander in Chief, and to my Premises and Declarations often repeated to you. Your Letter, of the 8th. of September, is far from removing the difficulty I am under. It recommends Major Barré in General Terms; but as no mention is made of his pretensions as Deputy adjutant General, or any intimation of your Opinion on that Subject, I cannot understand from it what your wishes are. I shall conform myself to them when they are known, and I beg you will by the first Opportunity acquaint me with them. If you chuse the Major Barré should have the Commission and Rank which he desires, he shall have my best Assistance towards obtaining them, but it is right that he should owe his good fortune to the explicit Recommendation of his General recommending and rewarding Merit.

That Major Barré (who is clearly of Opinion that you meant this Promotion for him, tho' you did not express it in your Letter to me) may be no sufferer by a delay arising from any Scruples, I will undertake to obtain the King's Leave that the Commission of Deputy Adjutant General, which he shall receive in Consequence of your Recommendation, shall be dated on the 20th October, which is the date of this Letter.

Ipswich 6a2, no. 349

242

Extract of a letter from General Amherst to Barrington

[Copy]   New York
                                                    6 January 1761

Major Barré served, my Lord, as Deputy Adjutant General on the Expedition up the River St. Laurence in the Army where Lieutenant Colonel Maitland acted as Major of Brigade, this must have been a heart burning to him and may have made him more anxious and urgent with your Lordship than he would otherwise have been: as your Lordship has in the kindest manner asked my opinion and what my wishes are on the Subject, I am glad to say Major Barré has great Merit, I think; from his Services, it is very natural that he should request a Commission of Deputy Adjutant General with the Rank of Lieutenant Colonel, and I really wish he may succeed in it as I think he deserves it, and that it will be for the good of His Majesty's Service.
[Added later, in another hand]:
L-Col. Barré's Comn. is dated Jan 29 1761

Ipswich 6a2, no. 350

243

Barrington to Lt.-Colonel Isaac Barré MP

[Copy]   Cavendish Square
                                                4 February 1773

According to your desire I have laid before the King your
Memorial to His Majesty. The Crown has an undoubted right to
confer Military preferment at pleasure: I am however permitted
to inform you, that the late promotion of Colonel Morrison arose
from the commendable manner in which he has conducted an
important branch of Military Service for more than nine years.
Upon that consideration His Majesty has thought fit to give him a
fresh Commission of Quarter Master General with the rank of
Colonel by which such Commissions have been frequently
accompanied; but the King by this promotion of Colonel Morrison does not mean to convey, or conceive that he does convey his
disapprobation of any other Officer's Services.

Ipswich 107

244

Barrington to Lord North

[Copy in Barrington's hand]   Cavendish Square
                                                5 May 1776

I am ashamed that you should have had the trouble of writing or
now have the trouble of reading another Letter about Mr. Carey: I
shall only add on his subject, that the Commission lying at the
War office will put him on a footing with all the Majors on half pay
promoted in 1772; none of whom were told that they should ever
be restored to Service on *any* terms: it is likewise all that I ever
understood him to desire till lately. He very justly calls it *a
Shadow*; but a brevet is in its' nature no more, and therefore he
now prudently endeavours to tack a substance to it. However this
Shadow the object of much desire, when bestow'd on him will
become the object of Envy; it will be treated by military men as an

unjust partiality shewn to a Member of Parliament, & by the News Papers as a fresh proof of the Servile complacency so long imputed to me by them. On the other hand all the ministers under whom I ever served have blamed my opposition to triffles necessary for the support of Government; & I have therefore been occasionally under the displeasure of them all with equal reason. During the Duke of Grafton's administration, or at least till towards the end of it, there was a Commander in Chief to whom all applications were made: Lord Granby's resignation was a fatal Event to me. It restored to the War Office an invidious patronage, which has cost me some old and valuable friendships not to be replaced at my time of life; and I have not suffered it to produce so much advantage to me, as to the Ministers. I have three Nephews in the Army: one a Captain of Dragoons bought all his Commissions, but not till they came to his turn in his own Regiment; the second lately purchased a Cornetcy; the third indeed obtain'd thro' the King's goodness a Commission in a Regiment in Canada, and is now a Prisoner with the Rebels. In the late reign my brother was a very old Lieutenant Colonel when I was placed in the War Office: He was not made aid de Camp to the King or obtaind a Regiment but in turn and with his Cotemporaries. The Expedition which he commanded made the first of our Conquests in the late War: He return'd from Guadeloupe as poor as he went thither with a good Constitution ruind by that Climate; left at his death a very bare subsistance for his Widow; and his four Children have since the year 1764 been educated and maintain'd by me. I do not mention this as a greivance; Complaint would be abominable when so many distinguished favours of a civil nature have been confer'd on me and my family by the Crown: Besides, I never made application to be releived from an Expense which my employment enabled me to support without inconvenience.

Pardon My Lord these details: I have in vain attempted to perswade by assurances, I now endeavour to convince by facts. This is an effort to shew that I am friendly to your person and administration; till then all my Conduct will appear to you thro' a false and injurious Medium.

Ipswich 6c3

7

The Health and Comfort of the Army

Any advances in army medicine or even in providing simple amenities for private soldiers in the eighteenth century are bound to seem meagre and derisory to modern ideas.[1] However, contemporary scientific capacities, as well as attitudes about what was rightly due to troops, have to be allowed for. Barrington cannot be called a great innovator in this area, but at least he tried to be effective and humane within guidelines already established. For example, chaplains were required for regiments, so they must be provided. He seems to have had little use for religion himself,[2] but it was the King's wish, so orders were issued (245), although Barrington was no more able than any other official in the eighteenth century to discover a way of overcoming the absenteeism of army chaplains. The King also interested himself in the diet of soldiers, and arranged through the War Office that in time of dearth and high prices they should be supplied with bread (246). Veterans were provided for, sometimes by a generous evasion of regulations, at Chelsea Hospital, of which Barrington was an *ex officio* governor (247), and soldiers disordered in their wits were given such treatment as the age afforded at public expense in the Bethlehem Hospital (248). He was also active in making the best available medical provision for foreign stations, and for campaigns[3] (249, 251) using his authority to get the best men for the job by preventing the purchase of staff posts (250). He also persuaded the Treasury to allow an extra shilling a day to surgeon's mates in order to attract good applicants.[4] In 1756 he and the Duke of Cumberland set up an unofficial but useful Hospital Board (252). Two years later he arranged for a hospital for the German campaign, from which arose one of several quarrels with Lord Ligonier about the extent of the authority of the Secretary at War (253, 254, 255, and see 12 above). Barrington took a good deal of trouble (and indeed plumed himself) over the German hospital, and felt a degree of personal responsibility when its shortcomings in the field came to light. Bureaucratic efficiency in London could not compensate for logistical problems and official incompetence in Germany. He was therefore relieved to receive a version of events full of indignation from the doctors of the Board, which he hurriedly accepted (256, 257, 258, 259). He was also much exercised by reports of the distresses of troops in stations further afield (260, 261, 262, 263, 264). Fortescue and other writers have been loud in blame of uncaring civilians at home who by their neglect permitted the military to be destroyed overseas, but enormous distances and poor technical knowledge were often as much to blame as official complacency. Ideas were not entirely lacking. An interesting document belonging to Barrington's second term indicates a real attempt to learn and apply lessons from past experience of the best seasons for landing fresh troops in unhealthy areas (265). But appalling disasters occurred and would continue to do so until far into the next century. The thought (even if it crossed their minds) that officials in London were doing their best can have been of little comfort to the wretched garrison of Pensacola 'encamped on a loose burning sand' in 1765, although significantly the first and most important form of consolation which the officers there requested was to be allowed to succeed to the vacant commissions of their dead colleagues (266, 267, 268, 269, 270). Perhaps they realized that this was the only relief which War Office bureaucracy could provide.

245

Barrington to Messrs Cox and Mair, Agents

[Copy]   War Office
                                                17 January 1777

* * *

By the enclosed Extract from Sir Guy Carleton's Letter you will
observe that, on the 17th November last, there was only one
Clergyman (beside the Chaplain of the Artillery) to officiate in the
whole British Army in Canada.

I understand that Mr Bruce Deputy Chaplain to the 31st was
certainly with his Regiment in Novr. and therefore think it most
probable that he was likewise employed and paid for doing the
duty of all the other Corps, a practice highly disapproved of by His
Majesty.

As the King expects that there shall be a Clergyman present
with each Regiment, I shall be under the Necessity of reporting to
His Majesty the Names of those Chaplains who shall appear
neither to have joined or [sic] provided proper Deputies by the
time the next Returns are received from Canada.

W.O. 4/99, pp. 29–30

246

Barrington to officer commanding troops
at Chatham Barracks

[Copy]   War Office
                                                10 July 1767

The King having been pleased to take into His Gracious consideration, the extraordinary high price of every kind of provision
at this time, as likewise the peculiar difficulties to which Soldiers
stationed in Barracks are subject (difficulties which do not equally
affect any other Troops in His Majesty's Service) has been
pleased to grant them the same allowance of Bread which is
delivered to Soldiers when they are encamped, to continue 'till

the 1st of December next, by which time it is hoped that the new wheat will be brought to market, and that the price of Bread will be considerably lower'd.

It must be clearly understood that this allowance arises entirely from the circumstances of the present time, and that it is not by any means intended to be a permanent Establishment.

For the better execution of His Majesty's gracious purpose, I have the honor to signify to you the King's Pleasure, that you do direct an account to be taken of the number of Men belonging to such of the Companies of the 12th and 13th Regiments of Foot, as shall be in the Garrison under your Command, who are desirous to receive their Bread upon the following Terms Vizt

That each Man shall receive a Loaf of Bread of six Pounds weight, which is to be the allowance for four days and for which he is to pay five pence.

It is proposed that the Loaf shall be of good brown Bread, without any mixture of Rye, and you will be pleased to make agreement with proper Bakers near Chatham Barracks for the regular delivery of such bread, to as many of your Men as may chuse to receive it on the above Terms.

The additional expence beyond what the Soldier contributes, is to be paid by Government, you will therefore order a regular account thereof to be kept by the Paymasters of the Regiments, who are to transmit the same, on the last day of each Month, to the Agent, signed by you, or the Commanding Officers in the Barracks in order to its being inserted in the Contingent Bills of the Regiment.

W.O. 4/82, pp. 168–169

247

Barrington to Commissioners of Chelsea Hospital

[Copy]   War Office
                                              18 July 1767

His Majesty having been moved in behalf of James Lee late an Out-Pensioner of Chelsea Hospital, who has been struck off the Out-Pension for having again entered into the Service without the Permission of the Board, His Majesty is graciously pleased in Consideration of his having served in the Army and Navy thirty two Years, his being rendered incapable of getting his Livelyhood and to keep him from want, to order that he shall be replaced on the Out-Pension of the said Hospital at his former Allowance, notwithstanding he may not be strictly entitled thereto agreeable to the Rules of the Board.

W.O. 4/82, p. 190

248

Barrington to Governors of Bethlehem Hospital

[Copy]   War Office
                                                      23 October 1765

It having been represented to me, that William Gumridge a private man in Lt Colo Nugent's Company, in the 1st Regt. of Foot Guards, is disordered in his Senses, I desire you will be pleased to direct him to be brought on Saturday next, in order to be received into your Hospital for Cure, if found to be a proper Object, that is, poor & mad, the proper Care shall be taken that the customary expence, as Bedding, Cloathing &c during his continuance in your said Hospital with the Charges of his Funeral (in case he dies there) shall be defrayed, and that he shall be received back, when you think proper to discharge him.

W.O. 4/78, p. 29

249

Barrington to the Apothecary General

[Copy]   War Office
                                                      17 January 1756

Mr Robert Mackinly, Surgeon to the 44th Regiment of Foot (late Halkets) having represented that in the late unfortunate Action under General Braddock, he not only lost his Baggage, Medicine

Chest with the Instruments sent him by the Govermt. but all his own Stock which was very Considerable; That at Philadelphia and New York he endeavoured to procure some to supply his present Necessity, but there was not a Tradesman in either of those places, nor in all America capable of making any kind of Chirurgical Instruments, I am commanded by His Majesty to acquaint you, It is His Pleasure that you do prepare with the utmost Expedition four Regimental Chests of good and whole-some Medicines as well Internal as External together with a Set of Instruments for the use of the said 44th Regt. serving in America, which Medicines are to be of such species as shall be thought most proper to be used in that Climate, and delivered to John Calcraft Esq. Agent to the said Regiment, the said Medicines being first viewed and approved by the Physitian and Surgeon General of the Army.

W.O. 4/51, p. 139

250

Barrington to Henry Drummond, Agent

[Copy]   Cavendish Square
                                                21 November 1766

I have so much esteem & regard for the 20th Regt that I am very sorry to find they earnestly desire a thing to which I cannot contribute my assistance. It has always been a principal Object of my care that the Army should be supply'd with the very best Surgeons, & my endeavours for that purpose have never fail'd of success, except in Corps where the Surgeoncy has been sold, in which case upon an Exchange it has been necessary to find a Man with Money; & it often happens that men who have none, possess the best talents: On this account I have always prevented buying & selling of Surgeoncies so far as the practice of the Army would allow, thinking they ought to be given and not purchas'd. I am fully persuaded that the person propos'd to buy the Surgeoncy of the 20th Regt. is an excellent man, & I shall be very glad whenever I can serve him without breaking a general rule establish'd for public benefit. I know that in this Country it is impossible to observe any rule, if any exceptions to it are once allowed.

I write all this upon a Supposition that Mr Fleming did not buy his Surgeoncy: if he bought he has a right to sell; and in that case I will recommend Mr Cahil. If Mr Fleming did not buy, & is unable to do his duty, he must exchange on half-pay; a method which will do perfectly well for the Regt, & I heartily wish it would do as well for Mr Cahill.

Ipswich 107

251

Barrington to William Young

[Copy]   War Office
                                                17 February 1757

'Instructions to William Young Esqr. Master Surgeon of the Hospital established for the Expedition under the Command of Major Genl. Hopson [to Martinique]'

When you want any Money for the use of the Hospital after you leave Portsmouth, the Commander in Chief on your applying to him will supply you with it.

You are to intimate to the Surgeons of the Several Regiments, that no patient will be admitted into the Hospital unless a Certificate is sent with him of his Name and the Company he belongs to, and of the Cloaths sent with him and specifying his Ailment; this to be signed by the Surgeon or his Mate and an Officer of the Company the patient belongs to; And you are not to admit with him any of his Arms or Accoutrements.

You are to Charge the Paymaster of his Regiment five pence per day Stoppages from the day of his Entry to the day of his Discharge or Death, reckoning the first and last day only as one day.

You are to see from time to time that your Instruments are kept Clean and in good Order and that there be always in readiness plenty of Lint and Bandages.

You are also to require the Master Apothecary and his Mates to take special Care of the Hospital Medicines, and from time to time to inspect the Medicinal Chests of the Surgeons of the several Regimts. that there be no Waste of Imbazlement.

You are to take as much Care as possible of the Hospital Bedding and Stores, and when you join Lord Loudoun, you are to deliver over to the Director of his Hospital all that remains of them and to take his Receipt for the Same, And you are to make up with him your Accompt of Receipts and payments of Money.

For which Extra Trouble you are allowed ten Shillings p day beside your Pay as Master Surgeon, to the time of your making up and finishing the Delivery and Accompt mentioned in the last Article.

W.O. 26/23, pp. 179–180

252

Directions to the Hospital Board

[Copy] N.d. [August, 1757]

'Instructions to the Physicians General, Physicians to the Hospitals, and Hospital Board &c'

The Physicians General, having Cõmissions as Physicians to the Hospital are together with the Physicians to the Hospital and Chief Surgeons to be Considered as the Principal Officers thereof.

The Office of the said Physicians General, when not Commanded to do Duty at the Headquarters, shall be to Attend the General Hospital, to Visit the Sick & prescribe for them such diet & Medicines as they shall judge most proper to give directions to have them Conveniently lodged in Wards with a free Air, kept Clean, and not Crowded, to Assign the Several parts of Duty to the other Physicians who may be employed, to the Master Apothecaries, and their Mates, & at such Times as no Physicians General shall be so Appointed, or in their Absence the Above Offices & Duties shall be discharged by the Physicians to the

Hospital; And in Order for the more effectual care of the Sick the Physicians or Surgeons to the Hospital or each of them respectively shall have the power of Suspending any of the Inferior Officers employed about the Sick, till the Hospital Board shall meet and judge of the Complaints which shall be then laid before them.

The Hospital Board shall consist of the Physicians General, the Physicians to the Hospital, the Chief Surgeon, and Master Surgeons with the Director of the Hospital. And if the Board shall pass any Sentence inferring dismission or longer Suspension of the person Complained of, the same shall be transmitted to the Commander in Chief, to be Confirmed or set aside According to His pleasure.

But if any Complaint be moved against the Mates, not put in by Warrants, or against any of the Servants officiating in the Hospital, the Board shall be allowed to Suspend for a longer Time or dismiss the Delinquents on their own Authority. And with regard to the Nurses any of the Physicians, Chief Surgeon or Master Surgeon shall be empowered to dismiss such of them as they shall find within their several departments improper for their Office without Application to the Board.

The Commander in Chief having issued his Orders for employing an additional Number of Mates to Attend the Sick as the Hospital Duty may require, the said Physicians General or in their Absence the Physicians to the Hospital, shall choose out of those recommended to them, such as they shall judge most proper for the Service and shall from Time to Time report to the Commander in Chief what abatement may Conveniently be made of that Number; In like manner the Chief Surgeons shall Act with regard to the Additional Mates of the Chirurgical department.

W.O. 26/23, pp. 209–210

337

253

Barrington to Major-General Napier, secretary to Lord Ligonier

[Copy in Clerk's hand]   War Office
                                                      12 July 1758

The Hospital for Germany has been settled some time, & I think so well settled, that I am willing to make myself answerable for its being well conducted.

I beg you will excuse me to Lord Ligonier for not changing the subdirection of the Hospital. Cathcart is used to the Business, & the country where he is going. I have besides great objection to a Surgeons being a subdirector, which is almost as improper as making a subdirector a surgeon. The Service is best perform'd when men keep intirely to the Business to which they were bred.

I was indeed prevail'd on to make Mr Coryn subdirector of the Hospital on the Expedition; I have since repented my having so done, because now every Surgeon wants the same Office, & will not rest contented nay happy with being on the Staff as they all were before, & as, I hope, they will be again when they find the precedent of Mr Coryn is not to be follow'd: However, as he went out director of the Expedition, he may possibly have attain'd some knowledge in that kind of Business at Sea, & I think it therefore more proper that he should continue with the Expedition.

I told Lord Ligonier yesterday that if the Duke of Marlborough would write me a Letter, desiring that Mr Bourleton might be his Surgeon, I would certainly take his Grace's recommendation; but I since find that there was no Surgeon allow'd to Lord Ligonier, when he commanded the British Troops in 1746 & this Establishment is the proper precedent for his Grace's. If my Lord Duke wants any augmentation, he will apply to the Treasury, without whose consent I must not venture to encrease it.

I beg you will represent all this to the Marshal in the most respectful manner, with my assurances of the most earnest desire to comply with his Commands.

I will take the King's pleasure on Capt. Gore, & notify him immediately after.

Ipswich 3b, no. 192

254

Barrington to Robert Adair

[Copy in Clerk's hand]   War Office
                                              4 September 1760

I send you the enclosed Letter which I have received from Mr John Cathcart Director of the Hospitals which I desire you will transmit to Doctor Wintringham for the opinion of the hospital board in Germany, on the two following Questions, which opinion should afterwards be laid before Lord Granby for his approbation.

1st: If the good of the Service requires a Purveyor and Two Deputies for the Hospital

2d If Mr Robert Cathcart deserves to be advanced from a Deputy to be principal Purveyor.

Ipswich 3b, no. 157

255

John Cathcart to Barrington enclosed with Document 254

[Copy in Clerk's hand]   Chandois Street
                                              2 September 1760

I beg leave humbly to represent to your Lordship that Our Army in Germany has of late become so great that their Hospitals cannot be properly managed by a Deputy and assistant, and I think from the Experience I have had in Hospitals that the Service must Suffer if a Principal Purveyor and Two Deputies be not now appointed.

Your Lordship certainly Judged right in allowing only a Deputy with two Clerks to go with the Six Regiments of Infantry and Six of Cavalry that went first to Germany because their Number was small but now being augmented to no less than Seventeen Regiments and Battalions of Infantry and Fifteen Regiments of Cavalry, I think there is a necessity for what I propose, for in the last War, when our Army in the Low Countrys was not so great, as it now is in Germany there was allowed for the management of the Hospitals one principal (then called a Director) and two Deputies, one to remain with the first Hospital and Magazine, the other to be with the Flying or detached Hospital, and the directors bussiness was to oversee both, to make contracts, provide Servants, procure money, and see the Books regularly kept up. This assistance I was allowed in Brabant, when We had Holland and Flanders near to supply us with all we wanted, and Our Army never at a great distance from Our first hospital, a Magazine but in Germany; where Our Army now is, it is the reverse; necessaries not easily to be come at, and Our Army frequently at a great distance from Our first Hospital, and Magazine, and therefore the like assistance of a Purveyor and Two deputies becomes necessary.

I hinted the above to your Lordship a few days ago, and desired that my deputy Mr Robt. Cathcart now serving in Germany might be appointed Purveyor of the hospital, that he might be intitled to a half pay of Ten Shillings p day at the End of the War, and this I did because I really think he deserves to be advanced when an opportunity offers on account of his long and faithful Service for he was my deputy as director of the hospital in the West Indies, and in the low Countrys, during the last War almost Nine Years, he has also in the same greatly served in Germany ever since Our Forces went over now above two Years, and your Lordship will remember that at his being appointed for Germany his Character was strictly inquired into of those he had served with in the last War particularly Doctor Wintringham, Doctor Clephane, Mr. Adair, and Mr Blith, and I believe they have not changed the opinion they then had of him.

I therefore humbly propose that your Lordship will be pleased to desire Mr. Adair to transmit this paper to Doctor Wintringham for the opinion of his hospital Board on these Two Questions.

1st: If the good of the Service requires a Purveyor and two Deputies for the hospital.

2d: If Mr Cathcart deserves to be advanced from a Deputy to be principal Purveyor, and that their opinion be laid before Lord Granby for his approbation.

Ipswich 3b, no. 157

256

Barrington to the Marquis of Granby

[Copy in Barrington's hand]   War Office
                                               2 January 1761

I have for some time had the mortification to hear various reports, to the disadvantage of the Hospital department in the Army under your Lordship's command. I cannot say that I have hitherto given much credit to them; but, as they have rather encreas'd than diminished, since the late arrival of several Officers from Germany, I think it right to impart my concern upon this head to your Lordship. I would not have you imagine that they who talk the loudest upon this Topick, impute any part of the Evil to the Commander in Chief; my reason for applying to your Lordship is, that I may know from authority whether it is true, that out of the great number of sick which have been in the Hospitals this Campaign, very few have ever rejoined the Army; And if so, to what cause this extraordinary mortality is to be attributed, whether to the peculiar malignity of their disorders, or to the want of proper Lodging & other necessaries, or to the negligence or incapacity of those who have the care of them. I heartily wish your Lordship may enable me to contradict their rumours in the main point, the number of the dead in Hospitals; but if that is too true, I shall be glad to learn from your Lordship, whether any thing can be done on my part more than has been done towards preventing this great evil another year, either by furnishing the Hospitals with any new Species of Stores or medicines, of which they may be in want, or by putting them under the care of persons of greater abilities and diligence, if any such can be found.

Ipswich 3b, no. 159

257

Barrington to the Marquis of Granby

[Copy]   War Office
                                            9 January 1761

Since my letter of the 2nd Inst. to yr. Lordship concerning the Hospitals in Germany, I have had the thoughts of the Hospital Board here on that Subject.

They seem to be of opinion that one great impediment to the cure of the Sick is the want of a sufficient number of Carriages with each Brigade, to transport them from time to time in the General Hospitals, which from the nature of the Service must often be at a great distance from the Army. If your Lordship finds this to be the case you will doubtless think it proper that the number of Waggons at present allowed to each Brigade should be encreased.

They also apprehend that many Patients who have been recovered from malignant disorders in the Hospitals may afterwards perish from rejoining the Army too soon, for want of proper quarters where the Convalescents, being well lodged, & dieted, might wait 'till their strength is entirely re established.

To remedy this inconvenience the King has been graciously pleased to consent that the Convalescents of the Army under your Lordship's Command may be sent off from time to time to such places in the interior parts of Hanover as yr Lordship and Prince Ferdinand think proper for their Quarters of refreshment.

If your Lordship approves of this Plan you will be pleased to concert measures for carrying it into execution with Prince Ferdinand, as the Regency of Hanover, have orders from H.M. to do everything which is necessary on their part for the reception and accommodation of the convalescent soldiers whom yr Lordship may think fit to send under the care of proper Officers into that Country.

W.O. 4/63, pp. 69–70

Dr Wintringham and Mr Burlton to Barrington

[Copy in Barrington's hand]   Corvey [near Höxter] Germany
23 January 1761

The Marquis of Granby having done us the honour of an Order, that we should transmit to your Lordship a faithful & succinct account of such facts and circumstances as come within our knowlege, and have an immediate relation to several Complaints set forth in your Lordship's Letter of the 2d instant, most notoriously affecting the conduct & characters of the Members in the Physical department of the British Hospital in Germany, we take the liberty to avow in the first place that we are, & must be ever at a loss how to express sufficiently our surprize at a charge so void of all real foundation, & that is so, we perswade ourselves will appear from the consideration of the following particulars.

It has been said, as your Lordship makes mention, that out of the great number of Sick which have been in the Hospital this Campaign, such has been the extraordinary mortality that very few have ever rejoin'd the Army. This, My Lord, is an assertion so contradictory to truth, that the weekly & monthly reports of Entries & discharges when compared together, will evince it to every Enquirer beyond the possibility of a doubt. The march of larger parties of Convalescents from the Hospital to the Army, during the Campaign was [no *omitted*] new or uncommon object, and when towards the latter part of it at the approach of Winter, it was not then thought prudent to hazard the relapse of such recover'd men by Field or Camp duty, it was not without some difficulty that Towns could be found sufficient & large enough to provide them with proper Quarters: A circumstance which we choose to mention, as it serves not only to prove, that the Numbers discharged from the Hospitals are very considerable, but further that there is a strict attention paid to the preservation of such as do recover.

It is a well known & a melancholy truth confirm'd by the experience of all Ages, that the British Troops soon after their

343

removal into this Climate, become very sickly, & that many of them die; many powerful reasons concurr to the producing this event, & many have been the efforts to prevent, or at least to lessen this grievous misfortune, too tedious to recite here, We shall only observe to your Lordship that such has been the zeal and care of the Physical Members of the Hospital in this respect, that they are ready to appeal to the records of any Campaign made in preceeding times under the same Circumstances, & to stand the decision whether they do not at least equal them in their successful treatment of their Patients, consider'd either as sick or as wounded.

It is not hereby meant to affirm that the Patients in the Hospital had not frequent and just cause for Complaint; these in almost every instance had their source in the distress, confusion, & embarrassment, in which the Civil department of the Hospital depending on it's Director or Purveyor, was frequently involved, & ever liable to from the insufficiency of the hands allow'd him by the Government, as well in their number, as in their qualifications to discharge the several duties to be perform'd by them. These grievances, My Lord, in this branch of the department, & by which many were sufferers, did not pass unoticed or uncensured by the Physicians & Surgeons, and who spared no pains or means within their power to accomplish, that might obviate & redress them, in which they have the concurrent testimony of the officers appointed by the Marquis from time to time, to inspect into the State of the British Hospitals.

It is lastly insinuated that the mortality of the Patients brought to the Hospital, is owing to the negligence or incapacity of those who have the care of them; to this, we in particular beg leave to observe to your Lordship, as worthy of remark; That as no Officers of what rank so ever for whom they have been concern'd have hitherto in any one instance, thought fit to make a complaint of this nature with propriety either as to time, place, or person, it should have been made in or address'd to. We cannot therefore consider such a charge as proceeding from any other Cause, than the effects of ignorant clamour & detraction: At the same time we are well assur'd that the Gentlemen in this branch of the Hospital department, are not possessed of so much vanity as to imagine they are free from errors & imperfections, or that persons of greater abilities than themselves in the respective Provinces they profess, are not to be found, into whose care, it is our firm belief, they would with the greatest satisfaction resign the Office they are now entrusted with, & which they have ever been zealous to discharge with fidelity & honour.

Ipswich 3b, no. 160

259

Barrington to the Marquis of Granby

[Copy in clerk's hand]   War Office
                                                            10 February 1761

I received yesterday a Letter written by your Lordship's order, and signed by Dr Wintringham and Mr Burlton. It relates to some of the Points mentioned in my Letter to you of the 2d January last. I will take the earliest opportunity of laying it before the King, and I am very glad that I am furnished with answers to several of the Clamours which have been raised here against the management of the Hospitals in Germany: Clamours, to which I never gave Credit myself, tho' they were proper Objects of my enquiries.

There is a part of that Letter, of which I must take particular notice, it is as follows 'It is not hereby meant to affirm that the Patients in the Hospital had not frequent, & just cause for Complaints, these in almost every instance had their Source in the distress, confusion, and embarrassment, in which the Civil Department of the Hospital depending on it's Director, or Purveyor, was frequently involved, and ever liable to from the insufficiency of the hands allowed him by the Government as well in their number as in their qualifications to discharge the several duties to be performed by them. These grievances, My Lord, in this branch of the department, and by which many were Sufferers, did not pass unnoticed, or uncensured by the Physicians, and Surgeons, and who spared no pains, or means within their power to accomplish that might obviate and redress them, in which they have the concurrent testimony of the Officers appointed by the Marquis, from time to time to inspect into the State of the British Hospitals'.

I am at a loss to imagine to whom the Physicians and Surgeons *noticed and censured the insufficiency of the persons employed in the Civil department both in number and qualifications.* Surely no Complaints as to these defects reached your Lordship, for it does not appear they were remedied on your side the Water & certainly were not represented on this. The least intimation to me would have produced an immediate recall of whoever was thought insufficient for his Office, and the utmost care & diligence would have been used in sending over such as both *in number and qualifications*, would have been sufficient for the Service required of them. In the Campaign of 1759, it was represented to me from Germany that the Director wanted Assistants, and I Immediately sent some over to him. Since that time till now, no representation has been made to me, against the conduct of the Civil department of the Hospital: On the contrary Mr Cathcart was lately promoted from Deputy, to principal Director on a representation of your Hospital Board in his favour, transmitted and approved by your Lordship.

I once more beg, My Lord, that I may know whom you think proper to be recalled, & what kind of Assistance you would have sent. My utmost diligence shall be exerted to forward whatever you deem expedient for this most useful and compassionate part of the Service. I never saw in my life one Man employed in the Civil department of the Hospitals of Germany. All those employed in that branch were recommended by the Hospital Board here, and were never protected by me farther than they appeared deserving. If they were my best Friends and nearest relations, the slightest representation of their insufficiency, from your Lordship, would produce their immediate removal.

Ipswich 3b, no. 161

260

Grey Cooper to Barrington

[In Clerk's hand, signed by Cooper]

Treasury Chambers
Whitehall
7 May 1766

In answer to your Lordship's Letter of 26th of last month concerning the deficiency in the Remittances made by the Contractor for the Subsistence of the 70th Regimt. at Grenada, I am order'd by the Lords Commissioners of His Majesty's Treasury to acquaint your Lordship, that Mr Bacon the Contractor for remitting money for the subsistence of the Troops in the ceded Islands had attended their Board; and Your Lordships Letter inclosing one from Major Fletcher having been read to him; he informed their Lordships, that by the death of both his Agents at St. Vincents, and other unavoidable accidents, the regularity of the remittance had been for some time interrupted, but that he had the greatest reason to believe from his last Accounts, that every cause of complaint had been for some time removed; and that he expected soon farther advices from his Agents, which My Lords have directed him to lay before them as soon as they arrived. My Lords have also ordered me to inform your Lordship that they have directed the Paymaster General to issue for the future the subsistence of the Regiments serving in the ceded Islands, to the Contractors, according to the effective State only of the said Regiments, agreable to the latest Returns received at your Office; for which purpose, My Lords desire your Lordship will transmit such Returns from time to time to the Paymaster; & My Lords have directed the Agents to issue the remainder of the subsistence of their Regiments, according to their Establishments, to the Agents of the respective Corps.

W.O. 1/873, no. 85

261

Governor Johnstone of Minorca to Barrington

[Holograph]   Port Mahon
                                                      12 January 1767

* * *

Inclosed I have the Honor of Sending you the Quarterly Returns of the Garrison, in which I am Sorry You will find so large a number of Sick, especially at this Season, but I can assure Your Lordship that it is neither owing to neglect in the Surgeon or Irregularity in the Men, but principally from the extream badness of the Weather which has been exceeding Wet attended with very high cold winds for near these two months past, which has been the occasion of a number of relapses amongst the Convalescents, and a little from the badness of the Quarters, particularly at St Philips, where the repeated care of Lt. Col. Mc.Kellar & the great expences of the repairs He had made has not been able to make them Wind and Water tight, which abstracted from the great hardship it is upon the poor Inhabitants, the being turn'd out of their Miserable Ruins will I hope be a Sufficient reason for the Immediate takeing into Consideration some of the proposals and Plans for Barracks and a New Town already sent over, and the sending of the necessary Orders in consequence of it.

W.O. 1/989, p. 721

262

Extract of a letter from Lieutenant Governor Johnstone to Barrington, sent to Henry Seymour Conway, Secretary of State

[Copy]   Port Mahon
                                                      29 January 1766

I must now (and indeed not before it is absolutely necessary) trouble you with the enclosed Representation, relating to the state of their Quarters in the Arreval of St. Philips, signed by the

Commanding Officers of the different Regiments, together with the Chief Engineer & the Fort Major, to which I must add my own Testimoney: and desire, that your Lordship will be so good as to take the affair into your consideration, & so state it to His Majesty, as to procure His Orders for some Relief, both to the Garrison & the Miserable Inhabitants turned out of their Houses without the least Consideration.

I wrote to Mr Ellis upon this same subject before I left the Island, and sent him a Scheme for removing the present arreval to a spot at some distance, with a Plan for a Town & Barracks for 1200 Men, & an Estimate of the whole, as also some Reasons shewing the necessity of some such measures being taken in case the Harbour & Fortress are thought of consequence enough to be defended; and the infinite use in point of time and security, the present Arreval was to the french in reducing it. All which papers are, as I know from His Majesty in his Hands, as also that Copies of them were sent to the Board of Ordnance by Lieutenant Colo McKellar, by my Orders, I have heard, that they have been more than once taken into consideration, & laid before the late Chancellor of the Exchequer, but were dropt on account of the expence, which might be easily defrayed by a Yearly allowance of four or five thousand Pounds. But this proportion I leave to abler heads, and only hope, that your Lordship will procure some Resolution to be taken upon it, as really no time ought to be lost, nor would, if His Majesty could see the very uncomfortable situation his Officers, Soldiers & Subjects are in for want of it, & the great risque of their health.

[Similar letter to the Master General of the Ordnance]

W.O. 4/78, pp. 491–492

263

Enclosure with Document 262

[Copy]   St Philip's Castle, Minorca
                                                              27 January 1766

Having pursuant to an Order from Colonel Johnstone Lieutenant
Governor & Commander in Chief, examined the state and
condition of the Soldiers Barracks in the Arraval of this place We
have found the same to be as follows.

1st Many of the Walls are shaken and crackt probably from the
Effects of the last Siege

2d The Roofs are in general too flat, and many of the Rafters
and Timbers are sagged & decayed

3rd Many of the Floors are sunk lower than the Street, &
consequently damp and unwholesome.

Though to our knowledge they have been frequently repaired
since our last taking possession of the Island, they are neither
wind nor water tight, and it is our opinion upon the whole, that
they are past repairing & being put into that habitable condition
that is necessary for the preservation of Men's healths, without
pulling them down & rebuilding them, and as they are dispersed
all over the Town, & in general contain only from four to about 8
or 10 Men each Barrack, it is further Our opinion that building
one Entire Pile to contain the same Number of Men, will not
exceed the expence of Rebuilding the present Barracks & that
such a building must tend to the ease of keeping up good Order &
discipline amongst the Men, & must consequently be more
advantageous to His Majesty's Service. Many of the Officers
Quarters are likewise in a very bad condition, and some of them
such as are not fit for Officers to live in, and the poor Inhabitants
both British and Natives are at the same time greatly distressed in
having had these Houses taken from them, for they received no
Consideration in lieu.

We find that the repairs of the Quarters and Barracks in the
Arraval have cost upwards of £500 a Year since we have been last
in possession of the Island, & it is very probable, they must cost at

least that Sum for Years to come, and still continue bad, & as this Sum wou'd in a few Years build such a pile of Barracks as is proposed, and if the proposal sent home, about two Years ago, for removing the Town (of which the Building of Barracks was a part) does not take place, It is Our opinion there ought to be Barracks built either within the works or Arraval as shall be found most convenient & without loss of time.

Signed as follows

Choly. Scott Lieut Colonel to the 11th Regt

Pat Mackellar, Lt. Colonel & Chief Engineer

Hild Oakes Lieut Colo 33d Regt.

Benj. Stehelin Captain & Commanding Officer of Artillery

John Gore Fort Major

[Similar paper to the Master General of the Ordnance]

W.O. 4/78, pp. 493–494

264

Governor Johnstone to Barrington

[Holograph]   Port Mahon, Minorca
                                               19 March 1767

*   *   *

And as I have had many complaints, that the Regiments quarter'd in the Arraval steal out of their Quarters and plunder the Country in the night; in order to prevent as much as I can any Thing of the sort for the time to come, I intend quartering, till some Barracks are built, the two Regiments forming that Garrison, the one in the Subterranean's in Charles Fort, and the other in those of the North West outward Ravelin, and have order'd them to be prepared for that Purpose. The Officers must still remain in the Town.

*   *   *

W.O. 1/989, p. 730

Abstract of opinions from the Colonies about the best seasons for landing troops

[Copy]   War Office
                                                N.d. [1767]

The King's Orders being sent in 1766 to the Governor or Commanding Officer of the following Stations vizt. Gibraltar, Grenada, Islands, Jamaica Antigua, St Augustine, Pensacola, Mobile and Senegal. To transmit a Report of the most Eligible Season for Landing Troops in each of their respective Districts. so as to avoid as much as possible the inconveniencys of the Climate The following are sent after a thorough Consultation with all the practitioners of Physick that cou'd be met with. N. the Governor or Commanding Officer, as also the several Practitioners of Physick have signed the Reports—Assigning their several Reasons for their Opinions.

Gibraltar	From the middle of November to the latter End of March, The best time for Landing—June, July August and September,—the worst,—The Garrison being very subject in those Months to Bilious and putrid disorders. April and May, are too near the Hot Season October – is rather too soon after.
Minorca	From the Month of December to March—The most Eligible time for Landing. April and May—too near the hot months. June, July, August, September and October absolutely improper. November improper—as the Rainy Season commences and the Sickness of the former Months are not entirely gone.
Grenada Islands	Between the 1st Jañry and the end of June.

Equal as to what time they land, during that period. If not for the Hurricanes – which are deemed to last from the 26th of July to the end of October, and during the greatest Heat and Rains, New Comers are exposed to the greatest inconveniences. the latter part of the Year would be equally eligible to the former part of it.

Excepting as to risque of Hurricanes—
Troops shou'd come from England in July or August in order to arrive there in September or October. If Troops are to be sent to perform Operations in the Field, or to remain only for the space of five or six Months. The Admirals, All the Land Officers and every Physical Person agree—That the earlier in January they arrive—the better.

Troops from Gibraltar and Minorca wou'd be more Seasoned for the Climate than those which arrive directly from Britain or Ireland.

Jamaica	November, December, January and February the best Months to Land—as coolest and most free from Rain.
	November—the best and most Cool time before the Heats come on.
	March, April—May and June—very hot and not proper on that account.
	July, August, September and October— Worst of all as there is much Rain and Heat.
N.	The Navigation is inconvenient in the 4 Months which are best for Landing the Troops.
Antigua	From the latter End of November, to the End of February—is the most proper time.
	Not very bad till the beginning of May.
	June, July, August and September very bad.
	Improper in October.
St. Augustine	April—May—June—July—August and

East Florida	September— are very improper Months. October—not good. November—best for Landing. December, January, February and March will do but the sooner Troops arrive after the beginning of November the better.
Pensacola	From the beginning of May—to the latter End of September—very improper. October and November—rather better. The beginning of December—the best. Not bad till April—but the nearer the beginning of December—the better.
Mobile	The latter End of November with all December and January the most proper time in the whole Year. February and the beginning of March—the next best Month. April and May to be avoided if possible. June, July, August and September and to the middle of October. Certain Destruction to Troops who arrive at that time.
Senegal	December, January, February, March, April The best Months to Land. From the beginning of May to the latter End of November—is the most sickly Season & to be avoided.
North America	—As the Climate is so good—It is near equal what time Troops Land. The River St. Laurence is certain to be free from Ice before the middle of May. But the sooner Ships go up after that time, the better, as the Easterly Winds generally Blow only till the Middle of June. After that time the Westerly are more frequent.

W.O.26/27, pp. 443–447

Barrington to Major–General Oughton

[Copy]   War Office
                                                    9 December 1765

I am to acknowledge the Honor of your Letter of the 3d instant, stating the great Loss your Regt. had sustained since its Arrival at Pensacola, and the distresses they had suffered. That they had Landed there the 25th of July in perfect Health and Spirits, but being encamped on a loose burning Sand, the weather being intensely hot and not having any vegetable Diet to refresh them, nor any sustenance but Salt Provisions and Water, the Calenture with Fluxes, Yellow Fevers, black Vomits, and Coups de Soleil raged in a few days with the Impetuosity of a Plague by which every Officer was infected but two, that the Regt. tho' landed compleat, could furnish but a Corporal and four Men for Guard; that in less than Six Weeks a Captain, Lieutenant, Surgeon, two Volunteers, five Officers Wives out of six, ninety five Men, and above forty Women and Children were swept away, and the rest left in a languid and dispirited State. That the only Consolation they now had was the Hope that His Majesty would out of His great Goodness and Compassion permit them to succeed to the vacant Commissions, and that you earnestly desired I would lay this before the King, in so favorable a Light as would procure them their Request, which would revive their drooping Spirits, and help to support them under the want of every Comfort & convenience, almost every Necessary of Life. In your Letter you have stated the Succession as follows, Vizt.

Captain Lieut Francis Vignoles to succeed Captain Hooker.
Licut. Edward Crofton, to be Captain Lieutenant
Ensign James Boucher to be Lieutenant.
Mr Charles Green to be Ensign.
Ensign John Darrell to succeed Lieutenant Farmer.
Mate Richard Deane to succeed Surgeon Chalmers.

I have laid this Letter before the King, who feels, to the utmost Extent, the melancholy Situation of a gallant Regt. perishing in His Service. His Majesty has ordered me to consider and report

355

to him what can be done for their Relief, and to prevent the like dreadful Calamity hereafter. But the best and most immediate Cordial to the surviving Officers is the willing Consent which the King has given to the Promotion you recommend, a most extraordinary Mark of Consideration, at a Time when the Half Pay List is so burthensome to the Public, and when so many deserving Officers are upon it, with undoubted Claims to be employed.

If your Regt. had been at home, or in a Place more Comfortable and less expensive to your Officers, and if this dreadful and unusual Mortality had not happened, such unexampled Favor could not have been obtained. I congratulate your Officers on a Distinction they so well deserve: I know you will communicate it to them in the properest manner, leaving the fullest Persuasion imprinted in their minds that they serve a King and Master, who always rewards suffering Merit, and never forgets his Troops because they are distant from his presence.

I have likewise endeavoured to do Justice to the Humane, Amiable, and Active Concern which you have expressed for your distressed Regts. and I am permitted to tell you that it is entirely satisfactory to His Majesty.

W.O. 4/78, pp. 160–162

267

Barrington to Charles Lowndes,
Secretary to the Treasury

[Copy] War Office
10 December 1765

Having received a Return from the 31st Regt. of Foot, which lately relieved the 35th at Pensacola, whereby it appears that 91 private men besides Officers, were then already dead, & Major Genl. Oughton, who commands the 31st Regt. having signified to me that He apprehends this great loss of Men is owing to the Want of proper Barracks for their Reception, as well as to that of fresh Provisions, I beg leave to send you inclosed a Copy of the above Return, [*in margin*: See the Return dated Pensacola 7th Septr. 1765, in the Return Book], & an Extract of the Letter I have received from Major Genl Oughton upon this subject, for the information of the Rt. Honble the Lords Commrs of H.M. Treasury, & submit it to their Lordships' consideration, whether, in Case it be deemed necessary that a Regt. should remain at Pensacola, it wou'd not be proper for their Lordships to give immediate Orders to the Commander in Chief in No. America, that if he thinks it necessary & practicable, sufficient Barracks may be, as soon as possible, erected there, for the Reception of the Troops, or at least an Hospital, & also to the Contractor for Provisions to supply the Regt. there with Fresh Provisions as often as he can possibly afford to do so.

W.O. 4/78, p. 174

268

Enclosure with Document 267

[Copy]   [4 December 1765]

'Extract of a Letter from Major Genl. Jas. Adolphus Oughton to the Secry. at War, dated 4th Decr. 1765'

All Accounts heretofore received agree in giving Pensacola the Character of a very healthy Place, though perfectly barren & incapable of Improvement, the former most probably the Effect of the latter. It is not therefore to the Nature of the Climate, but to other Contingencies that We are to impute the Disorders which seized the Troops immediately after their landing. The Regt. arrived there in the hotest Season of a Summer uncommonly hot, & being obliged to encamp in a loose burning Sand, were exposed without Shade or Shelter to the accumulated Force of intense heat both direct & refracted, so that several Men apparently well when they came off Duty, dropped down dead in half an hour after. Proper Cover therefore appears to be the first Object of considn. Barracks: What serve for Barracks at present are Huts built of Logs or Piles, covered with Bark, which being exsiccated

& warped, are equally incapable of sheltering the Wretched Inhabitants from Heat & Cold, nor, during the Rainy Season is there a Possibility of lying dry in those assigned to the Officers, which are doubtless the best of them. Brigr. Bouquet was preparing to remedy this Evil, but his sudden & unfortunate death put a Stop to all the salutary Plans he had formed for that Settlement. To build Barracks of Brick or Stone would require much Time in a Country so totally devoid of Materials & Artificers, nor would it perhaps be adviseable for Government to be at that Expence till a proper place be determined on for erecting a Fort; the present situation, being most injudiciously chosen, among many material Objections it may suffice to observe that there is not a drop of fresh Water in it. Wood likewise, proper for building, is at some considerable Distance, requires time to season, much labour to fell, carry, & saw, & Artificers to square, mortice, frame & erect into Houses. All this however may be done in the Northern Colonies with much Facility & agreable to any Plan given them, it being the common Practice in that Country as well as in Russia, to sell Wooden houses ready made. They have the further conveniency of being removeable at Pleasure. Mr. Adair Director of the Hospital, carried one with him to the Siege of Quebec, capable of containing 300 Men which he erected in two days time & Mr Napier sent one of the same construction for 400 Men, to the Hospital at Martinico. Nails, Hinges, & other Iron Work should be sent along with them.

Provisions: It is evident that Health can neither be preserved nor restored in hot Climates, while Men are reduced to a Necessity of living on Salt Provisions alone, & those recessarily tending to a State of Putridity. Live Cattle may be supplied at a reasonable rate from New York so as to furnish Broth &c for the sick & allow fresh Provisions in lieu of Salt, to be served out to the Garrison twice a Week, till such time as they can be supplied by Contract with the French Settlers at Mobille. It would likewise be adviseable to send Sheep & Hogs for Breed as after the rainy Season there must certainly be Grass in the Woody Parts of the Country. Hay in the mean Time must be sent with them. Potatoes, Onions, Turnips, & Carrots would be of infinite Service & may be had in great plenty at New York. It would be kind to furnish the Officers with Poultry for Breed, at Prime Cost, it being impossible for them to pay a Dollar for a Fowl, three for a Turkey &c as is the Case when they get any to buy from the Soi-disants Merchants there.

Liquors: The Scurvy is the only endemical Distemper peculiar to Pensacola & such is the inveteracy of it, as I have been assured by a Gentleman who was there some time, that Men have died of an universal Mortification in two days from a broken Shin & other trifling Accidents, Spruce Beer is allowed by all the Physical Gentlemen to be an excellent Antisceptick, & has been found by Experience in No. America to be the best preservative agst. that Disorder. The black Pine is the fittest for that Purpose, & may together with the Molasses, be furnished from New York, where they are in the constant Practice of making it, as it is universally drank by the Troops in the Northern Colonies. The best black Pine is, indeed, at Newfoundland, where they make Extracts of it which will keep some years. The Scurvey is known to rage with equal Violence in extreme hot & extreme Cold Climates. Before they fell on the Practice of making Spruce Beer, they usually buried one third of their Servants &c every Winter, now that Distemper is totally unknown among them: They may be furnished with extract of Pine from thence, (should that be thought more adviseable) so as to make their Beer for a penny a Quart: Cyder which is next in Merit, may be had very cheap at New York, till they can be supplied with Spruce Beer, Lime Juice is cheap at Jamaica, & is likewise an excellent Antiscorbutic. Vinegar is absolutely necessary to be delivered out with their Salt Provisions, they make it of Cyder at New York, & sell it very cheap. The waste of Spirits by Perspiration during the heats is excessive, & Nature so exhausted by it as to be unable to bear up against any Disorder, that Attacks them in that languid State. Wine was found to be the best restorative, & performed amazing Cures at the Havannah &c but as that is too expensive an Article, the Physical Gentlemen that I have consulted, agree that Rum mixed with Water will answer the End. This my Officers found so necessary, that they have hitherto supplied the Men with it at their own Expence, I am an humble Suitor to your Lordship that they may be reimbursed this Expence, as their Circumstances can by no means afford

359

what their Humanity prompted them to. Half a pint p diem till they get the Spruce Beer & a Gill afterwards, Mr Adair tells me is a Sufficient Quantity. It should be two years old Rum, as new Spirits are found to be fatally pernicious. New York appears to be Our properest Pointe D'Appuy for these purposes as it abounds with most of the above Particulars, has great Convenience of Shiping & is the Residence of the Commander in Chief, Quarter Master General, Barrack Master General, Commissary General & Contractor.

W.O. 4/78, pp. 175–179

269

Barrington to Lieutenant-Colonel Walsh of the 31st Regiment of Foot [at Pensacola]

[Copy]   War Office
                                                  12 December 1765

I am to acknowledge the Receipt of your Letter of the 7th Septemr. last, with the State of the 31st Regiment inclosed. It gave me the greatest concern to hear of the extraordinary loss the Regiment had suffered, and the melancholy circumstances you were then in, but I flatter myself that these distresses will be gradually alleviated, as well by your becoming every day better inured to the Climate, as by every Assistance and Relief that can be furnished by Government. General Oughton will inform You at large of the gracious manner in which His Majesty has consented that the Succession to the Vacant Commissions shall go in the Regiment, and I make no doubt that this extraordinary Mark of His Majesty's Royal favor will be received with due Gratitude by the whole Corps.

In answer to that part of your Letter, wherein you take Notice of the want of Bedding and Medicines, I must observe to you that the Stock provided for the use of the 31st Regt. was as large if not larger than what is commonly supplied for Regts. on the like Service, as will appear by the Invoices which I send you enclosed.

W.O. 4/78, pp. 187–188

Extract of a letter from Major-General Oughton to Barrington, sent to Henry Seymour Conway, Secretary of State

[Copy]
N.p.
10 February 1766

I have this instant received Letters of October 25th from my unfortunate Regimt. at Pensacola, by which I find that, tho' the Sickness and Mortality was considerably abated, it still continued to so dispiriting a degree as to reduce the Survivors almost to despair. The Scurvy too tho' so early in the Year, was begining to rage wt. Violence, and the small quantity of fresh provisions they could procure being reserved for the Hospital, there was nothing to obstruct the progress of that disorder. The Captains had already advanced so much to purchase wine, Spirits, Vinegar &c. for the Relief of their Men, that their Credit was exhausted, and no means left of continuing it for Self preservation.

What, my good Lord, is to be done in this calamitous Affair? Is a Regiment totally to perish without the smallest prospect, nay without a possibility of being in the least useful to their Country? And must the Nation sustain such a loss of Men, many worthy Families sustain the Loss of their Relations, from a mistaken Idea, from a Misrepresentation, or perhaps from want of a due Attention to the Importance of the Object?

I know Your Lordship's humanity and zealous regard to the good of His Majesty's Service, I know too you are well acquainted with the Inutility of keeping Troops, I should say, of exposing them to perish there. I therefore make no Scruple of pouring out my Grief to You, and no doubt of using your Endeavours to preserve the Remainder of them from destruction.

I am well aware of the busy Bustle of the times, and that His Majesty's Ministers can ill afford to give attention to any but the important Objects now under consideration. But in this case, My Lord, Delays are not only dangerous, but fatal, the time requisite to carry any Measures into execution is, (from their distance) so very long, that every Pacquet which sails without Orders for removing the Regiment, carries a Death Warrant for so many gallant Men.

W.O. 4/78, pp. 386–388

Notes to the Barrington Papers

Full publication details are given at the first mention of a particular book or article. In subsequent references an abbreviated citation is given. Unless otherwise expressed, the place of publication is London.

Other Abbreviations

C.J.	*Journals of the House of Commons*
EHR	*English Historical Review*
JMH	*Journal of Modern History*
JSAHR	*Journal of the Society for Army Historical Research*
P.H.	William Cobbett and T. C. Hansard eds., *The Parliamentary History of England . . . to 1803*

1 Clarence E. Carter ed., *The Correspondence of General Thomas Gage with the Secretaries of State and with the War Office and the Treasury, 1763–1775* (2 vols., New Haven Conn. 1931–2, repr. 1969); John Shy, 'Confronting Rebellion: Private Correspondence of Lord Barrington with General Gage, 1765–1775' in Howard Peckham ed., *Sources of American Independence: Selected Manuscripts from the Collections of the William L. Clements Library* (2 vols., Chicago, 1978).

2 E. Channing and A. C. Coolidge eds., *The Barrington–Bernard Correspondence and Illustrative Matter, 1760–1770* (Cambridge, Mass., 1912).

3 *Gentleman's Magazine* (1793), Part I, p. 187.

4 Shute Barrington, *The Political Life of William Wildman Viscount Barrington, compiled from original papers* (1814).

5 Sir Lewis Namier and John Brooke eds., *The History of Parliament: The House of Commons, 1754–1790* (3 vols., 1964), II, pp. 55–59.

Notes to Section 1

1 For an account of the first Lord Barrington see Romney Sedgwick ed., *The History of Parliament: The House of Commons, 1715–1754* (2 vols., 1971), I, p. 437.

2 John Brooke ed., Horace Walpole, *Memoirs of the Reign of George II* (3 vols., 1985), I, p. 237, n. 4.

3 See e.g. Nemesis to the *Public Advertiser* May 12 1772. John Cannon ed., *The Letters of Junius* (Oxford 1978), p. 510.

4 Horace Walpole to Lady Ossory, 30 June 1785. W. S. Lewis *et al.* eds., *Horace Walpole's Correspondence* (40 vols., 1937–1983), XXXIII, pp. 469–470.

5 Horace Walpole to Montague, 23 December 1759. Ibid., IX, p. 265. This liaison lasted for a long time, apparently until 1770. *Town & Country Magazine* (January 1771), III, p. 9, where he is called the Hostile Scribe, and she the Stableyard Messalina.

6 Housekeeping accounts *passim*. Ipswich 17. See also Ipswich 18 for rents of Lady Barrington's London properties (sugar houses, warehouses, an alehouse, and several wharfages and private dwellings).

7 Number 16 on the west side of the square, partially on the site later occupied by Asquith's town house. After his death Shute Barrington occupied the house until 1803. Hugh Phillips, *Mid-Georgian London* (1964), p. 302.

8 He paid 20 guineas a year for the opera subscription, beginning in 1756. Drummond's Account Book. Ipswich 23/1.

9 *Gentleman's Magazine* (1756), pp. 395–6.

10 *C.J.* XXVII, pp. 315–320.

11 See e.g. *P.H.* XV, p. 486.

12 Calcraft to the Earl of Loudoun, 12 November 1756. Add. MSS. 17,493, ff. 17–21, at 18v.

13 'The man who stands not forth in support of the King and the constitution of his country in time of publick difficulties and violence, without the lure of reward, is in my opinion base indeed.' Robinson to Jenkinson. Add. MSS. 38206, f. 207, quoted in I.R. Christie, *Myth and Reality in Late-Eighteenth-Century British Politics* (1970), p. 156.

14 A. F. Steuart ed., *The Last Journals of Horace Walpole during the Reign of George III from 1771–1783* (2 vols., 1910), I, p. 70.

15 Ibid., p. 233.

16 5 January 1761, in H. Ellis, ed., *Letters Illustrative of English History* (4 vols., 1824), IV, p. 432.

17 Shute Barrington, *Life*, pp. 73–85, 95–100.

18 Ibid., p. 80.

19 Bradshaw to Barrington, 13 September 1767. Ipswich 112/11.

20 Thomas Whateley to George Grenville, 4 June 1768. W. J. Smith ed., *The Grenville Papers: Being the Correspondence of Richard Grenville, Earl Temple K.G., and the Right Hon. George Grenville, Their Friends and Contemporaries* (4 vols., 1852–3), IV, p. 300.

21 Knox to G. Grenville, 8 September 1768. Ibid., IV, p. 360.

22 C.O.5/84, ff. 114–127. Printed in C. W. Alvord and C. E. Carter eds., *The New Regime 1765–1767* (vol. XI of *Illinois State Historical Library: British Series*), pp. 234–243; See John Shy, *Toward Lexington* (Princeton, N.J., 1965). pp. 232–237; John Shy, *A People Numerous and Armed* (Oxford, 1976), pp. 87–89.

23 The term 'desert' needs to be interpreted in the eighteenth-century sense of a wilderness outside civilisation.

24 There exists a tradition in the Barrington family that Francis was Junius. Ipswich 92 (an account of the rebuilding of Beckett by George Viscount Barrington, 1882). But nothing else in the family papers bears on this.

25 Edmund Burke to Dr William Markham, post 9 November 1771, Lucy S. Sutherland ed., *The Correspondence of Edmund Burke*, vol. II., *July 1768–June 1774* (Cambridge, 1960), pp. 268–269.

26 December 7 1770. John Wright ed., *Sir Henry Cavendish's Debates of the House of Commons, During the Thirteenth Parliament . . . Commonly called the Unreported Parliament . . . 1768–1771* (2 vols., 1841–43), I, p. 189.

27 Testis to the *Public Advertiser* 19 November 1770. Testiculus to the *Public Advertiser*, 24 November 1770. See also John Calcraft to Chatham, 'Lord Barrington is heartbroken at his nonsensical speech in parliament; the army affronted, and Hervey full of resentment, at being hung out in the envious colours his Lordship chose for him.' W. S. Taylor and J. H. Pringle eds., *Correspondence of William Pitt, Earl of Chatham* (4 vols., 1838–40), III, p. 494.

28 Junius to Woodfall. Private letters no. 53. Professor Cannon dates this 25 January 1772. Cannon, *Junius*, p. 386.

29 According to Junius, Barrington expelled Francis. Veteran to the *Public Advertiser*, 23 March 1772. Cannon, *Junius*, pp. 506–507.

30 Veteran to the *Public Advertiser* 28 January, 17 and 27 February, 10 and 23 March 1772. Two more appeared under different pseudonyms, viz. Scotus, taking exception to Barrington's supposed

enmity towards Scotsmen, 4 May; and Nemesis, who computed that Barrington, having complained to friends that he was insufficiently rewarded, had in fact received £53,000 of public money during his combined periods of office, 12 May 1772. Cannon, *Junius*, passim and particularly pp. 496–512, 547–557.

31 Francis left for India in 1773 to take up his appointment on the Supreme Council, largely due to Barrington's influence. Junius students have adapted this fact to argue for or against the Francis ascription. Cannon, *Junius*, p. 551 et seq.

32 The King to Barrington 27 and 28 January 1770. Sir John Fortescue ed., *The Correspondence of King George III* (6 vols., 1927–8), III, pp. 15 and 16. For other examples see Walpole, *Memoirs of George II*, I, p. 147 (Barrington as a negotiator for the King with Halifax in 1751); Walpole, *Last Journals*, I, p. 388 (as a messenger from the King to Lady Ailesbury).

33 Shute Barrington, *Life*, pp. 153–157. The documents printed in the present work should be read with those in the *Life*, pp. 140–157.

34 Ibid., p. 165.

35 Ibid., p. 161.

36 Ibid., pp. 161–182. This is another of Barrington's long descriptive memoranda on crucial parts of his public life.

37 Barrington to the Earl of Buckinghamshire, December 1777. *H.M.C. Lothian*, p. 325.

38 Barrington's engagement diaries for 1777–1792 are all classified under Ipswich 37.

39 'Lord Barrington is to wait on Lord North, to know what is to be done for him; I therefore authorize You to make Such a provision as You may think right, though it should be handsome it ought not to be extravagant.' The King to North, 12 December 1778. Fortescue, *Correspondence*, IV, p. 231.

40 Barrington MSS., Berwick Place.

41 'I shall keep an ensigncy in a good Regt. for my Cousin and namesake.' Barrington to Bernard, 10 March 1772. Channing and Coolidge, *Barrington–Bernard Correspondence*, p. 214. See also R. A. Bowler, *Logistics and the Failure of the British Army in America 1775–1783* (Princeton, N.J., 1975), pp. 29–30 and 252 for the appointment of Daniel Chamier, the brother of Barrington's protégé and Deputy Secretary, to be Commissary in North America in 1773.

42 Certificate of 8 August 1792, covering period 1 January to 9 August 1765. Barrington MSS., Berwick Place.

43 Horace Walpole to Lady Ossory, 30 January 1794. Lewis, *Walpole Correspondence*, XXXIV, p. 197.

44 See Ipswich 79.

45 E.g. Newcastle, Dodington, Henry Fox (at least in earlier years), Halifax, Botetourt, Hillsborough, Bradshaw.

Notes to Section 2

1 The office of Secretary at War has been discussed by several historians: C. M. Clode, *The Military Forces of the Crown* (2 vols., 1869), II, Chapter XXI; M. A. Thomson, *The Secretaries of State, 1681–1782* (1932), pp. 65–77; Olive Anderson, 'The Constitutional Position of the Secretary at War 1643–1855', *Journal of the Society for Army Historical Research*, XXXVI (1958), pp. 165–9; Olive Gee, 'The British War Office in the Later Years of the American War of Independence', *Journal of Modern History*, XXVI (1954), pp. 123–136; I. F. Burton, 'The Secretary at War and the Administration of the Army during the War of the Spanish Succession' (unpublished Ph.D. thesis, London 1960). For comparison with a later period chapters 3 and 4 of K. Bourne, *Palmerston* (1982) are valuable. Interesting references to Barrington are to be found in Piers Mackesy, *The War for America* (1964), A. J. Guy, *Oeconomy and Discipline* (Manchester 1985), and Shy, *Lexington*.

2 Anderson, op. cit., p. 166.

3 Sir William Holdsworth, *A History of English Law* (17 vols., 1903–72), XII, p. 729.

4 *P.H*, XX, p. 1253.

5 *Brickdale's Debates*, 9 December 1770, quoted in Namier and Brooke, *Parliament*, II, p. 58.

6 See also Barrington to Ligonier, 19 July 1758, and to Granby, 17 June 1760, on the civilian control of hospitals. Shute Barrington, *Life*, pp. 41–42, 58–62. R. Whitworth, *Field-Marshal Lord Ligonier. A Story of the British Army, 1702–1770* (Oxford, 1958), p. 230 for a view sympathetic to Ligonier. The quarrel over the hospital for curing ruptured soldiers, set up by Dr Lee, regarded by Ligonier as a genius and by Barrington as a fraud, can be found in R. A. Roberts ed.,

Calendar of Home Office Papers of the Reign of George III, 1770–1772 (1881), pp. 187, 189, 308, 321.

7 Bourne, *Palmerston*, pp. 161–180.

8 See Barrington to the King, tentatively dated, probably wrongly 12 (Dec?) 1773 by Fortescue, *Correspondence*, III, p. 41: document 31 is correctly dated.

Notes to Section 3

1 E.g. Barrington to Thomas Bernard, 7 September 1769. Channing and Coolidge, *Barrington–Bernard Correspondence*, p. 208.

2 Sherwin was appointed 24 December 1755. *London Gazette* no. 9540; he died in office on 28 November 1756. *Gentleman's Magazine* (1756), p. 573.

3 Appointed 2 December 1756.

4 Several lengthy surveys by Tyrwhitt survive, e.g., 'Mr Tyrwhitts' History of the Press Act', which traces the subject back to the wars of Queen Anne, n.d. (but apparently 1757), Ipswich 3b, no. 276. See also the 'Extract from the History of Q. Elizabeth concerning Subsidiary Treaties', n.d. (probably 1755), Ipswich 3c, no. 60.

5 Appointed 1 January 1763. *London Gazette* no. 10274.

6 Appointed 21 January 1772. Ibid., no. 11215.

7 See L. Scott, 'The Undersecretaries of State, 1755–1775', (Manchester M.A. Thesis, 1950), p. 117.

8 Appointed 1 December 1775. Ibid., no. 11618, He left office on 22 August 1803. *London Gazette*, no. 15613.

9 Add. MSS. 40759, ff. 221–263.

10 Joseph Parkes and H. Merivale eds., *Memoirs of Sir Philip Francis, K.C.B., with Correspondence and Journals* (2 vols., 1867), p. 66.

11 P.M.G. 2/10, p. 121. Barrington complained that he was taxed at 5% of his salary in his civil capacity and 5% as a military man. Barrington to Newcastle, 24 December 1760. W.O. 4/63, p. 16.

12 Nemesis to the *Public Advertiser*, 12 May 1772. Cannon, *Junius*, pp. 509–512.

13 *Reports from Committees of the House of Commons* (15 vols., 1803), V, XII, pp. 358, 359, 404.

Notes to Section 4

1 Clode, *Military Forces*, II, p. 182.
2 H. M. Little, 'The Treasury, the Commissariat and the Supply of the Combined Army in Germany, during the Seven Years War (1756–1763)' (London Ph.D. thesis 1981), passim.
3 Although the detailed finance records have mostly been destroyed Barrington kept some: they now survive in the archive at Ipswich, especially in Ipswich 6e.
4 These can be followed in the *Journal of the House of Commons* and in Estimates for the Land Forces, W.O. 25/3209.
5 *C.J.* XXXI, p. 53.
6 For this and much of the ensuing account I rely upon Guy, *Oeconomy*, chapter 3.
7 G. A. Steppler, 'The Common Soldier in the Reign of George III', (London Ph.D. thesis, 1985), p. 61.
8 See Section 1, footnote 22; for Shelburne's reception of and research into Barrington's plan, and its subsequent fate, see Shy, *Lexington*, Chapter VI, *passim*.
9 T.29/38, pp. 78, 190, 204, 235, 276, 279; W.O. 4/82, p. 193.
10 *C.J.*, XXI, p. 51. See Shy, *Lexington*, pp. 244–247 for the presentation of Estimates and Extraordinaries.
11 Establishments can be found in W.O. 24/287.
12 Guy, *Oeconomy*, pp. 27–28.
13 Ibid., pp. 32–35.
14 E.g. Barrington to Calcraft, requiring a return of equipment lost on campaign, so that he might obtain a warrant for reimbursement, 5 December 1759. W.O. 4/59, p. 362.
15 Guy, *Oeconomy*, pp. 143–146.
16 The foreign troops also objected to being quartered in farms. Barrington to Cornet Abercrombie, 21 May 1756. W.O. 4/51, p. 511.
17 See Little, op. cit., pp. 137–141, 205–214.
18 See also Newcastle to Barrington, 12 October 1763. Ipswich 112, no. 42. The fair copies of documents 94 and 95 are Add. MSS. 32951, ff. 381–382, 432–433.
19 T. 29/37, p. 264. See also draft estimates, upon which document 100 was based, in Ipswich 6e, nos. 31 and 32; for the question of precedence in rank of these officers see Judge Advocate General to

Barrington, 29 January, 1766. W.O. 26/27, p. 220; for the application of the solution in Ireland see Barrington to Lord Beauchamp, 18 June, 1766. W.O.4/80, p. 47; and Barrington to John Lamb (agent), 15 July, 1767, W.O. 4/82, p. 175.

20 See R. Middleton, *The Bells of Victory. The Pitt-Newcastle Ministry and the Conduct of the Seven Years' War, 1757–1762* (Cambridge, 1985), p. 34. For the financial implications for colonel and agent of transferring companies to the new regiments see Barrington to officers commanding 19 infantry regiments, 26 April, 1756. W.O. 4/51, p. 398.

21 For Barrington's presentation of estimates, including proposed augmentations, in 1770, see Cavendish, *Debates*, II, pp. 184–189.

22 Estimates of many types, varying from the global year-estimate to a small-scale estimate for a new regiment, can be found in the *Journals of the House of Commons*, but the Barrington archive at Ipswich contains a number of examples of preparatory exercises and parts of estimates—abstracts, 'states' and other statistical comparisons, which have an added value because of the absence of such papers in the W.O. series.

23 Guy, *Oeconomy*, p. 110; see also Barrington to Samuel Martin, 21 May, 1760. W.O. 4/60, p. 585.

24 Minutes of meeting of Board of General Officers, 20 June, 1760. W.O. 71/10, pp. 43–45; Barrington to Judge Advocate General, 27 June, 1760. W.O. 4/61, p. 339.

25 Barrington to Major-General Whitmore and nine other colonels of regiments, 27 June, 1760. Ibid., pp. 340–343.

26 Guy, *Oeconomy*, pp. 147–157 is required reading for the complex procedure of settling clothing patterns and arranging the finance.

27 Ibid., pp. 80–81.

28 Barrington to G. Ross (agent), 17 July, 1767. W.O. 4/82, p. 189.

Notes to Section 5

1 See Houlding, *Fit for Service*, pp. 38–39.

2 It is not clear from the existing documents when this happened. Clode thought that it was in 1717 (II, pp. 131–132), but it must have been earlier than that. The use of the army in aid of the civil power and of the police role of the Secretary at War is discussed in T. Hayter, *The Army and the Crowd in Mid-Georgian England*, (1978).

3 For the distribution and rotation of the army in Great Britain see Houlding, *Fit for Service*, pp. 23–45.

4 8 George II, c. 30.

5 See e.g. Barrington to Postmasters at Oxford and Eye, Suffolk. W.O. 4/59, p. 540. Earlier Secretaries at War were careful to respond to appeals to enlarge quarters for the convenience of towns. William Strickland to Mayor of Portsmouth, 7 July 1730. W.O. 4/32, p. 47.

6 Houlding, *Fit for Service*, Chapter 1.

7 Barrington had a copy (now with the Barrington MSS. at Berwick Place) of John Senex, *The Roads through England Delineated, or Ogilby's Survey, Revised, Improved, and Reduced to a Size portable for the Pocket* (1759).

8 A large number of innkeepers' letters and petitions are in the Public Record Office, e.g. W.O. 40/1, 2 and 3.

9 Clode thought that public opinion was against barracks (I, pp. 221–225), without specifying any examples. It would seem that he derived this material from certain individuals—Marshal Wade, Blackstone—and from proceedings in Parliament. Under increasing pressure of quartering the people did not always agree.

10 Representation of the inhabitants of Guildford to Lord George Onslow (n.d. but 1759). W.O. 40/3 (unnumbered bundles).

11 Beckford's complaint and Barrington's reply were printed in Burke's *Annual Register*, XII, (1769), p. 187.

12 The peacetime activities of the army have been recorded in a series of tables in Houlding, *Fit for Service*, Appendix A, pp. 396–408.

13 Hayter, *Army*, chapter 5.

14 Barrington to Harvey, 27 August 1756. W.O. 4/52, p. 184; see Hayter, *Army*, chapter 7 for the 1756 rioting, only a small fraction of which can be touched upon in this present work.

15 C. D'Oyly to William How, 6 October 1766. W.O. 4/80, p. 399.

16 Barrington to Lieutenant-Colonel James Wolfe, 8 January, 1757. W.O. 4/53, p. 40.

17 G. Rudé, *Wilkes and Liberty. A Social Study of 1763 to 1774* (Oxford, 1962); Hayter, *Army*, chapter 11.

18 Cavendish, *Debates*, I.

19 Shute Barrington, *Life*, pp. 113–120.

20 Houlding, *Fit for Service*, Appendix A.

21 Ibid., pp. 75–90.

22 J. Freemantle to C. D'Oyly, 22 March, 1766; William Burton and other excise officers to Barrington, 26 November 1766. W.O. 1/989, p. 349.

Notes to Section 6

1 Barrington to Townshend, 30 August 1771, Ipswich 107.

2 Barrington to William Pitt, offering the post of commissary of stores in Gibraltar to a connection, 22 March, 1766. Taylor and Pringle, *Chatham Correspondence*, II, pp. 404–405.

3 Barrington to Bernard, 3 June, 1760. Channing and Coolidge, *Barrington-Bernard Correspondence*, p. 14.

4 Barrington to Bernard, 7 January 1772. Ibid., p. 211.

5 Lord Anson to Barrington, 4 February, 1761, Ipswich 3b. An interesting example, as Anson was generally against 'Borough recommendations' at least in the Navy. Middleton, *Bells of Victory*, p. 104.

6 Some of these lists are in Ipswich 3a, nos. 16–20.

7 Barrington to William Adair and seventeen other agents, 21 January 1760. W.O. 4/59, p. 561.

8 S.P. 41/5, pp. 1–8, quoted in A. Bruce, *The Purchase System in the British Army, 1660–1871* (1980), p. 25.

9 W.O. 71/10, p. 232; see also Barrington to Charles Gould enquiring the grounds on which the new rates were computed, 2 February, 1766, and Gould to Barrington explaining the method, 3 February, 1766. Ibid., pp. 238–239; Bruce, *Purchase*, pp. 32–33.

10 'I entirely approve of Your intended letter & think no occasion could be more proper thus Authenticaly to declare my resolution of not permitting Officers to sell any more than those Commissions they bought.' The King to Barrington, 7 February 1766; Fortescue, *Correspondence*, I, no. 241. The original is in Ipswich 111. See also Barrington to the King, 7 February 1766. Ibid., no. 240.

11 Printed in Shute Barrington, *Life*, pp. 131–137, and in Bruce, *Purchase*, pp. 173–175, but is reproduced in the present work because it was one of the most important statements of Barrington's view of his position.

12 Granby died in October 1770; the King gave his regiment (the Royal

Regiment of Horse Guards) to Henry Seymour Conway, but declined to appoint another Commander-in-Chief. The King to Lord North, 21 October 1770. Fortescue, *Correspondence*, II. no. 619.

13 Bute to Barrington, soliciting help for John Wemyss, a lieutenant on half-pay, 3 March 1760. Ipswich 3d.

14 The examples (215, 216) come from a large class, many of them in the private letter book numbered 107 at Ipswich. See also Barrington to Major-General Burton, apologising for being unable to prevent Sir Edward Hawke's young nephew (a Granby nominee) from being promoted over the heads of six older and more experienced captains in the 5th Regiment of Foot. Ipswich 107.

15 For example the case of Captain Hill. Barrington to Hill, 23 May 1772; same to same, 6 September 1772; same to same 3 November 1772; Barrington to Count La Lippe, 10 November 1772. Ipswich 107.

16 See Ipswich 6a2, *passim*.

17 W.O. 26/28, p. 478.

18 Barrington to Singleton, 23 November 1765. W.O. 4/78, p. 110.

19 For example the case of Bryce McCumming, quartermaster of the 31st Regiment. Barrington sent him some money, being unable to help him in any other way. McCumming to Barrington, 19 August 1791; Barrington to McCumming (a draft) n.d.; McCumming to Barrington 28 August 1791; same to same 19 February 1792. Ipswich 7.

20 See also Barrington to Lieutenant Browne (of the invalids at Hull), stating that the rule against promotion in the invalid corps was 'fully established when I came to the War Office in 1755 and constantly practised since', 10 March 1773. Ipswich 6a2, no. 33.

21 See for example C. D'Oyly to Lieutenant-Colonel Ogilvy (13th Foot), 22 November; Barrington to Ogilvy, 22 November; same to same, 30 November, 1765. W.O. 4/78, pp. 107, 108, 130.

22 'The rule which prevents the proposed Exchange is not of novel Institution; I found it established when I first came to the War Office in 1755, & invariably observed by the late Duke of Cumberland.' Barrington to the Archbishop of York, 8 May, 1773. Ipswich 6a2, no. 90.

23 Barrington to Elliot, 25 December 1773. Ipswich 107.

24 Same to same, 31 December 1773. Ipswich 107. See also

Barrington to Earl of Pembroke, objecting to an exchange where no money had originally been given for the commission, 20 January 1766. W.O. 4/78, pp. 320–321.

25 Barré to William Pitt, 8 October 1760; P.R.O. 30/8/18; same to Bute, 21 December 1760. Fortescue, *Correspondence*, I, no. 10.

26 Peter Brown, *The Chathamites* (1967), p. 211.

27 Taylor and Pringle, *Chatham Correspondence*, IV, p. 250–251.

28 Shute Barrington, *Life*, p. 206.

29 'Copy of Words dictated by Sir John Dalrymple' (to Lieutenant-General Mackay, Barrington's second), 19 September 1778. Berwick Place MSS. The quarrel did not arise directly out of promotion, having more to do with alleged difficulties made by Barrington in the equipping of a new regiment. Rank was however involved in several alleged injuries done at earlier times to the family.

30 E.g. 'Rules observed by Lord Barrington when Secretary at War', n.d. but in a 1780 bundle. W.O. 1/890, f. 139.

Notes to Section 7

1 For army medicine see Sylvia Frey, *The British Soldier in America: A Social History of Military Life in the Revolutionary Period* (Austin, Texas 1981), chapter 2; P.E. Kopperman, 'Medical Services in the British Army 1742–1783', *Journal of the History of Medicine and Allied Sciences*, XXXIV, (1979), pp. 436–443; U. Troehler, 'Quantification in British Medicine and Surgery 1750–1830, with Special Reference to its Introduction into Therapeutics' (London Ph.D. thesis, 1978). None of these dwells much upon the part played by the War Office.

2 There is no sign of any feeling for religion in anything ever written by Barrington. His brother the Bishop made a successful career in the Church without any sincere subscription to the Thirty-Nine Articles.

3 During the American War Barrington defended himself angrily against Barré's accusations about expensive medical establishments by explaining that additional surgeons should always be sent with any expedition going to unhealthy stations in the West Indies. *P.H.*, XIX, p. 54.

4 Barrington to Henry Fox (a warrant), 3 November 1758. W.O. 26/23, pp. 471–472.

Biographical Notes

This list contains most of the more important persons figuring in the text, including officers who attained the rank of lieutenant-colonel, more senior officials, prominent medical men, and members of parliament.

Abercrombie, James. Ensign 1725, lieutenant 1727, captain 1736, first lieutenant-colonel 1 Foot Guards 1742, colonel 44 Foot 1756, major-general 1756, lieutenant-general 1759, general 1772.

A'Court Ashe, William (1708–81). Ensign 11 Foot 1726, lieutenant 2 Foot Guards 1738, M. P. Heytesbury 1751–81, captain and lieutenant-colonel 2 Foot Guards 1745, major-general 1759, lieutenant-general 1765, colonel 11 Foot 1765–81, general 1778.

Adair, Robert (d. 1790). Staff Surgeon Flanders 1742, Chief Surgeon to Hospital for Forces in Great Britain and Inspector of Regimental Infirmaries 1756, Surgeon-General of H.M. Forces 1786.

Albemarle, George Keppel, Earl of (1724–70). Ensign 2 Foot Guards 1738, captain-lieutenant 1 Dragoons 1741, captain and lieutenant-colonel 2 Foot Guards 1743, Lord of the Bedchamber to Duke of Cumberland 1746–65, M.P. for Chichester 1746–54, colonel 3 Dragoons 1755–72, major-general 1756, lieutenant-general 1759, Privy Council 1761, Governor of Jersey 1761–72, commanded at capture of Havana 1762, general 1772.

Amherst, Jeffrey Lord (1717–97). Ensign 1731, cornet Ligonier's Horse 1735, colonel 15 Foot 1756, Commander in Chief Canada 1758–63, major-general 1759, lieutenant-general 1761, Governor Virginia 1768, colonel-in-chief 60 Foot 1768, Governor Guernsey 1770, Privy Council 1772, general 1778, colonel 2 Horse Grenadier Guards 1779, colonel 2 Horse Guards 1782, Commander in chief 1793, field-marshal 1796.

Ancram, William Kerr, Earl of, Marquess of Lothian (c. 1710–75). Cornet 11 Dragoons 1735, captain 11 Foot 1739, captain and lieutenant-colonel 1 Foot Guards 1741, lieutenant-colonel 11 Dragoons 1745, colonel 24 Foot 1747–52, aide-de-camp to Duke of Cumberland 1745–46, M.P. Richmond 1747–63, colonel 11 Dragoons 1752, major-general 1755, lieutenant-general 1758, general 1770.

Argyll (or Argyle), John Campbell, Duke of (1723–1806). Lieutenant 21 Foot 1739, captain 1741, major 1743, M.P. Glasgow Burghs 1744–61, lieutenant-

375

colonel 30 Foot 1745, lieutenant-colonel 42 Foot 1749, aide-de-camp to George II 1755–59, colonel of 56 (afterward 54) Foot 1755–57, colonel of 14 Dragoons 1757–65, major-general 1759, lieutenant-general 1761, deputy Commander in Chief Scotland 1762–65, M.P. Dover 1756–66, colonel of 1 Foot 1765–82, Commander in Chief Scotland 1767–78, general 1778, colonel 3 Foot Guards 1782–1806, Lord-Lieutenant Argyll 1794–1800.

Atholl, John Murray, Duke of (1729–74). Göttingen University 1751–53, captain 54 Foot 1745–46, M.P. Preston 1761–64, Scottish representative peer 1766–74.

Barré, Isaac (1726–1802). Trinity College Dublin 1745, ensign 32 Foot 1746, lieutenant 1755, captain 1758, captain 28 Foot 1760, lieutenant-colonel 106 Foot 1761, M.P. Chipping Wycombe 1761–74, Adjutant-General 1763, Governor Stirling Castle 1763, dismissed from appointments by Grenville government 1764, Privy Council 1766–68, Vice-Treasurer of Ireland 1766–68, retired from army 1773, Treasurer of the Navy 1782, Paymaster General 1783, Clerk of the Pells 1784–1802.

Barrington, Daines (1727–1800). Oxford University, Marshal of High Court of Admiralty 1751, judge on Welsh circuit 1757, recorder of Bristol, Second Justice of Palatine court of Chester 1778, author of *Observations on the Statutes* (1766).

Barrington, George, fifth Viscount (d. 1829). Prebendary of Durham and rector of Sedgfield.

Barrington, John Shute, first viscount (1678–1734). Utrecht University 1694–98, Inner Temple 1698, Commissioner of Customs 1708–11, assumed name of Barrington under terms of a will, M.P. Berwick upon Tweed 1715–23, Irish peerage 1720, expelled from House of Commons after a lottery scandal 1723, author of tracts on behalf of protestant dissenters.

Barrington, Mary, Viscountess (d. 1764). Wife of William Wildman, 2nd Viscount Barrington.

Barrington, Richard, fourth Viscount Barrington (d. 1813). Ensign 3 Foot Guards 1777.

Barrington, Samuel (1729–1800). Entered navy 1740, lieutenant 1745, captain and continuously employed until 1763, rear admiral of the White and Commander in Chief West Indies 1778, commanded at capture of St. Lucia 1778, repulsed fleet of D'Estaing and Suffren, second-in-command Channel Fleet 1782, admiral 1787.

Barrington, Shute (1734–1826). Merton College Oxford 1755, ordained 1756, canon of Christ Church 1760, canon of St Paul's 1762, canon of Windsor 1766, bishop of Llandaff 1769, bishop of Salisbury 1782, bishop of Durham 1791, author of biography of his brother William, Lord Barrington, and of sermons and tracts.

Barrington, William, 3rd Viscount (d. 1801). Lieutenant 7 Foot 1775, captain 70 Foot 1777–79.

Beauclerk, Lord George (1704–68). Ensign 1 Foot Guards 1723, lieutenant 11 Dragoons 1726, captain and lieutenant-colonel 1 Foot Guards 1736, M.P. New Windsor 1744–54, colonel 1745, colonel 8 Marines 1747–48, colonel 19 foot 1748–68, Governor Landguard Fort 1753–68, major-general 1755, Commander in Chief Scotland 1756–67, lieutenant-general 1758, M.P. New Windsor 1768.

Beckford, William (1709–70). Balliol College Oxford 1725, Leyden 1731, M.P. Shaftesbury 1747–54, alderman Billingsgate Ward 1752, Master of Ironmongers' Company 1753, M.P. for City of London 1754–70, Sheriff of City of London, Lord Mayor of London 1762–63 and 1769–70.

Bentinck, Lord George (1715–59). Ensign 1 Foot Guards 1735, M.P. Droitwich 1742–47, captain-lieutenant and lieutenant-colonel 1 Foot Guards 1743, M.P. Grampound 1747–54, colonel 1752, colonel 5 Foot 1754–59, M.P. Malmesbury 1754–59.

Bernard, Sir Francis (1711–79). Christ Church Oxford 1736, called to the bar, Governor of New Jersey 1758, Governor of Massachusetts Bay 1760, recalled 1769.

Blackett, William. Lieutenant Robinson's Marines 1740, captain 22 Foot 1744, captain Invalids at Chester 1759, lieutenant-colonel 1761.

Blackstone, Sir William (1723–80). Pembroke College Oxford 1738, Middle Temple 1741–46, Fellow of All Souls 1744, first Vinerian Professor of English Law at Oxford 1758–66, M.P. Hindon 1761–68, M.P. Westbury 1768–70, Judge of Common Pleas and King's Bench 1770, author of *Commentaries on the Laws of England.*

Bland, Humphrey (1686–1763). Commissioned 1704, major Honeywood's regiment, lieutenant-colonel King's Regiment of Horse, colonel 36 Foot 1737, colonel 13 Dragoons 1741, colonel 3 Dragoons, Governor of Fort William 1743–52, Governor of Gibraltar 1749, colonel 1 Dragoon Guards 1752, Governor Edinburgh Castle, Commander in Chief Scotland 1753, author of *Treatise on Military Discipline,* (1727; nine editions to 1762).

Blaney (or Blainey, or Blayney), Hon. Cadwallader. Lieutenant 45 foot 1741, captain and lieutenant-colonel 2 foot guard 1753, colonel 91 foot 1761.

Blaquiere (or Blacquiere), Sir John, later Lord de Blaquiere of Ardkill (1732–1812). Ensign 37 Foot 1750, cornet 11 Dragoons 1752, captain 23 Foot 1756, major 18 Dragoons 1759, lieutenant-colonel of 17 Dragoons 1763, Secretary of Legation in France 1771, Chief Secretary in Ireland 1772–77, M.P. Rye 1801, M.P. Downton 1803.

Blathwayt, William (c.1649–1717). Middle Temple 1665, Clerk of Embassy at The Hague 1668–72, and at Copenhagen and Stockholm 1668–72, Assistant Secretary of Trade and Plantations 1675–79, Clerk of the Privy Council 1678–86, Auditor-General of Plantations 1680–1717, Under Secretary of State (North) 1681–83, Secretary at War 1683–89, 1689–1704, Lord of

Trade 1696–1707, M.P. for Newton, I.O.W. 1685, 1693, 1695, 1698, 1701, 1702, 1705, 1708.

Bocland (or Bockland), Maurice. Cornet 1715, captain and lieutenant-colonel 2 Foot Guards 1738, first major 2 Foot Guards, colonel 11 Foot 1747, major-general 1755, lieutenant-general 1758.

Bouquet, Henry (d. 1765). Lieutenant-colonel 60 Foot 1756, colonel 60 Foot 1762.

Bowles, William. Clerk in War Office from 1750, franking clerk 1756, First Clerk 1757–59.

Braddock, Edward (1695–1755). Ensign 2 Foot Guards 1710, lieutenant 2 Foot Guards 1727, captain 2 Foot Guards 1736, second major and colonel 2 Foot Guards 1743, colonel 14 Foot 1753, major-general 1754, killed at Battle of the Monongahela.

Bradshaw, Thomas (1733–74). Clerk in War Office 1757–59, First Clerk 1759–61, Chief Clerk at the Treasury 1761–63, commissioner of taxes 1763–67, M.P. Harwich 1767–68, Secretary to the Treasury 1767–70, M.P. Saltash 1768–72, 1772–74, Lord of the Admiralty 1772–74.

Breadalbane, John Campbell, Lord (1696–1782). Christ Church Oxford 1711, Master of the Horse to Princess of Wales 1718, Minister Copenhagen 1720–30, St. Petersburg 1731, M.P. Saltash 1727–41, Lord of the Admiralty 1741–42, M.P. Orford 1741–45, Master of the Jewel Office 1745–56, Scottish representative peer 1752–68, 1774–80, Chief Justice south of the Trent 1756–65, Keeper of the Privy Seal (Scotland) 1765–66, Privy Council 1766.

Brudenell, Thomas. Lieutenant in Campbells' Foot 1740, captain Marines 1741, colonel 51 Foot 1757, major-general 1759.

Burghersh, John Fane, Lord (1728–74). M.P. Lyme Regis 1762–71, commissioner of taxes 1760–62.

Burgoyne, John (1722–92). Sub-brigadier 3 Horse Guards, cornet 1 Dragoons 1740, lieutenant 1741, captain 13 Dragoons, captain 11 Dragoons 1756, captain and lieutenant-colonel 2 Foot Guards 1758, raised and commanded 16 Light Dragoons in 1759, M.P. Midhurst 1761, colonel 1762, M.P. Preston 1768, Governor of Fort William 1769, major-general 1772, second in command to Carleton in America 1776, commanded column of invasion from Canada 1777, lieutenant-general 1777, surrendered at Saratoga 1777, deprived of command of 16 Light Dragoons, wrote *The Maid of the Oaks* and other plays.

Burke, Edmund (1729–97). Trinity College Dublin 1744–50, Middle Temple 1747, began to edit *Annual Register* 1759, M.P. Wendover 1765–74, private secretary to Rockingham 1765–66, M.P. Bristol 1774–80, M.P. Malton 1780–94, Privy Council 1782, Paymaster-General 1782, 1783, author of *Reflections on the Revolution in France* (1790) and other writings upon politics and aesthetics.

Burleton, Philip (d. 1790). Master Surgeon Flanders before 1750, Staff-Surgeon Germany 1758, surgeon to Commander in Chief (Ligonier), Inspector of Regimental Infirmaries and Chief Director of Hospitals in Germany 1761.

Bute, John Stuart, Earl of (1713–92). Representative peer of Scotland 1737, Lord of Bedchamber to Princess of Wales 1750, tutor to Prince of Wales, Privy Council 1760, Groom of the Stole 1760, Secretary of State (North) 1761, First Lord of the Treasury 1762–63.

Byng, John (1704–57). Entered navy 1718, lieutenant 1724, captain 1727, Governor and Commander in Chief Newfoundland 1741–44, rear-admiral 1745, Vice-Admiral of the Blue 1746, M.P. Rochester 1751, Admiral of the Blue 1758, court-martialled and shot 1757 after loss of Minorca.

Cadogan, Charles Lord (1685–1776). Captain and lieutenant-colonel 2 Foot Guards 1715, colonel 4 Foot 1719–34, colonel 6 Dragoons 1734–42, major-general 1739, colonel 2 Horse Guards 1742–76, lieutenant-general 1745, Governor Sheerness 1749–52, Governor Gravesend and Tilbury Fort 1752–76, general 1761.

Calcraft, John (1726–72). Clerk in Pay Office, 1745–47, clerk in War Office 1747–56, Paymaster of Widows' Pensions 1757–62, Deputy Commissioner of Musters, 1756–63, agent for sixty-three regiments at height of Seven Years' War, M.P. Calne 1766–68, M.P. Rochester 1768–72.

Campbell, see Fletcher.

Carleton, Sir Guy, later Lord Dorchester (1724–1808). Ensign 25 Foot 1742, lieutenant 25 Foot 1745, captain-lieutenant 1 Foot Guards 1751, lieutenant-colonel 72 Foot 1758, captain 93 Foot 1763, colonel 47 Foot 1772, major-general 1772, Lieutenant-Governor Quebec 1775, Commander in Chief Canada 1775, colonel 84 Foot 1782, Commander in Chief America 1782, colonel 15 Dragoons 1790, general 1793, colonel 27 Dragoons 1801, colonel 4 Dragoons 1802.

Carpenter, Benjamin (d. 1789). Sub-brigadier 2 Horse Guards 1738, second major 2 Horse Guards 1749, first major 2 Horse Guards 1754, colonel 12 Dragoons 1760, major-general 1762, colonel 4 Dragoons 1770, lieutenant-general 1772, general 1789.

Cary, Hon. George. Captain and lieutenant-colonel 1 Foot Guards 1750, colonel 64 Foot 1759, major-general 1761, colonel 43 Foot 1766, lieutenant-general 1770.

Cathcart, Robert (d. 1773). Purveyor for hospital for British forces in Germany 1760.

Cavendish, Lord John (1732–96). Peterhouse Cambridge, M.P. Weymouth and Melcome Regis 1754–61, M.P. Knaresborough 1761–68, Lord of the Treasury 1765–66, M.P. York 1768–84, Privy Council 1782, Chancellor of the Exchequer 1782 and 1783, M.P. Derbyshire 1784–96.

Chamier, Anthony (1725–80). Prominent banker during Seven Years' War, secretary to Commander in Chief 1763–72, Deputy Secretary at War 1772–75, Undersecretary of State 1775–80, M.P. Tamworth 1778–80.

Chesterfield, Philip Dormer, Earl of (1694–1773). Trinity Hall Cambridge, M.P. St. Germans 1715–22, Lord of the Bedchamber to Prince of Wales 1715–27, M.P. Lostwithiel 1722–23, captain of Yeoman of the Guard 1723–25, Lord of the Bedchamber to the King 1727–30, Privy Council 1728, Ambassador to The Hague 1728–32, Lord Steward of the Household 1730–33, Lord-Lieutenant Ireland 1745–46, Lord Justice of the Realm 1745, Secretary of State (North) 1746–48, author of *Chesterfield's Letters to his Son*.

Cholmondeley, Hon. James (1708–75). Major 1725, lieutenant-colonel Albemarle's regiment 1731, Lieutenant-Governor Chester Castle 1731–70, M.P. Bossiney 1731–34, M.P. Camelford 1734–41, colonel 48 Foot 1741, M.P. Montgomery 1741–47, colonel 34 Foot 1742, major-general 1747, colonel 12 Lancers 1749, colonel 6 Dragoons 1750, lieutenant-general 1754, general 1770, Governor Chester Castle 1770–75.

Clarke, Thomas. Lieutenant and captain 2 Foot Guards 1749, captain and lieutenant-colonel 1761, first major 1777, major-general 1777, colonel 31 Foot 1780, lieutenant-general 1782.

Clavering, Sir John (1722–77). Ensign 1736, captain and lieutenant-colonel 2 Foot Guards 1752, brigadier in Guadeloupe expedition 1759, colonel 52 Foot 1762, Governor of Landguard Fort 1770, lieutenant-general 1770, member of Council of Bengal, unofficial acting Governor-General 1777.

Clephane, John (d. 1758). M.D. St. Andrews 1729, Physician to British army in Flanders in Austrian Succession War F.R.S. 1749, Physician St. George's Hospital 1751, L.R.C.P. 1752, member of Hospital Board 1757.

Clinton, Lord Thomas Pelham (1752–95). Ensign 12 Foot 1769, captain 1 Dragoon Guards 1770, M.P. Westminster 1774–80, captain and lieutenant-colonel 1 Foot Guards 1775, colonel 1780, M.P. East Retford 1781–94, colonel 75 Foot 1782–85, colonel 17 Light Dragoons 1785–95, major-general 1787.

Conway, Henry Seymour (1719–95). Lieutenant 5 Dragoons 1737, captain-lieutenant 8 Dragoons 1740, captain-lieutenant and lieutenant-colonel 1 Foot Guards 1741, M.P. Higham Ferrers 1741–47, captain and lieutenant-colonel 1 Foot Guards 1742, colonel 48 Foot 1746–49, M.P. Penryn 1747–54, colonel 34 Foot 1749–51, colonel 13 Dragoons 1751–54, M.P. St. Mawes 1754–61, colonel 4 Horse 1754–59, major-general 1756, second in command Rochefort expedition 1757, lieutenant-general 1759, colonel 1 Dragoons 1759–64, M.P. Thetford 1761–74, Secretary of State (South) 1765–66, (North) 1766–68, colonel Royal Regiment of Horse Guards 1770–95, Governor Jersey 1772–95, M.P. Bury St. Edmunds 1775–84, field-marshal 1793.

Conyngham, Henry, Viscount. Lieutenant 4 Dragoon Guards 1725, captain 1 Dragoons 1725, M.P. Tiverton 1747–54, M.P. Sandwich 1756–74.

Cooper, Sir Grey (c. 1726–1801). Middle Temple 1747–51, Joint Secretary to the Treasury 1765–82, M.P. Rochester 1765–68, M.P. Grampound 1768–74, M.P. Saltash 1774–84, Lord of the Treasury 1783, M.P. Richmond (Yorks) 1786–90, Privy Council 1796.

Coote, Sir Eyre (1726–83). Captain 39 Foot 1755, at Plassey 1757, lieutenant-colonel commandant 84 Foot 1759, at Wandewash 1760, colonel 27 Foot 1765, M.P. Leicester 1768–74, Commander in Chief Madras 1769–1770, major-general 1775, colonel 27 Foot 1771–73, colonel 6 Dragoons 1773, M.P. Poole 1774–80, Commander in Chief Bengal 1777, lieutenant-general 1777.

Cope, Sir John (d. 1760). Cornet 1 Dragoons 1707, captain 33 Foot 1709, captain and lieutenant-colonel 1710, lieutenant-colonel Macartney's Foot 1712, lieutenant-colonel 2 Foot Guards 1719, lieutenant-colonel 1 Horse Grenadier Guards 1720, M.P. Queenborough 1722–27, Liskeard 1727–34, colonel 39 Foot 1730–32, colonel 5 Foot 1732–37, colonel 9 Dragoons 1737–41, M.P. Orford 1738–41, major-general 1739, colonel 7 Dragoons 1741–60, lieutenant-general 1743, Commander in Chief Scotland 1745.

Cornwallis, Hon. Edward (1713–76). Ensign 1730, lieutenant 1731, captain 8 Foot 1734, major 20 Foot 1742, M.P. Eye 1743–49, lieutenant-colonel 1745, Groom of the Bedchamber 1747–63, Governor Nova Scotia 1749–52, colonel 40 Foot 1749–52, colonel 24 Foot 1752–76, M.P. Hastings 1753–62, major-general 1757, Governor Gibraltar 1762–76, lieutenant-general 1760.

Coryn, George (d. 1780). Surgeon to 20 Foot 1732–52, Staff-Surgeon in Great Britain 1756, Subdirector of German hospital, purveyor in General Hopson's expedition 1758.

Cosne, Ruvigny de. Captain and lieutenant-colonel 2 Foot Guards 1755, colonel 2 Foot Guards 1762.

Cox, Richard. Agent in Albemarle Street to five regiments in 1761, later Cox and Drummond, Cox and Mair at Craig's Court, and Cox and Kings.

Craig, Francis. Lieutenant and captain 2 Foot Guards 1746, captain and lieutenant-colonel 2 Foot Guards 1758, colonel 1763, second major 2 Foot Guards 1769, major-general 1775, lieutenant-general 1777.

Craufurd, John (c. 1725–64). Ensign 13 Foot 1738, captain 1743, major 1747, lieutenant-colonel 1749, colonel 85 Foot 1759–63, M.P. Berwick upon Tweed 1761–64, colonel 3 Foot 1763–64, Lieutenant-Governor Berwick 1764, Lieutenant-Governor Minorca 1764.

Cumberland, William Augustus, Duke of (1721–65). Colonel 2 Foot Guards 1740, colonel 1 Foot Guards 1742, Privy Council 1742, major-general 1742, at Dettingen 1743, lieutenant-general 1743, Captain-General of British forces at home and abroad 1745, at Fontenoy 1745 and Culloden 1746, Lord

Justice of the Realm 1755, resigned all commands after Klosterseven 1757.

Cunninghame (or Cuninghame), James (1731–88). Captain 45 Foot 1755, lieutenant-colonel 1758, colonel 1772, major-general 1777, Governor Barbados 1780, lieutenant-general 1782, M.P. East Grinstead 1786–88, colonel 45 Foot 1787–88.

Dalrymple, Sir John (1726–1810). Edinburgh and Trinity Hall Cambridge, advocate at Scottish bar 1748, Baron of the Exchequer 1776, wrote *Memoirs of Great Britain and Ireland* (1771).

Dalrymple, William. Captain in Loudoun's Foot (broke 1748), major 14 Foot 1764, lieutenant-colonel 1765, colonel in army 1777, Quartermaster-General in America 1780, major-general 1782, lieutenant-general 1793, general 1798.

Dalrymple, William. Lieutenant 20 Foot 1763, captain 1772, major 1779, captain-commandant corps of foot serving in Jamaica 1776.

Darlington, Henry Vane, Earl of (c. 1705–58). M.P. Launceston 1726–27, M.P. St. Mawes 1727–41, M.P. Ripon 1741–47, M.P.Co. Durham 1747–53, Lord of the Treasury 1749–55, Joint Paymaster-General 1755–56, Lord Lieutenant Co. Durham.

Dartmouth, William Legge, Earl of (1730–1801). Trinity College Oxford 1749, Recorder Lichfield, Privy Council 1765, First Lord of Trade 1765–66, 1772–75, Secretary of State (America) 1772–75, Privy Seal 1775–82, Steward of the Household 1783.

De La Warr, John, Lord. Major 1715, lieutenant-colonel 1717, colonel 1 Horse Guards 1737, major-general 1745, lieutenant-general 1747.

Dodd, John. Lieutenant and captain 1 Foot Guards 1763, captain and lieutenant-colonel 1775.

Dowdeswell, William, (1721–75). Christ Church Oxford 1737, Leyden 1745, M.P. Tewkesbury 1747–54, Worcestershire 1761–75, Chancellor of the Exchequer 1765–66, Privy Council 1765.

D'Oyly, Christopher (c. 1717–95). Inner Temple 1741–44, First Clerk at the War Office 1761–62, Deputy Secretary 1763–72, M.P. Wareham 1774–80, under-secretary in Colonial Department 1776–78, Commissary-General of Musters 1776–80, M.P. Seaford 1780–84.

Draper, Sir William (1721–87). King's College Cambridge, ensign 48 Foot 1744, lieutenant and captain 1 Foot Guards 1749, raised and commanded 79 Foot for E. Indies 1757, Governor of Great Yarmouth 1761, commander of Manila expedition 1762, colonel 16 Foot 1765, major-general 1772, lieutenant-general 1777, Lieutenant-Governor of Minorca 1779, which he defended at sieges of 1781 and 1782.

Drummond, Robert Hay (1711–76). Christ Church Oxford 1731, royal chaplain to George II 1736, Bishop of St. Asaph 1748, of Salisbury 1761, of York 1761.

Dundas, Sir Laurence (c. 1710–81). Commissary for Bread and Forage in Scotland 1746–48, M.P. for Linlithgow Burghs 1747–48, Commissary for Stores and Provisions in Flanders 1747–49, Commissary of Stores in Scotland 1748–57, Keeper of Forage and Magazines 1757–58, Commissary of Bread for Foreign Levies in Germany 1759, Contractor for Transport for the Hanoverian Troops 1760–62, Governor Royal Bank of Scotland 1764–77, M.P. Edinburgh 1768–80, Privy Council 1771, M.P. Richmond 1780–81, M.P. Edinburgh 1781.

Dupplin, see Kinnoul.

Duroure, Alexander (d. 1765). Ensign 1714, lieutenant 1714, major Douglas' Marines 1739, lieutenant-colonel 24 Foot 1741, colonel 38 Foot 1751, colonel 4 Foot 1756, major-general 1758, lieutenant-general 1760.

Effingham, Francis Howard, Earl of (d. 1760). Cornet 1733, captain 1739, second lieutenant-colonel 2 Horse Guards 1743, first lieutenant-colonel 2 Horse Guards 1749, colonel 34 Foot 1754.

Eliot, George Augustus, late Lord Heathfield (1717–90). Academy of la Fère, volunteer with Prussian army 1735–36, cornet 2 Horse Grenadier Guards 1739, captain 1745, major 1749, lieutenant-colonel 1754, aide-de-camp to George II 1756, raised 15 Light Dragoons 1759, major-general 1759, second in command Havana 1762, lieutenant-general 1765, Commander in Chief Ireland 1774, Governor of Gibraltar 1775 and during the siege 1779–1781.

Elliot, Sir Gilbert, later Lord Minto (1727–77). Edinburgh 1735, Leyden, Scottish bar 1742, M.P. Selkirk county 1762, M.P. Roxburgh county 1765, Lord of Admiralty 1756–57, 1757–61, Lord of Trade 1761–62, Treasurer of the Chamber 1762–70, Keeper of the Signet in Scotland 1767, Treasurer of the Navy from 1770, Privy Council 1777.

Ellis, Welbore, later Lord Mendip (1713–1802). Christ Church Oxford 1732, M.P. Cricklade 1741–47, Lord of the Admiralty 1747–55, M.P. Weymouth and Melcombe Regis 1747–61, Vice-Treasurer of Ireland 1755–62, Privy Council 1760, M.P. Aylesbury 1761–68, Secretary at War 1762–65, M.P. Petersfield 1768–74, Joint Vice-Treasurer Ireland 1770–77, M.P. Weymouth and Melcombe Regis 1774–90, Treasurer of the Navy 1777–82, Secretary of State (America) 1782, M.P. Petersfield 1791–94.

Fazakerley, Nicholas (1685–1767). Brasenose College Oxford 1702, Middle Temple 1707, M.P. Preston 1732–67, Recorder of Preston 1742–67, Treasurer of Lincoln's Inn 1747.

Fletcher (afterwards Fletcher Campbell), Henry. Captain 2 Foot 1745, lieutenant-colonel 35 Foot 1758, colonel 35 Foot 1764, major-general 1772, lieutenant-general 1777.

Fox, Henry, Lord Holland (1705–74). Christ Church Oxford, M.P. Hindon 1735–41, M.P. Windsor 1741–61, Lord of Trade 1743–46, Privy Council 1746, Secretary at War 1746–55, Secretary of State (South) 1755–56, Paymaster-General 1757–65, M.P. Dunwich 1761–63.

Fox, Henry Edward (1755–1811). Cornet 1 Dragoon Guards 1770, lieutenant 38 Foot 1773, captain 38 Foot 1774, major 49 Foot 1777, lieutenant-colonel 38 Foot 1778, colonel and aide-de-camp to George III 1783, major-general 1793, colonel 10 Foot 1795, lieutenant-general 1799, Commander in Chief Ireland 1803, Lieutenant-Governor Gibraltar 1804, Commander in Chief British forces in Sicily 1806, general 1808, Governor of Portsmouth.

Francis, Sir Philip (1740–1818). Clerk in Secretary of State's office 1758, First Clerk at War Office 1762, member of Bengal Council 1773, M.P. Yarmouth I.O.W. 1784–90, M.P. Bletchingley 1790–96, M.P. Appleby 1802–07, probably the author of the Junius letters.

Fraser, Simon (1726–82). St. Andrews 1743–45, Glasgow 1748, Middle Temple 1752–56, lieutenant-colonel commandant 78 Foot, M.P. Inverness shire 1761–82, colonel 1762, major-general 1772, colonel 71 Foot 1777, lieutenant-general 1777.

Frederick, Sir Charles (1709–85). New College Oxford, Middle Temple 1728, Clerk of Deliveries for Ordnance 1746–50, Surveyor-General of Ordnance 1750–80, M.P. New Shoreham 1741–54, M.P. Queenborough 1754–84.

Gage, Thomas (1721–87). Lieutenant 48 Foot 1741, captain 62 Foot (broke 1748), major 55 Foot 1748, lieutenant-colonel 44 Foot 1751, raised and commanded 80 Foot 1758, Governor Montreal 1760, major-general 1761, Commander in Chief America 1763, colonel of 60 Foot 1770, lieutenant-general 1770, Governor and Captain-General of Massachusetts Bay (after Hutchinson) 1774–75, general 1782.

Gansell, William. Ensign 1734, lieutenant 2 Foot Guards 1739, captain and lieutenant 2 Foot Guards 1749, colonel 55 Foot 1762, major-general 1762, lieutenant-general 1772.

Garth, George. Ensign 1 Foot Guards 1775, lieutenant and captain 1758, captain and lieutenant-colonel 1772, third major 1 Foot Guards 1782, second major 1784, colonel 17 Foot, Lieutenant-Governor Placentia, lieutenant-general 1796, general 1801.

Germain, see Sackville.

Gloucester, Prince William Henry, Duke of (1743–1805). Privy Council 1764, colonel of 13 Foot 1766–67, major-general 1767, colonel 3 Foot Guards 1768–70, lieutenant-general 1770, colonel 1 Foot Guards 1770–1805, general 1772, field-marshal 1793.

Gordon, Lord Adam (1726–1801). Ensign 2 Dragoons 1741, lieutenant 1743, captain 18 Foot 1746, M.P. Aberdeenshire 1754–68, captain 3 Foot Guards 1756, colonel 1762, colonel 66 Foot 1763–75, major-general 1772, M.P. Kincardineshire 1774–88, colonel 26 Foot 1775–82, lieutenant-general 1777, Governor Tynemouth Castle 1778–96, colonel 1 Foot 1782–1801, Commander in Chief Scotland 1789–98, general 1793, Governor Edinburgh Castle 1796–1801.

Gore, Thomas (c. 1694–1777). M.P. Cricklade 1722–27, M.P. Amersham

1735–46, M.P. Portsmouth 1746–47, M.P. Bedford 1747–54, M.P. Cricklade 1754–68, Commissary-General of Musters 1746–77.

Gorham (or Goreham), Joseph. Major-commandant of corps of rangers in America 1761, lieutenant-colonel 1772, Lieutenant-Governor Placentia 1774, colonel 1782.

Gould, Sir Charles (1726–1806). Christ Church Oxford 1743–47, called to the bar 1750, K.C. 1754, Judge-Advocate-General 1771, M.P. Brecon 1778 –87, M.P. county of Brecon 1787–1806, Privy Council 1802.

Grafton, Augustus Henry Fitzroy, Duke of (1735–1811). Peterhouse Cambridge 1753, M.P. Boroughbridge 1756, M.P. Bury St. Edmunds 1756–57, Lord of the Bedchamber to Prince of Wales 1756–57, Lord-Lieutenant Suffolk 1757–63, 1769–70, Privy Council 1765, Secretary of State (North) 1765–66, First Lord of the Treasury 1766–70, Lord Privy Seal 1771–75, 1782–83.

Granby, John Manners, Marquess of (1721–70). Trinity College Cambridge 1738, M.P. Grantham 1741–54, colonel 1745, M.P. Cambridgeshire 1754–70, major-general 1755, colonel Royal Regiment of Horse Guards 1758–70, lieutenant-general 1759, Lieutenant-General of the Ordnance 1759–63, colonel 21 Dragoons 1760–63, Master-General of the Ordnance 1763 –70, Commander in Chief 1766–1770.

Grant, James (1720–1806). Ensign 2 Foot 1730, ensign 1 Foot Guards 1734, captain 47 Foot 1741, captain 18 Foot 1743, major 1745, lieutenant-colonel 1 Horse Guards 1749, colonel 61 Foot 1759–68, M.P. Winchelsea 1759–60, colonel 37 Foot 1769–73, lieutenant-general 1770.

Grenville, George (1712–70). Christ Church Oxford, Inner Temple 1729 (called 1735), M.P. Buckingham 1741–70, Lord of the Admiralty 1744–47, Lord of the Treasury 1747–54, Privy Council 1754, Treasurer of the Navy 1754–55, 1756–57, 1757–62, Secretary of State (North) 1762, First Lord of the Treasury 1763–65.

Grenville, James (1715–83). Inner Temple, 1734 (called 1738), M.P. Old Sarum 1742–47, Deputy Paymaster of Forces 1745–55, Lord of Trade 1746–55, M.P. Bridport 1747–54, M.P. Buckingham 1754–68, Lord of Trade 1756–57, 1757–61, Cofferer of the Household 1761, Privy Council 1761, Joint Vice-Treasurer of Ireland 1766–70, M.P. for Horsham 1768–70.

Haldimand, Frederick (1718–91). Born in Switzerland, served in Dutch army, lieutenant-colonel 60 Foot 1756, major-general in America 1762, colonel-commandant 60 Foot 1772, major-general 1772, lieutenant-general 1777, Governor and Commander in Chief Canada 1778–84.

Hamilton, Hon. Charles. Captain 1 Dragoons 1755, major 1 Dragoons 1766, lieutenant-colonel 1772.

Harrington, Lady Caroline (d. 1784). Daughter of second duke of Grafton, wife of William Earl of Harrington (colonel of 2 Horse Grenadier Guards 1745–79).

Harvey, Edward (1718–78). Lincoln's Inn 1736, cornet 10 Dragoons 1741, captain 7 Dragoons 1747, major 1751, lieutenant-colonel 6 Dragoons 1754, colonel 1760, M.P. Gatton 1761–68, major-general 1762, colonel 12 Dragoons 1763–64, colonel 3 Horse 1764–75, Adjutant-General 1765–78, M.P. Harwich 1768–78, Governor of Portsmouth 1773–78, colonel 6 Dragoons 1775–78.

Hawley, Henry (1679–1759). Ensign Erle's Foot 1694, captain Queen Anne of Denmark's Dragoons 1706, Major 1711, lieutenant-colonel 1712, brevet colonel 1712, lieutenant-colonel 4 Dragoons 1717, colonel 13 Dragoons 1730, major-general 1739, colonel 1 Dragoons 1740, lieutenant-general 1743, Commander in Chief Scotland 1745, defeated at Falkirk Muir 1746, Commander in Chief allied cavalry in Germany 1740–47, Governor of Inverness and Fort Augustus 1747, Governor of Portsmouth 1752.

Hay, Lord Charles (d. 1760). Ensign 1722, captain 9 Dragoons 1729, M.P. shire of Haddington 1741, captain 3 Foot Guards 1743, colonel 33 Foot 1752, major-general 1757.

Henniker, John (1724–1803). Merchant and purveyor to the army in Seven Years' War and American War of Independence, M.P. Sudbury 1761–68, Dover 1774–84.

Herbert, Hon. William (c. 1696–1757). Lieutenant 1 Life Guards 1722, M.P. Wilton 1734–57, captain and lieutenant-colonel 1 Foot Guards 1738, Groom of the Bedchamber 1740–57, paymaster at Gibraltar 1740–57, aide-de-camp to George II 1745, colonel 14 Foot 1747–53, colonel 6 Marines 1747, colonel 2 Dragoon Guards 1753–57, major-general 1755.

Hillsborough, Wills Hill, Earl of, and Marquess of Downshire (1718–93). M.P. Warwick 1741–56, Privy Council 1754, Treasurer of the Chamber 1755–56, First Lord of Trade 1763–65, Joint Postmaster General 1766–58, Secretary of State (America) 1768–72, Secretary of State (North) 1779–82.

Hodgson, Studholme. Ensign 1 Foot Guards 1728, lieutenant and captain 1 Foot Guards 1741, captain and lieutenant-colonel 1747, colonel 50 Foot 1756, major-general 1759, colonel 5 Foot 1759, commanded Belle Isle expedition, lieutenant-general 1761, colonel 4 Foot 1768, general 1778, field-marshal 1796.

Holdernesse, Robert Darcy, Earl of (1718–78). Trinity College Cambridge, Lord Lieutenant of North Riding 1740–77, Lord of the Bedchamber 1741–51, Ambassador to Venice 1744–46, Minister at The Hague 1749–51, Privy Council 1751, Lord Justice of the Realm 1752 and 1755, Secretary of State (South) 1751–54, Secretary of State (North) 1754–61, Lord Warden of the Cinque Ports.

Home, William, Earl of. Second major 3 Foot Guards, colonel 48 Foot 1750, colonel 25 Foot 1752, major-general 1755.

Hopson, Peregrine (d. 1759). Lieutenant 1703, major 14 Foot 1739, lieutenant-colonel 48 Foot 1741, lieutenant-colonel 29 Foot 1743, colonel 29 Foot

1748, colonel 40 Foot 1752, major-general 1757, commanded Guadeloupe expedition 1759, succeeded in command on his death by John Barrington.

Howard, Sir Charles (d. 1765). Ensign 2 Foot Guards 1715, captain and lieutenant-colonel 1719, M.P. Carlisle 1727–61, colonel 1734, colonel 19 Foot 1738–48, major-general 1743, lieutenant-general 1747, colonel 3 Dragoon Guards 1748–65, general 1765, Lieutenant-Governor Carlisle 1724–49, Governor Carlisle 1749–52, Governor Inverness 1752–65.

Howe, Sir William (1729–1814). Cornet 15 Dragoons 1746, lieutenant 1747, captain-lieutenant 20 Foot 1750, captain 1750, major 60 Foot 1756, lieutenant-colonel 58 Foot 1757, M.P. Nottingham 1758–80, colonel 46 Foot 1764–75, major-general 1772, Commander in Chief America 1775 –78, colonel 23 Foot 1775–86, lieutenant-general 1777, Privy Council 1782, Lieutenant-General of the Ordnance 1782–1804, colonel 19 Light Dragoons 1786–1814, general 1793, Governor Berwick 1795–1808, Governor Plymouth 1808–14.

Huck, Richard (d. 1787). Surgeon Independent Companies 1745, Surgeon to Loudoun's Foot 1747, surgeon 33 Foot 1750, Staff-Surgeon North America 1756, Physician North America 1757, F.R.C.P. 1784.

Hume, Abraham (1703–72). Director South Sea Company and Exchange Assurance Company, Commissary of Forces Abroad 1742, Commissary-General of Stores at Home and Abroad 1746–47, M.P. Steyning 1747–54, Commissary-General of Stores at Home and Abroad 1756, M.P. Tregony 1761–68.

Jefferys, Charles. Ensign 1710, major Battereau's Foot (broke 1748) 1742, lieutenant-colonel 1734–46, colonel 14 Foot 1756, major-general 1759.

Jenkinson, Charles (1729–1808). University College Oxford 1746, Lincoln's Inn 1747, M.P. Cockermouth 1761–66, Undersecretary of State 1761–62, Joint Secretary to the Treasury 1763–65, Lord of the Admiralty 1766–67, M.P. Appleby 1767–72, Lord of Trade 1767–73, M.P. Harwich 1772–74, Vice-Treasurer Ireland 1773–75, Privy Council 1773, M.P. Hastings 1774–80, Secretary at War 1778–82, M.P. Saltash 1780–86, Member of Board of Trade 1784, President of Board of Trade 1786–1804, Chancellor of Duchy of Lancaster 1786–1803.

Kellet, John. Captain Royal Regiment of Horse Guards 1754, major Royal Regiment of Horse Guards 1758, lieutenant-colonel Royal Regiment of Horse Guards 1761.

Keppel, Hon. William (1727–82). Ensign 2 Foot Guards 1744, lieutenant and captain 1745, captain and lieutenant-colonel 1 Foot Guards 1751, second major and colonel 1 Foot Guards 1760, colonel 14 Foot 1765–75, major-general 1762, lieutenant-general 1772, colonel 12 Light Dragoons 1775–82.

Kerr, Lord Robert. Ensign 1 Foot Guards 1764, major 6 Dragoons 1768, lieutenant-colonel 6 Dragoons 1773.

Kingsley, William. Lieutenant 1721, colonel in the army 1750, colonel 20 Foot 1756, lieutenant-general 1760.

Kinnoul, Thomas Hay, Earl of, and styled Viscount Dupplin until 1758 (1710–87). Christ Church Oxford 1726, M.P. Scarborough 1736, M.P. Cambridge 1741–58, Lord of Trade 1740–54, Lord of the Treasury 1754–55, Joint Paymaster General 1755–57, Privy Council 1758, Chancellor of the Duchy of Lancaster 1758–62, Ambassador to Portugal 1759–62.

Knox, William (1732–1810). Member of council for Georgia 1757–61, agent for Florida and East Florida, undersecretary in Secretary of State's office 1770–1782.

La Fausille, John. Ensign 1708, lieutenant 1726, captain-lieutenant 8 Foot 1743, captain 1743, lieutenant-colonel 8 Foot 1749, colonel 66 Foot 1758.

Lambton, John (1710–94). Ensign 2 Foot Guards 1732, lieutenant and captain 2 Foot Guards 1739, captain and lieutenant-colonel 1746, colonel 68 Foot 1758, major-general 1761, M.P. Durham 1762–87, lieutenant-general 1770, general 1782.

Leece, Harman. Clerk in War Office from 1746, Principal Clerk 1782–95.

Legge, Hon. Henry Bilson (1708–64). Christ Church Oxford 1726, M.P. East Looe 1740–41, Junior Secretary to the Treasury 1741–42, M.P. Orford 1741–59, Lord of the Admiralty 1745–46, Lord of the Treasury 1746–49, Treasurer of the Navy 1749–54, Chancellor of the Exchequer 1754–55, 1756–57, 1757–61, M.P. Hampshire 1759–64.

Lennox, see Richmond.

Lennox, Lord George Henry (1737–1805). Ensign 2 Foot Guards 1754, aide-de-camp to Duke of Cumberland 1757, lieutenant-colonel 33 Foot 1758, M.P. Chichester 1761–67, colonel 25 Foot 1762–1805, secretary at British Embassy Paris 1765–66, M.P. Sussex 1767–90, major-general 1772, lieutenant-general 1777, Governor Plymouth 1784–1805, Privy Council 1784, Constable of the Tower 1784–85, general 1793.

Lewis, Matthew. First Clerk in War Office 1772, Deputy Secretary at War 1775–1803.

Ligonier, John Louis, Earl of (1680–1770). Captain 1703, brevet-major 1706, brevet colonel 1711, lieutenant-colonel 12 Foot 1712, Lieutenant-Governor Minorca 1713–16, lieutenant-colonel 4 Horse 1716, colonel 8 Horse 1720–49, major-general 1739, lieutenant-general 1743, general 1746, M.P. Bath 1748–63, colonel 2 Dragoon Guards 1749–53, Governor Guernsey 1750–52, Governor Plymouth 1752–59, colonel Royal Regiment of Horse Guards 1753–57, field-marshal 1757, colonel 1 Foot Guards 1757–70, Commander in Chief 1757–66, Master-General of the Ordnance 1759–63.

Loudoun, John Campbell, Earl of (1705–82). Cornet 1727, captain 1739, colonel 54 Foot (broke 1748), colonel 30 Foot 1749, colonel 60 Foot 1755–57, major-general 1755, Captain-General and Governor of Virginia

1756, Commander in Chief America 1756–58, lieutenant-general 1758, colonel 3 Foot Guards 1770–82, general 1770.

Lovibond, Anthony. Lieutenant 10 Dragoons 1755, captain 1 Dragoon Guards 1759, major 1 Dragoon Guards 1776, lieutenant-colonel 1 Dragoon Guards 1778, colonel 1782.

Lowndes, Charles (1699–1783). Chief Clerk to the Treasury 1755–62, Keeper of Treasury Papers 1762–65, Secretary to the Treasury 1765–67, M.P. Bramber 1768–69.

Mackay, Hon. Alexander (1717–89). Ensign 25 Foot 1737, lieutenant 47 Foot 1740, captain Loudoun's Foot 1745, major 3 Foot 1749, lieutenant-colonel 52 Foot 1755, lieutenant-colonel 39 Foot 1760, M.P. Sutherland 1761–68, raised and commanded 122 Foot 1762 (broke 1763), colonel 65 Foot 1764–70, M.P. Tain Burghs 1768–73, major-general 1770, colonel 21 Foot 1770–89, Governor Tynemouth 1771–78, lieutenant-general 1777, Governor Landguard Fort 1778–88, Commander in Chief Scotland 1780–89, Governor Stirling 1788–89.

McKellar, Patrick. Major (engineers) 1758, lieutenant-colonel (engineers) 1762, Director of Engineers 1775, colonel 1777.

Maitland, Hon. Alexander. Lieutenant and captain 1 Foot Guards 1747, captain and lieutenant-colonel 1 Foot Guards 1756, colonel 49 Foot 1768, major-general 1722, lieutenant-general 1777.

Maitland, Hon. Richard. Lieutenant 1 Foot 1749, captain-lieutenant 43 Foot 1752, captain 43 Foot 1754, lieutenant-colonel 1760, Deputy Adjutant-General at Quebec.

Manners, Lord Charles. Ensign 1741, ensign Pulteney's Foot 1742, captain 3 Foot Guards 1745, colonel 56 Foot 1755.

Manners, Lord Robert (c. 1717–82). Ensign 2 Foot Guards 1735, lieutenant and captain 1 Foot Guards 1742, colonel 1747, Lieutenant-Governor Hull 1749–82, colonel 36 Foot 1751–65, major-general 1757, lieutenant-general 1759, colonel 3 Dragoon Guards 1765–82, general 1771.

Mansfield, see Murray.

Marlborough, Charles Spencer, Duke of (1706–58). Colonel 38 Foot 1738, Lord of the Bedchamber 1738–43, Lord Lieutenant Oxfordshire and Buckinghamshire 1738–58, colonel 1 Dragoons 1739–40, colonel 2 Horse Guards 1740–42, colonel 2 Foot Guards 1742–44, major-general 1745, Privy Council 1749, Master General of the Ordnance 1755–58, lieutenant-general 1758, commanded Cherbourg/St. Malo expedition 1758, Commander in Chief British forces in Germany 1758.

Martin, Samuel (1714–88). Trinity College Cambridge 1729, Inner Temple 1729 (called 1736), agent for Montserrat 1742–49, M.P. Camelford 1747–68, Secretary to the Treasury, 1756–57, 1758–63, M.P. Hastings 1768–74.

Maxwell, Edward. Ensign 1741, lieutenant 21 Foot 1742, captain 21 Foot 1749, lieutenant-colonel 21 Foot 1758, colonel 67 Foot 1774, major-general 1777, lieutenant-general 1782, general 1796.

Mitchell, Andrew (1708–71). Edinburgh University, Leyden 1730–31, Middle Temple 1734 (called 1738), Under Secretary for Scotland 1742–46, M.P. Aberdeenshire 1747–54, M.P. Elgin Burghs 1755–71, envoy to Prussia 1756–65.

Munroe, Hector (1726–1805). Ensign Loudoun's Foot 1747, ensign 48 Foot 1749, lieutenant 31 Foot 1754, captain 1756, major 89 Foot 1759, M.P. Inverness Burghs 1768–1802, colonel 1777, major-general in India 1777, major-general 1782, colonel 42 Foot 1787–1805, lieutenant-general 1793, general 1798.

Montague, Charles. Ensign 1739, lieutenant 11 Foot 1741, captain 11 Foot 1743, major 11 Foot 1744, colonel 59 Foot 1755, major-general 1759, colonel 2 Foot 1760, major-general 1761.

Montgomery (or Montgomerie), Hon. Archibald (1726–96). Ensign 1743, captain 43 Foot 1744, major 36 Foot 1751, lieutenant-colonel commandant 62 Foot 1757–63, M.P. Ayrshire 1761–68, Governor Dunbarton Castle 1764–82, colonel 51 Foot 1767–95, major-general 1772, lieutenant-general 1777, Governor Edinburgh Castle 1782–96, colonel 2 Dragoons 1795–96.

Mordaunt, Sir John (1697–1780). Captain 3 Dragoons 1726, M.P. Pontefract 1730–34, captain and lieutenant-colonel 3 Foot Guards 1731, M.P. Whitchurch 1735–41, colonel 58 Foot 1741–42, M.P. Cockermouth 1741–68, colonel 18 Foot 1742–47, colonel 12 Dragoons 1747–49, major-general 1747, colonel 10 Dragoons 1749–80, Governor Sheerness 1752–78, lieutenant-general 1754, commanded Rochefort expedition 1757 (acquitted after subsequent court-martial), general 1770, Governor Berwick 1778–80.

Morris, Staats Long (1728–1800). Yale University, lieutenant in Independent Company of New York 1748, captain-lieutenant 1751, captain 50 Foot 1755, captain 36 Foot 1756, raised and commanded 89 Foot 1759 (broke 1763), brigadier in East Indies 1763, colonel 1772, major-general 1777, colonel 61 Foot 1778–1800, lieutenant-general 1782, general 1796, Governor Quebec 1797–1800.

Morrison, George. Captain 89 Foot 1759, lieutenant-colonel 1761, Quartermaster-General 1768, colonel 1772, major-general 1777, colonel 75 Foot 1779, lieutenant-general 1782, general 1796.

Morse, Leonard. Clerk in War Office 1757, franking clerk 1783, Senior Clerk 1797–1807, F.R.S.

Mostyn, John (1709–79). Christ Church Oxford 1728, ensign 16 Foot 1733, captain 1736, M.P. Malton 1741–68, captain-lieutenant 2 Foot 1742, captain and lieutenant-colonel, 1743, Groom of the Bedchamber 1747–79, colonel 7 Foot 1751–54, colonel 13 Dragoons 1754–58, major-general 1757, colonel 5 Dragoons 1758–60, commanded cavalry in Germany 1759–60, colonel 7 Dragoons 1760–63, Governor Minorca 1768–79, general 1772.

Murray, William, Earl of Mansfield (1705–93). Christ Church Oxford 1723–27, Lincoln's Inn (called 1730), K.C. 1742, M.P. Boroughbridge 1742–56, Solicitor-General 1742–54, Attorney-General 1754–56, Privy Council 1756, Lord Chief Justice 1756–88.

Napier, Robert (d.1766). Ensign 5 Foot 1722, lieutenant 1723, lieutenant 2 Foot 1728, captain-lieutenant 1736, captain 1738, Deputy Quartermaster-General Flanders 1742, Deputy Quartermaster-General Austrian Netherlands 1745, Adjutant-General Flanders 1746, Adjutant-General 1748–63, colonel 53 Foot 1755, major-general 1756, lieutenant-general 1759.

Newcastle, Thomas Pelham-Holles, Duke of (1693–1768). Clare Hall Cambridge 1710, Lord Lieutenant Middlesex 1714–62, Lord Lieutenant Nottinghamshire 1714–62, Lord Chamberlain of the Household 1717–24, Privy Council 1717, Secretary of State (South) 1724–48, Secretary of State (North) 1748–55, First Lord of the Treasury 1754–56, 1757–62.

Noel, Bennet. Lieutenant 2 Foot Guards 1731, first major 2 Foot Guards 1753, lieutenant-colonel 2 Foot Guards 1755, major-general 1758.

North, Frederick Lord, later Lord Guildford (1732–92). Trinity College Oxford 1749, M.P. Banbury 1754–90, Lord of the Treasury 1759–65, Joint Paymaster-General 1766–67, Privy Council 1766, Chancellor of the Exchequer 1767–82, First Lord of the Treasury 1770–82, Lord-Lieutenant of Somerset 1774–92, Home Secretary 1783.

Oakes, Hildebrand. Ensign 23 Foot 1746, lieutenant 23 Foot 1748, captain 51 Foot 1755, major 51 Foot 1759, lieutenant-colonel 33 Foot 1762.

Onslow, George (1731–1814). Peterhouse Cambridge 1749, M.P. Rye 1754–61, M.P. Surrey 1761–77, Lord of Treasury 1765–77, Lord-Lieutenant Surrey 1776–1814, Privy Council 1777, Comptroller of the Household 1777–79, Lord of the Bedchamber 1780–1814.

Onslow, Richard (c. 1697–1760). Captain 11 Foot 1716, captain 30 Foot 1718, Receiver General of Post Office 1720–27, captain 15 Foot 1721, captain and lieutenant-colonel 1 Foot Guards 1724, M.P. Guildford 1727–60, colonel 1732, Paymaster of the Navy 1732–42, colonel 39 Foot 1738, colonel 8 Foot 1739–45, major-general 1743, colonel of 1 Horse Grenadier Guards 1745–60, lieutenant-general 1747, Governor Fort William 1752–59, Governor Plymouth 1759–60.

Oswald, Thomas. Lieutenant-colonel commandant 103 Foot 1760 (broke 1763), lieutenant-colonel 1761, lieutenant-colonel 2 Foot 1774.

Oughton, Sir James Adolphus Dickenson. Captain 37 Foot 1742, major 37 Foot 1747, lieutenant-colonel 37 Foot 1749, colonel 55 Foot 1759, major-general 1761, lieutenant-general 1770.

Owen, Sir William (c. 1697–1781). New College Oxford 1713, M.P. Pembroke Boroughs 1722–47, M.P. Pembrokeshire 1747–61, M.P. Pembroke Boroughs 1761–74, Lord-Lieutenant Pembrokeshire 1761–78.

Parslow, John. Ensign 1 Foot Guards 1715, lieutenant and captain 1 Foot

Guards 1736, captain and lieutenant-colonel 1 Foot Guards 1747, colonel 54 Foot 1760, major-general 1761.

Pelham, Hon. Henry (1695–1754). Hart Hall Oxford, M.P. Seaford 1717–24, Treasurer of the Chamber 1720–22, Lord of the Treasury 1721–24, M.P. Sussex 1722–54, Secretary at War 1724–30, Privy Council 1725, Paymaster General 1730–43, First Lord of the Treasury 1743–54, Chancellor of the Exchequer 1743–54.

Pierson (or Peirson), Richard. Captain and lieutenant-colonel 1 Foot Guards 1752, Superintendent of Commissariat in Germany 1760, second major 1 Foot Guards 1761, major-general 1762, colonel 36 Foot 1765, lieutenant-general 1772.

Pigot, Sir Robert (1720–96). Ensign 31 Foot 1741, lieutenant 1744, captain 1751, major 70 Foot 1758, lieutenant-colonel 70 Foot 1760, lieutenant-colonel 38 Foot 1764, M.P. Wallingford 1768–72, colonel 1772, Warden of the Mint 1772–96, colonel 38 Foot 1775, major-general 1777, lieutenant-general 1782, general 1796.

Pitt, John, Viscount (1756–1835). Ensign 47 Foot 1774, lieutenant 39 Foot 1778, captain 80 Foot 1779, captain and lieutenant-colonel 3 Foot Guards 1782, First Lord of the Admiralty 1788–94, Privy Council 1789, colonel 1793, Lord Privy Seal 1794, major-general 1795, colonel 4 Foot 1799, Master-General of the Ordnance 1801-06, lieutenant-general 1802, Governor Plymouth 1805, Governor Jersey 1807, commanded Walcheren expedition 1809, general 1812, Governor Gibraltar 1820.

Pitt, William, Earl of Chatham (1708–78). Trinity College Oxford 1727, cornet Cobham's Horse 1731–36, M.P. Old Sarum 1735–47, Groom of the Bedchamber to Prince of Wales 1737–45, Privy Council 1746, M.P. Seaford 1747–54, Vice-Treasurer of Ireland 1747, Paymaster-General 1746–55, M.P. Aldborough 1754–56, Secretary of State (South) 1756–57, M.P. Buckingham 1756, M.P. Okehampton 1756–57, Secretary of State (South) 1757–61, M.P. Bath 1757–66, Lord Privy Seal 1766–68.

Powis, Henry Arthur Herbert, Earl of (1703–72). Lord Lieutenant Shropshire 1734–61, colonel of regiment raised in 1745, major-general 1755, lieutenant-general 1759, Comptroller of the Household 1761, Privy Council 1761, Lord Lieutenant Montgomeryshire 1761–72, Treasurer of the Household 1761–65, Treasurer to Prince of Wales 1764–72, general 1772.

Pownall, Thomas (1722–1805). Trinity College Cambridge 1740, clerk at Board of Trade 1743–54, secretary to Governor of New York 1753, Lieutenant-Governor New Jersey 1755, Governor Massachussetts Bay 1757–9, Governor South Carolina 1760, First Commissioner of Control in Germany 1761–3, Commissioner for Investigating Accounts in Germany 1763–66, M.P. Tregony 1767–74, M.P. Minehead 1774–80.

Pringle, Sir John (1707–82). M.D. Leyden 1730, F.R.C.P. Edinburgh 1735, Physician Flanders 1742, F.R.S. 1745, Physician to the Duke of Cumberland

1749, Physician to the Queen's Household 1761, Physician in Ordinary to the Queen 1763, F.R.C.P. London 1763, P.R.S. 1772, Physician in Ordinary to the King 1774, Author of *Diseases of Armies*.

Rainsford, Charles (1728–1809). Cornet 2 Dragoons 1774, ensign 1 Foot Guards 1745, lieutenant 1751, captain and lieutenant-colonel 1761, equerry to Duke of Gloucester 1766–80, M.P. Maldon 1772–74, colonel 1774, Governor Chester 1776–96, major-general 1777, colonel 44 Foot 1781–1809, lieutenant-general 1782, M.P. Bere Alston 1787–88, M.P. Newport 1790–96, general 1796, Governor Tynemouth 1796–1809.

Rich, Sir Robert (1685–1768). Ensign 1 Foot Guards 1700, captain 24 Foot 1704, captain and lieutenant-colonel 1 Foot Guards 1708, colonel 1710, M.P. Dunwich 1715–22, colonel 13 Dragoons 1722, M.P. Bere Alston 1724–27, colonel 8 Dragoons 1725, M.P. St Ives 1727–41, colonel 8 Dragoons 1731, colonel 4 Dragoons 1735–68, major-general 1735, lieutenant-general 1739, general 1745, field-marshal 1757.

Rich, Sir Robert (1714–85). Ensign 1 Foot Guards 1735, lieutenant and captain 1739, lieutenant-colonel 4 Foot, colonel 4 Foot 1749, Governor Londonderry and Culmore Fort, major-general 1758, lieutenant-general 1760, dismissed after dispute with War Office 1770.

Richmond, Charles Lennox, Duke of (1735–1806). Leyden 1753, captain 20 Foot 1753, lieutenant-colonel 33 Foot 1756, colonel 72 Foot 1758, Lord of the Bedchamber 1760, major-general 1761, Lord Lieutenant of Sussex 1763, Ambassador to Paris 1765, Privy Council 1765, Secretary of State (South) 1766, lieutenant-general 1770, general 1782, Master-General of the Ordnance 1782, colonel Royal Regiment of Horse Guards 1795, field-marshal 1796.

Rigby, Richard (1722–88). Corpus Christi Cambridge 1738, Middle Temple 1738, M.P. Castle Rising 1745–47, M.P. Sudbury 1747–54, M.P. Tavistock 1754–88, Lord of Trade 1755–60, Joint Vice-Treasurer of Ireland 1762–65, 1768, Paymaster General 1768–82.

Robinson, Robert. Ensign 18 Foot 1740, lieutenant 18 Foot 1744, captain 18 Foot 1745, colonel 1763, colonel 32 Foot 1773, major-general 1775, lieutenant-general 1777.

Rochford, William Henry Nassau de Zuylenstein, Earl of (1717–81). Lord of the Bedchamber 1738–55, Envoy Turin 1749–55, Groom of the Stable and 1st Lord of the Bedchamber 1755–60, Privy Council 1755, Lord-Lieutenant of Essex 1756–81, Ambassador Madrid 1763–66, Ambassador Paris 1766–68, Secretary of State (North) 1766–70, Secretary of State (South) 1770–75, Master of Trinity House 1771–81.

Rockingham, Charles Watson Wentworth, Marquess of (1730–82). Lord-Lieutenant North and West Ridings 1751–62, Lord of the Bedchamber to George II 1751–60, F.R.S. 1751, Lord of the Bedchamber to George III 1760–62, Privy Council 1765, 1st Lord of the Treasury 1765–66, 1782.

Ross, George (1700–86). Agent for eleven regiments in 1762, later amalgamated as Ross and Gray of Conduit Street, M.P. Cromartyshire 1780–84, M.P. Tain Burghs 1786.

Rufane, William. Ensign 1722, captain 24 Foot 1737, major 24 Foot 1741, lieutenant-colonel 24 Foot 1751, colonel 6 Foot 1761, major-general 1762.

Sackville (afterwards Germain), George Viscount (1716–85). Trinity College Dublin 1731, captain 3 Horse 1737, lieutenant-colonel 28 Foot 1740, M.P. Dover 1746–9, colonel 12 Dragoons 1749, colonel 3 Horse 1750–57, Chief Secretary Ireland 1751–5, major-general 1755, colonel 2 Dragoon Guards 1757–59, lieutenant-general 1758, Lieutenant-General of Ordnance 1758 –59, Privy Council 1758–60, court-martialled after Minden and stripped of his appointments, M.P. Hythe 1761, Privy Council 1765–85, M.P. East Grinstead 1768, First Lord of Trade 1775–79, Secretary of State (America) 1775–82.

Sandwich, John Montague, Earl of (1718–92). Trinity College Cambridge 1735, F.R.S. 1740, Lord of the Admiralty 1744–46, colonel 22 Foot 1745, Minister Plenipotentiary at The Hague 1746–49, Privy Council 1749, First Lord of the Admiralty 1749–51, major-general 1755, lieutenant-general 1759, First Lord of the Admiralty 1763, Secretary of State (North) 1763–65, Secretary of State (North) 1768–70, 70–71, First Lord of the Admiralty 1771–82, general 1772.

Sandys, Edwin Lord (1726–97). New College Oxford 1743, M.P. Droitwich 1747–54, M.P. Bossiney 1754–61, Lord of the Admiralty 1757, M.P. Westminster 1762–70.

Shelburne, William Petty, Earl of, late Viscount Fitzmaurice and Marquess of Lansdowne (1737–1805). Christ Church Oxford 1755, lieutenant 20 Foot 1757, colonel 1760, M.P. Chipping Wycombe 1760–61, First Lord of Trade 1763, major-general 1765, Secretary of State (South) 1766–68, lieutenant-general 1772, Secretary of State (Home) 1782, First Lord of the Treasury 1782–83, general 1783.

Sherwin, Thomas. Clerk at the War Office 1731, First Clerk 1745–1755, Deputy Secretary at War 1755–56.

Sloper, Robert. Major 10 Dragoons 1755, lieutenant-colonel 1 Dragoon Guards 1759, colonel 1772, major-general 1777, lieutenant-general 1782, colonel 14 Light Dragoons 1788, general 1796, Governor Hurst Castle.

Stehelin, Benjamin. Second captain-lieutenant R.R.A. 1757, third captain R.R.A. 1761, major R.R.A. 1777, lieutenant-colonel R.R.A. 1782, colonel 1782.

Strange, James Smith Stanley, Lord (1717–71). Leyden 1735, M.P. Lancashire 1741–71, Lord Lieutenant Lancashire 1757–71, Privy Council 1762, Chancellor Duchy of Lancaster 1762–71.

Stuart (or Stewart), Hon. Charles (1735–1801). Ensign 37 Foot 1768, lieutenant 7 Foot 1770, captain 35 Foot 1773, M.P. Bossiney 1776–90, lieutenant-colonel 26 Foot 1777, lieutenant-colonel 101 Foot 1784, M.P. Ayr Burghs 1790-94, major-general 1793, colonel 26 Foot 1795, M.P. Poole 1796-1801, lieutenant-general 1798.

Suffolk, Henry Howard, Earl of (1739-79). Magdalen College Oxford 1757, Privy Council 1771, Lord Privy Seal 1771, Secretary of State (North) 1771-9.

Taylor, Peter (1714-77). Deputy Paymaster in Germany 1757-63, M.P. Wells 1765-66, M.P. Portsmouth 1774-77.

Toovey, John. Ensign 1719, captain-lieutenant Hawley's Dragoons 1739, lieutenant-colonel 1 Dragoons 1754, colonel 1759, major-general 1761.

Townshend, Charles (1725-67). Clare College Cambridge 1742-45, Leyden 1745-46, Lincoln's Inn (called 1747), M.P. Great Yarmouth 1747-56, Lord of Trade 1749-54, Lord of the Admiralty 1754-55, M.P. Saltash 1756-61, Treasurer of the Chamber 1756-61, M.P. Harwich 1761-67, Secretary at War 1761-62, First Lord of Trade 1763, Paymaster-General 1765-66, Chancellor of the Exchequer 1766-67.

Trapaud, Cyrus. Ensign 3 Foot 1735, lieutenant-colonel 3 Foot 1749, colonel 70 Foot 1762, major-general 1762, lieutenant-general 1772, general 1783.

Tyrawley, James O'Hara, Lord (1682-1773). Lieutenant 7 Foot 1703, captain 1705, captain 2 Dragoon Guards 1709, colonel 7 Foot 1713-39, aide de camp to George I and George II 1724-43, Envoy Extraordinary to Portugal 1728-41, major-general 1739, colonel 5 Horse 1739, lieutenant-general 1743, colonel 2 Horse Grenadier Guards 1743, Ambassador Extraordinary to Russia 1743-45, colonel 3 Life Guards 1745, colonel 10 Foot 1746, Governor Minorca 1747-56, colonel 14 Dragoons 1749, colonel 3 Dragoon 1752, colonel 2 Foot Guards 1755-73, Governor Gibraltar 1756-57, Governor Portsmouth 1759-73, Privy Council 1762, field-marshal 1763.

Tyrwhitt, Thomas (1730-86). Queen's College Oxford 1747-50, Middle Temple 1755, Deputy Secretary at War 1756-62, Clerk House of Commons 1762-68, F.R.S. 1771, Trustee of British Museum 1784.

Vignoles, Charles. Ensign 1718, lieutenant 31 Foot 1723, captain 31 Foot 1742, major 31 Foot 1751, lieutenant-colonel 70 Foot 1758.

Waldegrave, James (1718-84). Ensign 1 Foot Guards 1735, captain-lieutenant and lieutenant-colonel 3 Foot Guards 1748, M.P. Oxford 1747-54, Groom of the Bedchamber 1747-63, colonel 9 Foot 1751-55, M.P. Newcastle-under-Lyme 1754-63, colonel 8 Dragoons 1755-59, major-general 1757, lieutenant-general 1759, colonel 2 Dragoon Guards 1759-73, governor Plymouth 1761, Master of the Horse to the Queen 1770, general 1772, colonel 2 Foot Guards 1773, Lord-Lieutenant Essex 1781.

Walpole, Sir Edward (1706-84). King's College Cambridge 1725, Lincoln's Inn 1723 (called 1727), M.P. Lostwithiel 1730-34, M.P. Great Yarmouth 1734-68, Secretary to Lord Lieutenant of Ireland 1737-39.

Walpole, Hon. Horatio (Horace) (1717-97). King's College Cambridge 1735-38, M.P. Callington 1741-54, M.P. Castle Rising 1754-57, M.P. King's

Lynn 1757–68, author of *Memoirs of George II* and *Memoirs of George III*.

Walshe, Ralph. Major 1761, major 31 Foot 1762, colonel 31 Foot 1765.

Warde, George. Brigadier 4 Troop Horse Guards 1742, captain 11 Dragoons 1748, major 11 Dragoons 1756, lieutenant-colonel 4 Dragoons 1758.

West, James (1703–72). Balliol College Oxford 1719, Inner Temple 1721 (called 1728), F.R.S. 1727, secretary to Chancellor of Exchequer 1743–52, Joint Secretary to Treasury 1746–56, 1757–62, Recorder Poole 1746–72, Bencher Inner Temple, 1761, Reader Inner Temple 1767, Treasurer Inner Temple 1767–68, P.R.S. 1768–72.

Weymouth, Thomas Thynne, Viscount later Marquess of Bath (1734–96). St John's College Cambridge 1753, Lord of the Bedchamber 1760–63, Master of the Horse to the Queen 1763–65, Lord-Lieutenant Ireland 1765, Privy Council 1765, Secretary of State (North) 1768, Secretary of State (South) 1768–1770, 1775–79.

Whitmore, William (1714–71). Captain 2 Foot 1735, M.P. Bridgnorth 1741–47, major 1743, captain and lieutenant-colonel 3 Foot Guards 1745, colonel in army 1751, M.P. Bridgnorth 1754–71, colonel 53 Foot 1755–71, major-general 1758, lieutenant-general 1760, Warden of the Mint 1766–71.

Wilkes, John (1725–97). Lincoln's Inn 1742, Leyden 1744–46, Sheriff of Buckinghamshire 1754–55, M.P. Aylesbury 1757–64, colonel Buckinghamshire militia 1762–63, M.P. Middlesex 1768–69, 74–90, Alderman of London 1769, Sheriff of London 1771–72, Lord Mayor of London 1774–75, City Chamberlain 1779–97.

Wintringham, Sir Clifton (1710–94). M.B. (Cantab) 1734, F.R.S. 1743, Physician in Germany 1743, Physician in Ordinary to the King 1762, Director-General of the Hospital and Chief Physician Albemarle's expedition to West Indies 1763, F.R.C.P. 1763, Physician-General Land Forces 1786.

Wolfe, James (1727–59). Ensign 12 Foot 1742, lieutenant 1743, captain 4 Foot 1744, brigade-major in Flanders 1745, major 20 Foot 1749, lieutenant-colonel 20 Foot 1750, Quartermaster General Ireland 1757, colonel 67 Foot 1757, Quartermaster General Rochefort expedition 1757, brigadier at Louisbourg 1758, major-general in Canada 1759, commanded St. Lawrence expedition 1759, killed at Quebec 1759.

Wood, Robert (c.1717–71). Glasgow University 1732, Middle Temple 1736, Under-Secretary of State 1757–62, M.P. Brackley 1761–71, Under-Secretary of State 1768–70, author of *Ruins of Palmyra, Ruins of Balbec*.

Yonge, Sir George (1733–1812). Leipzig University, secretary at Turin embassy 1753, M.P. Honiton 1754–61, 1763–96, Lord of the Admiralty 1766–70, Privy Council 1782, Joint Vice-Treasurer of Ireland 1782, Secretary at War 1782–83, 83–94, Master of the Mint 1794–99, M.P. Old Sarum 1799–1801, Governor Cape of Good Hope 1799–1801, Governor-General Tortola (Virgin Islands) 1801–1812.

Bibliography

1 **Manuscript Sources**

Public Record Office

War Office Papers:

W.O. 1/873, 874, 890, 976, 989.
2/42.
4/51, 52, 59, 60, 61, 62, 63, 77,
78, 80, 82, 83, 85, 86, 87, 90, 99,
100, 104, 600, 981, 988, 989, 1044.
5/54, 55.
26/22, 23, 24, 25, 27, 29, 30.
30/49, 105.
34/86, 90.
40/1, 2, 3, 17.
71/10.

Colonial Office Papers:

C.O. 5/84

State Papers:

S.P. 41/22, 23.
44/189.

Paymaster Generals' Papers:

P.M.G.2/10.

Treasury Papers:

T. 1/514.
26/37
29/37, 38, 39, 46.

Chatham Papers:

P.R.O.30/8/18, 75, 76, 187, 231.

British Library

Newcastle Papers:
Add. MSS. 32734, 32874, 32859, 32910, 32911,
32912.
Calcraft Papers:
Add. MSS. 17493

Suffolk Record Office, Ipswich

Barrington Papers:
H.A.174/1026 (expressed throughout this book as 'Ipswich', e.g.
Ipswich 3b no. 1 is H.A. 174/1026/3b/1)

3a, b, c, d,	– correspondence 1755–1761.
6a, b, c, d,	– correspondence 1765–1778.
7	– correspondence 1779–1793.
111	– Letters from George III.
112	– correspondence with Chatham, Newcastle, the King and others.
13	– Commissariat 1757–1761.
16	– Rent account 1765–1777.
17	– Housekeeping and stable expenses 1740–1763.
18	– Rental of London Estate 1745–1762.
23/1	– Account books with Drummond's Bank 1756–1788.
23/2	– Account books 1763–1775.
28	– Household accounts 1731–1764.
33	– Inventories of Beckett.
36	– Correspondence and dispatches of General Barrington (Guadeloupe).
37	– Engagement diaries 1777–1792.
38	– Correspondence of General Barrington (West Indies, 1759).

51   – Account book.
66   – Copy Abstract of
                  Barrington's Will 1787.
100   – Secretary at War's Commission 1765.
107   – Private letter book (numbering
                  of pages unreliable).

Berwick Place, Hatfield Peverel

Barrington MSS. (not classified).

2 Printed Sources

Newspapers and Periodicals

The Annual Register
The Gentleman's Magazine
The London Gazette
The Public Advertiser
The Town and Country Magazine

Correspondence and Memoirs

Barrington. Shute, *The Political Life of William Wildman, Viscount Barrington* (1814).

Barrington. Channing, E. and Coolidge, A. E. eds., *The Barrington-Bernard Correspondence* (1912).

Barrington. Shy, John ed., 'Confronting Rebellion: Private Correspondence of Lord Barrington with General Gage, 1765–1775,' in Peckham, Howard H. ed., *Sources of American Independence: Selected Manuscripts from the Collections of the William L. Clements Library* (2 vols.: Chicago 1978).

Burke. L. S. Sutherland ed., *Correspondence of Edmund Burke, II, July 1768–June 1774* (Cambridge, 1960).

Chatham. Taylor, W. S. and Pringle, J. H. eds., *Correspondence of William Pitt, Earl of Chatham* (4 vols., 1838–1840).

Ellis, Sir Henry ed., *Letters Illustrative of English History* (4 vols., 1824).

Fox. Ilchester, Lord ed., *Letters to Henry Fox* (1915).

Francis. Parkes, J. and Merivale, H. eds., *Memoirs of Sir Philip Francis, K.C.B., with correspondence and journals* (2 vols., 1867).

Gage. Carter, C.E. ed., *The Correspondence of General Thomas Gage with the Secretaries of State 1763–1775* (2 vols., 1931–1934).

George III. Fortescue, Sir John ed., *The Correspondence of King George the Third from 1760 to December 1783* (6 vols., 1927–1928).

Grafton. Anson, Sir W. R. ed., *Autobiography and Political Correspondence of Augustus Henry, third Duke of Grafton* (1898).

Grenville. Smith, W. J. ed., *The Grenville Papers: being the Correspondence of Richard Grenville, Earl Temple, K. G., and the Right Hon. George Grenville, their Friends and Contemporaries* (4 vols., 1852–1853).

Hardwicke. Yorke, P. C. ed., *Life and Correspondence of Philip Yorke, Lord Chancellor Hardwicke* (3 vols., 1913).

Junius. Cannon, John ed., *The Letters of Junius* (Oxford, 1978).

Minorca. Richmond, Sir H. W. ed., *Papers relating to the Loss of Minorca in 1756* (1913).

Mitchell. Bisset, Andrew ed., *The Memoirs and Papers of Sir Andrew Mitchell, K. B., Envoy Extraordinary and Minister Plenipotentiary from the Court of Great Britain to the Court of Prussia, 1756–1771* (2 vols., 1850).

Roberts, R. A. ed., *Calendar of Home Office Papers of the Reign of George III, 1770–1772* (1881).

Walpole. Brooke, John ed., Horace Walpole, *Memoirs of the Reign of George III* (3 vols., 1985).

Walpole, Lewis, W. S. et al. eds., *Horace Walpole's Correspondence* (34 vols., 1937–1983).

Walpole. Steuart, A. Francis ed., *The Last Journals of Horace Walpole during the Reign of George III from 1771–1783* (2 vols., 1910).

Printed Collections and other Printed Sources

(Army Lists) *A List of the Officers of the Army and of the Corps of the Royal Marines* (from 1754).

Cavendish. Wright, John ed., *Sir Henry Cavendish: Debates of the House of Commons, During the Thirteenth Parliament . . . . commonly called the Unreported Parliament . . . 1768–1771* (2 vols., 1841–1843).

Cobbett, William and T.C. Hansard eds., *Cobbett's Parliamentary Mystery of England* (36 vols., 1806–1820).

The Court and City Kalendar (1755–1778).

The Court and City Register (1755–1778).

Cuthbertson, Bennett, *A System for the Compleat Interior Management and Economy of a Battalion of Infantry* (Dublin, 1768).

Dalrymple, Campbell, *A Military Essay* (1781).

Dalrymple, Sir John, *Three Letters to Lord Barrington* (1778).

(Erskine, T.), *Observations on the Prevailing Abuses in the British Army* (1775).

Journals of the House of Commons.

Report of the Committee Appointed to Consider the State of His Majesty's Land Forces and Marines, 6 June, 1746: *Reports from Committees of the House of Commons, II, pp. 75–211.*

The Royal Kalendar (1767–1778).

Senex, John, *The Roads through England Delineated, or Ogilby's Survey, Revised, Improved, and Reduced to a size portable for the Pocket* (1759).

(Williamson, J.), *A Treatise of Military Finance* (1782).

3 Secondary Works: Books

Alvord, C. W., *The Mississipi Valley in British Politics* (Cleveland, Ohio, 1917).

Ashton, T.S., *Economic Fluctuations in England, 1700–1800* (1959).

Baker, N., *Government and Contractors: The British Treasury and War Supplies, 1775–1783* (1971).

Barnett, Correlli, *Britain and her Army, 1509–1970* (1970).

Binney, J. E. D., *British Public Finance and Administration, 1774–1792* (Oxford, 1958).

Bowler, R. A., *Logistics and the Failure of the British Army in America 1775–1783* (Princeton, N. J., 1975).

Brooke, J., *The Chatham Administration* (1956).

Brown, P., *The Chathamites* (1967).

Bruce, A., *The Purchase System in the British Army, 1660–1871* (1980).

Cantlie, Sir Neil, *A History of the Army Medical Department* (20 vols., Edinburgh, 1974).

Christie, I. R., *Myth and Reality in Late-Eighteenth Century British Politics* (1970).

Clode, C. M., *The Military Forces of the Crown* (2 vols., 1869).

Curtis, E. E., *The Organization of the British Army in the American Revolution* (New Haven and London, 1926).

Fortescue, Sir John, *A History of the British Army* (13 vols., 1899–1930).

Frey, S. R., *The British Soldier in America* (Austin, Texas, 1981).

Guy, A. J., *Oeconomy and Discipline. Officership and Administration in the British Army, 1714–1763* (Manchester 1985).

Hayter, Tony, *The Army and the Crowd in Mid-Georgian England* (1978).

Holdsworth, Sir William, *A History of English Law* (17 vols., 1903–1972).

Hoon, E., *The Organization of the English Customs System, 1696–1786* (Newton Abbot, 1968).

Houlding, J. A., *Fit for Service. The Training of the British Army, 1715–1795* (Oxford, 1981).

Jacobsen, G. A., *William Blathwayt, a late Seventeenth-Century Administrator* (New Haven, 1932).

Mackesy, P., *The Coward of Minden* (1979).

Mackesy, P., *The War for America 1775–1783* (1964).

Middleton, R., *The Bells of Victory* (Cambridge, 1985).

Namier, L. B. and Brooke, J., *Charles Townshend* (1964).

Namier, L. B. and Brooke, J., *The History of Parliament: the House of Commons 1754–90* (3 vols., 1964).

Phillips, Hugh, *Mid-Georgian London* (1964).

Radzinowicz, L., *A History of English Criminal Law* (4 vols., 1948–1968).

Roseveare, Henry, *The Treasury: The Evolution of a British Institution* (1969).

Rudé, George, *Wilkes and Liberty. A Social Study of 1763–74* (Oxford, 1962).

Savory, Sir Reginald, *His Britannic Majesty's Army in Germany during the Seven Years' War* (Oxford, 1966).

Scouller, R. E., *The Armies of Queen Anne* (Oxford, 1966).

Sedgwick, Romney, *The History of Parliament: The House of Commons 1715–1754* (2 vols., 1971).

Shelton, W. J., *English Hunger and Industrial Disorders* (1973).

Shy, John, *A People Numerous and Armed* (Oxford, 1984).

Shy, John, *Towards Lexington: the Role of the British Army in the Coming of the American Revolution* (Princeton, N.J., 1965).

Sosin, J. M., *Whitehall and Wilderness* (Lincoln, Nebraska, 1961).

Thomson, M. A., *The Secretaries of State, 1681–1782* (Oxford, 1932).

Wheeler, O., *The War Office Past and Present* (1914).

Whitworth, R. H., *Field Marshal Lord Ligonier: The British Army 1702–1770* (Oxford, 1958).

Wiener, Frederick B., *Civilians under Military Justice* (Chicago, 1967).

4 Secondary Works: Articles

Anderson, Olive, 'The Constitutional Position of the Secretary at War, 1642–1855', *Journal of the Society for Army Historical Research*, XXXVI (1958), pp. 165–169.

Baker, N., 'Changing Attitudes towards Government in Eighteenth-Century Britain', in A. Whiteman et al. eds., *Statesmen, Scholars and Merchants* (Oxford, 1973), pp. 202–219.

Burton, I. F. and Newman, A. N., 'Sir John Cope: Promotion in the Eighteenth Century', *English Historical Review*, LXXVIII (1963), pp. 655–668.

Gee, Olive, 'The British War Office in the Later Years of the American War of Independence', *Journal of Modern History*, XXVI (July 1954), pp. 123–136.

Guy, A. J., 'Regimental Agency in the British Standing Army 1714–1763', *BJRL*, LXII (1980), pp. 31–57.

Hayes, J., 'The Purchase of Colonelcies in the Army, 1714–1763', *JSAHR*, XXXIX (1961), pp. 3–10.

Kopperman, P., 'Medical Services in the British Army', *Journal of the History of Medicine*, XXXIV (1979), pp. 436–443.

Muskett, P., 'Military Operations against Smugglers in Kent and Sussex, 1698–1750', *JSAHR*, LII (1974), pp. 89–110.

Sutherland, L. S., and Binney, J., 'Henry Fox as Paymaster to the Forces', in R. Mitchison ed., *Essays in Eighteenth Century History* (1966), pp. 231–259.

5 Secondary Works: Theses

Bruce, A. P. C., 'The System of Purchase and Sale of Commissions in the British Army and the Campaign for its Abolition, 1660–1871' (Manchester Ph.D., 1973).

Burton, I. F., 'The Secretary at War and the Administration of the Army during the War of the Spanish Succession' (London Ph.D., 1960).

Hayes, J. W., 'The Social and Professional Backgrounds of the Officers of the British Army, 1714–1763' (London M. A. thesis, 1956).

Little, H. M., 'The Treasury, the Commissariat and the Supply of the Combined Army in Germany during the Seven Years War (1756–1763)' (London Ph.D., 1981).

Pimlott, J. L., 'The Administration of the British Army 1783–1793' (Leicester Ph.D., 1975).

Scott, L., 'Under-Secretaries of State, 1755–1775' (Manchester M. A., 1950).

Steppler, Glenn A., 'The Common Soldier in the Reign of George III, 1760–1792' (Oxford D. Phil., 1985).

Troehler, U., 'Quantification in British Medicine and Surgery with special Reference to its Introduction into Therapeutics' (London Ph.D., 1978).

Index

Officers are shown with the last rank they attained.

ARMY RECORDS SOCIETY
(FOUNDED 1984)

Members of the Society are entitled to purchase back
volumes at reduced prices.
Orders should be sent to the Hon. Treasurer, Army Records Society,
c/o National Army Museum,
Royal Hospital Road,
London SW3 4HT.

The Society has already issued:

Vol. I:
*The Military Correspondence of
Field Marshal Sir Henry Wilson 1918–1922*
Edited by Dr Keith Jeffery

Vol. II:
*The Army and the
Curragh Incident, 1914*
Edited by Dr Ian F. W. Beckett

Vol. III:
*The Napoleonic War Journal of
Captain Thomas Henry Browne, 1807–1816*
Edited by Roger Norman Buckley